AAK - 8551

W9-CAD-140

WITHDRAWN

17.75 75p

MEDITERRANEAN AFRICA

Monir S. Girgis

Professor of Geography
Edinboro University

WITHDRAWN

UNIVERSITY
PRESS OF
AMERICA

LANHAM • NEW YORK • LONDON

Copyright © 1987 by

University Press of America,® Inc.

4720 Boston Way
Lanham, MD 20706

3 Henrietta Street
London WC2E 8LU England

All rights reserved

Printed in the United States of America

British Cataloging in Publication Information Available

Library of Congress Cataloging in Publication Data

Girgis, Monir S., 1923-
    Mediterranean Africa.

    Bibliography: p.
    Includes index.
    1. Africa, North.   I. Title.
DT162.G57   1987   961   86-28150
ISBN 0-8191-5955-7 (pbk. : alk. paper)

All University Press of America books are produced on acid-free
paper which exceeds the minimum standards set by the National
Historical Publication and Records Commission.

PREFACE

This book which represents many years of teaching and field work, is an interdisciplinary and comprehensive study of the countries of Mediterranean Africa from the earliest times to the present. It includes detailed discussions of geography, history, politics, economics and populations of the area, and is designed to meet the needs of students, teachers and cultivated laymen who are interested in African, Middle Eastern and international relations studies.

Most works about Africa deal mainly with the countries south of the Sahara, or at best cover selected elements about the Mediterranean countries. There are several books about North Africa by French authors; however, to them the North African countries are the three Maghreb countries where French political influence prevailed. It is the impression of the author that there is an urgent need for a study of this important region which comprehensively combines and updates the scattered information on Mediterranean Africa using an interdisciplinary approach. This method clearly shows the inter-action between the environment and the inhabitants as well as between the national interests and global politics. Mediterranean Africa is a part of the world, not apart from it.

These countries were among the leaders in developing the stages of the ancient civilization, and carried the torch of culture during the Middle Ages. They became the prey of colonization in one form or another during modern history. The nationalists diligently resisted their foreign masters and struggled to obtain independence which was achieved very recently. Although these countries have had similar experiences, there are clear historical and cultural differences among them.

Finally free of the many years of foreign domination associated with political decay and economic decline, these countries now are striving to develop their economies through carefully planned fiscal policies. They are experiencing varying degrees of success due to their different mineral and financial resources, population problems and international relations. The strategic location of these African countries on the southern shore of the Mediterranean Sea continues to be important to the worlds' great powers.

I

The international relations of these countries with both the West and East varies from one country to another.

This comparative study presents an analysis of the similarities and differences of the countries and includes topical as well as regional chapters. The topical chapters deal with the geology, surface features, climate, vegetation, history and general economics of the whole area. The regional chapters discuss each country separately.

In researching material for this study, careful consideration was given to recently researched articles appearing in professional journals as well as new publications. Communications with governmental officials of these countries provided the most currently available statistics, and an exchange of letters with friends who live or teach in the region were very helpful. Having been born and raised in Egypt, the author has kept abreast of the development within these countries through continued research during the many visits to his homeland and the other countries.

TABLE OF CONTENTS

III

IV

MAPS

CHAPTER 1

INTRODUCTION

The region of Mediterranean Africa has its own
geographical personality and a distinctive geographic
orientation that makes it different from the rest of
the countries of Africa that are located south of the
Sahara.

Mediterranean Africa is comprised of the countries
of Egypt (Arab Republic of Egypt), Libya (Socialist
People's Libyan Arab Jamahiriya), Tunisia (Republic of
Tunisia), Algeria (Popular Republic of Algeria) known
in the Arab World as El Djezair, and Morocco (The
Kingdom of Morocco) known also as El Maghreb. Each of
these countries has a long sea front extending along
the Mediterranean Sea. Egypt has another sea front on
the Red Sea and Morocco has a second sea front on the
eastern shores of the Atlantic Ocean. This region
extends from longitude 35° E to about 17° W and from
south of latitude 20° N to about 36° N. The total area
of these countries is about 2,331,000 square miles,
most of it is part of the Sahara.

The Sahara, the largest and driest desert in the
world is located within and southern to the countries
of Mediterranean Africa, eastward across the Red Sea as
well as from the coast of the Mediterranean southward
to the shores of the sea of sand (the Sahel region) has
been very effective in separating the region from
Sub-Sahara Africa. Not only its climate, vegetation,
and production are different but also its ethnic,
linguistic and cultural characteristics do not show any
considerable similarity. However, the Nile river in
the east and several of the oases in the Sahara allowed
the seepage of culture from the lands of Mediterranean
Africa to the people living south of the Sahara.

The most tangible cultural elements that were
carried southward are the Islamic religion and the
Arabic language. The Nile, that mighty river that runs
from the heart of Africa south of the equator northward
to empty into the Mediterranean, while carrying the
life-giving water northward to Egypt, served as a route
carrying cultural influence southward. The Nile has
never been an easy highway, the six cataracts (rapids)
that are located between Aswan in southern Egypt and
Khartum, the capital of Sudan, have prevented
navigation in that part of the river and consequently
did not allow free large scale movements of people.

1

Through movements that lasted for a long time the religion of Islam and the Arabic language spread slowly in the Nile Valley as far south as the Sudd region of southern Sudan. The Sudd region, a large swamp, prevented the people of southern Sudan to move northward.

The caravanees, mostly from the Tuareg and other oases' dwellers, crossed the Sahara from north to south, back and forth for hundreds of years. Their means of transportation were camels, animals that naturally adapted well to the sandy, harsh deserts and dry climate and rightly named the ships of deserts. The oases were used as stations to supply the caravenees with water and limited provisions and allowed them to cross these huge expanses of deserts carrying the trade between the Mediterranean and Tropical Africa. While exchanging textiles, salt and glass for slaves, gold and cola nuts they were carrying too, the Islamic religion to the people in the Sahel region.

Although the Sahara acted as a barrier and separation between the two parts of Africa, the Mediterranean Sea, with its islands and straits, served since the early history as a highway connecting the cultures on its southern shores in Africa with the European cultures on its northern shores. The ancient Egyptions were in direct contact with the Greek islands; Alexander the Great built Alexandria on the Mediterranean coast of Egypt that became the most famous center of Hellenic civilization after the decline of Athens. The Greeks also crossed the sea to Libya and established settlements in Cyrenaica. The Phoenician colonies were on both the European and African coasts of the sea, in fact, the archeological sites of those colonies in Libya and Tunisia are among the tourist attractions. The Roman Empire turned the Mediterranean into a Roman lake, the southern coastal area of the sea in Tunisia was named Africa for the first time and Morocco was named Mauretania.

When the Roman Empire degenerated under the severe and successive hammering of the "Barbarians", the Ostrogoths, the Visigoths, the Lombards, the Huns, the Franks and the Vandals, Northern Africa did not escape their invasion. The Vandals crossed the Straits of Sicily and Gibraltar and devastated the northwestern region of Africa.

2

The Mediterranean was keeping North Africa in direct and continuous contact with Europe, even during that ancient age of history, the Suez isthmus simultaneously formed an important bridge connecting Africa with Asia and carried armies, waves of imigrants, trade and culture between Mediterranean Africa and Asia in general and the Middle East in particular. One of these military-cultural waves that crossed the vital bridge was the Arab invasion. It affected the linguistic, religious, social and political system of the entire region to this day. The Islamic religion that was carried by the invaders became the State religion of all the countries of North Africa, Arabic became their official language.

Under Arab leadership the Moors crossed the Mediterranean straits to Spain and Sicily to establish Islamic states that lasted for centuries - Islamic monuments and shrines are still there to witness the glorious age of Islamic expansion and culture.

The crusaders sailed on the Mediterranean not only to fight in the Holy Land and the Levant[1], but also in Egypt and Tunisia. The Ottomans (Turks) crossed the Suez isthmus to conquer North Africa as far west as Algeria. When the Ottoman Empire started to go downhill, the European influence started again to cross the Mediterranean to establish itself clearly and tangiably in North Africa. The French, under the leadership of General Bonaparte, invaded Egypt. Although the French did not stay more than three years, their language, schools, archeological institute are still very important in Egypt. In fact the modern administrative system in Egypt and the judical system owe their existance to that short period of French occupation. Later the French helped in improving irrigation in Egypt and built the Suez Canal that has been a vital international waterway and tremendously increased the strategic importance of Egypt that led to the British occupation of that country that remained until 1956.

The Italians colonized Libya and the French did not only impose themselves on Tunisia and Morocco, but also annexed Algeria as a French province until the day of its independence. Spain also crossed the Strait of Gibraltar and colonized the northern part of Morocco (El Rif), in fact they still have their two Spanish exclaves; Ceuta and Melilla.

3

The countries of the region, with the exception of Eygpt, owe their present international boundary lines to the colonial powers.

These strong ties between Mediterranean Europe and Mediterrranean Africa, as well as with the Middle East, gives the region its distinctive geographical personality that separates it from the rest of the African continent.

The extension of Mediterranean Europe in Mediterranean Africa^2, has made the countries of that region of Africa aware not only of world affairs, but of the national problems facing them. As soon as the Europeans stepped in to colonize these countries in one form or another, the national and resistance movements started and the national aspiration of independence began to gain momentum. Although colonization slowed down the pace of development and progress among the nations, the cultural contact introduced modern education, modern administrative systems, modern transportation and communication systems, banking and financial institutions and above all modern technology. In other words, that contact prepared these countries to handle their own affairs and tackle their economic problems effectively and efficiently as soon as they achieved their political independence.

The Arab invasion gave the region a cultural unity, the overwhelming majority of the population are Moslems and all the countries are members of the Organization of the Islamic Conference. The Arab invaders imposed the Arabic language as well as Islam, encouraged learning it since it is the language of the Qoran and prayers; almost the total population is Arabic Speaking and all the countries are members of the Arab League.

Even the physical environment is showing some similarity, all the countries have large areas that are parts of the Sahara, dotted with oases and very sparcely populated.

Within this physical and cultural unity there is a considerable diversity and clear differences among these countries. While Egypt is a river country, depending almost entirely on the Nile for its agriculture and very existence, the Maghrab states are predominatly mountainous countries without any large rivers and their population depends on the winter rainfall. Libya has neither rivers, nor appreciable

4

rainfall and is mostly a desert country. While all the countries are Islamic by religion and Arabic is the official language, Egypt has a strong Christian minority of the Coptic Orthodox church that was founded in the very early decades of Christianity. Morocco has a strong linguistic minority that is about 30 percent of the population, they are the Berbers of the Atlas mountains. The Berbers in Algeria are about 20 percent of the population. In Algeria too, the Tuareg of the Hoggar mountains are of a different ethnic group with a language, economic, and social system different from the northern Algerians. Libya, due to labor shortage, has a relatively high number of foreign residents of different nationalities.

Within this diversity, the countries are depending on different resources. Egypt is depending on agriculture, limited resources of oil, developing industry that is facing considerable problems and the Suez Canal revenues. Libya has huge oil and natural gas resources. Tunisia is mainly agricultural. Morocco depends on agriculture and large wealth of phosphates. The Algerian economy combines both agriculture and oil and natural gas.

In the field of foreign policies and international relations, there is also diversity within the general unity. Officially all the countries are following a neutral policy and have not joined any Western or Communist alliances and are members of the Third World Group that was founded originally by India, Yugoslavia, Egypt and Indonesia. Their shores and lands along the Mediterranean have no foreign naval, air, or army bases, unlike the Northern Mediterranean countries where NATO and the United States maintain important military bases. However, each of the countries is following its own foreign policy. Egypt is the only country not only of the region, but also of the Arab World that has recognized Israel and has a peace treaty with that country. Libya is following a very hard line policy toward Israel and discourages any peace movement toward it, in fact it is supporting financially and politically all hard line policies against Israel. Morocco and Tunisia, although never recognized Israel, they are in favor of peaceful political solutions for the Arab-Israeli problem. Algeria is supporting the Palestinian Liberation Organization (PLO).

Egypt has been following a pro-American policy since 1974. It is receiving from the U.S.A. financial, economic aid and buys American equipment for its

military forces. American and Egyptian forces are
cooperating in military exercises. Libya, since
President Qaddafi came to power, has been following a
very strong anti-American policy - he belives not only
that the U.S.A. is supporting Israel all the way, but
also using Israel as an American base and enclave in
the Arab World to resist pan Arabism. Both Moroccco
and Tunisia follow pro-American policy and keeping
strong ties with France. Algeria is rather neutral in
dealing with foreign affairs.

The region as a whole has important strategic
location concerning geopolitics and world and
transportation. The region's countries are alined
along the southern shores of the Mediterranean - one of
the busiest world routes for international trade and
navigation. They are facing the southern flank of NATO
and very close to the Turkish Straits that are of
utmost importance for the Soviet Union. Two of the
countries have unmatched location, Egypt in the east
has the Suez Canal, close to the oil fields around the
Persian Gulf; Morocco in the west looks on the Strait
of Gibraltar, that narrow bottle neck that controls the
navigation between the Mediterranean Sea and the
Atlantic Ocean.

That continuous and steady contact between the
more developed countries of Europe in general, and the
North Mediterranean countries in particular, and the
less developed countries on the southern flank of the
sea through the different ages of history, especially
the modern ages, has contributed to accelerate the rate
of development in North Africa. Indeed it is more
developed than the rest of the African countries with
the exception of the very rich Republic of South
Africa. On the whole, the people have higher standards
of living compared to most of the African population,
with the exception of the European settlers of the
Republic of South Africa. These countries will do
better through growing in age especially if they will
be able to control the high growth rate of population
that is tied with culture and tradition.

6

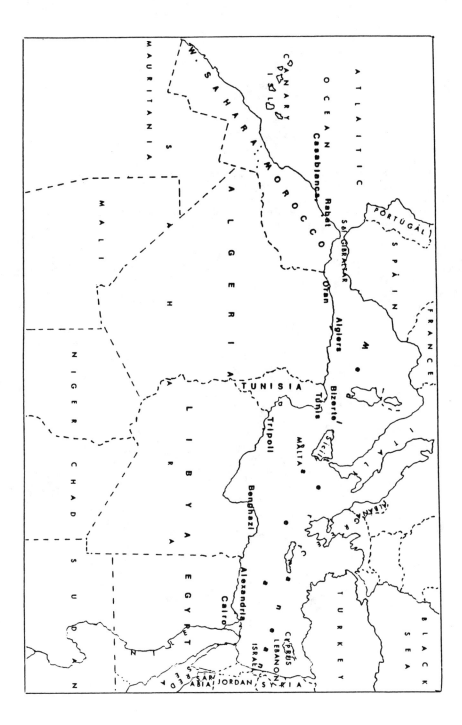

REFERENCES

[1] The countries of the Levant are: Syria, Lebanon, "Palestine" and Jordan.

[2] Other writers consider that North Africa extends northward to southern Europe.

CHAPER 2

STRUCTURE AND GEOLOGICAL MAP

The geological structure of Mediterranean Africa
is a simple form if compared with the other
Mediterranean countries or with Africa south of the
Sahara.

Most of Mediterranean Africa, with the exception
of the Atlas region, forms a part of the African
plateau. The ancient Tethys Sea invaded the northern
parts of Mediterranean Africa many times since Cambrian
time. On the floor of that ancient sea, marine
sediments accumulated and bear witness to the sea's
invasion.

The Archean platform of Mediterranean Africa,
which was a part of Gondwanaland, is exposed at the
surface in many areas, but it is covered with younger
sedimentary rocks in most of the region.

The Precambrian surface is widely exposed in the
Red Sea Mountains of eastern Egypt. The rocks include
granite, gabbro, schist, and gneiss. Precambrian
outdrops and metamorphic rocks form the high peaks of
El Dokhan and Hamada. These rocks also form most of
the high southern part of the Sinai peninsula where the
two lofty peaks of Djebel Musa and Mount St. Catherine
are located.

The Nile River has eroded the sedimentary cover
that conceals the Pre-cambrian rocks at Aswan in
southern Egypt to form the first cataract.

The Archean rocks crop out also at Djebel
El-Oweinat which is a small, mountainous massif
situated at the junction of the Libyan-Egyptian-
Sudanese borders. The rocks here are mostly
crystalline schists intruded by granite.

It is believed that the Archean rocks in the Red
Sea Mountains, Sinai Peninsula, and Djebel El-Oweinat
have never been submerged[1].

In the southern part of Cyrenaica and across the
Libya-Chad political boundary line, the Tibesti Massisf
crystalline basement crops out in a wide area in the
northern part of the massif, whereas schists dominate
in the northwest and granites in the northeast.

The Hoggar (El Hoggar, or Ahoggar) Massif that dominates the Central Sahara is a great inlier of igneous and metamorphic rocks that have been bared by erosion. This crystalline basement rises to an elevation of 7670 feet in the Tefedest. These mountains were partly submerged during the Cretaceous when the sea covered the lower areas of the Southern Sahara. Crystalline basement is also exposed in the Western Sahara at Eglab Massif. The Archean rocks are also involved in the deformation which produced the Atlas ranges. They form the core of the Great Atlas of Morocco (Haut Atlas), where overlying younger sediments are intensely folded and were subjected to erosion, exposing the up-thrust crystalline rocks. The Anti Atlas forms an elevated escarpment edge of the Saharan platform which was uplifted when the Great Atlas was formed. The rocks here consist largely of crystalline rocks which are well exposed at or in the viciniity of Kurdois, Qurzazate, and near Zanago[2]. The crystalline rocks are also exposed in the Moroccan Meseta where the Umm El Rabia river has eroded the Paleozoic sedimentary cover. These Precambrian rocks are also exposed in two other small areas of northern Algera near the Mediterranean coast where the rivers Ramah and Somma have eroded the Harinean sediments that cover the uplifted crystalline rocks.

Precambrian volcanic rocks are widely distributed in Mediterranean Africa. These rocks cover many parts of the Red Sea Mountains and the southern highlands of the Sinai Peninsula. Volcanic rocks are also exposed in the Ahaggar Mountains at the eastern edge of the Eglab Massif, in the Great Atlas, and in the Tel Atlas, where they were uplifted during the building of the ranges.

The Cambrian transgression spread over the greater part of northwest Africa. In the High Atlas of Morocco, the Cambrian sediments reach 1000 m. in thickness. They cover an area extending to Djeblet and the meseta in the north and to the Anti Atlas in the south. The most common lithologies are limestone and green and grey shale. The sea did not extend eastward beyond the Hoggar Massif and the rest of Mediterranean Africa remained above the sea level.

The sea covered the whole of Western Africa during the Ordovician Period. The sea was shallow with almost sandy sedimentation. The only area not submerged was central Hoggar. In Algeria, the Ordovician sediments are exposed in the north near Algiers and Bougie

(Bejaia). In Morocco, they are present in the vicinity of Imini, Tafilalet, and Dra. Most of the Ordovician rocks are sandstone is exposed in the northern part of the Hoggar and Tassilis Massifs. It is clear from an examination of the geologic structure that the eastern part of Mediterranean Africa has stayed above sea level during this age, also[3].

The Silurian sea also covered western Mediterranean Africa, but no rocks of Silurian age are known in either Egypt or Libya, except near Fezzan.

Silurian sediments are exposed in Algeria in the Beni-Afeur area, in the Oran area, in the Djorf Quzzene near the Moroccan borders, and the Great Kabylie. In eastern Morocco, they are present south of Oudja, in the northern slopes of the High Atlas, in central Morocco south of Naima, and in the Meseta. Silurian limestone is present in the Sahara in the Tassila des Ajjer and between Sardeles and Ghat. The eastern limit of the Silurian depostion is in Hamada el Homra in Central Fezzan in Libya.

There is a widespread evidence that the Caledonian tectonism that formed the Caledonian Mountains of northwestern Europe also influenced Silurian events of Morocco and the Sahara. The oldest movements were Post-Ordovician and were followed by the second series of movements in Post-Silurian. These deformational events did not form high mountains, but caused the erosion of older Paleozoic sediments so that the continental Upper Devonian and Carboniferous sediments were deposited directly on the precambrian basement.

The Devonian sea covered most of Northwest Africa and the western part of the Sahara, but did not extend to the east until Fezzan at the Silurian Sea. Devonian sediments of limestone, sandstone, and coral limestone are present in Morocco and Tafilalet. In the Sahara, blue limestone is present in the Saoura Trough and sandstone in Tindouf Syncline.

The Carboniferous sea covered all of Northwest Africa and some parts of the Northeast. The Atlas region was submerged during the early Carboniferous. The seas retreated from the western parts of Algeria near Kenadaza and the Colom-Bechar and Kenadaza basins around Djerada during the late Carboniferous, and their sediments are continental with important coal seams and fresh water sediments. An arm of the sea extended far

southward into the Sahara during the Lower-Carbon-
iferous and marine deposits are present from Saoura
Trough and Hamada de Tindouf north to the Hoggar. This
gulf extended eastward to Fezzan. Another embayment
extended from Tethys Sea southward to cover the present
Gulf of Suez and North Sinai Peninsula; marl and
sandstone are present along the Gulf of Suez, limestone
and coal are present in Gabel Maghara in Northern
Sinai[4]. Another arm of the sea extended along the
western borders of Egypt to reach Gabel O Uweinat,
where marine sediments are exposed.

The folded strata in parts of the Atlas Mountains
and the Moroccan Meseta were deformed by the Harcnian
tectonism; the present Uplands in the Sahara were
produced by these movements during the Carboniferous.

During the Permian Period, all of North Africa
with the exception of Tunisia stood above sea level.
Tunisia was covered by a Permian sea, and marine
sediments of marl, sandstone, and limestone are present
at Djebel Tabaga and in the neighboring hills of
Souinia and Saikara. The rest of the rocks are of
continental origin.

The Mesozoic Era: When the Mesozoic Era began,
all of North Africa was above sea level with the
exception of a small region in northeast Egypt around
Djebel Araf al Naga in the Sinai Peninsula where
Triassic marine limestones are present.

During the Jurassic the northeast part of
Mediterranean Africa was submerged as far south as Al
Galala El Baharia Plateau: Jurassic limestone present
in the plateau and near Djebel Maghara in Northern
Sinai indicates the former presence of the Jurassic
Sea. Marine Jurassic deposits are also present
southwest of Tripoli in Libya which indicates that the
Tethys Sea covered the northern part of this area. It
is also believed that the sea covered all northwest
Africa during this time. The southern shoreline of the
sea extended from Djefferea Dome to Bou-Annane in
eastern Morocco to Agadeer on the Atlantic.

The Cretaceous sea covered all of Mediterranean
Africa, extending to the east as far as northern
Sudan. It also covered Libya, northwest Africa, and
the Sahara south to the Hoggar. During the early
Cretaceous, the sea was shallow, consequently
sandstones are present throughout the southern part of
the region with the exception of the Red Sea Mountains,

the Ouynat, and the Hoggar Massif which were not submerged. During the Middle and late Cretaceous, the sea became deeper, and vast amounts of marine sediments were deposited. They are present throughout most of Mediterranean Africa.

In Egypt, the Nubian Sandstone[5] extends from Sinai Peninsula southward into northern Sudan. It is believed that these deposits extend under the younger rocks in southern Sudan as well. The thickness of the sandstone increases northward, from about 166 feet at Aswan to more than 2000 feet in northeastern Sinai. The sandstone in Egypt rests directly on the crystalline Precambrian basement, because the sea did not cover this area previously. The Nubian Sandstone covers most of the middle and northeastern parts of Sinai Peninsula and a narrow strip along the western slopes of the Red Sea Mountains. In addition, it is present throughout the southwestern part of the Western Desert forming the wide plateau of El Gilf and westward into Libya. Erosion has exposed the Nubian Sandstone in both Wadi Araba on the western side of the Gulf of Suez and in the Baharya Oasis in the Western Desert.

During middle and late Cretaceous, the sea became deeper and covered most of Eygpt. Cretaceous chalky limestone, marl and paper shales are present on the sides of the Nile Valley as far south as Louqsor and in the Western Desert as far south as Karkour and Doungol Oasis. In Egypt, these middle and upper Cretaceous formations are represented by a narrow outcrop belt between the Nubian Sandstone and the overlying Cenozoic sediments.

In Libya, cretaceous rocks are sandstones deposited in the shallow sea and deeper water limestones. The sandstone is exposed in the southern part of Cyrenaica as an extension to the Nubian Sandstone of the Egyptian Western Desert. It extends southward to the margin of the Tibesti Massif. In Fezzan, this sandstone covers most of the southern and western parts of the province and extending westward into the Algerian Sahara. It is obvious from the deposit sand structures in Libya that the Cretaceous sea retreated northward during the Middle Cretaceous. (Turoni[6]) Continental sediments of clay and sandstone containing plant remains and silicified wood crop out in many areas, particulary between Homs and the Algerian and Tunisian borders. These continental sediments extend southward and cover many parts of the

13

lower Cretaceous sandstone, but in the north they are
covered by Cretaceous maring limestone.

It is clear from the geological studies in both
Algeria and Morocco that the Cretaceous sea did not
cover the Sahara in that region before the middle
Cretaceous. Continental sediments were deposited
during this time and are exposed in many areas. These
beds are present in the 140 mile depression that
extends from Fort-Flalters to Ohrant along the Hoggar
Desert road from Ein Saleh to El Golia. Similar rocks
are also exposed in Eastern Morocco at the base of the
Hamada de Guir. Other areas where these Cretaceous
beds are present in the region are between Wadi Saoura
and the borders of the Hoggar Massif and in the
Meguiden Plateaux that extend between the Timimoun salt
lake to the Tademait Plateau. Most of these sediments
are red and purple clay, white and red sandstone, hared
and gravelly sandstone and quartzite. The thickness of
these beds varies from 930 feet to 80 feet. They
contain fossils of reptiles, crocodiles, and
dinosaurian theropods and silicified rocks that
indicate that the region was humid during this part of
early Cretaceous. During the middle part of the
Cretaceous, this part of the Sahara in both Algeria and
Morocco as well as in Egypt and Libya was submerged
beneath the Cretaceous sea. This transgression reached
its zenith during the late Cretaceous when the Tethys
Sea waters penetrated far into the Sahara south of the
Hoggar Massif. The Tethys Sea joined the lower Miger
by two routes, to the east through the western borders
of the Hogar. These upper Cretaceous rocks are also[7]
exposed in the Atlas Mountains and the Shotts plateau,
particular in the western part of El Rif[8] Atlas between
Oujida and Sidi bel Abbas, in the region extending from
AinBeida to Maktar and the region from Louis Gentil to
Ounara in the western slopes of the High Atlas.

Of particular significance is the fact that the
northwestern coast of Africa and the modern Atlantic
coast were formed during this part of late Cretaceous.

During the early and middle Eocene, the sea
invaded north Africa again. Eocene sediments are
exposed near Taza in the southern Rif, in Wadi Ladhar,
and in the area near El Kasr in Morocco. Most of these
sediments are sandstone, marble, limestone and
phosphates. These early Eocene marine sediments are
also present in the Tadla and Sous regions of Atlantic
Morocco where the sea formed two gulfs south of the
Morocco Meseta. These rocks are very rich in

14

phosphates, especially in the Tadla region north to the Grand Atlas at Awlad Abdoun, Meskala, and Ganntour.

In Algeria aand Tunisia, these lower and middle Eocene formations are well represented in the Tel region and the northern part of the Sahara. These sediments are exposed at Awlad Djellal in the Aures, Negrine, and the Gafsa Mountains. Some of these deposits are also rich in phosphates as in Djebel Onq, Djebel Kouif, Mazita, and Tocqueville. In the Guelma and Constantine regions, the middle Eocene is represented by limestones and marl.

Important folding in the Mediterranean and Sahara Atlas began as early as the middle Eocene. In the north and in the ancient rigid massifs of the Qabylie and northern Moroccan Rif have been raised. In the south, uplift also occurred along the Saharan border. In the Aures, middle Eocene deformation produced hills of 1000-17000 feet. The formation of these folds was accompanied by some faulting.

The Upper Eocene transgression covered the northern Tunisia and the Tel region in Algeria with the exception of two areas which stood as islands: The Qabyla in the Biban Range and the coast of Oran. Most of the sediments are sandstones, marls, and clays. The Lallemand and the Tunisian salt lakes in the north extend eastward to the Libyan frontier which is covered by complexes of dunes reaching 700 feet in height, resting mostly on marine Eocene deposits of sandstone and limestone.

In Libya, the Eocene is extensively exposed to the north and east of Djebel Soda as well as on the coast in the Djebel El Akhdar east to Benghazi. Eocene deposits also crop out in the southern part of Libya at Djebel Nero in the Serir Tibesi. The presence of these formations in this area suggests that the Eocene sea covered most of the eastern parts of Mediterranean Africa in both Egypt and Libya.

In Egypt the Eocene sea covered about a fifth of the country. Eocene sediments of limestone, clay, and marl underly most of the deserts flanking the Nile valley and most of the Tih Plateau in the Sinai Peninsula. In the western desert they are present westward to the Farafra oasis and southwestward to the Qattara depression. Similar rocks are present to the east of Wadi El Hamamat in the eastern desert. In many cases, these formations rest on Cretaceous rocks but in

15

some other areas on older formations. The lower Eocene limestone in Egypt is usually hard and white, whereas the middle Eocene limestone is characterized by its bright white color.

The Oligocene Sea did not cover as large an area of Mediterranean Africa as the Eocene sea did. The character of the Oligocene deposits shows that the northern part of Africa was bordered by an uneven continental shelf bounded by low-lying coasts. The southern most Oligocene deposits are in the south Tellian ranges in Algeria and near the Fayoum depression in Egypt. Most of these deposits are sandstone.

In Egypt, the Oligocene sea formed a huge gulf that covered the northern parts of the country south to the area of Cairo. Sediments deposited in this embayment are exposed in the area between Cairo and Suez in the eastern desert as well as in the region between Cairo and Fayum in the western desert. They also crop out at Gebel El Kashab, west of the Gizeh (Giza) pyramids, and at Borg El Arab on the northwestern shores near Lake Maryut. It is believed that during the Oligocene, a major river crossed Egypt, rising in the Red Sea Mountains and emptying into the Maryut Gulf. Sediments transported by this drainage are comprised mostly of gravels and sand but also contain petrified trees and the remnants of the arsinoitherium.

In Libya, the Oligocene sediments indicate the presence of a deep gulf south of the gulf of Sidra, but not extending as far south as that of the Eocene. In Tunisia, the Oligocene is represented in the central part of the coastal plain, especially around Cape Bon, by sandstone. In Algeria, Oligocene sandstone crops out in the south Telliam ranges particularly near Djelfa and Aflou.

By the end of the Oligocene the first major Alpine tectonism that built the Atlas Mountains occurred. It is believed that the northeastern region of Africa during this time was also subjected to tectonic movements that formed an internal lake (the Red Sea) and uplifted the Red Sea Mountains.

The marine Miocene sediments are present only in the Rif region of Morocco, most of these deposits in the southern Rif through are calcareous, sandy molasses, and limestone with green marls. The Miocene

16

sea covered almost the same area as the Eocene sea. Further to the south it invaded the valleys on the northern border of the Aures Mountains. In Tunisia, although the Miocene Sea penetrated into the Bizarta and the central regions and even reached the Biskara Depression, large islands (the high hills) remained emergent.

When the Alpine deformation reached its maximum, the sea retreated from North Africa. The Mediterranean joined the Atlantic by the southern Rif strait which passed through the Gharb. The channel was not closed until near the end of the Miocene.

The Miocene Sea covered the eastern part of Libya in Cyrenaica and extended southward to Jalo Oasis and Aujola. In Tripolitannia, Miocene deposits are rather limited and concentrated on the coastal plain near Misrata.

Miocene deposits are found throughout the Mediterranean region in Egypt. The rocks are mostly limestone and reach 700 feet in thickness in the Moghara Oases (90 miles west of Cairo). Limestone deposits are also present in the Fayum Depression. In the Eastern Desert, they are present southward along the Red Sea coast as far as Ras Benas and the Tropic of Cancer. These deposits include oil-bearing dolomites and gypsiferous marls.

Miocene continental sediments are found in northwestern Africa (the Barbary States) and throughout the Sahara where they form the Hamadas. Most of the sediments are red sandstone and lacustrine limestone.

By the beginning of the Quaternary, the mountain zones underwent further uplift which raised the peaks of the Atlas ranges to their present height. The Strait of Gibraltar and Sicily were formed during this period[10] and the Red Sea attained its present shape.

During the Quaternary, North Africa and the Sahara were subjected to a pluvial age parallel to the European ice age, alteration of wet and dry periods prevailed, as proven by the fossil record of fauna and prehistoric industries.

The major tectonic activity that occurred during the Tertiary and Quaternary was accompanied by extensive volcanic activity. This is represented by the basaltic rocks on the El Hoggar dome, the Fezzan volcanoes, and some active volcanoes in the Tibesti Massif. The tectonism is represented by the instability of the land in the Maghreb States, as demonstrated by the destructive earthquakes such as the one which partially destroyed the town of Orleansville in western Algeria in 1956 and the one that destroyed the port of Agadir in south Morocco in 1960.

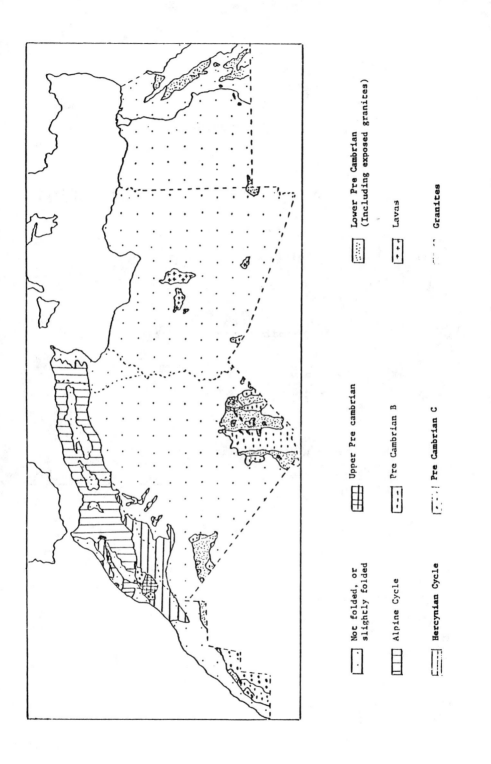

Not folded, or slightly folded

Upper Pre cambrian

Lower Pre Cambrian
(Including exposed granites)

Alpine Cycle

Pre Cambrian B

Lavas

Hercynian Cycle

Pre Cambrian C

Granites

REFERENCES

[1] For more details, see Hume, W.F., Geology of Egypt, p.67.

[2] Raymond Furon: Geology of Africa, p. 109.

[3] Raymond Furon: Geology of Africa, p. 108.

[4] See: Ball, John, Contributions to the Geography of Egypt, pp. 135-138.

[5] The term "Nubian Sandstone" was adopted by Lartet after studying this formation Nubia, and is still in use.

[6] See Furon, pp. 98-101.

[7] Chotts Plateau

[8] Er Rif

[9] Grande Kabylie and Petite Kabylie.

[10] For more details see Fallot, P. Essai sur la geolgie du Rif Septentrional.

CHAPTER 3

SURFACE FEATURES

The Atlas Mountains in the western part and the
Nile Valley in the eastern part are the two dominating
geographical features of this region of Africa.

The Atlas ranges are the result of a phase of
mountain building that took place in the geologically
recent Teretary Era when sediments deposited beneath
the ancestral Mediterranean Sea were uplifted, folded
and fractured. The mountains remain geologically
unstable and the region is liable to severe
earthquakes.

The Atlas Mountains do not form a complete and
isolated mountain group, but rather, an African
extension of the Alpine system which is most
extensively developed in Europe and Asia and encloses
the western basin of the Mediterranean. It is thought
that these mountains were continuous across the
Sicilian Channel to Sicily and the Strait of Messina to
the Apennines in the Italian Peninsula in the east and
in the west they were also continuous across the Strait
of Gibraltar to the Sierra Nevada range of southeastern
Iberia and eventually to reappear in the Balearic
Islands.

The Atlas system comprises two main ranges: The
northern Atlas range (Mediterranean of Tell Atlas
bifurcates in northern Morocco, one branch curving
around in the Rif Atlas[1], the other curving south in
the Middle Atlas[2]. The southern range (Saharan Atlas)
becomes the Higher Atlas in Morocco[3], The two ranges
enclose the high plateau of the Shotts (Chotts), a
region of internal drainage with numerous salt lakes.
The two ranges approach close to one another in the
east, to the extent of eliminating the plateau of the
Shotts which disappears in Tunisia. The mountains
reach the eastern shores of Tunisia in high cliffs,
Cape Blanco marking the termination of the northern
range and Cape Bon that of the southern range. Between
those two promontories is the Gulf of Tunisia.

MOROCCO comprises the highest and most rugged
ranges in the Atlas Mountain system of northwest
Africa. They form four distinct massifs which are
surrounded and partially separated by lowland plains
and plateaux. In the north, the Rif Atlas forms a
rugged arc of mountains that rise steeply from the

21

Mediterranean coast to heights of over 7,300 feet. Their limestone and sandstone ranges are difficult to penetrate and have functioned as a barrier to east-west communications.[4]

The Middle Atlas lies immediately south of the Rif from which they are separated by the Col of Taza, a narrow gap which affords the only easy route between western Algeria and Atlantic Morocco. They rise to nearly 10,000 feet and form a broad barrier between the two countries. They also function as a major drainage divide and are flanked by the basins of Morocco's two principal rivers, the Oum er Rbia which flows west to the Atlantic and the Moulouya which flows north east to the Mediterranean.

Southward the Middle Atlas chain merges into the High Atlas, the most formidable of the mountain massifs, which rises to over 13,000 feet. The mountains are aligned in a chain from southwest to northeast and they rise precipitously from both the Atlantic lowland to the north and the desert plain of the Sahara in the south. Eastward, the chain loses height and continues into Algeria as the Saharan Atlas. The central part of the massif has been eroded by former glaciers and present streams into a wilderness of sharp peaks and steep-sided valleys. There are no easily accessible routes across the High Atlas, but numerous mountain trails make possible exchange of goods between Atlantic and Sahara Morocco.

The Anti Atlas is the lowest and most southerly of the mountain massifs. Structurally, it is considered an elevated edge of the Saharan platform which was uplifted when the High Atlas was formed. It consists largely of crystaline rocks and is joined to the southern margin of the High Atlas by a mass of volcanic lava which separated the Sous River that runs westward to the Atlantic at Agadir from the upper Dra River which runs southeast to the Sahara.

The wide valley of the river Sebou and the valley of the river Moulouya, make a strait that connected the old ancestral Mediterranean (Tethys Sea) with the Atlantic before the opening of the Strait of Gibraltar and are covered with a thick layer of marl and clay.

The only extensive area of lowland in Morocco stretches inland from the Atlantic coast and is enclosed in the north, east and south by the Rif, Middle and High Atlas. It consists of the Rharb Plain

and the Sebou River valley in the north and of the
plateaux and plains of Meseta, the Tadla, the Rhemna,
the Sous valley, the Djebilet and the Haouz further
south.

The Atlas Mountain system in Algeria is made up of
three broad zones running parallel to the coast: the
Tell Atlas, the High Plateaux and the Sahara Atlas. In
the north, and separated from the Mediterranean by only
a narrow and discontinuous coastal plain, is the
complex series of mountains and valleys that comprise
the Tell Atlas. Here, individual ranges, plateaux and
massifs vary in height from about 13,000 to 17,000
feet, and are frequently separated from one another by
deep valleys and gorges which divide the country into
self-contained topographic and economic units. Most
distinctive of these are the massifs of the Great and
Little Qabylie[5] between Algers and the Tunisian
frontier.

South of the Tell Atlas lies a zone of featureless
plains known as the High Plateau of the Shotts. To the
west, near the Moroccan frontier, they form a broad,
monotonous expanse of level terrain about 100 miles
across and over 3,500 feet high. They gradually narrow
and fall in height eastward and end in the Hodna Basin,
a huge enclosed depression, the bottom of which is only
1,375 feet above sea level. The surface of the plateau
consists of alluvial debris derived from erosion of the
mountains to north and south and only here and there do
minor ridges project through the thick mouth of
alluvium to break the monotony of the level horizons.
The plateaux owe their name to the presence of several
vast basins of internal drainage, known as shotts, the
largest of which is the Hodna Basin. During the rainy
periods, water accumulates in the shotts to form
expansive shallow lakes which give way, as the water is
absorbed and evaporated, to saline mud flats and
swamps.

The southern margin of the High plateau is marked
by a series of mountain chains and massifs that form
the Saharan Atlas. They are more broken than the Tell
Atlas and present no serious barrier to the
communications between the High Plateaux and the
Sahara. From west to east the chief mountain chains
are the Ksour, Amour, Ouled Nail, Ziban and Aures. The
latter is the most impressive massif in the whole
Algerian Atlas system and includes the highest peak:
Djebel Chelia, 7,638 feet. The relief of the Aures is
very bold, with narrow gorges cut between sheer cliffs
23

surmounted by steep bare slopes, and to the east and north of the Hodna Basin its ridges merge with the southernmost folds of the Tell Atlas. Northeastern Algeria forms, therefore, a compact block of high relief in which the two Atlas Mountain systems cease to be clearly separated. Within it there are a number of high plains studded with salt flats but their size is insignificant compared with the enormous shotts of the west.

South of the High Atlas, Algeria extends for over 900 miles into the heart of the Sahara. Structurally, this huge area consists of a resistant platform of geologically ancient rocks against which the Atlas Mountains were folded. Over most of the area relief is slight, with occasional plateaux, such as those of Eglab, Tademait and Tassili-n-Ajjer, rising above vast spreads of gravel (regs) such as the Tanezrouft plain and huge sand accumulations such as the Great Western and Eastern Ergs. In the southeast, however, the great massif of Ahaggar rises to heights of 9,050 feet. Here erosion of volcanic and crystaline rocks has produced a lunar landscape of extreme ruggedness (Hamadas). Southward from the Ahaggar the massifs of Adrar des Iforas and Air extend across the Algerian frontier into the neighboring countries of Mali and Niger.

TUNISIA includes the easternmost ridges of the Atlas Mountains, but most of it is low-lying and bordered by a long and sinuous Mediterranean coastline that faces both north and east. The country comprises three main topographic regions[6]: mountainous northern region, central region of low plateaux and plains and the Saharan region in the south. The northern region is dominated by the eastern folds of the Atlas Mountain system which form two separate chains, the northern and High Tell, separated by the valley of the River Medjerda, the only perennially flowing river in Tunisia. The northern Tell, which is a continuation of the Algerian Tell Atlas, consists mainly of sandstone and extends along the north coast at heights of between 1,000 and 2,000 feet. South of the Medjerda valley the much broader Tell Atlas, which is a continuation of the Saharan Atlas of Algeria, is made up of successions of rugged sandstone and limestone ridges. Near the Algerian frontier they reach a maximum height of 5,065 feet in Djebel Chambi, the highest point in Tunisia, but the folds die away eastward towards the Cape Bon peninsula which extends northeast to within 90 miles of Sicily.

24

South of the High Tell or Dorsale (backbone) central Tunisia consists of an extensive platform sloping gently towards the east coast. Its western half, known as the High Steppe, is made up of alluvial basins rimmed by low, barren mountains, but eastward, the mountains give way first to the low Steppe, which is a mountainous gravel-covered plateau, and ultimately to the flat coastal plain of the Sahel. Occasional water courses cross the Steppes, but they only flow after heavy rain and usually fan out and evaporate in salt flats, or sebakhad, before reaching the sea.

The central Steppes give way southward to a broad depression occupied by two great seasonal salt lakes or shotts. The largest of these, the Shott Djerid, lies at 52 feet below sea level and is normally covered by a salt crust. It extends from close to the Mediterranean coast near Gabes, almost to the Algerian frontier, and is adjoined on the northwest by the Shott of Rharsa which lies at 69 feet below sea level. South of the shotts, Tunisia extends for over 200 miles into the Sahara. Rocky, flat topped mountains, the Monts des Ksour, separates a flat plain, known as the Djeffara which borders the coast south of Gabes, from a sandy lowland which is partly covered by the dunes of the Great Eastern Erg.

LIBYA is a part of the vast plateau of North Africa but there are certain minor geographical features which give individuality to three component areas of Libya: Tripolitania, Fezzan and Cyrenaica. Tripolitania consists of a series of regions of different levels, rising in the main, towards the south. In the extreme north along the Mediterranean coast, there is a low-lying coastal plain called the Jefara. This is succeeded inland by a line of hills or rather a scarp edge, that has several distinguishing local names, but is usually alluded to merely as the Jebel. Here and there in the Jebel occur evidence of former volcanic activity - old craters, and sheets of lava.

South of the Jebel there is an upland plateau - a dreary desert landscape of sand, scrub and scattered irregualr masses of stone. After several hundred miles, the plateau gives place to a series of east-west running depressions, where artesian water, and hence oases, are found. These depressions make up the region of Fezzan, which is merely a collection of oasis on a fairly large scale, interspersed with areas of desert. In the extreme south, the land rises considerably to

form the mountains of the central Sahara, here some
peaks reach 12,000 feet in height.

Cyrenaica has a slightly different physical
pattern. In the north, along the Mediterranean, there
is an upland plateau that rises to 2,000 feet in two
very narrow steps, each only a few miles wide. This
gives a broad prominent coastline to much of Cyrenaica,
and so there is a marked contrast with Tripolitania
where the coast is low-lying and in parts fringed with
lagoons. The northern upland of Cyrenaica are called
the Jebel Akhdar (Green Mountains). On its western
side it drops steeply to the shores of the Gulf of
Sirte, but on the east it falls more gradually, and is
traceable as a series of ridges, only a few hundred
feet in altitude, that extend as far as the Egyptian
frontier. This eastern district, consisting of low
ridges aligned parallel to the coast, is known as
Marmarica.

South of the Jebel Akhdar, the land falls in
elevation, producing an extensive lowland, which except
for its northern fringe, is mainly desert. Here and
there occur a few oasis. In the same region, and
becoming more widespread toward the east, is the Sand
Sea, an expanse of fine, mobile sand, easily lifted by
the wind into dunes that can sometimes reach several
hundred feet in height and over 100 miles in length.
Finally, in the far south of Cyrenaica lie the central
Saharan mountains the Tibests Range, continuous with
these to the south of the Fezzan.

EYGPT consists, essentially, of a narrow valley,
some 2 to 10 miles wide, cut by the River Nile in the
plateau of northeast Africa. At an earlier geological
period, a gulf of the Mediterranean Sea extended as far
south as Cairo[8], but deposition of silt by the Nile has
entirely filled up this gulf, producing the fan-like
shaped delta region, through which flow the two
branches of the Nile, the eastern, or Damietta branch,
and the western, or Rosetta branch. As deposition of
silt takes place, large stretches of water are
gradually impounded to form shallow lakes, which later
become firm ground. At the present time there are four
such stretches of water in the north of the Delta:
from east to west, and in order of size, Lakes
Menzaleh, Brullos, Idko and Mariut[9].

Upstream from Cairo, the Nile Valley is at first 6
to 10 miles in width, as the river tends to lie close
to the eastern side, much of the cultivated land lies

26

on the western bank. Towards the south the river valley gradually narrows until, at about 250 miles from the frontier of the Sudan, it is no more than 2 miles wide. Near Aswan there is an outcrop of resistant rock, chiefly granite, which the river has not been able to erode as quickly as the rest of the valley. This gives rise to a region of cascades and rapids which is known as the First Cataract. The part of the valley south to Aswan has been turned into an artificial lake that forms a huge reservoir after building the High Aswan Dam.

The land immediately to the east of the Nile Valley, spoken of as the Eastern Plateau (Eastern Desert) is a complex region with peaks that rise 6,000 to 7,000 feet. Gebel Shayeb is the highest (7,207 feet), and Gebel Hamata is (6,527), also much broken up by deep valleys that make travel difficult. Limestone predominates in the northwest, the two extensive lofty plateaus of North Galala and South Galala and Gebel Ataqa are built of limestone. Elsewhere are the igneous and metamorphic rocks along with sandstone and coral reefs extend along the arid Red Sea shore. The most important valleys that dissect the plateau are those that run towards the Nile valley such as Wadi Oena, Allaqi, Shait and Kharit, all were formed during the Pluvial age that took place in the lower Pleistocene. The Red Sea mountains form the western horst of the Rift Valley which is occupied here by the Red Sea and its two arms: The Gulf of Suez and the Gulf of Aqaba.

The Sinai Peninsula, separated from the Eastern Highlands by the Gulf of Suez, is structurally very similar, but the general plateau level is titled, giving the highest land (again nearly 7,000 feet in elevation) in the extreme south, where it rises in bold scarps from sea level. That southern part of the peninsula, triangular in shape, is built mainly of igneous rock, attains its highest level in Gebel Katherina (7,150 feet). Towards the north, the land gradually slopes down, ultimately forming the low-living sandy plain of the Sinai Desert which fringes the Mediterranean Sea. It is mostly built of limestone. One of the most important features of the Plateau is Wadi El Arish (El-Arish Valley) that runs northward to the Mediterranean Sea. Because of its low latitude and accessibliity, the Sinai, in spite of its desert nature, has been for many centuries, an important corridor linking Egypt with Asia.

West of the Nile occur the vast expanses known as
the Western Plateau (Western Desert). Although by no
means uniform in height, the land surface is much lower
than that east of the Nile and rarely exceeds 1,000
feet above sea level. It attains its greatest altitude
in the Southwest where Gebel Oweinat is located just
outside Egypt, but the northeastern flanks of the
mountain are within the borders of Egypt. To the
northeast from Gebel Oweinat is the sandstone plateau
of Gilf-El-Kebir. The plateau slopes gradually to the
depression where the oases of Dakhla and Kharga are
located. North of these oases is an escarpement that
forms the southern edge of the limestone plateau that
extends northward to the Mediterranean Sea. In this
plateau are situated the great hollows containing the
oases of Farafra, Baharia and Siwa, the Qattara
depression, the Faium depression and the smaller
depressions of Rayan and Natrun. These depressions
seem to have been hollowed out by wind action, breaking
up rock strata that were weakened by the presence of
underground water, and most hollows still contain
supplies of artesian water. In some instances (as for
example, the Quattara depression and the Wadi Natrun)
the subterranean water is highly saline and
consequently useless for agriculture, but in others –
notable the oases of Siwa, Behariya, Dakhla, Kharga and
Farafra – the water is sufficently fresh to allow for
irrigation and settlements have grown up within the
desert.

One of the main features of the Western desert,
which is just an extension of the Sahara, is the
occurrence of parallel belts of sandy dunes running
generally in a south southeasterly direction. Besides
these dunes, there are extensive flat areas covered
with drifted sand; but the total area covered by sand
is in fact less than that occupied by bare rocks[10].

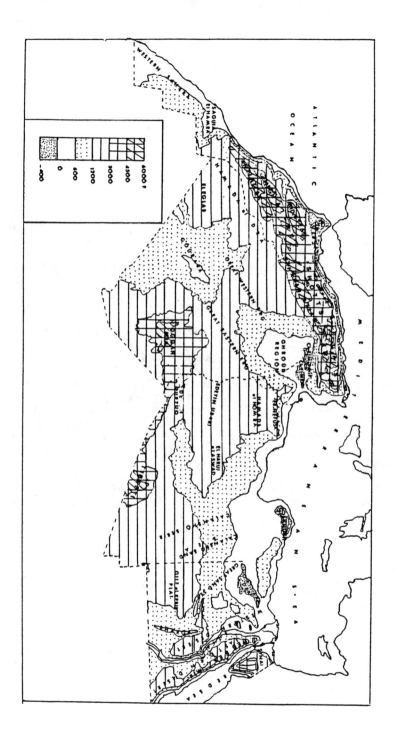

REFERENCES

[1] El Rif

[2] Moyen Atlas

[3] Haut Atlas

[4] Depois, Jean and Raynal, Rene, Geographie De L'Afrique du Nord-Ouest.

[5] Grande Kabylie and Petite Kabylie

[6] Depois, Jean. La Tunisie, ses regions, pp. 57-67.

[7] Blansum, T. Libya: The Country and Its People.

[8] Some studies have shown that the Mediterranean Sea has extended as far south as Isna. See John Ball: Contribution to the Geography of Egypt, pp. 32-54.

[9] There are some evidences that these lakes were the result of the submergence of the northern part of the delta under the sea.

[10] For more details about the formations of the oases and depressions see Said, R., Geology of Egypt, pp. 12-15.

CHAPTER 4

CLIMATE

Northern Africa that lies south to the
Mediterranean Sea and the Tropic of Cancer runs through
the very southern margin of its lands has
Mediterranean, semi arid, and arid climates. Its
climatic conditions are considerable influenced by the
Mediterranean Sea which plays a great role in the
pressure and wind systems as well as modifying the
temperature patterns. Along the west coast the cold
Canaries current flows southward, it is responsible for
the coastal fogs, the relatively low summer temperature
in the Western Maghrab and the offshore winds make the
coastlands rather arid. The location of the Atlas
ranges in the west and the effect of the Eurasian land
mass in the east and the extension of the region for
more than 2400 miles are other factors that leave their
imprints on the climatic maps and characteristics of
this part of Africa.

Air Masses:
    The main air-masses that reach North Africa and
have influence on its climates are: 1-Polar Continental
(cP) air reaches the region in winter time and its
source is Siberia and European Russia. This air is
cold, dry and stable. In reaching Africa much of it
crosses the Mediterranean Sea, where it acquires some
moisture, and this may give rise to precipitation as it
moves southward. The effect of this air decreases
westward. A similar type of air-mass forms in the
Atlas which is ice capped, but Affects only small
areas. 2-Polar maritime (mP) air reaches northern
Africa from the north Atlantic ocean. It occurs
frequently after the Mediterranean and north Africa,
when it is introduced in the depression that traverse
the Mediterranean in winter, this air is typically
cool, moist and unstable. 3-Subsident tropical
maritime (mTs) air appears on the west coast of Maghreb
southern to latitude 30°N all year. Stratus clouds and
coastal fogs are frequent, but rain never falls from
this type of air-mass. 4-Tropical continental (cT) air
derived chiefly from the Sahara, when the air subsides
upon a relatively uniform surface, and a dry stable
air-mass results. Surface turbulance resulting from
intense solar heating by day caused hazy, dusty
conditions up to almost 4,900 feet. This air mass is
associated with the north side of the Inter-Tropical
Convergence Zone (ITCZ).

31

In summer the Mediterranean Sea is usually covered by fair uniform pressure above the average and the prevailing winds are northerly. In winter the Basin is covered by a succession of depressions traveling from the west and the prevailing winds over much of the Basin are westerly.

It must be added the fact that in winter season conditions are always favorable for frontgenesis over the Basin. The main factor favoring much frontgenesis is the temperature contrast between cP and mPk air-masses over Europe and warm mPW air over the Mediterranean. If however, there is cyclogensis from other causes over the Basin, the frontgenetic temperature field helps to give the young cyclones energy. Most cool season cyclones are formed orographically, and are not wave-cyclones in the ordinary sense.

Climatic Conditions:
The Summer Drought: In all the coastal regions of the Maghreb states, June, July and August are almost rainless. In Tripoli and Benghazi of Libya the months of May and September are added. In the rest of the region arid conditions prevail most of the year.

Heat, blue skies, and blazing sunlight are the ruling qualities of summer weather in general. The return of moisture to the air by evaporation and transpiration far exceeds in amount whatever moisture is produced by precipitation and dewfall. Even the Mediterranean Sea itself loses more moisture than it receives, both from rainfall and stream runoff, a fact attested to by the prevailing eastward flow of water through the Straits of Gibraltar and the very high salinity of more than 37 parts per thousand for surface water along the Maghreb States shores. Over 39 parts per thousand is the value along the Egyptian Coast (Mean surface salinites for the world's oceans as a whole average 35 part per thousand).

During May the thermometer begins to rise regularly above 70° almost everyday and mean monthly temperatures average more than 60°. Mean monthly values increase steadily as the sun's rays reach the earth through cloudless skies, attaining maximum at most stations in August, along the Mediterranean coast. July, however is often only a degree or two cooler, and in some places both months are equally hot. In the interior, the maximum is mostly in July. Summers intend to be increasingly hotter and longer from west

32

to east and from north to south, partly because of increasing remoteness from the Atlantic's cooling influence, and partly because the effect of the intensified desert heat. The nocturnal temperatures along the coast are prevented from dropping much below 70°, ranging from about 70° at the Straits of Gibraltar to about 77° near Tunis and increasing eastern-wards to 81° near Benghasi and 84° at Port Said.

In most places of the region the dry land may heat to over 150°, the air temperature in the shade rising to over 100°, and since the air is calm, a shimmering radiation of heat from the sun-baked land creates a mirage phenomena. Many streams diminish in size, some cease flowing altogether, leaving only stagnant muddy pools. But the air is seldom saltry and oppressive. It is typically dry, and is usually in motion near the sea. Only in the interior valleys and depressions does it often attain a stifling quality that may remain unrelived until nightfall.

Relative humidity is characteristically low during summer in most localities that lie sheltered from the sea, but generally the relative humidity, like the rainfall decreases eastward and southward. The average relative humidity during July and August is 72 percent in Casablanca, 67 percent in Rabat, 65 percent in Tunis, 42 percent in Alexandria, 42 percent in Marakesh, 32 percent in Ouada (Morocco), 17 percent in Tamanrasset (Algeria), 26 percent in Kufra Libya and 14 percent in Aswan (Egypt).

Summer drought although attributable in part to the powerful evaporative effect of persistently high temperatures and intensive solar radiation, arise primarily from a pronounced scarcity of rainfall. As spring advances, showers fall on an ever diminishing number of days and bring smaller amounts of rain when they do occur. Casablanca, Rabat, Tangier, Algeris, Tunis, and Tripoli have less than .03 inches of rain and each less than one rainy day in July. Alexandria reports no rain at all in July and August.

What is the background of this spell of dry, hot sunny weather? On the face of it we might expect considerable rainfall of the thunderstorm type; the air is moist at low levels, and the sun is very strong. The answer appears to lie in the dryness of the upper atmosphere, and is the stability of the air-column. Even more significant, however, is the absence of any real source for cold air which might penetrate into the

basin and start cyclogenesis. Europe to the north is
warm in the summer months, and the chances of polar
outbreak reaching the Mediterranean in a tolerably cool
condition are remote. Algeria for example, has never
recorded temperatures below 62°F in July. The
temperature contrast associated with strong cyclonic
development are hence lacking.

Strong and persistent winds are rare up to great
heights. Only in Egypt is there to be seen any
persistant circulation. Here the circulation of
northerly and northwesterly winds form part of the
great monsoonal circulation of Asia.

The Rainy Months:
Some time during September the cold front of an
Atlantic depression will sweep south-eastwards across
France and penetrate through the gap of Province and
sweep out in the western Mediterranean, usually
reaching the coast of Algeria and the northern coast of
Tunisia. The sudden injection of cold air into an area
which is covered by warm and moist air released enough
energy for cyclone formation, and heavy rain occurs
over most of the coast of the Maghreb. The summer
drought and sluggish circulation are banished, and the
rainy season begins. As autumn goes on, the invasions
of polar air southward into the Mediterranean become
more vigorous and more frequent, and the resulting
cyclogenesis is correspondingly increased. From
mid-October until the following May, the climate
retains this rather stormy, cyclonic aspect, so
strikingly different from the quiet of summer. The
winter cyclones that are responsible for this wet
season are of three types. The first type is Atlantic
storms which enter the Mediterranean through the
Province gap, across the Spanish mesita, or through the
Straits of Gibraltar. The second type is waves or
fronts formed in the frontogenetic zone over the
Mediterranean Basin itself when pressure is high over
continental Europe and a flow of cP air moves towards
the sea while the Mediterranean Sea is relatively warm
and shallow depressions are formed[1]. Heavy and
frequent showers occur within these depressions,
presumably because of convergence and the heating of cP
air by the sea as it circulates around the centers.
Occasionally true eastward-moving wave cyclones develop
in these circumstances. The Siberian anticyclone is
the source region for genuine Pc air masses. The
coldest spells experienced in Egypt are on the arrival
of such air masses. The synoptic conditions that favor
the invasion of this Pc air occur when a deep

depression with tight pressure gradient (usually centered over Cyprus) covers the Mediterranean Sea at the time that the Siberia anticyclone extends westward to cover the Balkans. The Bc air starts as a north-easterly current in the rear of the depression over the east Mediterranean but reaches Egypt as a cold northwesterly wind. The third class of cyclone is the Saharan type. These are storms forming as frontal cyclones over the northern Sahara with warm sectors of cT air. Saharan depressions form chiefly in the trough south of the Atlas on fronts separating mP from cT air. As they move north-eastward into the Mediterranean they bring a wave of cT air out across the African coast. Though they give little rain, the weather of the warm sector is a characteristic weather type of the southern Mediterranean. The hot, dusty, desert winds from the southwest which blow as soon as the warm front is past, are known as the Samoom in Algeria and Tunisia, Gibli in Libya, Khamasin in Egypt and Sahat in Morocco. High temperatures, very low humidities and thick dust haze are characteristic. If the winds are strong, actual dust-storms or sand-storms occur, especially just before the arrival of the cold front. It is worth noting that the very dry character of this air precludes heavy precipitation. The moisture added at low levels does not affect the body of the airmass, which is too stable, for convection to carry the moisture upwards.

In Mediterranean Africa, unlike northwest Europe, inclement weather lasts only a few hours, to be followed by the return of clear, sunny skies and bracing air, for indigenous depressions are typically smaller and shallower than those of higher latitudes. Furthermore, whereas the warm sectors of a normal polar front depression farther north bring extensive cloud cover and higher relative humidity, the warm sector in the Mediterranean is often clear and dry. And the north winds of the trailing cold sector in the Mediterranean usually bring clear, bright weather unlike the unsettled storminess elsewhere in Europe.

Mention has been made of the general decrease in yearly rainfall from west to east and from north to south, and of the fact that maritime slopes are wetter than interior slopes in the lee of prevailing storm paths. Tangier has 35.5", Algeria 30.0", Tunis 16.5", Tipoli 15.2", Benghasi 10.5", Alexandria 7.0", Port Said 2.2", Casablanca 15.6", Agadin 8.9", Marakesh 9.3", Greyville 15.3", Biskara 6.9", Ein Salah 0.8", Kufra 0.4", Cairo 1.3", and Aswan 0.1" of rain^2.

35

The mean number of days on which rain falls with an amount of 0.05 inches or more are :   78 days for Tangier, 77 days for Casablanca, 70 days for Robat, 51 days for Marakesh, 35 days for Agadin, 76 days for Algers, 85 days for Tunis, 45 days for Tripoli, 43 days for Alexandria and 10 days for Cairo.

But it should be noted that in the arid and semi-arid regions where rainfall is less than 15 inches "mean annual rainfall" or "number of rainy days" are terms of little practical significance. Black clouds sometimes pass over, but the trails of rains that can be seen descending from them are evaporated by the thirsty desert air before they can reach the ground. If the air is sufficiently cooled by ascent up mountains, or by cyclonic or convectional influences, there may be violent downpours of rain - as much as 2 inches in a single storm in regions which are quite rainless for years.

The Ahaggar mountains in south east Algeria is an exception in all the region; it is fortunate in getting a share both of the summer air from the south monsoon winds and the winter rains from the Mediterranean cyclones and there are many running streams in its deep valleys. It is estimated that a mean annual rainfall of about 10 inches falls in the Ahagger region.

Snow is not a common occurance in North Africa but at elevations about 3500 feet it is likely to be reported during winter[3]. On the peaks of the High and Middle Atlas in Morocco snow may be seen as early as October while at heights of 3500-7000 feet it may lie for a week or so in the winter. Occasional snow is noted down to about 1800 feet but it is a very rare phenomenon at the coast. In the High Atlas winter blizzards are frequent and the snow can lie 4 feet or more in depth, while some north and west facing slopes can retain a snow cover for 6-8 months. Snow is never seen at Rabat or Casablanca but occurs one year in five at Tangier, once in two years at Algiers and nearly every year at Oran. Meknes and highland stations experience snow almost every year. In the eastern part of the zone snow is extremely rare beyond Susa but in Tunisian highlands, above 3500 feet, snow is reported about 10 days each year. Snow is very uncommon in Libya, except in the higher ground where accumulation of 6 to 8 inches may happen. Except for the mountain peaks in Sinai snow is an extremely rare phenomenon in Egypt. It occurs about once in ten years, mainly on the Mediterranean coast. Very rare

36

inland, in the 50 years, 1918-1968, snow fell on 5 occassions, but it never stayed on the ground. On the summits of the Sinai Mountains snow falls every year during the period between November and April. The depth of snow there may reach 3 feet and can remain for a long time.

Despite the occurence of most of the year's precipition during the winter months, skies are surprisingly free of could cover most of the time. Even in the cloudiest months, December through February, the mean cloud cover rarely amounts to more than 55% of the sky during the day (except for the western coast of Morocco because of the effect of the Canaries Cold Current where it amounts to 65%). Just north to the Atlas Mountains in the Maghreb and a few miles south to latitude 30° N., in Libya and Egypt the cloud covers is less than 30% and decreases fast southward.

Rabat's humidity increases in wintertime even at some highland stations where daily temperatures drop below the dew point after dark. Fog and mist thus occur during the night with considerable frequency.

And so, for five or six months, the winter goes. Rainy or showery weather with cyclones alternating with bright weather in the intervening periods in the northern section of the region, cool dry with irregular rain in the southern section. By May the sun has restored temperatures to near summer level. Toward the end of the month the last major polar outbreak and the final cyclonic rains are experienced. Then the atmosphere settles down to fourteen or fifteen weeks of unbroken tranquility that brings the hot and arid summer.

Climatic data for selected stations that cover the different climatic types in North Africa. Elevations are in feet, temperatures are in Fahrenheit degrees and rainfall in inches. The stations are arranged alphabetically.

Station	Elevation		Jan.	Feb.	Mar.	Apr.	May	Jun.	Jul.	Aug.	Sep.	Oct.	Nov.	Dec.	Ann.
MOROCCO															
Maghreb															
Agadir	89	T	57	59	62	65	67	70	72	73	71	69	64	58	
		R	1.5	1.1	0.9	0.7	0.2	0.0	0.0	0.1	0.3	0.8	1.3	1.6	8.6
Ben Gueria	1471	T	52	56	60	63	70	74	81	82	76	69	61	56	
		R	1.1	1.2	1.1	0.5	0.3	0.2	0.0	0.0	0.2	0.9	0.8	2.0	8.3
Cassablanca	203	T	54	55	58	60	64	68	71	73	71	67	60	56	
		R	2.1	1.9	2.2	1.6	0.7	0.2	0.0	0.	0.3	1.5	2.6	2.9	16.7
Essaouria (Magador)	33	T	57	59	60	64	65	67	68	67	67	64	61	53	
		R	2.2	1.5	2.2	0.7	0.6	0.1	0.0	0.0	0.2	1.3	2.4	2.0	13.2
Fez (Fes)	1368	T	50	51	56	59	66	73	80	81	75	67	57	51	
		R	2.0	2.5	2.5	2.4	1.4	0.6	0.0	0.2	0.5	1.9	2.8	3.1	19.9
Marrakesh	1542	T	52	55	59	67	70	77	82	85	76	70	63	54	
		R	0.8	0.9	1.7	1.3	0.4	0.4	0.0	0.2	0.4	0.9	1.3	0.7	9.2
Melilla	10	T	54	53	58	61	66	71	76	78	74	68	61	56	
		R	2.6	1.6	1.4	1.4	0.7	0.3	0.0	0.1	0.8	1.2	2.8	2.6	15.3
Midalt	4987	T	43	45	50	56	61	69	77	76	68	59	51	44	
		R	0.4	0.8	0.9	1.3	1.0	0.5	0.3	0.3	0.9	0.9	0.9	0.8	9.0
Ouarzazate	3717	T	49	58	59	65	72	80	86	85	77	67	58	50	
		R	0.3	0.2	0.5	0.2	0.1	0.1	0.1	0.2	0.6	0.6	0.6	0.5	4.0
Rabat	276	T	54	56	59	61	66	69	72	74	71	68	68	56	
		R	2.6	2.5	2.6	1.7	1.1	0.3	0.0	0.0	0.5	1.9	3.3	3.4	19.9
Tangier	56	T	54	55	57	59	68	68	72	74	71	65	58	55	
		R	4.5	4.2	4.8	3.5	1.7	0.6	0.0	0.0	1.0	3.9	3.8	3.4	33.5
Taroudant	89	T	56	60	64	68	69	74	79	80	76	71	67	59	
		R	1.1	1.2	1.0	0.8	0.2	0.0	0.0	0.0	0.3	0.9	1.5	1.2	8.2
ALGERIA															
Aflou	4547	T	39	38	47	51	60	69	75	76	66	57	45	41	
		R	1.2	1.3	1.5	1.3	1.1	1.1	0.3	0.4	1.0	1.8	1.2	1.3	13.5

Station	Elevation		Jan.	Feb.	Mar.	Apr.	May	Jun.	Jul.	Aug.	Sep.	Oct.	Nov.	Dec.	Ann.
Ain (Constantine)	2165	T	44	47	51	54	63	71	79	78	72	61	52	44	20.8
		R	3.3	2.5	2.2	1.8	1.7	1.0	0.2	0.4	0.9	1.7	1.9	2.7	
Algeris	194	T	54	55	58	61	66	72	78	77	75	68	61	55	30.0
		R	4.5	3.3	2.9	1.6	1.8	0.6	0.1	0.2	1.6	3.1	5.1	5.4	
Annaba (Bone)	13	T	52	53	56	60	70	71	77	78	74	68	61	55	31
		R	5.6	4.1	2.9	2.2	1.5	0.6	0.1	0.3	1.2	3.0	4.3	5.2	
BISKARA Biskara	410	T	53	56	61	68	77	85	92	91	85	73	61	55	6.9
		R	0.5	0.7	0.8	1.2	0.6	0.4	0.2	0.1	0.6	0.8	0.4	0.6	
Colombishar	2661	T	47	53	59	67	75	84	91	89	81	69	57	49	3.4
		R	0.3	0.3	0.5	0.3	0.1	0.1	0.0	0.1	0.3	0.5	0.6	0.4	
El Baydah (Greyville)	4280	T	39	43	46	52	60	70	79	76	68	54	51	47	15.3
		R	0.9	1.2	2.4	1.7	2.2	0.7	0.2	0.5	1.2	1.5	1.3	1.5	
Hassi Messaaud	460	T	51	56	21	70	77	89	93	92	86	74	62	54	1.4
		R	0.2	0.1	0.2	0.1	0.0	0.0	0.0	0.0	0.0	0.1	0.3	0.3	
In Salah	919	T	55	60	68	76	86	94	99	97	92	80	68	58	0.8
		R	0.0	0.0	0.0	0.0	0.0	0.0	0.1	0.3	0.4	0.0	0.0	0.0	
Skikda (Philipville)	26	T	51	52	55	58	63	69	75	76	73	66	59	53	32.8
		R	6.7	4.3	2.8	1.9	1.9	0.4	0.2	0.3	1.4	3.3	2.7	5.9	
Tindof	1453	T	56	61	68	72	77	81	95	94	86	73	66	57	1.7
		R	0.0	0.0	0.2	0.1	0.0	0.0	0.5	0.4	0.3	0.1	0.0	0.1	
TUNISIA Bizerte	20	T	57	53	56	60	65	73	77	79	76	69	61	54	24.7
		R	4.2	2.0	2.0	1.6	0.8	0.5	0.2	0.2	1.2	2.7	3.4	4.8	
Gobes	7	T	52	54	59	64	70	74	80	82	78	72	62	54	6.8
		R	0.8	0.7	0.8	0.4	0.3	0.0	0.0	0.1	0.6	1.2	1.3	0.6	
Gufsa	1030	T	48	51	57	64	72	80	86	85	78	69	59	49	6.0
		R	0.7	0.5	0.9	0.5	2.4	0.3	0.1	0.2	0.5	0.6	0.7	0.5	
Tunis	116	T	51	52	58	60	66	74	79	80	76	68	59	52	16.5
		R	2.5	2.1	1.6	1.4	0.8	0.4	0.1	0.3	1.3	2.0	1.9	2.4	

Station	Elevation		Jan.	Feb.	Mar.	Apr.	May	Jun.	Jul.	Aug.	Sep.	Oct.	Nov.	Dec.	Ann.
LIBYA															
Agedabia	18	T	55	57	62	69	75	78	79	80	79	73	68	59	
		R	1.6	0.9	0.2	0.1	0.1	0.0	0.0	0.0	0.0	0.4	0.9	1.1	5.3
Banghasi	82	T	56	57	60	65	71	75	77	78	76	73	67	59	
		R	2.7	1.6	0.8	0.2	0.1	0.0	0.0	0.0	0.1	0.7	1.8	2.6	10.6
Derna	30	T	56	57	59	64	68	73	76	78	75	72	66	59	
		R	2.6	1.8	1.1	0.4	0.2	0.0	0.0	0.0	0.1	1.0	1.7	2.5	11.4
Kufra (Oasis)	1254	T	55	59	66	75	82	87	87	88	83	76	67	59	
		R	0.06	0.0	0.0	0.0	0.02	0.0	0.0	0.0	0.0	0.0	0.0	0.02	0.1
Misurata	19	T	54	56	60	65	69	75	79	81	78	74	66	57	
		R	2.1	1.3	0.5	0.3	0.2	0.0	0.0	0.0	0.5	1.3	1.7	1.9	9.7
Sabha	1444	T	53	59	65	75	84	89	88	87	83	78	68	54	
		R	0.03	0.02	0.03	0.01	0.14	0.01	0.0	0.0	0.0	0.0	0.07	0.04	0.35
Sirte	71	T	56	57	61	67	71	75	78	80	79	76	67	58	
		R	1.6	1.1	0.5	0.1	0.1	0.0	0.0	0.0	0.3	0.7	1.0	1.4	6.8
Tripoli	56	T	54	56	60	65	69	74	79	80	78	74	65	58	
		R	3.3	1.8	0.9	0.5	0.3	0.1	0.0	0.0	0.5	1.8	2.4	4.7	16.3
EGYPT															
Alexandria	105	T	56	57	60	64	69	74	77	78	76	73	66	60	
		R	1.9	0.9	0.4	0.1	0.0	0.0	0.0	0.0	0.0	0.2	1.3	2.2	7.0
Aswan	400	T	59	63	70	78	85	90	91	90	88	82	72	62	
		R	0.0	0.05	0.0	0.0	0.05	0.0	0.0	0.0	0.0	0.0	0.0	0.0	0.1
Baharia	420	T	54	57	63	70	78	81	83	84	79	73	66	57	
		R	0.0	0.0	0.0	0.0	0.0	0.0	0.0	0.0	0.0	0.0	0.04	0.06	0.1
Bilbies	160	T	56	58	62	69	77	82	84	84	80	75	64	60	
		R	0.05	0.07	0.09	0.0	0.05	0.0	0.0	0.0	0.0	0.0	0.07	0.47	1.8
Cairo	98	T	53	55	61	68	74	70	81	80	76	72	64	60	
		R	0.4	0.2	0.2	0.1	0.0	0.0	0.0	0.0	0.0	0.1	0.1	0.2	1.3
El Arish	150	T	57	59	62	66	71	77	79	81	78	76	68	61	
		R	1.3	0.6	0.5	0.4	0.1	0.0	0.0	0.0	0.0	0.3	0.6	0.8	4.4

Station	Elevation		Jan.	Feb.	Mar.	Apr.	May	Jun.	Jul.	Aug.	Sep.	Oct.	Nov.	Dec.	Ann.
El Nakhl	1380	T	48	50	56	64	71	74	76	79	74	66	59	49	
		R	0.3	0.3	0.2	0.1	0.0	0.0	0.0	0.0	0.0	0.0	0.0	0.1	1.0
El Tor	6	T	50	60	65	71	78	82	84	85	81	75	69	62	
		R	0.1	0.1	0.0	0.0	0.0	0.0	0.0	0.0	0.0	0.1	0.1	0.1	0.5
Kafr Daud	80	T	56	58	62	68	74	79	81	80	77	73	67	59	
		R	0.1	0.1	0.0	0.0	0.0	0.0	0.0	0.0	0.0	0.2	0.1	0.2	0.5
Mansura	13	T	55	58	61	68	75	79	81	82	77	70	64	60	
		R	0.5	0.4	0.3	0.2	0.1	0.0	0.0	0.0	0.0	0.1	0.2	0.3	2.1
Marsas (Metrah)	93	T	55	57	60	64	68	73	76	78	76	72	67	59	
		R	2.1	1.7	1.5	1.0	0.6	0.2	0.0	0.4	0.4	3.0	1.6	3.9	16.4
Port Said	11	T	56	57	60	65	70	75	78	80	78	74	65	59	
		R	0.9	0.4	0.4	0.2	0.1	0.0	0.0	0.0	0.0	0.1	0.5	0.7	3.3
Salum	571	T	55	56	60	65	69	74	77	78	75	71	65	58	
		R	0.9	0.5	0.3	0.0	0.2	0.0	0.0	0.0	0.0	0.1	0.9	0.8	3.7
Siwa	49	T	58	56	62	69	75	83	85	84	79	74	65	56	
		R	0.04	0.04	0.04	0.04	0.08	0.0	0.0	0.0	0.0	0.0	0.04	0.12	0.4

REFERANCES

[1] Thompson, B.W.   The Climate of Africa.

[2] U.S. Naval Weather Service.   Vol. IX, Part I.

[3] Griffths, J.F. Climates of Africa.

CHAPTER 5

VEGETATION

Vegetation of North Africa is the result of the
climatic conditions and topographic features as well as
man's interference. In fact, vegetation has suffered
widely from destructive effects of overgrazing, defor-
estration and mismanagement.

The Sahara occupies most of North Africa, it
extends southward from the Atlas Mountains, the
Mediterranean coast of Libya on the Gulf of Sidra and
the Mediterranean coast of Egypt, it extends in length
for about 3500 miles from the Atlantic caost of Morrocco
to the Red Sea shores of Egypt. Only a single
persistent river, the Nile, traverses this mighty arid
realm, taking its rise in the lake district of east
Africa and the Ethiopian highlands, where it is supplied
with all the water it requires to maintain its steady
northward flow.

Vast tracts of the Sahara is considered lifeless.
Such regions, entirely without accessible water
resources, are regarded as maximum or absoulutely without a single tuft of grass. The only signs of life in
this region are in the oasis where there are some
settled cultivations dependent on permanent supplies of
underground water. In fissures and ravines and on the
beds of the wadis especially in the valleys within the
highlands there are dry tufted grasses with woody root
stocks, acasia bushes, all of which flourish after the
suddden, irregular rainstorms.

Along the Mediterranean coast in Cyrenaica and
Egypt, and along the feet of the southern Atlas, there
is another vegetative region that may be called
semi-desert. It is this coastal strip where the rainfall
is between 5 and 8 inches, very irregular and very
unreliable. During the rainy winter, short grasses grow
on which considerable numbers of sheep, goats and camels
are raised by the nomadic and semi-nomadic tribes living
in the region. Streams from the Atlas that lose
themselves in the desert still support tufted bushes and
grass along the line of their beds after their waters
have seeped below the surface, while at intervals,
depressions facilitating well digging support date
palms, gardens and population.

Although the Nile valley and delta are located
within these arid regions, it is quite different because

43

it is a region of intensive farming depending on highly developed systems of irrigation except along the shores of the delta where plants are found.

The Shotts plateau is covered with coarse grasses scrub and other herbaceous vegetation including esparto grass which is widespread, especially in the eastern part where rainfall is more and, because of its use in manufacturing paper, important commericially. This same type of coarse grass and scrub is found also on the Red Sea mountains and in the northern section of the Sinai peninsula where it helps the few nomads there to keep their herds of goats, sheep and camels.

The coastal plain and the Atlas Mountains of the Maghreb and the Nefusa Plateau of Tripolitanica and the Achoar Plateau of Cyrenaica are the regions of Mediterranean vegetation in North Africa. This type of vegetation due to the different climatic and topographic differences, is far from simple or uniform in nature.

The portion of the Maghreb coast from the Gulf of Gabes in Tunisia, to the Atlantic shores of Morocco possesses a broad, well developed variety of Mediter- ranean landscape, virtually uninterrupted for 1,200 miles. Here the qualities of the Mediterranean environment are extended inland about 100 miles in Tunisia and up to 200 miles in Morocco, by virtue of the Atlas Mountains. On these coastal plains cork oak, holm oak, olive and allepo pine along with juniper and the sandarac tree, are important scrub forest species. On the lower mountian slopes other species like the zeen oak combine with the more common members of maquis formation. On the upper slopes of the mountinas near the sea are found the more common Mediterranean oaks (cork, evergreen, and holm), along with chestnut oak, cedar, fir and pine. It should be noted that much of the former forest cover, however, has been destroyed by the collecting of firewood and overgrazing by goats and sheep through many centuries. This has led to soil erosion and an arid appearance of the mountainsides which is not justified by the actual rainfall. The Moroccoan government, aware of the importance of forest industry, has encouraged reforestation projects to restore the cork trees and started eucalyptus plantations which are covering now more than 100,000 acres.

Southward to the High Atlas and in the Meseta in Morocco as well as north to the Dorrale and west to the

Sahal in Tunisia, where rainfall is less than 10 inches, steppes grasses are found. Camel, goat and sheep-owning nomads are found.

Soils

Soils of North Africa as well as the water problem are among the physical factors that handicap agricultural development and expansion in the countries of the region.

The first feature of note is the enormous area which is virtually devoid of soil, amounting to 92.5 percent of the region. This huge desert area is regarded as non-soil. It includes bare rock, fernuginous and calcareous crusts, ergs, regs and desert.

Grey and reddish soils of desert steppe are found on the Shotts plateaus and at the southern feet of the Desert Atlas. This type of soil is calcareous and may have gypsum from the surface or at no great depth, saline patches are fairly common in this area especially around the Shotts.

Chestnut soils of dry steppes; brownish or greyish brown and slightly leached are found in the south part of the Sahal region in Tunisia along the coast of Tripolitania in Libya and in four other separate parts in Morocco; north to Fez and Marrakech, south of middle Sous Valley and east to the High Atlas in the area extending from Kaser to Bou Anane. Under irrigation, this soil can be very fertile and productive.

Pedzolic soils that show strong leaching of nutrients and are acid to strongly acid are found on the high elevations on the eastern sections of the Mediterranean Atlas in both Algeria and Tunisia, as well as on the Rif Atlas and the High Atlas. This soil is not suitable for agricultural production and their region is mostly used for grazing.

The northeastern coastal plain of Tunisia, the lower slopes of the Mediterranean Atlas and the western coastal plain of Algeria, the lower slopes of the Rif Atlas as well as the northern portion of the Moroccoan Meseta is covered with humus-carbonate soil. It is dark grey or dark brown, shallow and highly calcareaous soil. On cultivation, the humus content may rapidly decrease. Under good management and with intensive use of fertilizers it can be very productive.

45

Covering the Algerian Mediterranean coastal plain from Algeris eastward to Skida (Philipeville) is a type of brown soil of the Mediterranean forests, it shows little leaching of plant nutrients, but it erodes easily on hill slopes, as around the region of Bejaia (Bougie), commonly this soil is intermixed with humuscarbonate soils. It is an area of vineyards and wheat.

An area of terra roasa soils covers most of the Jabelel. Akhdar east to Benghazi and extends to Derna in Libya, although it is moderately fertile soil but it is eroded from many parts due to the semi-arid condition, it is mostly used for olive tree, palm trees and barely productive.

Aluviun soil of volcanic origin is covering the Nile valley and its delta in Egypt, it is of high fertile quality, very productive although it is not naturally rich, considering organic content. Close to Mediterranean coast this soil shows some salinity but it may be cured with proper drainage systems.

The oasis of the Sahara have local aluvium soils derived from the local rocks with high salinity and mixed with sand. They are suitable for palm trees, olive trees and barley.

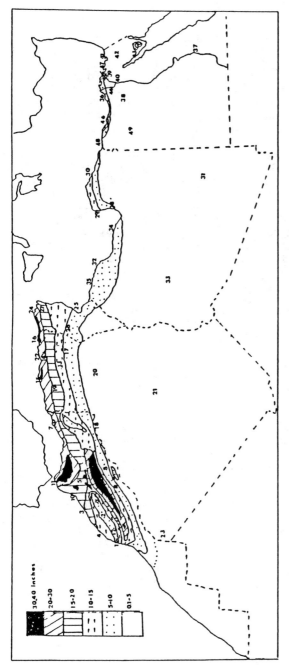

30,40 inches
20-30
15-20
10-15
5-10
01-5

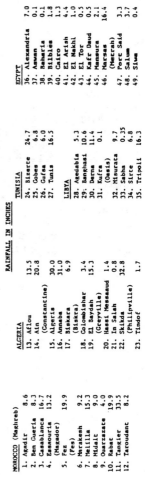

RAINFALL IN INCHES

MOROCCO (Maghreb)

1. Agadir	8.6
2. Ben Guerir	8.3
3. Casablanca	16.7
4. Essaouria (Mogador)	13.2
5. Fez (Fes)	19.9
6. Marrakesh	9.2
7. Melilla	15.3
8. Midalt	9.0
9. Ouarzazate	4.0
10. Rabat	19.9
11. Tangier	33.5
12. Taroudanc	8.2

ALGERIA

13. Aflou	13.5
14. Ain (Constantine)	20.8
15. Algeria	30.0
16. Annaba	31.0
17. Biskara (Biskra)	6.9
18. Colomb-Bashar	3.4
19. El Baydah (Greyville)	15.3
20. Hassi Messaaud	1.4
21. In Salah	0.8
22. Skikda (Philipville)	32.8
23. Tindof	1.7

TUNISIA

24. Bizerte	24.7
25. Gobes	6.8
26. Gufsa	6.0
27. Tunis	16.5

LIBYA

28. Agedabia	5.3
29. Banghasi	10.6
30. Derna	11.4
31. Kufra (Oasis)	0.1
32. Misurata	9.7
33. Sabha	0.35
34. Sirte	6.8
35. Tripoli	16.3

EGYPT

36. Alexandria	7.0
37. Aswan	0.1
38. Bahaeria	0.1
39. Bibbles	1.8
40. Cairo	1.3
41. El Arish	4.4
42. El Makhi	1.0
43. El Tor	0.5
44. Kafr Daud	0.5
45. Mansaura	2.1
46. Marsam (Matrah)	16.4
47. Port Said	3.3
48. Salum	3.7
49. Siwm	0.4

CHAPTER 6

ASPECTS OF THE HISTORICAL GEOGRAPHY

The excavation of the prehistoric sites in Egypt, especially those at Neqada, El Badari, and Ma'adi show as an established fact that domestication of plants and animals first appeared in Egypt around 5000 B.C., but it is possible that intensive hunting and gathering in the Nile Valley in Egypt as well as in the Sahara go back much further in time. The Sahara, as it has been mentioned, had more rain during the Pluvial age than it has now. The Neolithic rock paintings in the Algerian Sahara show that cattle and herdsmen lived about 10,000 years ago, in what is now a very dry region. As the climate deteriorated, the inhabitants of the Sahara retreated to the Nile Valley where water is available, or to the coastal areas where the winter rain is adequate to support human habitation, or to the south were there is rain in the summer that increases southward.

North Africa was probably occupied at that time by Caucasoid Mediterranean people with Hamitic language. About 5000 B.C., several waves of immigrants, pushed out of their original habitat in the southwest Asia by cycles of dry climates, crossed the Sinai Peninsula and moved to Egypt and along the Mediterranean coast. Through cultural contact, new crops and animals were introduced to Africa north of the Sahara.

Agriculture started in the Nile Valley on the levees bordering the main river channels, and crops were grown on the adjacent soils as the flood waters retreated in autumn, and in the lower parts of the flood plain later during the low water season of he year[1]. Gradually the system was refined. Banks were constructed to control the flooding, and to ensure the proper irrigation of the cropland, channels were dug through the natural levees. Cropping was extended into the spring and early summer, depending on ground water. The human population increased, urban centers began to develop, great strides were very rapidly made in political and religious thinking, great artistic achievements occurred, and economic activity was carried further than ever. Political unity was acheived in a very short period.

The inhabitants of the rest of the region were primarily herdsmen, but also practiced agriuclture as a secondary activity, especially along the coast between the Atlas Mountains and the Mediterranean Sea. Tree crops and cereals were grown on the coastal plain and on terraces built on the northern slopes of the Atlas Mountains.

While the ancient history of Egypt is clear and well documented, the ancient history of the rest of the region before the Roman era is obscure. This is because in the case of Egypt, pictorial records, hieroglyphics on monuments and lay tablets, households and state accounts, laws and obituaries provided a political and social history over a period of 5000 years that is unrivalled elsewhere in the world.

Dynastic Egypt was the heart of power and the source of ideas not only for Mediterranean Africa but for all the known world. During the Old Kingdom (2650 - 2350 B.C.), Egypt had a strong government that exercised control over all the country and established the political unity. A vast system of dikes and irrigation cannals were built to regulate the annual floods of the Nile. Prosperous farming and a surplus of food led to an expanding population, stimualted commerce, building of urban centers, and paid for Pyramids, temples, and other great monuments which are considered the most prominent and spectacular of the architectural engineer-ing structures of the ancient world. It was during the Middle Kingdom (2100 - 1650 B.C.) that the Egyptian armies moved westward to control parts of Libya and southward into Nubia. That Middle Kingdom came to an end when pastoral semetic people from the north invaded Egypt. The Hyksos or Shepard Kings from Eastern Syria crossed the Sinai Peninsula and because of political weakness and disunity during the last years of that Middle Kingdom, they were able to conquer the country. Although the Hyksos invasion was a major political setback, it still contributed to the Egyptian civilization. They introduced to Egypt the wheel and the horse. Egypt used both later during the New Kingdom, not only to expel the Hyksos invaders, but also to expand northward to build their huge empire that extended to upper Mesopotamia. It was during that New Kingdom that the Egyptiona cluture and civilization reached their peaks and diffused through trade and cultural contact to the other parts of the world. By the seventh century B.C., Egypt stared to lose power, ending its first political cycle, and was eventually conquered by the Assyrians and Persians, who left no imprint on the political and social activity of the country.

It was the Greek era that was responsible for the revival of Egypt in general and Alexandria in particular as a new center of world cultural radiation. The coming of Alexander the Great and the rule of Ptolemy, one of his generals, who with his successors ruled Egypt for 300 years, rebuilt the administration and the urban life in the country after the decay that prevailed during the Assyrian and Persian conquest. The drainage and irrigation of the Faiyum depression was extended. The supply of water by the great stream, Bahr Yousef, was improved; Alexandria, a new city built on the Mediterranean became the new capital and the center of political, social, and cultural activities.

The history of the rest of the region of Mediterranean Africa is rather obscure due to the lack of documentation. The earliest documented history shows that during the second millennium B.C., the Phoenicians established a number of city-states along the African Mediterranean coast from the Gulf of Sirte to the Atlantic coast of Morocco; those include Utica (on the coast of Tunisia), Cyrene (on the coast of Cyrenaica) and Carthage (close to where the city of Tunis is now located). The largest and most important of those city-states was Carthage, which was established around 800 B.C. It is estimated that the population of Carthage exceeded a half million people at its high noon age. The city was dependent on trade and on the immediate surrounding areas for grain.

The rise of Rome and the establishment of the huge Roman Empire that turned the Mediterranean Sea to a Roman lake led to more agriculture and economic expansion in all of Mediterranean Africa in order to meet the continuous and increasing need of its metropole. In fact, North Africa in general and Egypt in particular were the graineries of both the Roman and Byzantine Empires for five centuries.

Whereas the Carthaginians had confined their activities to the coast, the Romans extended their rule far inland; especially in Utica (what is now Tunisia), not merely to the eastern part of the Maghreb. Extensive areas of steppe in central Tunisia and along the coast of the Gulf of Gabes were planted with olive trees; the oil was refined locally and exported to Rome, and large quantities of wheat were shipped to Italy. In Algeria, the Romans irrigated the land in Numidia (eastern half of Algeria) and for the first time, established a settled agricultural way of life among the Berbers (aboriginal inhabitants of North West Africa),

In the semi-steppe areas of Libya and Eastern Maghreb, dams were built across wadis (dry valleys) to trap sediments on which crops were grown.

In Egypt, the already successful agriculture was intensified, more new canals were built to ensure better irrigation, swamps of the northern Delta were drained and claimed for agriculture, old canals were dredged, and in the Faiyum depression, crop areas were expanded after using the Maurice Lake (Lake Qarun) as a reservoir. All these improvements were carried on in order to supply Rome with more wheat, olives and olive oil, and more flax and textiles.

As early as 55 A.D. when St. Mark the Evangelist started to preach Christinaity in Egypt, and especially after Emperor Constantine of Byzantium adopted Christianity (approximately 312 A.D.), all the Egyptians and most of the population of the Maghreb region and Libya were converted to Christianity. Also, both the Greek and Latin languages became the official languages, the languages of learning and of the elite.

While the trade and cultural contact between Mediterranean Africa and the rest of the Middle East was, on a large scale, encouraged by the political stability and unity of the Roman Empire, the relations between these countries and the rest of Africa, south of the Sahara, was on a rather limited scale, due to its dryness and vastness. In fact, neither Carthaginian nor Roman rule ever reached across the Sahhara. However, there were some commercial links with points to the south. Carthage was linked with Giao, while the Roman city of Leptis Magna, close to modern Tripoli, was the northern terminus for the trans-Saharan caravan routes through Fezzan, and Marrakech was the Moroccan terminus of a trade route across the Mauritanian desert. Berber pastoralists were the agents of this contact. The Egyptians were in close contact with the Nubians in the north of what is now Sudan , but the Nile, because of its cataracts, and the Sudd did not provide an easy route to the south. Most of the trade between Egypt and Africa south of the Sahara was made by sea. To serve this purpose, a canal was built connecting the Nile near present Cairo with the Red Sea near present Suez. The Egyptians did not only trade with the Red Sea countries, but it is documented that they toured around Africa. Throughout the centuries, the main exports of Africa south of the Sahara to the Mediterranean countries were gold, ivory, ostrich feathers, hides and slaves; these were in exchange for slat, cloth, iron and copper goods.

51

The western Roman Empire collapsed under the heavy strokes of the Barbarians of east and central Europe as well as of the Vandals who settled in Tunisia. The Byzantine Empire was weakened by its continuous wars with the Persians in the East and the Europeans in the west as well as by the theological confusion and disputes and the persecution of those who opposed their religious dogma or political ideas especially in Egypt, where they were facing strong opposition from the Coptic Church. Consequently, the economic situation rapidly deteriorated. It is estimated that the wheat production in Egypt alone decreased about thirty percent during the last three decades of the Byzantine rule. Many of the land owners as well as the peasants deserted the land to the various monasteries or fled away being unable to pay th very high taxes. The canals were neglected and filled with silt. In the Maghreb region, the pastoral Berbers of the Atlas used the political instabiluty and raided the coastal agricultural land.

The Arabs, after defeating the Byzantine forces in Palestine and Syria, were attracted to Egypt by its wealth, especially its agricultural production. In 641, the Arab army crossed the Sinai Peninsula and conquered Egypt. A camp-city at Al-Fustat (the southeastern district of Cairo), in the strategic position near the apex of the Nile Delta, became the headquarters of the Muslim army and the new capital. The Copts, who disliked Byzantine rule, had not opposed the conquest. Under the Arabs, they found less oppression and at first paid lower taxes than under Constantinople. In the course of time, the taxes were grossly increased, conversion to Islam was either encouraged or imposed, and Egypt became an Arabic speaking country with a Muslim majority. But to this day, the Coptic Christian minority of more than eight million remains and uses the ancient Coptic language in its liturgy.[2]

For over two centuries Egypt was administered as a province of the Arab Empire. By the middle of the ninth century, the empire started to show symptoms of old age and signs of decay; the more remote territories were slipping from the grasp of the Abbasid Caliphs of Baghdad. Between 868 and 969, Egypt was ruled by two dynasties, the Tulunids and the Ikshidids, in virtual independence of the Caliphs.

In 969, Egypt, for the first and last time, was invaded from the west. The Fatimides, a Shiaite Dynasty founded in Tunisia, terminated the Ikhshidid rule and became the master of Egypt. Cairo (Al Qahirah) was built to be the new captial, and the mosque of Al-Azhar was founded and became the greatest center of Islamic theological learning. Under the Fatimides, Egypt was the center of an Empire that at its zenith included most of North Africa, Sicily, Syria and western Arabia.[3]

For more than three decades under that Dynasty, Egypt enjoyed a good degree of prosperity: agriculture and industry were encouraged. Trade with the Mediterranean countries and India brought wealth to the country and the ruler. By the beginning of the eleventh century, Fatimide rule and trade rapidly declined not only because of the negligence of a weak governor, but also because Egypt suffered for several successive years from low flood seasons that decreased the areas of cultivated land as well as the crops. Besides the poor economic conditions and the sociopolitical instability, the country came under another kind of political and military pressure from the Crusaders who, due to weakness of both the Baghdad and Cairo rulers, were able to establish along the Syrian coast feudal Western Christian states.

The defeat of the Crusaders in Syria by Egypt was due to the enegry and ability of Salah Al Din ibn Ayub (Saladin)[4] who was a minister to the Fatimid Caleph. Later, Salah Al Din deposed the caliph-ruled Egypt and founded the Ayubid Dynasty. The Ayubids strengthened the army and built up body guards by purchasing large numbers of slave-troops. Those were mostly of Asiatic origin from Turkestan, Mongolia, and the Caucas. The slave-troops (Mamluks) increased their power as that of their masters declined.

In 1250 one of the Mamluks (Aybuk ousted the last Aybid ruler and became the first Mamluk ruler (Sultan). Those Mamluks ruled Egypt from 1250 - 1517 and their ranks were replenished by fresh purchases. They were an alien element who exploited the country for their own benefit. Nevertheless, they were able to protect Egypt as well as their own interest against the two devastating Mongol invasions. In 1260 the Mamluks defeated Hulagu (grandson of Jeghiz Khan) and in 1401 they defeated Tamerlane and saved Egypt from their devastating advance.[5]

The numerous mosques built by the Mamluks indicate the wealth of th rulers and not necessarily the prosperity of the Egyptians: they oppressed all classes of native Egyptians. Most of the income was from taxing the active trade between Europe and the Far East crossing the Suez isthmus. Finally, Vascode Gama's voyage to India around the Cape of Good Hope (1446 - 1499) sounded the doom of the Egyptian prosperity. European ships henceforward by-passed Egypt and traded directly with the east. In 1517 the young and powerful Ottoman Empire invaded Egypt and ruled it from 1517-1798.

The history of Libya cannot be separated from the larger accounts of North Africa. When the Byzantine empire showed signs of decay, the Barbarians broke into the countryside, destorying its agricultural system and spreading insecurity which caused depopulation. In 431 the Vandals appeared, overran the country and ruined everything in their train. They were the first to introduce that piracy for which its harbours became notorious. In fact, the country before the Arab invasion was reduced to anarchy.

In this condition the first Arab invaders found it. In 643 the Arab army that conquered Egypt overran the country as far as Tripoli and Fezzan. The population rapily embraced Islam and adopted the Arabic language although some oasis residents still use Berber languages. Libya enjoyed peace and prosperity during the first decades after the Arab invasion but when the Bedouin Arab tribes, the Banu Hilal and the Banu Suleim invaded Libya and the rest of the Maghreb region, it brought the final catastrophe for medieval Libya. The country was devastated, agriculture abandoned. The only city that was spared and retained some vestiges of civilization was the fortfied city, Tripoli. Under these conditions the Ottomans invaded the country.

Tunisia, as the rest of Mediterranean Africa, was invaded by the Arabs. In 647 the Arabs were able to conquer the coastal plain and built the town of Tunis, and in 670 they founded Qairawan and made it the center of the Arab Rule in northwest Africa. The Berbers, although converted to Islam, did not yield to the Arab domination and made several attempts to regain their independence. They showed their resistance by sometimes adopting sects of Islam not approved by the central Islamic government such as Kharijites, Shiites or Ibadites. In the year 800 the Caliph in Baghdad appointed Ibrahimibn Aghlab as a tributary ruler of Ifriqia (Tunisia) and he succeeded in restoring peace. The Aghlubs became strong enough that they became virtually independent from the Islamic empire. During their time Tunisia enjoyed a relatively stable and prosperous existence. In 827 Aghlabid forces began the conquest of Sicily and it was completed in 878. In 905 the Fatimides ousted the Aghlabid dynasty and ruled all North Africa and Sicily. The new dyansty established a new capital on the coast, Mahdiya, before they moved the capital again eastward to Cairo, Egypt in 970. When the Fatimids moved to Cairo, they handed their rule of Tunisia to the Berber Family, the Zirids who were their supporters, and under their rule Tunisia enjoyed great prosperity. Arts, sciences, agriculture, commerce, and industry all flourished, but this golden age was suddenly brought to an end when the Bedouin tribes of Beni Hilal destroyed Libya on their way. The economy collapsed and the political power of the Berbers crumbled and the whole country lapsed into politcal fragmentation. After a short Norman rule that lasted only for twelve years (1143-1160), Tunisia became a part of the empire of the Caliphs of Marrakech (the Al Mohads, or Al Muawahhidun).[6] When the influence of that empire declined, another Berber family (the Hafsids) ruled the country until the Ottoman invasion in the sixteenth century.

The Islamic history if Maghreb started with the Arab invasion in the middle of the seventh century, but it met strong resistance from the Berbers as well as by the Byzantine Garrison who were in control of the coastal towns. But by 962, the Berber resistance yielded and the Byzantines were dislodged. In a short time, the Berbers did not only convert en masses to Islam, but also joined the Arabs and went along with them to the conquest of the western Maghreb and of Spain.

This new-found Islamic unity came to an end as fast as it was born. The Berbers, being dissatisfied with their inferior position as non-Arabs in an Arab empire, rebelled in 756 against the central Islamic authorities in Damascus, and in 756 they completely destroyed the authority of the recently established authority of the Abasid Calpithe. This was followed by a long period of anarchy, civil wars, and the rise and fall of some short-lived independent dynasties. The most important of these were the Aghlabids who, as mentioned before. were able to invade Sicily. In 910 the Fatimide dynasty rose to power and restored peace and prosperity to central and east Maghreb. When the Fatimides transferred their capital to Cairo, Egypt in 973, the power in the Maghreb was again disputed between various Berber confederacies. In 1050 the invasion of the Banu Hilal Bedouins brought, as it did in the rest of North Africa, devastation and anarchy. Fortunately for

Algeria, the Almoravids, who came from Morocco, brought to the area some kind of peace and prosperity. They were followed by the Almohads, who, although their power was short-lived, were able to expand trade to the north Mediterranean shores and their time was of cultural and economic prospoerity. But by 1250, the area was again in political chaos and instablility; in the interior, various minor princes asserted their independence while the coastal towns organized themselves into independent city states; their main source of income came from piracy.

Early in the sixteenth century, another strong power entered on the political stage of Mediterranean Africa and dominated the scene. It was the Ottoman Empire whose armies conquered Egypt in 1517 and advanced westward to reach Algeria. The Ottoman Sultans were mostly uncultured, and their empire was depending on military strength. They were only interested in extracting from the conquered countries the most revenues they could get without introducing any new economic or social projects or even encouraging keeping the existing ones. No wonder that all the countries that came under their domain in Europe, Asia, or Mediterranean Africa entered their darkest historical ages. This happened in the time when the European countries were gaining more strength building their industry, improving their agriculture, building their infrastructure, and establishing colonies everywhere in the world. The only strength in the Ottomans was their military strength, so as soon as that strength showed signs of decay, all Mediterranean Africa, like most of the other parts of their Empire, fell under one form or another of European control.

During the Ottoman era in Egypt, the Sultan and his agents rarely interfered with the local administration as long as they receive the amount of revenues levied on the country. The real governors of Egypt, the Mamluk soldiery and their leaders, the Beys, were allowed to continue receiving constant recruiting from the slave markets (especially from the Balkans) and kept the Mamluks in unimpaired vigor. From time to time, Mamluk grandees were virtually sovereign in Egypt. One of them, Ali Bey, ousted the official Ottoman governor and even invaded Syria, threatening the capital Istanbul; but one of his generals (a Mamluk) betrayed him, and Egypt was restored as a part of that sick empire. The Egyptians viewed with indifference the struggle of the Mamluks for mastery, as they were very unpopular by the extortions which they practiced on all classes of the native Egyptians.

During the eighteenth century, as a result of the French Revolution and the European power struggle between France and Britian, the French decided that the occupation of Egypt with its unique strategic location might lead to the overthrow of the British rule in India. General Bonaparte landed at Alexandria in 1798. The French stayed in Egypt for only three years (1798-1801), but their imprint and their great effect on the history of the country is still tangible to this day. The shock to Egypt of the French occupation was tremendous. The Mamluk ruling class was humiliated by the defeat and was unseated. The Egyptian Moselm leaders, were associated with the administration and consulted on public matters, something the Egyptians never knew during all the Mamluk and Ottoman reign and the idea of nationalism was reborn. The way to future development had been opened. French scholars who had accompanied Bonaparte produced monographs which became the basis of modern studies of the country. The discovery of the Rosetta Stone by the French during their campaign and Champollion success in solving and reading its languages, gained the world the archaeo-logical aspects of the ancient civilization and created the famous subject of Egyptology. French schools, institutes, newspapers, and the French language are still very popular in Egypt. The French engineer, DeLesseps was the man who got the concession of building the Suez Canal.

As soon as the French were forced to evacuate Egypt, a power struggle arose between the various forces: the British, who were responsible for dislodging the French, the Ottomans, who wanted to restore their authority in Egypt, the Mamluks, who wanted to regain their government seat, and the officers of the Ottoman army who had their own personal ambitions. The victor was Mohammed Ali, an Albanian officer of the Ottoman force. He defeated the British who had occupied Alexandria, massacred the Mamluks, formed an army whose majority were recruited from Egyptian natives and fought the Ottoman Empire, invaded Syria, defeated the Ottomans, advanced into Anatolia, and threatened the Ottoman capital Istanbul (formerly Constantinople). International intervention resulted in restricting Mohammed Ali's domain to Egypt and the Sudan.

57

Mohammed Ali is the founder of Modern Egypt. He organized the Administration on western style. The first railroad in all of Africa and Asia was built in Egypt to connect Cairo, Alexandria, and later the Suez. an ambitious educational system was organized under European teachers, and Egyptian students were sent abroad, especially to France. A press was set up primarily for the production of textbooks and manuals. As a result of his efforts and statesmanship, the political personality and the dignity of the Egyptian natives was restored; a Western educated class was emerging and the ferment of ideas characteristic of modern intellectual life had begun.[8]

In 1864, Mohammed Ali's grandson, Ismail, regined. He wanted to make from Egypt "a piece of Europe." The Suez canal was built. Argiculture was improved, new canals were cut, railways and telegraph lines were constructed, education was expaneded, and young women were encouraged to go to schools. The famous Egyptian museum, the National Library, the Opera House were built, and the modern districts of Cairo were planned and constructed. Expeditions to discover the upper sources of the Nile were sent, and the domain of Egypt in the Sudan and the Red Sea region was extended. However, the price for that rapid progress was very high. The huge international debts and the failure to repay them led to the declaration of bankruptcy by the Egyptian treasury. Both France and Britian picked this chance to intervene and control the financial system of the country to "ensure" payment of the debt. Britian, never lost interest in the strategic location in Egypt since the Suez Canal was built and proved to be the main vein of the Imperical transportation to India and the Far East. The British picked the chance of a rebellious movement against Tawfiq, Ismail's successor as the governor of Egypt, and occupied Egypt in July 1892. The British occupied the country practically until June 1956. Faced by a very strong nationalist movement, the British Government in February 1922 issued a declaraion unilaterally approving the recognition of Egypt as an independent sovereign state. The many restrictions on the independence made it nothing more than limited autonomous independence. In 1936 an Anglo-Egyptian treaty was signed which formally terminated the British occupation but allowed Britian to station forces in the Suez Canal Zone "until the Egyptian army will be in a position to secure the security of the canal." In the same year, Egypt became a member of the League of Nations.

The following years were marked by continuous
political struggle between the king, the political
parties, and the British government. The political
parties fought against each other for authority; the
king thought that the political parties, especially the
(WAFD), would rob him of his authority by insisting on
democratic process, and the British government that
never liked to see a strong Egypt that would threaten
its strategic interests. Another problem added to these
difficulties was the defeat of the ill-equipped army by
the newly established state of Israel. The corruption
in the government, the supply of faulty arms to the
Egyptian forces by the King and his circles, the
humiliation of defeat, the inflation, the negligence of
the economic projects, and the failure of the government
to negotiate with the British a new treaty for the
evacuation of the British forces from the canal zone all
of them foiled a revolution.

A group of young army officers, who had long been
planning a coup d'etat, overthrew the government, ousted
the king in July 1952, and later on June 18, 1953 Egypt
became a republic. The first major success of the
revolutionary government was signing a treaty with the
British in 1954 that provided for the withdrawal of
British troops from the Canal Zone within 20 months and
giving the Sudanese the right of self-determination.[9]

The general political atmosphere in the Middle East
and the ambitions of the revolutionary government did
not help to improve the relations between Egypt and the
west. The government committed itself to the "Arab
cause" and followed a clear, hard policy against the
State of Israel and its supporters. It led the
opposition to n the Baghdad pact and the Central Treaty
Organization (CENTO). Egypt tried to rebuild its army;
when the Americans refused to sell Egypt the arms, a
deal was made with Czechoslovakia which was to supply
large quantities of military equipment in return for
cotton and rice.

One of the main national goals of the government
was to build the High Aswan Dam. The aim of this
project was to increase cultivatable land and generate
hydroelectic power for industrialization, which was seen
as the main solution to Egypt's increasing population
problem. The United States, the International Bank of
Reconstruction, and Britain had offered loans to build
the dam, but when Egypt made the arms deal with the East
Bloc, the U.S.A., Britain, and the International Bank
withdrew their offers of finance for the High Dam. On

July 26, 1956 President Nasser of Egypt announced that the Suez Canal Company had been nationalized and the revenue from the canal would be used to finance the High Dam.

Britain and France, who tried to retain the control of the Canal, and Israel, who tried to defeat the Egyptian army before they could handle the new weaponry and impose a peace treaty on Egypt, reached a secret agreement to invade Egypt. The opinion of the world, U.S.A., and U.S.S.R. was to vigourously oppose that violent action, an the armed forces of Britain, France, and Israel were forced to withdraw.

On February 1, 1958, Egypt and Syria were united under one centralized government under the title of the United Arab Republic (U.A.R). In fact, the unity was ill-conceived, based on emotions, and led to miscarriage. It was a short-lived unity that came to an end in October 1961. The failure of the unity was a practical proof that Arab unity is an illusive dream.

The following six years saw further deterioration of U.A.R. relations with the West, increasing dependence on the Soviet Union and in general, an unstable relation with the Arab countries.

The relation between Egypt and the Arab countries, in general, and Saudi Arabia, in particular, and between Egypt and the Western countries still worsened as a result of the coup d'etat in Yemen, Egypt did not only support the Republicians led by Colonel Elsallal politically, but sent a huge force to fight the royalists who were financially supported and suppled with arms by Saudia Arabia.

Egypt kept more than 50,000 soldiers in Yemen without actually winning any clear victory in such a rugged terrain country. This Yemenese campaign was an economic as well as a military disaster to Egypt. It tied up in Yemen a large force badly needed, to defend the Egyptian territories against Israel. It did not make secret which its intentions of using force to impose a peace treaty on Egypt in particular and the Arab countries in general. The Yemenese war showed that although the Egyptian forces were equipped with Soviet-made arms, they lacked the discipline, the morale, and the trained leadership. Economically, the war was an immense, unbearable burden on the already weak and very shaky Egyptian economy. It led to a very high rate of inflation that the country had never before practiced; in fact, the effect of that inflation is still felt today. It made it impossible to carry on with the economic plans, and the deficit in the balance of payments became worse. In spite of continous American wheat supplies in 1964-65, credits from France, Japan, Italy, a loan from Kuwait and increased drawings from the International Monetary Fund, the country defaulted on repayments due to the IMF. In December 1966, Egypt seemes to be on the verge of bankruptcy. In spite of all this difficulties, Nasser, then President of Egypt, carried on simply by emotions and pride, kept the armed forces in Yemen until he was forced to withdraw them in August 1967. It may be said that this imprint of the Egyptian campaign on Yemen was not less than the imprint of the French campaign of 1798 on Egypt; it did not only help ousting a feudal monarchy, but it opened Yemen for the first time to the outside world. But, nevertheless, its effect on Egypt was disastrous.

The Egyptian-Israeli War was really ambigious. Although Nasser was aware of the intentions of Israel, he never stopped his anti-Israeli slogans, he did not plan for the war; he neither chose the time nor decided the strategy or the tactics of the war. When Syria-Israeli boundary skirmishes started, Nasser was again controlled by emotions; he closed the Straits of Tiran for navigation into and out of Israel, thus giving Israel the excuse to attack Egypt and practically annihilate its armed forces, especially the air force which was destroyed on the air fields by not having the chance to fight or even to fly. This outcome of the war proved the lack of a professional leadership for the armed forces and the maleficence of the political dectatorship. Egypt lost not only its armed forces but the entire Sinai Peninsula, the income from the Suez Canal that was closed, and its oil field. Although the military and economics losses were huge, the Egyptians (as a nation) neither lost their pride nor their determination to reclaim the Sinai Peninsula.

The Egyptian-American relations continued to deteriorate. Egypt always looked to the U.S.A. as a third party in the Egyptian-Israeli relation as being directly or indirectly involved with Israel in supplying it with the most advanced weaponary, backing it financially, helping it economically and supporting it politically.

One of the results of the 1967 was more involement of the U.S.S.R. in Egyptian affairs and policies. The

Soviet Union reequipped the Egyptian forces, provided other military supplies and instructors, and offered more economic aid especially by constructing a steel complex at Helwan (South of Cairo) and an aluminum factory at Naga Hamadi in upper Egypt.

On the other hand, Israel realized that although it was victorious in 1967, it was not able to impose a peace treaty on Egypt. Violation of the cease-fire agreement from both sides led to war of attrition by Egypt and bombardment of Egyptian targets by the Israelis. In November 1967. the U.N. Security Council adopted a British Resolution (Resolution 242) laying down the principles for a "Just and Lasting Peace in the Middle East". Dr. Gunnar Jarring was appointed Special U.N. Representative. The Palestinians, for their own reasons, rejected the resolution. The Israelis interpreted the resolution in a way which was never intended, and Dr. Jarring never succeeded in his mission. In 1969, the U.S.S.R., France, Britain and the U.S.A. began talks at the U.N. to promote a steelement, but unfortunately they failed. In 1970, the U.S. State Department Secretary, William Rogers, put forth a set of proposals for solving the continuing crisis, but again no solution was reached.[10]

After that war of 1967, it seemed that the Egyptian public was very dissatisfied with the political regime. The trial of officers and civilians responsible for the defeat was considered only to find some scapegoat for the regime. The bad and serious economic situation continued to slide downward. Widespread demonstrations by students and workers took place, something that had never been known in Nasser's time, and universities were closed. The change of governments and the announcement of March 30 of a new plan for building a modern state in Egypt based on democracy, science, and technology, was considered as just a change of the paint and not of the substances. Egypt's dependency on the regular financial aid payments from Saudi Arabia, Kuwait, and Libya, and on Soviet assistance was humiliating to Egyptians, who were and are very strongly nationalists in outlook. The economic crisis of Egypt was a little bit softened by the completion of the high dam; it increased the agricultural production and the industrial output, although the continuous increase in the growth rate of population did not only consume the fruits of the economic expansion but forced the country to import more consuming goods, especially grains and food stuff.

On September 28, 1970 Mohamed Anwar El Sadat, then Vice President, succeeded Nasser as a provisional President. In mid-1971, he was firmly in control of the government of Egypt, after comprehensive purging of his opponents at all levels of the government.

In 1971 Sadat made repeated declarations of his intention to fight Israel and get back the Sinai Peninsula, but only when the time was ripe. During 1972, Egypt intensified its efforts to diversify sources of aid and armament development, rather than depending heavily on the Soviet Union. The Suez-Alexandria (Sumed) pipeline, to carry oil from Suez to the Mediterranean Sea, received promises of Western backing. And in May 1972, a five-year preferential trade agreement was concluded with the E.E.C.

The year of 1972 was a year marked by the striking event of the dismisal of Soviet military advisers from Egypt in July. They were being accused of interfering too much in the military decisions. The military installations were manned by Egyptian personnel. This movement did not rupture the Soviet Egyptian relations, but neither did it improve the Western relations with Egypt, although President Sadat's main intention in that approach was too improve his country's relation with the United States, a chance that the American policy makers missed. During that year, the ecomomic difficulties were as bad as they had been for a long time. The case of "no-war-no-peace" led to more internal political unrest. Under such conditions, as it always was for ages in the past, relations between the two communites of Egypt, the Moslems and the Copts, became rather tense. The Moslem extremists burned down some churches and provoked the Christian population. At first, Sadat tried to prevent the dangerous split by passing a law providing harsh penalties for offenses endangering national unity. The law had little or no effect because the Moslem extremists abused the loosening of the political ties concerning their personal freedoms, and at the same time the Copts were trying to defend their rights and freedom.

In spite of all those political, economical, national and international difficulties, and in order to regain their pride and reclaim the Sinai Peninsula, the Egyptians were able to build professional fighting forces with a fresh leadership and isolate them against politics and political ambitions.

On the sixth of October 1973, Egypt impressed the world by its surprise and successful attack against Isreal. The Egyptain forces crossed the Suez Canal, destroyed the Bar lev lines of fortification, and pierced the defense lines of the Israelies in a few hours. After the American intervention to prevent the total defeat of Israel, it began to be clear that Egypt would be fighting in practicality not Israel but the American armament and the American prestige. Egypt accepted the cease-fire proposal[11].

The 1973 war had important result. Psychologically, it restored the Egyptian confidence and the Egyptian pride, militarily it proved their ability to fight and defeat an army well-equipped with the most sophisticated American armament, and politically the war altered the whole structure in the Middle East and forced Israel to realize that peace could not be obtained on their terms only.

It is of significance to mention that the cease-fire agreement and the following disengagemet talks were opposed by both Syria and Libya. However, Egypt's insistance in reaching an agreement with Israel showed that Egypt, for the first time since the rise of the Israeli problem, would follow a policy of national interest and would not be carried away by emotions, flared up by illusions about Arab unity.

That war had results on the national, political, and economic scenes. Politically it led to extending an amnesty to many important political prisoners, press censorship was lifted, and police interference was limited in everyday life. Economically it led to the establishment of a program of economic and social reform which concentrated on reconstruction, attracting foreign investment, and the introduction of a private enterprise sector in the economy, while still maintaining the public sector.

The history of Libya under Ottoman rule was marked with the same political and economic deterioration that prevailed in the other countires of that empire. Spain, after ridding itself completely from Islamic rule, was politically interested in Northwest Africa and Libya. In 1510 Spain conquered Tripoli. But the Spaniards became heavily involved in European politics and they could not extend their control beyond the city itself due to the resistance of the Libyans who were helped and encouraged by the Ottomans. Therefore, they conceded the lordship and the defense of Tripoli to the knights of Malta. Although the Turks were not able to capture the island of Malta, they were able to oust the knights from Tripoli. The Turks made Libya an Ottoman province that included Tripoli, Cyrenaica, and Fezzan, with Tripoli a seat of the Pasha (the title of the Turkish governor). In fact, the Turks never administered the interior part, and as in all parts of that empire, collecting the levied tribute was the most important task of a few regular troops or certain assigned tribes. All other aspects of economic activities were neglected. The main source of income for the Pasha, his circles, and the Ottomans was the revenue from piracy. The maritime powers tried in vain to stop or even reduce piracy by bombarding Tripoli several times. Admiral Blake was the first to bombard the town in 1654, the great de Ruter of Holland followed in 1669 and 1672. In 1711, Ahmed Karamanli, a Turkish officer, succeeded in ousting the Pasha and proclaiming himself a Pasha. Although he was later recognized by Istanbul as the legal Pasha, he governed Libya independently. That Karamanli Dynasty was able to govern Libya until 1835. Several of those governors were capable statesman who improved the political and economical conditions in the country. Although they, like the former rulers, relied on piracy for much of their revenue, they made treaties with the maritime powers, bargaining with them to refrain from attacking their ships for a consideration. When they were not able to restrain their captains from breaking such treaties, the powers took strong action, as did the United States in 1805. Since piracy was a continual threat to the fast-growing maritime trade and transportation in the Mediterranean Sea, the European powers decided to end it completely by any means. They entrusted Britian with the suppression of those evils. It took ten years of naval and diplomatic action to effect this. The suppresion of piracy meant the ruin and end of the Karamanlis. The Ottoman Sultan picked the chance of the fall of that strong dynasty to reoccupy Libya and to bring it back under his direct control. He succeeded in doing that in 1835. The Libyan history during the rest of the nineteenth century was not different from the history of the rest of the countries under the rule of "The Sick Man of Europe": corruption, poverty, revolts, and economic negligence.

As in most of the Moslem countries, political chaos and economic failure led to the rise of religious movements. During that period of Libyan history the Sanuse brotherhood was founded by Mohammed ibn Ali al Sanusi in 1834. The center of the movement was on Jebel al Akhdar in Cyrenaica. From there the movement quickly diffused throughout Libya. In order to avoid the opposition of the Turks and to some extent the Europeans, the movement transferred its headquarters inland to the oasis of Jaghbub. In 1859 Mohammed al Mahdi al Sanusi succeeded his father as the leader of the movement.

Italy, for its national problems, came quite late to the colonization table, and in order to acquire some colonies, it had to be content with poor areas that did not interest the great powers. One of these areas was Libya, although it is a desert region and the best of it in the norhtwest is a semi-desert area. From an Italian viewpoint, however, it had two advantages: the first is its closeness to Italy itself, and by occupying it Italy would be in a good strategic location in the middle of the Mediterranean Sea; the second, it could be used later as a jumping point to invade Egypt which was once an important part of the Roman Empire and recently of excellent strategic value. Italy thought that conquering Libya would be an easy operation since Libya itself was in disarray, and Turkey was heavily involved in the Balkan War. On October 3, 1911 the Italians occupied Tripoli; they were also able to seize Misarata, but every where else they suffered considerable reverse. The Libyans joined the Turks to resist the Italians and succeeded in preventing them from stretching their bridgeheads inland. The defeat of Turkey in the Balkans and its very unstable national affairs were the main reasons for signing a peace treaty with Italy on October 12, 1912. The main condition in the treaty was that the Libyans should be allowed "administrative autonomy". This condition was never realized. Signing a peace treaty did not mean that Libya was conquered, in fact with the outbreak of World War I, Italy was only in control of the coastal towns of Tripoli, Benghazi, and Tobruk. During the years of World War I, the Germans joined the Libyans, led by the Sanusis and the Turks, in tying up Italian forces in Libya and British forces in the Western desert of Egypt and prevented them from fighting in the main western front. Although the Sanusi-led Libyan resistance movement was deserted by the Turks, they were still able to restrict the Italian conquest in the coastal towns after the war. Fascists made a great effort to occupy all of Tripolitania and Fezzan in 1922. It took them until 1925 to occupy Tipolitania, but the struggle in Cyrenaica and Fezzan went on. Sayed Omar El Mokhtar, representing the Sanusis, kept on the struggle until he was captured and hanged in 1931.

Although the Italians considered that occupying of Libya was just one step forward in building an African empire, and in spite of the fact that Libya, as was mentioned, is a desert or semi-desert region, without any minerals then, they proceeded with an extensive and expensive colonizing program. Italy's aim was as much as possible, the settlement of the Italian peasant population in Libya. Water wells were bored, water reservoirs were built, and the cultivatible area was expanded. An excellent network of roads was extended. The best of the productive land was taken from the original Libyan owners and given to skilled Italian cultivators of olives, vines, figs, tobacco, and barley. The Libyans were left to be bedouins, and illiteracy was widespread among them; in general, they were treated as second class citizens.

Italy lost World War II, and consequently lost its colonies including Libya. In 1942 the British occupied Cyrenaica and Tripolitania, and the French occupied Fezzan. The United Nations decreed Libya's independence in 1952. Mohammed Idris Al Sanusi, a hero of the resistance and backed by the British, declared himself the first king of Libya with a federal constitution to rule the three provinces of the country.[12]

Libya, as a young political country and with practically no natural resources during the fifties, went through political and economic hardships. The rivalries between the three provinces and the different political parties led to continuous political unrest. Libyan loyalties were with the tribes rather than the newly founded state. Lack of national unity, unexperienced government officials, and widespread illiteracy added to the political and administrative problems. The lack of resources forced the king and the government to depend almost entirely on economic and financial aid from Britain and the United States in return for permission to maintain militarty bases in Libya. Under such conditions, the economic development was negligible and the population was among those having the lowest standard of living in the world.

The economic situation changed dramatically in the early sixties when oil was discovered, produced, and exported on a large scale. The first oil well was discovered at Zelten in Cyrenaica in June 1959, and within 12 months, in June 1960, there were thirty-five wells in production yielding approximately 93,000 barrels of oil per day. The production increased steadily and fast, making Libya one of the most

67

important oil exporting countries. The tremendous new wealth did not only increase the gross national product of the country and the per capita income of the limited popluation, but also produced a complexity of national and international problems.

In April 1963 Libya was transformed from a federal state into a unitary state. The change was intended to build up a national unity by preventing the rivalry of the three regions ad to let all of the regions and the entire population enjoy a share in the new wealth. Women were allowed to vote, and elementary education became compulsory in 1968.

In the international affairs, Libya, being financially independent, made it clear that it would not propose the renewal or the extension of the military agreements with Britain and the United States. The 1955 agreement with France, that allowed France to retain certain military facilities, was cancelled as well. The oil wealth made Libya's voice heard quite well in other parts of the world. It joined the rest of the African countries in closing its air and sea ports to Portuguese and South African ships and planes. The outbreak of the Arab-Israeli war in June 1967 caused serious disturbances in Tripoli and Benghazi in which students, oil, and port workers played a prominent part. However, the closing of the Suez Canal increased the country's oil production and exports to Europe. With the great advantage of being on the right side of the Canal, Libya became the second largest producer in the Arab world only preceeded by Saudi Arabia. The government, like all of the governments of the Arab oil producing countries, agreed to make annual aid payments, totalling 30 million sterling pounds, to both Eypt and Jordan for alleviation the consequences of the war.

In 1967 the government initiated a program aimed to rapidly change Libya to a modernized country. The program was to expand education, improve the civil service, and develop the transportation and communication system. The government also sought to build modern armed forces, provided with up-to-date equipment, and sent some of the young Libyan men to Britain to be trained to handle the new weapons. One of those who were sent there was Muamar Elgaddafi, who later led the 1969 coup.

Elgaddafi[13], then 27 years old, was emotionally fascinated by Gamal Abdel Nasser's dictatorship, socialist national policies, slogans of Arab unity, and

68

his very anti-Israel militant attitude. In September of 1969 Elgaddafi led a bloodless coup that met no opposition or resistance while King Idris was in Turkey for medication. Within a few days, the new regime was in full control of the entire country which was proclaimed the Libyan Arab Republic. Following the same steps that Nasser made in Egypt in 1952, Gaddafi announced that a "Revolution Command Council" (RCC) took power. A largely civilian cabinet was appointed under the close supervision of RCC, political parties were banned, censorship was imposed on the press, and the royal constitution was cancelled. In January Gaddafi proclaimed himself Prime Minister, besides being head of the state and the army commander, and some of his colleagues joined the cabinet. In his first year, Gaddafi crushed two anti-government plots.

The revolutionary government of Libya had certain national and international policies to apply. Although the principles of these policies were rather general and obscure in the beginning, they became specific and clear later. In national affairs, the policy was to run the government in accordance with the Islamic law as Gaddafi himself understood and interpreted it. Alcoholic drinks and certain western clothes were prohibited. Property of the Jewish and Italian minority was confiscated. The Arabic language was to be the only language in use, and the law of amputation of thieves' hands was revived. In April 1973 Gaddafi called for an immediate "cultural revolution to destroy imported ideologies, whether they are eastern or western".

In May 1973 he presented his theory which was a call for a return to "Moslem Fundamentalism," and he urged all the Moslems to impose that theory on all their governments (a call since echoed in some other Moslem countries and Moslem parties and fraternities). Libyan banks were nationalized, businesses operating in Libya were to be controlled by Libyans, and the oil compaines were also nationalized.

Gaddafi's international policies followed three tracks:

I. The close ties with the western countries were abandoned, especially with the United States as the "main backer for Isreal." On the other hand, he established close relatins with the Arab countries, especially Egypt. (Nasser, with whom he was fascinated and whose steps he was trying to follow, was still the President of Egypt.) Later on he tried many times, but

69

in vain, to form an Arab unity or merge with some Arab countries. The main reasons for the failure of such a merger or unity were not only because Gaddafi wanted it to be on his own terms in applying his own national and international policies, but also because there was no logical, geographical, or political basis for such a merger; Gaddafi like Nasser was and still is carried by emotions that are based on unfounded slogans. In 1969 there was the proposal of forming a federation with both Egypt (United Arab Republic) and Sudan, but that has never materialized. Another attempt was in 1972 when Egypt and Libya agreed in principle to form a federated republic, but the attempt failed. When Gaddafi was frustrated by the failure of his attempt, he tried to put pressure on Egypt by staging a "March on Cairo". The marchers were halted 200 miles from Cairo. Gaddafi's failure to merge with Egypt turned him westward; in 1974 Tunisia and Libya announced that they had formed a unity. A referendum to approve the unity was to be held later, that referendum was postponed indefinitely and so was the unity.

The continuous attempts and failures to unite with Arab countries brought Gaddafi in direct confrontations with many Arab governments whom he thought did not support or obstruct that unity. His speeches attacked most of the Arab leaders, and he provided money, training, and arms for revolutionary movements to achieve Arab unity by "popular pressure". Many times diplomatic relations were severed with Tunisia, Morocco, Saui Arabia, Syria, Egypt, Sudan and Jordan. War of words between Libya and those countries was great, especially between Libya and Egypt after Egypt signed the record interim disengagement with Israel. The war of words turned to serious frontier clashes that had all the appearances of open, hot war. In 1980 Libya completed building a 200 mile wall of fortification to defend its border with Egypt.

II. The complete destruction of the state of Israel was and still remains the most important goal of Gaddafi's Libyan international goals. In fact, the aim of creating an Arab unity was always the first step toward achieving that goal. To that extent, Gaddafi supported or disapproved different Arab policies depending on their political handling of the problem and their demagogue attitudes toward the state of Israel.

When Gaddafi's coup of 1969 brought him to power, the Arab-Israeli war of 1967 had already given Israel a strong grip, as stated before, on the West Bank of the

Jordan River, the Gaza Strip, and the Sinai Pensula. In order to go along with Nasser, his most favorite leader in the world, Gaddafi accepted the American proposal for a cease-fire with Israel but rejected the United Nations Security Council Resolution 242 on the Roger's peace plan. In fact, he stated that a peaceful solution for the Arab-Israel problem was impossible. During the fighting between the Palestinian Liberation Army and the Jordanian Army in 1973, Libya withdrew its financial aid from Jordan and directed it to the Palestinian Organization and broke off the diplomatic relation with Jordan and started a media war with King Hussein.

Before the 1973 Arab-Israeli War, Gaddafi accused the Arab countries, particularly Egypt, Syria, and Jordan, of being more interested in recovering the territories they had lost during the 1967 war than in serving the Palestinian cause and helping the resistance movement. He did and still accuses the Arab countries of conspiring with Israel to destroy the resistance movement!!!

During the 1973 war, because Egypt and Syria did not inform Gaddafi of their intention to launch a war against Israel, he was very critical of the war plans. When Egypt and Syria accepted the U.N. cease-fire resolution, he accused the leaders of both countries of treason. The bad relations between Egypt and Libya further deteriorated in November 1977 when President Sadat of Egypt showed his peace initiative by visiting Jerusalem. Gaddafi condemned Sadat's move and was the engineer of the Tripoli Meeting of the "rejectionist" states who formed the "front of steadfastness and confrontation" against Israel in December 1977. When the Arab countries held a meeting in Baghdad to condemn the Egyptian-Israeli peace treaty signed in Camp David, U.S.A., and took harsh steps to isolate Egypt from the Arab world and impose economic and financial sanction on it, Libya walked out of the meeting on the grounds that the contemplated sanctions were insufficient.

In 1980 there was a split in the ranks of the Palestinian Liberation Organization (PLO) between the moderates and the left wings within the movement who rejected any movement to solve the Arab-Israeli problem peacefully. Gaddafi adopted the left wings leaders, continued to help them and suspended the financial aid to the moderates. He accused Arafat, the leader of the PLO, of being too soft on Israel and of having abandoned the armed struggle in favor of a strategy of diplomacy.

71

In 1983 Israel invaded Lebanon to eliminate the PLO existance there. The Palestinian Organization resisted the invasion, but at last they were not a match to the heavily-equipped Israeli army and accepted the cease-fire proposed by the United States, including evacuating the Beirut area. Gaddafi was very critical of Arafat and urged the Palestinians to fight (for the last crop of blood). In fact, he arranged and encouraged a meeting against Arafat and his moderate faction (Alfatah) and broke off relations with him.

Libya itself never joined in a war against Israel, "for reasons of geography", meaning that Libya is far from Israel. Libya's help was limited to financial aid and to supplying light arms for those whom it favored.

III. Gaddafi followed a policy of supporting "Islamic cause" and "liberation organization". The support was mostly in the form of financial help. He supported Pakistan in its war against India and supported the Pakistani government of General Zia El Haq who claimed establishing an Islamic government based on Qoranic rules. He supported the government of Indonesia when it invaded East Timor Island. It is said that he is partly financing the Pakistani nuclear program to build an "Islamic atomic bomb". He is still supporting the Moslem rebels in the Philippines. Gaddafi's support to Idi Amin of Uganda, being a Moslem leader, included sending some of his troops. Gaddafi did not only support the "liberation movement" in Morocco, but arranged for a coup to oust King Hassan; the coup failed. He is a supporter for the "liberation movemnet" in the former Spanish Sahara that was annexed to Morocco. Egypt is continuously accusing Libya of supporting the Islamic extremist parties that intend to topple the Egyptian political regime. The government of Sudan was also accusing Gaddafi that he was not only supporting the Sudanese underground parties but was preparing to invade Sudan.

In 1980 a raid on Gafsa in Tunisia was attributed to Libya. Although Libya denied it, the relations between the two countries were strained. France sent military aid to back the Tunisian government against the potential Libyan threat. The French embassy in Tripoli an the consulate in Benghazi were burned to demonstrate Libya's anger at the French action.

One of the areas Gaddafi got involved in is Chad. He started helping the rebels against the legal government in 1973 by supplying them with money and arms. In 1973 Libya occupied the uranium-rich Aouzu region in northern Chad, adjacent to the Libyan border. Gaddafi based his action on an agreement made between the Vichy government of France and Italy during World War II. It should be noted that France, as a colonial power, had no power to secede any part of a colony without the consent of its popluation; as well as the fact that the Vichy government was not recognized internationally. Libya is still meddling in the national affairs of Chad by helping the rebels, although Gaddafi denied that Neva interfered in Chad's national affairs. France sent French troops and an air force to back Chad's government against the Libyan and rebel forces.

Libyan relation under the Gaddafi regime was and is still very friendly with the Soviet Union. This does not mean that Gaddafi is a Communist. In fact, the reason for the close ties with the U.S.S.R. is the material benefits; the U.S.S.R. is providing the Libyan forces with arms, and Libya is paying large amounts of cash that the Soviet Union badly needs. Another reason for their friendship is that both Libya and the Soviet Union are following a policy against both Israel and the United States.

Libya's relation with the United States turned bad as soon as Gaddafi's regime took over in 1969. He terminated Libya's treaty with the United States and deprived it from using the military bases. Gaddafi always accused the United States of backing, supporting, financing, and arming Israel while following an anti-Arab policy. In 1973 he joined the rest of the Arab countries imposing an Arab oil embargo on the United States and the other countries that supported Israel. He was very critical of the United States for its role in the cease-fire and the disengagement agreement between Israel and Egypt and was bitter towards the Camp David Treaty.

When Libya declared that the Serta Gulf was Libyan's national waters, the Americans challenged the legality of that claim, orderd its Mediterranean Sea navy to enter the Gulf, and shot down two Libyan fighters that tried to approach the American ships. There is no diplomatic relation between the two countries at this time. The relation became worse early in 1986 and the United States severed all its economic relation with Libya.

Libya's relation with the United Kingdom is no better than that with the United States. Gaddafi terminated the British-Libyan treaty that allowed Britain to keep military bases in Cyrenaica, nationalized the British oil companies that were working in Libya, and announced that he was exacting compensations to the value of thousands of millions of dollars from Britain and Italy for damage susained by Libya during the north African campaigns of the Second World War.

Gaddafi's relation with France is mostly based on trade relation. France is buying the Libyan oil of high quality, which costs less to be shipped to France, in exchange for French arms, especially the Mirage planes. But on the political stage, France is not allowing Gaddafi to expand either in North Africa (Tunisia) or in Saharan Africa (Chad).

Tunisia, like the rest of North West Africa, became a battleground region of confrontation between the Spanish monarchy and the Ottoman empire. When the Spaniards succeeded in completely recontrolling their own country in 1492, they started to conquer North Africa. Naturally, they were opposed by the Ottomans who were advancing westward: The struggle between the two powers lasted until 1574 when Spain gave up its attempts to conquer North West Africa, and they became heavily involved in European politics and in their vast rich empire in the Americas and the Pacific Ocean. Tunisia was directly ruled by the Ottomans for almost seventeen years. In 1591 a military revolt against the "Pasha" (the representative of the Ottoman sultan) reduced the authority of Istanbul to Cipher. The real governors of the country were the "beys", the commanders of the amy. The decline of the army allowed the "beys", subordinate in rank, to grasp the authority and keep it in their hands. Hamouda bey and his family governed Tunisia from 1659 to 1702, and the family of Huseyn Ali Turki governed the country until it passed under French control in 1881. Tunisia was invaded in April 1881 and the French invaders met no serious resistance. Then, two other great western powers, Germany and Britain, encouraged the French invasion to all North West Africa. Germany's encouragement was to distract the French politics from German-European affairs, after their 1870 victory and the occupation of the French provinces of Alsase and Loraine, Britain did not contest France in North West Africa so that the French would not oppose the British occupation of Egypt. The bey was forced to accept the terms of the Treaty of Kasser Said (Treaty of

74

Bardo) under which he remained the nominal ruler of the country, while the French officials governed the country. In 1883 Tunisia, under the terms of the treaty of Mersa, became a French protectorate.

The French authorities encouraged a considerable number of French citizens to settle in Tunisia by offering them large scale grants of land. The Tunisian cultural and social life absored many French ideas. French became the official language, and the educational and administrative systems were reformed to follow the French systems.

After World War I, the achievement of independence in eastern Arab countries and the rise of the nationalist movement in Egypt inspired the Tunisians with a national consciousness; and in 1920 the Destour (Constitution) Political Party was formed under the leadership of Shaikh Al-Thaalibi. The party called for a self-governing constitutional regime with a legislative assembly. The French, in response for these national aspirations, formed economic councils on which Tunisian citizens and French settlers were equally represented. That French movement did not satisfy the strong, national elements in the party who took further nationalist activities. The French, in 1923, defended their colonial interests, resorted to repressive measures, broke the Destour Party; and its leader, Shaikh Tha'alibi, was exiled. The party was reestablished in 1934, but the young nationalists in the party accused the older leaders of collaborating with the French; they split and formed another[14] party, the "Neo-Destour", led by Habib Bourguiba (now the President of the country). The new party gained popularity in all parts of the country, and its strength was proved when it called for a national strike in 1938 to demonstrate the people's dissatisfaction with the French policies. The strike was successful, and again, the French resorted to more repressive methods; they proclaimed martial law, and the new party was dissolved.

After the defeat of France in World War Two, Tunisia came under the control of the Vichy government; then it became a battleground between the Axis army and the allies. With the defeat of th Axis, the Paris government regained control of the country. The "bey" Mohammed Al-Monsif was accused of collaboration with the Axis and was deposed and replaced by Mohammed Al-Amin, who reigned until Tunisia became a republic in 1957.

After the war, the nationalists resumed their struggle. Faced with stiff French repression, Habib Bourguiba moved to Cairo in 1945; his chief aid, Saleh Ben Yousef, stayed in Tunisia. The French authorities introduced some minor political reforms that included the reorganization of the council of ministries, but they did not satisfy the nationalists ambitions. In 1946 a national council demanded complete independence. Bourguiba returned to Tunisia in 1949 and proposed that the French authorities transfer sovereignty and executive control to Tunisian hands, under a responsible government with a prime minister appointed by the "bey", and with an elected National Assembly which will draw up a democratic constitution. Local French residents interests would be protected by representation on municipal councils. The Paris government responded reasonably for the proposals, and a new Tunisian government was formed in which the Neo-Destour Party was represented. Saleh Ben Yousif was the Minister of Justice, and the purpose of the government was stated as transferring the aurthority to the Tunisians gradually. Although the French settlers were opposing any "concessions" to the Tunisians, the French government proceeded with more reforms and removed the French advisors for Tunisian ministers.

Further peaceful progress toward independence came to a halt in 1952, as a result of strong French settlers opposition. Tunisian resentment errupted in strikes and demonstrations. Bourguiba and other leaders of the Neo-Destour Party were arrested, and military control was imposed. The situation became tense; the Tunisians resorted to terrorism, and the French settlers resorted to counter-terrorism. In July 1954 Mendes-France, the French Prime Minister, offered the Tunisians internal autonomy, while defense and foreign affairs were retained by France. A new Tunisian government was formed, accepting the offer, and a treaty was signed in Paris in July 1955. the treaty was opposed by the extremists, communists, and the French settlers, while the Neo-Destour Party, including Bourguiba, accepted it. Although the new treaty was accepted by most of the population, the Neo-Destour Party, in its congress held in Safax in November 1955, declared that they accepted the treaty only as a first step toward full independence. A delegatioon, led by Bourguiba, started independence negotiations in Paris; and in March 1956, France signed a protocol, recognizing the independence of Tunisia and its rights to exercise responsibility over foreign affairs and defense, and recognizing the fact that the French forces would be withdrawn from the country. In the early years of independence, Tunisia was very occupied by the withdrawal of the French forces. In July 1956, Bourguiba, as a Prime Minister, demanded the French government to withdraw its forces. France, who was fighting the nationalist movement in Algeria, rejected the Tunisia demand. The French-Tunisian relation became tense again, and Tunisia took its case to the United Nations Security Council in February and May 1958.

The situation improved when General de Gaulle came in power in June 1958. An agreement was reached under which French troops outside Bizerta would be withdrawn within four months while negotiations for a provisional agreement on Bizerta were to follow. The final settlement came after signing the Algerian-French cease-fire in March 1962. In June of the same year, the French agreed to evacuate Bizerta, and Tunisia had full control on all its land.

Considering the national affairs, Bourguiba started to consolidate his political power as early as 1955 by getting rid of his rivals in the party and by becoming Prime Minister in 1956. In 1957 he accused the "bey" Mohammed El Amin of having been unwilling to participate actively in the struggle for independence. On July 1957 the "bey" was ousted, and Tunisia became a republic with Bourguiba the Head of State. a new constitution came into effect in 1959 that gave him extensive authority in governing the country, and the Neo-Destour Party was practically the only political party. During the sixties all those who tried to liberalize the government or the party, whose name was changed to Parti Socialiste Destourien (PSD), were imprisoned or fled from the country. In 1974 Bourguiba was elected President for life, for both the party and the state.

While Bourguiba was able to suppress all opposition forces in the country and make an absolute government regime from the presidential regime, his internal trouble came from another direction. the General Union of Tunisian Workers, after several strikes, forced the government, in 1976, to agree on a "social contract" that involved some economic gains for the labor force. In spite of the agreement there were further strikes, and the Union became, through its weekly newspaper (Ach-Chaab), a vocal critic of government's policy and an outlet for action by political dissenters in the absence of recognized opposition political parties. The government decided to use force to bring the Union under direct government control. The Union in January 1978,

77

urged the government to change its policy that
intimidated the labor movement, and called a national
strike as a warning to the government which attacked its
offices. There were riots in most of the cities. the
army was called in to stop the riots, the number of
casualties was high, many were arrested and imprisoned,
and the government accused the Union of conspiring
against the state.

In January 1980, around the time of the second
anniversary of the 1978 strike, the town of Gafsa came
under guerilla attack; the army was called in and
regained control of the town. "Tunisian Armed
Resistance," an unknown group, claimed responibility,
declaring that their goal was to free the country from
Bourguiba's "dictatorship." Algeria denied any relation
with such a group, and the Libyan government claimed
that it was a "popular uprising" against an "unpopular
regime." the Gafsa attack drew international attention;
the French government sent forces to back the Tunisian
government, that upset the Libyan government. The
United States reponded by delivering supplies and arms
to Tunisia.

A limited degree of political liberalization was
applied in April 1980 when the government was changed.
Most political prisoners were released, about 1,000
imprisoned trade union members were pardoned, and
permission was granted to publish two weekly political
perodicals. In 1981 Bourguiba announced that he would
not oppose the emergence of political parties, provided
that they rejected violence and religious fanaticism and
were not dependent "ideologically or materially" on any
foreign group or country.

In the field of foreign policy, Tunisia followed a
pro-western policy. When Tunisia took its case against
France to the U.N. security Council in 1958, it accepted
the mediation of Britain and the United States but never
asked for help from the Soviet Union or the eastern
bloc.

That foreign policy was also inspired by the need
for economic aid; it kept good relations with not only
the United States, who offered most of the loans and
grants, but also with West Germany, who offered economic
and technical aid. When West Germany exchanged
diplomatic relations with the State of Israel and the
Arab countries decided to sever their relations with
Germany, Tunisia refused to do so. Most of the Arab
countries led by Egypt (U.A.R. then) severed their

diplomatic relations with Tunisia. Tunisia kept close
relations with France; although it was the former
colonial power, it backed Tunisia politically and
militarily as in the case of the Gafsa incident. In the
same time, Bourguiba was very cautious in his relation
with the Soviet Union, although Tunisia got some
economic help from it. Also, although Tunisia
recognized the People's Republic of China and both
exchanged diplomatic relations, Bourguiba never
hesitated to criticize the Chinese policy, especially in
encouraging revolutions.

Considering the Arab-Israeli problem, Bourguiba
followed an independent policy different from that of
the Arab League. In 1956 he openly criticized the Arab
policy and suggested that the Arabs should negotiate
with Israel in the basis of the United Nations'
political plan of 1948. In 1956 Bourguiba, in an open
letter to the heads of the Arab states that were
conferring in Casa Blanca, criticized Nasser (then
President of Egypt) that he was using the Arab League to
promote his own political ambitions. He also
recommended direct negotiations with Israel, although
Tunisia condemned Israel for its invasion of the Arab
countries in 1967 and was ready to send Tunisian troops
to the battlefield. Syria attacked the Tunisian policy
and later withdrew its ambassador from Tunis. Ironic-
ally enough, when the Arab countries turned against
Egypt after it signed the Camp David peace treaty with
Israel, the Arab League decided to move its headquarters
from Cairo to Tunis.

In January 1970 Tunisia and Algeria signed a
"Treaty of Cooperation and Friendship." It provided for
collaboration in the exploitation of the El Borma oil
field which straddles the Tunisia-Algeria border. The
boundaries between the two countries was demarcated and
the economic problems between both of them were solved.

As soon as the Spaniards completed the task of
driving Muslim power from Spain in 1492, they proceeded
to invade the Muslim countries of North Africa. Mers El
Kebir was captured in 1505, followed by Oran in 1509 and
Bougie (Bejaia) in 1510. The Algerians and the Ottomans
cooperated to drive away the Spaniards. In 1541 all of
Algeria came under the Ottoman rule.

The Ottoman direct rule did not last long, in fact,
the real authority on this land was in the hands of ten
"beys" (commanders of the local army divisions), while
the supporters of the regime were the pirates who used

all the shores of North Africa as their nests, and the towns as slave markets to sell the unfortunate sailors of the ships of the European Christian countries that they captured, as well as for African slaves that were carried by the desert caravans across the Sahara.

While the British fleet bombarded Algiers in 1816 trying to force the "beys" to abandon piracy, France took advantage of the anti-slavery movement in Europe and moved to occupy Algeria.

In 1630 the French, moved by national policy, occupied Algiers and exiled the bey and the few Turkish officials. Political unrest in France halted the extension of the French rule to other coastal towns. Under such conditions, and in the absence of any strong political authority outside Algiers, the chiefs of the tribes strengthened their positions. As soon as the political situation stabilized in France, the French government decided to resume the conquest of Algeria, and in 1834 a governor general was appointed. Most of the eastern part of the country was captured by 1844, while in the west the French were faced by the forceful and strong resistance of Abd Elqader. He was a Berber leader who was able to unite both the Arabs and the Berbers of the country to resist the French invaders by the help of the Moroccans. The ruthless tactics and persistance of General Bugeard, the architect of the French rule in Algeria, defeated the Algerians and the country was annexed to France.

The French pushed a strong policy of colonization based on encouraging French and European immigrants to settle in Algeria, and on confiscation of the good land to give as grants to the settlers. By 1860 practically all the best land was in the hands of Europeans. Napoleon III tried to protect the natives against settler encroachments and allowed them to acquire French nationality. These steps provoked the settlers, and in 1870, in the confusion of the French-Prussian War, they set up a revolutionary commune. In 1871 the new French government set up a new civil administration that continued the forceful colonization policy. Widespread confiscation of the remaining good land was applied, following the natives' unsuccessful rebellion. That policy was accompanied with repressive methods (civilizing campaigns) to break the traditional social and tribal systems.

During the years before World War I, there was considerable agricultural and industrial development that concentrated more power in the hands of the settlers while the natives (Muslims) had been reduced socially, culturally, and economicallly to second class.

The nationalist movements that started and spread rapidly in the Eastern Arab world in general and especially in Egypt has its echoes in North West Africa. Nationalist aspirations began to be voiced among the Algerian World War I veterans who fought in Europe defending France; freedoms and the right to self-determination, and they rightly demanded that they should have the same rights they fought for. These nationalists also included Algerians that were employed in France and students that went to France to study. In 1924 Messali Hadj, one of these students, founded in Paris the first Algerian newspaper to defend Algerian national rights. Messali was cooperating with the French communist party, although he severed his relation with that party in 1927, and the French government pushed him and his group underground. In 1933 Messali reappeared sponsoring a congress to discuss the future of Algeria, calling for independence, the establishment of a revolutionary government, large scale reforms on land ownership, and nationalization of industrial enterprises. In 1933, under the leadership of Farahat Abbas, another group that had moderate goals was formed, called the Federation of Muslim Counselors, and they called for integration with France on the basis of complete equality. The French settlers fiercely opposed such an idea. In 1936 Messali Hadj played a significant role in the formation of the Party of the Algerian People (PPA).

Although the second World War put a temporary lead on the nationalists' activities, it strenghtened their hand for the future. And although the Vichy government was antipathetic to nationalist sentiments, the allied landings in North Africa in 1942 provided an opportunity for the Algerian nationalists to put forward constitutional demands. Farahat Abbas presented to the French authority and the allied military command a memorandum, for the post-war establishment of an Algerian consitituent assembly. It is clear that it was a very moderate demand since there was no plan for independence outside the French framework. The French did not respond to that moderate demand and the military command did not like to provoke the French by interfering in what it considered as French affairs. The nationalists, trying to push their cause, presented the "Manifesto of the Algerian People" in 1943, which called for introduction of the Arabic language as an

81

official language and the creation of an Algerian State with a constitution to be determined by constituent assembly. The then Free French administration rejeceted the Manifesto out of hand. Farahat Abbas founded the Friends of the Manifesto of Freedom (AML) to work for the foundation of an autonomous Algerian republic linked federally with France. The AML was supported by middle-class Muslims while the PPA gained many followers among the masses[15].

The resistance of the French settlers to grant the natives their political and social rights and the post-war French policy made it hard for the nationalist to believe that a peaceful and evolutionary solution could be reached. The French crushed the riots of May 1945 at Setif so fiercely that the number of casualties exceeded 15,000; the AML was dissolved and Farahat Abbas was arrested. The nationalists regarded force as the only means to gain their rights.

Attempts to achieve a compromise solution did not succeed. In 1946, Farahat Abbas, after his release, formed the Democratic Union of the Algerian Manifesto (UDMA) with a program identical to that of the AML. Although some members of the UDMA were elected to the French assembly, they withdrew after it became clear to them that they would achieve nothing. The French government offered a solution in 1947. This gave the Muslims French citizenship with the right to vote (including women) and recognized Arabic as an official language along with French. The proposed Algerian Assembly would be of two colleges each of 60 members, one to represent the Europeans and the other to represent the Muslims. The proposals ruled out any possibility of anti-French settlers legislations. Although the authors of that last compromise were the French, they never intended to put it into operation. They openly interfered in the election arrested nationalist candidates, political meetings were forbidden, with the purpose of destroying any opposition to direct French rule.

In reaction to these French actions and continuous intimidation the nationalists set up in 1953 "The Revolutionary Council for Unity and Action" (CRUA) to prepare for an immediate revolt against French rule. Plans for the revolution and war were arranged in meetings that were held in Switzerland in 1954. Algeria was divided into six wilayas (zones); each had its own military commander. When the war started in November 1954, the CRUA changed its name to the National

Liberation Front (Front de Liberation National of FLN). The war started in the Aures in early 1955 and by the end of 1956 it spread to all the settled areas of Algeria. In 1956 Farahat Abbes, leader of the UDMA, and the religious leaders joined the FLN, making it representative of all shades of Algerian nationalist feeling except the Algerian National Front headed by Messali Hadj. In 1956, the FLN drew up a soicalist program for the future Algerain Republic[16].

The French government believed that the FLN was kept active and alive by external support only, and Egypt was the main supporter. When France failed to convince Nasser (then the president of Egypt) to withdraw his support to the FLN, it joined the U.K. and Israel in attacking Egypt in October 1956, picking the chance of Egypt's nationalization of the Suez Canal. The attack failed and the international sympathy for Egypt and the Algerian situation grew stronger. In order to isolate Algeria from Tunisia and Morrocco, the French set up electrified barriers along the boundary lines of both countries, but these barriers did not restrict the movement of military aid to the Algerian fighters. Ben Bella, one of the leaders of the revolution, and some of his companions were interned in France when the French pilot of their plane en route from Morocco to Tunisia landed at Algiers.

All these desperate measures failed to reduce the Algerian fighters capacity to continue the war. In response to the French actions, the FLN established in Tunis the Provisional Government of the Algerian Republic (GPRA) headed by Farahat Abbes. It became clear to the French government that the only solution for the Algerian problem was to negotiate faithfully with the FLN.

The Algerian problem was the main reason for the overthrow of the Fourth French Republic and the reinstatement of General de Gaulle as the President of France. The French settlers hoped that de Gaulle, as a strong man, would support their cause and crush the revolution. De Gaulle, indeed, stepped up the military action against the FLN, but the FLN responded in 1958 by establishing the Provisional Government of the Algerain Republic in Tunis (GPRA) headed by Farahat Abbes. The resistance to de Gaull's offensive action was so strong that he began to recognize the strength of the Algerians in their determination to liberate their country and to achieve complete sovereignty. De Gaulle started to move

83

cautiously toward accepting that reality and to negotiate with the nationalists.

In September 1959 de Gaulle, in a public statement, made it clear that he believed that the Algerians had the right of self-determination. The negotiations were tedious and took a long time and in many cases were broken off. Some officers, including generals, in the French army in Algeria rebelled against their government, joined the settlers and formed the "Secret Army Organization" (OAS), but that did not change the outcome. On March 18, 1962, a cease-fire agreement and a declaration of future policy were signed. The declaration provided for the establishment of an independent Algerian state after a transitional period, for safeguarding of individual rights and the rights of French settlers, for the retention of the French naval base at Mersel-Kebir for 15 years and the nuclear testing site in the Sahara for five years. The OAS tried vainly to undermine the agreement by attacks on the Muslim population and destruction of public buildings, they failed and their leader General Salan was captured. On July 3, 1962, General de Gualle proclaimed the independence of Algeria. In spite of assurances that had been given to the European settlers considering respect of their rights, they began to leave Algeria to France en masse.

As soon as the Algerians achieved their aspiration of establishing an independent Algeria, they faced the problem of forming a strong national government that would be able to solve political, economical and social problems facing the young state that was in war for eight years. The rivalries between different personalities and ideologies within the FLN, the GPRA and the commanders of the army were sharp and threatened to start another war between the Algerians themselves. Thanks to efforts of the Algerain General Workers Union (UGTA) which organized mass demonstrations against fighting, the war was avoided. After many political maneuvers and activities, a Constituent Assembly was elected which took over the functions of the GPRA and Ben Bella was elected Prime Minister.

Ben Bella consolidated his position by forming a cabinent drawn from his personal associates, discredited Messali Hadj's communist party and the Party of the Socialist Revolution headed by Boudiaf who also had been detained in France. Ben Bella considered the two parties and their leaders as a strong threat and challengers to his own authority and the FLN. He

84

abolished the wilaya system, claiming that its function was very suitable for the war of independence, but the continuation of such a system would disrupt the country's unity. Ben Bella also managed to pack the UGTA with his followers and to gain control of that labor organization which had been opposing the dictatorial nature of his government. Ben Bella increased his powers even more by taking over the post of general secretray of the FLN, changing the government system to a presidentail regime, making the FLN the only political party, assuming the title of commander-in-chief as well as becoming head of state and head of government. He suppressed all the revolts and all signs of discontent and shelved or detained all those who showed signs of opposition.

In June 1965, Colonel Houari Boumedienne, then the Minsiter of Defense, led a coup d'etat, ousted Ben Bella and put him under arrest. The coup was bloodless and faced no oppostion; in fact, because of the very poor economic conditions of the country under Ben Bella, and because of his dictorial policies, the Algerians did not support Boumedienne or defend Ben Bella. Boumedienne was no more democratic than Ben Bella; he never sought popular mandate. The Algerian National Assembly remained in abeyance; he formed a Council of Revolution, whose members were mostly army officers, to govern the country, and he presided over it; he was also the Prime Minister and the Minister of Defense,; the FLN was still the sole political party.

Opposition to Boumedienne's regime was from various groups: politicians, who found no difference beween his regime and that of Ben Bella; the UGTA which found no improvement in the employment situation or in the economic conditions; some army officers, especially those leaders of units that carried most of the burden of the revolutionary war; and students who opposed and demonstrated against his policies, especially because of the poor employment prospects. An attempt to assassinate Boumedienne in April 1968 failed, and he escaped without serious injuries. This attempt was followed by a high wave of arrest in the unions and the administration by selective dismissals in the FLN and the army in order to secure his positions. After he held a strong grip on the country, he eliminated the other members of the party and the government who showed any tendency to oppose him, although they were his colleagues in the struggle against the French.

85

By 1971 Boumedienne introduced a more active social policy; a program of agrarian reform was instated, centralized bureaucratic state-controlled economy and industry especially was established, and he reorganized the FLN as a leading and guiding radical force in the life of all Algerians. The determination of Boumedienne's government to establish a socialist society and his unyielding, persistant effort to consolidate his personal power provoked a resurgence of opposition. In March 1976 two former presidents of the Algerian government-in-exile, Farahat Abbes and Youssef Ben Khedda among others, signed and circulated a manifesto that criticized Boumedienne for totalitarian rule and personality cult. Boumedienne's reaction was fast and sharp; he rejected the criticism of his rule, condemned the signatories as "bourgeois reactionaries" and placed all of them under house arrest. At the same time as a concession to conservative sentiment, Islam was recognized as the state religion, and Mohammed Seleh, known for his "Islamic Socialism", was installed as the administrative head of the FLN.

In November 1978 Boumedienne died, and since he never allowed any politician with any considerable stature to emerge, there was anxious speculation as to who should succeed him. The Council of the Revolution, although it had no official status, took over the government temporarily and succeeded in bringing a smooth transfer of power. Two of the Council members competed for the presidential position: Abdelaziz Bouteflika, then the Minister of Foreign Affairs, who was able to keep close association with Boumedienne and was considered a moderate, and Mohammed Saleh Yahiaoui, the adnministrative head of the FLN who favored and worked for Islamic Socialism. As a compromise between the two, Colonel Bendjedid Chadli, the commander of the Oran military district, was chosen as the new President.

Colonel Chadli appointed a Prime Minister for the first time since independence. Colonel Mohammed Ben Ahmed Abdelghani was chosen for the position; Bouteflika, who served as a Minister of Foreign Affairs for 15 years, was exluded. Although President Chadli made it clear, by making the post of Prime Minister obligatory, that it was not his intention to monopolize power to the extent that his predecessor did, he strengthened his grip in the FLN, he purged his rivals, especially Bouteflika and Yahiaoui, and changed the rules to make himself the real controller of the FLN and hence the main planner of the govenment's policies.

The new government followed the same guidelines of the former government with a few changes. Many of the political opponents of Boumedienne who were not considered a threat to Chadli were amnested, restrictions on Algerians to travel abroad were cancelled, income taxes were reduced, restrictions on owning property were eased, and above all the industrial policy was reviewed.

The industrialization program was scaled down, and the large state companies were reorganized into smaller units; the new policy shifted to social areas such as education, health, and infrastructure, raising agricultural production and consumer goods were given more attention, and the private sector was considerably liberalized.

In the area of foreign affairs, Algeria followed a rather cautious policy in spite of the slogans of "Anti-Imperialism", and a militant stand on the question of Palestine was taken.

The relation with France was very strong: France provided technical and educational assistance, cancelled all Algeria's pre-independence debt, and reduced the Algerian debt to France to only 400 million dollars. On the other hand, the French cultural influence in Algeria remained strong, and the French language remained the language of business, government, and education, although the teaching of Arabic was expanded. French consumer goods received preference, and the Algerian armed forces were trained by French officers and, to a large extent, equipped by French-made arms.

Considering the Palestinian problem, Algeria called for a People's War against Israel, supported the Palestinians in the United Nations and in all political conferences, and they attacked the United States for its continuous support of Israel.

Although Algeria was very critical of the United States and its "neo-colonial" policies and its "imperialistic attitude", it encouraged American investment in the oil industry and was the main supplier of the United States with liquified natural gas. In other words, Algeria made a clear distinction between political slogans and economic interest.

In African affairs, Algeria supported and helped independence movements, followed and anti-colonial

87

policy, and provided training and other facilities for the liberation movement of Southern Africa, Eritrea, and Chad. Algeria lost no time after independence in improving its relations with the neighboring countries. In 1972 an agreement settling the Morcoccan-Algerian boundary line was signed between the two countries, another agreement provided for joint exploitation of the Gara-Djebilet iron ore mines in the border region. Similar friendship agreements were signed with Mauritania and Tunisia. An agreement with Libya was signed to coordinate oil policies.

Algeria's relation with the colonial power, France, immediately after independence, was conducted with caution. France was Algeria's main customer and the main source of financial and technical help. France cancelled all the Algerian pre-independence debts. The French cultural influence in Algeria remained strong although the teaching of Arabic was being extended in the schools. Large numbers of Algerians (700,00) worked in France, and the Algerians had preference for French consumer goods. France also supplied the Algerian army with equipment.

Since Boumedienne improved his position at home and tightened his grip on national affairs, he changed his policy towards France. He demanded more money for the Algerian oil. The dispute over the price to be paid by the French oil companies gave him the excuse to take control of them by nationalization in February 1971. The French government regarded this move as a breach of the 1965 agreement but could only ask for fair compensation. Agreements for compensation and for guaranteed oil supplies for France were reached in December 1971. Solving that problem of oil interests seemed to put the Algerian-French relation back on track especially after President Valery Giseard d'Estaing visited Algeria in April 1975. Unfortunately those relations became cloudy again because the Algerian government resented the French support to Morocco over the problem of the former Spanish Sahara, especially when France started to equip the Moroccan armed forces with large quantities of arms. The problem became more complicated when France air-raided and bombed the Polisario troops in December 1977 although the French government announced that the raids were solely for the protection of the French citizens working in that area.

In September 1980 an agreement concluded between the two countries on a system of incentives to be provided by the French government for repatriating

Algeria workers; their number then reached 800,000. In
return Algeria was to release French bank accounts which
had been "frozen" since independence. Agreement on the
price of Algerian gas was also reached in 1982. The
only problem that was still hanging on from the Algerian
viewpoint was the French backing of Morocco in the
Saharan dispute.

The first strong dynasty to govern Morocco was the
Idrisid, founded by Idris in 788 and lasting until 986.
Idris, with the aid of the Berbers, was able to unite
most of Morocco; his son Idris II founded Fez, an
important center of Islamic culture and civilization.
During the last eighty years the Idrisid regime was
suffering from tribal revolts, warring principalities
that led to economic decline and external pressure from
the Molsem Caliphite of Cordoba in Spain from the north
and from the Fatimide dynasty that was established in
Tunisia and East Algeria.

After a period of fragmentation and turmoil, a
Berber dynasty, al-Murabitan (Almoravids), was able to
control Morocco and build a splendid medieval empire.
The empire reached its high noon under the leadership of
Yusef ibn Tashufin who in 1062 built Marrakesh and
extended the empire eastward to include most of Algeria.
In 1086 ibn Tashufin annexed the Muslim lands in Spain
to his empire and was able to halt the southward advance
of the Christian reconqusita. As the Almorravids
expanded fast, the decline of their dynasty was also
fast. They and their supporters were originally hard
Sahara nomads, but during the time of the prosperity of
their empire, they became absorbed in the rich milieu of
the Andalusian Muslim civilization. Incompetence and
dynastic discord among the leaders of their dynasty were
among the reasons responsible for the collapse of them
dynasty. In 1118 the Spaniards were able to take back
Saragossa and began a new phase of their reconquista.

The Almoravids were succeeded by another Berber
dynasty from the High Atlas, al-Muwahhiden (Almohads),
the "Unitarians". The dynasty was established by a
religious leader, Muhammed ibn Tumart al-Mahdi. His
successor Abd al-Mumin took Marrakesh in 1147 and
controlled all Morocco. By 1159 he was able to overrun
all north Africa as far as Cyrenaica. The Almohads
reached the zenith of their glory under the leadership
of al-Mansur who brought Muslim Spain under his control
and was able to check the Christians' southward advance
at the battle of Alarces in 1196. After al-Mansur, the
Almohads' empire began to decline because in the time of

89

his successor, al-Nasir, the Moroccans suffered a serious defeat in battle against the Spaniards at Los Navas de Tolosa in 1212. The Hafsids of Tunisia were able, after they overran Algeria, to control most of Morocco.[17]

Another Berber dynasty, the Merinids, came into power in 1248. Although their power lasted for almost a century, and in spite of their efforts to revive the empire, they had no tangible success. Rebellious movements against their domination in southern Morocco were frequent, and in east Morocco resistance to their lordship was so strong that the country was united only for short periods of time. Nevertheless their intervention in Spain helped the Muslim state of Granada prolong its existance for some more years. Another factor that brought the Merinids regime to its fatal end was the ability of the Badawi tribes of beni Hilal and beni Suleim to penetrate the Atlas mountains and reach the heart of Morocco; they detroyed the political regime and devastated the agricultural system. From another viewpoint, these Badawi tribes contributed much to the Arabization of Morocco. Again Morocco went into political fragmention, dynastic rivalries, and economic chaos. Another Berber regime, the Waltasid regime, came to existance in 1465 but did not last long; it collapsed under the Spaniards and Portuguese pressure. They were able, after ridding Spain of Muslim influence, to establish themselves along the Atlantic and Mediterranean shores of Morocco. By 1500 the Portuguese were rooted in Ceuta, Tangier, Arcila, Agadir, Mazagan and Safi.

A new strong movement among the "Shorfa" (descendants of Prophet Mohammed) in Morocco led the "Jehad" (holy war) against the christians. The leaders of these Shorfa were the Saadians who established their movement in Wadi Draa on the desert side of the Atlas mountains. Their claimed status as descendants of the Prophet gave them the prestige that enabled them to control the country and mobilize the people to oust the Portuguese from their possessions on the Moroccan Atlantic coast. They were also able to resist the Ottoman pressure on their eastern region; in fact, due to their resistance, Morocco was the only country in all Mediterranean Africa that escaped the Turkish colonization. During the reign of Ahmad al-Mansur (1578-1603) Morocco extended its control in western Sahara and seized Timbuktu and Gao (now Mali). The Saadians, who had no tribal support, based their regime on a new policy that they initiated (the Makhzan); under this policy the regime offered several Arab tribes exemptions from taxes in return for armed service to the state. That new policy succeeded only when the central government was strong. Tribal rivalaries and rivalaries between Arabs and berbers led to the disintegration of the regime. Tensions between the nomads and settled elements of the population intensified.

A new leadership among the Alawi Sharifs was able in 1644 to establish another dynasty, the Hassani or Filali, who still reign in Morocco. They started their movement in the oasis of Tafilalet; by 1668 they were able to gain control of all Morocco. A strong leader of that house was Mulai (my lord) Ismail who reigned from 1672-1727. Morocco enjoyed peace and prosperity.[18] He was able to occupy Tangier in 1684 and ousted the British who were occupying it since 1662. He also occupied Larache which was in the hands of the Spaniard since 1610. He was also able to control the Berber nomads who used to raid the sedentary agricultural areas. Mulai Ismail was depending on a hired corps of black troops who were stationed near his capital, Meknes, and on a network of Qasabahs (fortresses). He also hired a strong force of European rengades. Morocco, during his reign, concluded the first commercial agreement with France, precedence being then accorded to the consuls of France over the consuls of all other countries. Another strong governor of the Alawi Sharifs was Mulai Muhammed Ibn Abdallah who founded Mogador in 1765 and drove the Portuguese from Mazagan in 1769. In 1780 he concluded a trade and friendship agreement with Spain. Ibn Abdalleh and his successors struggled hard but in vain to prevent foreign interference in their country; when France invaded Algeria, Morocco offered Abd al-Qadir, the hero of Algerian resisitance, financial and military help to fight the French invaders. During the French war against Abd al-Qadir they met and defeated a Moroccan force at Wadi Isaly in 1844; that was the first conflict between France and Morocco.

Another international conflict was with Spain in 1860 in a dispute over the limits of the Spanish Ceuta bridgehead. Morocco was defeated, and Ceuta was enlarged. In the same year, Spain seized Tetuan (the two bridgeheads are still in the hands of Spain who considers them part of Spain's mainland). Spain also got Ifni, another bridgehead on the Atlantic coast, and occupied the area south of Morocco (Spainsh Sahara) which was an area under Moroccan influence.

France, with her firm grip on Algeria, turned westward with the intention to occupy Morocco; but the international situation in the beginning of the century, the rivalaries among the great powers and the clouds preceeding World War One delayed the French intervention in Morocco. In 1904 an agreement between France and Britain, putting aside their rivalaries and differences, provided the British recognition of the French interests in all Maghreb in return for French recognition of the British interests in Egypt. In the same year France reached an agreement with Spain; according to the agreement, France (not Morocco) granted to Spain areas of influence, one in northern Morocco and the other in the southern part of the country; the southern boundary of Morocco was set at 27° 40"N. Lands south of that latitude would be under Spanish colonization. The only remaining great power that was interested in the region was Germany. In the conference of Algeciras in 1906, Germany suggested the economic internationalization of Morocco (economic opendoor policy) when it became clear to Germany that France was resisting the idea. It sent its gunboat, Panther, to Agadir waters. In 1911 France reached an agreement with Germany: France gave Germany some territorial concessions in the Congo in return for German recognition of the French interests in Morocco. In March 1912 Morocco became a French Protectorate with a French Resident-General empowered to direct foreign affairs, defense, finance, and to introduce internal "reforms." A new agreement with Spain was signed in 1912, it revised the former agreement of 1906. Spain received its areas of influence directly from France as the protecting power.

The first Resident-General in Morocco was General Lyutey (1912-1925). With vigor, effort, and unbending determination he was able to establish effective control of most of Morocco. He also helped the Spainiards to subdue the heroic resistance of the Rif tribesmen under Abd al-Karim. In fact, the national resistance to the French colonization lasted until 1934 when the pacification of Morocco could be regarded complete.[19]

The Moroccan nationalist movement started in the same time when France thought that the problems of being in full control of the country were over. A "Comite d'Action Morocaine" was formed and demanded a limitation of the protectorate. The French authority dissolved the "Comite" in 1937. Although the Moroccans rallied to the cause of France during World War II, the national movement was growing. In 1943 the "Istiqlal" party (Party of Independence) was formed, demanded full independence for Morocco with a constitutional form of government under Sultan Mohammed ibn Yusuf, who backed the party and its demands. The independence movement and the Istiqlal party were popular in the towns but not among the Berber tribesmen who did not like to reform on Western line. The Berbers led by Thami al-Glawi picked the chance of the deteriorating relation between Sultan Mohammed and the French administration over the Sultan's refusal of issuing decrees demanded by the French and converged in force towards the main towns, demanding the removal of the Sultan. The Sultan in 1953 agreed to go into exile in Europe but not to abdicate. He was succeeded by Mohammed ibn Arafa who was unpopular and lucky enough to survive two assassination attempts in 1953 and 1954. Under popular pressure, ibn Arafa renounced the throne and withdraw to Tangier in 1955. The former Sultan Mohammed ibn Yusuf was recognized as the legitimate Sultan. On March 2, 1956 a Franco-Moroccan declaration was issued stating that the protectorate agreement of 1912 was obsolete and that the French goverment recognized the independence of Morocco in October 1956. Tangier, which was an international port since 1906, was restored to Morocco, and in 1963, for economic reasons, it was made a free port. Morocco had envisioned the creation of "Great Morocco" that would include the Spanish territories in northwest Africa that were considered as originally a part of Morocco. Mauritania, Mali, and southwest Algeria were all claimed on historical basis.

Spain recognized Morocco as an independent country and gave back the northern zone of the protectorate assigned to her according to the Franco-Spainsh agreement of 1912, but it kept the two bridgeheads, Ceuta and Melilla. The problems of the bridgehead of Ifni in southern Morocco and the Spanish Sahara were not solved at that time. Moroccan raids on Ifni and the Sahara by the "Armee de liberation du Grand Sahara" (Moroccan irregulars) clouded the Spanish-Moroccan relation. In 1969 Spain gave back Ifni.

Morocco dropped its claim to Mauritania, recognized its independence, the two countries exchanged ambassadors, and signed a treaty of friendship and cooperation in 1970.

Another problem which faced the newly independent state of Morocco was its boundary line with its neighbor Algeria that had just emerged from the age of colonization. since France was the colonial power that colonized both countries, France had not bothered to

93

specifically demarcate the boundary line between the two
countries. the problem was complicated further by the
psychopolitical attitude of both of them, each was
trying to assert its claims and to show its strength by
defending its territorial rights. In July 1962 Moroccan
troops entered the region south of Colomb-Bechar, an
area that had never been specifically demarcated. The
Moroccan Press, directed by the government and inflaming
the situation by patriotic and national slogans,
organized a strong campaign in support of the view that
the Tindouf region in the southwest of Algeria should
belong to Morocco; although the region is merely desert,
it is important because it has large deposits of
high-grade iron ore.

    Thanks to the efforts of the Organiztion for
African Unity (OAU), an arbitration commission was
established. After lengthy negotiations, an agreement
was reached in the frontier dispute and a joint
comission mapped out a delination maintaining the
boundaries of the colonial period. Both Colomb-Becher
and Tindouf remained with Algeria; however, Morocco was
to have a share in a joint company to be established to
exploit the iron ore deposits. The agreement was a
well-planned compromise and relation between the two
countries improved fast, but unfortunately, for a short
while. The Spanish Sahara and the claims of both
countries led to open war.

    The problem of the Western Sahara-Spanish Sahara
(Saguia el Hamra and Rio de Oro) started as soon as
Spain declared its intention to withdraw from the
region.²⁶ The problem was not, as in such cases, between
the colonial power and the population; it was between
the rival countries of the region, Morocco, Algeria, and
Mauritania as well as between the political parties of
Spanish Sahara. In a country of a population estimated
to be 160,000 and illiteracy very high, such political
parties were set up and backed by the rival countries.
The problem developed rapidly and engulfed the area in a
hot war that affected the political, economic, and
social life of these countries as well as the
international relationship in Africa and with other
countries.

    On October 15, 1975, a United Nations investigating
mission reported that the majority of the population of
the western Sahara favored independence and the World
Court confirmed the mission's report by ruling in favor
of self-determination. King Hassan, whose claim in the
region is based on history and relic features, responded

94

by organizing a march of 350,00 unarmed civilians to take possession of the Spanish Sahara. The marchers crossed the boundary line and advanced few miles before both the Spanish authorities stopped them and the King called off the march, claiming that it had achieved its objective. On November 14, 1975, a tripartite agreement was signed in Madrid by which Spain agreed to withdraw from the Sahara in February 1976 and to hand it over to a joint Morocco-Mauritanian administration. Algeria declared that the tripartite agreement was invalid because it was in direct violation of the U.N. mission report and the World Court ruling and stepped up its support for "Frente Popular para la Liberation de Saguia el Hamra y Rio de Oro" (Polisario), a Sahara liberation movement hostile to Moroccan claims and making threats of direct military intervention. Morocco escalated the dispute by occupying the area militarily and entering the capital, El Aaiun, on December 11. The Moroccans met sharp resistance from Polisario fighters who were forced to retreat toward the Algerian border. Early in 1976 Moroccan and Algerian forces clashed at Amgalla inside the western Sahara, further fighting continued in that year. France, who from the beginning, favored for economic and strategic interests Moroccan expansion in the area rather than Algerian, stepped its arms supplies to Morocco. In February 1976, the Sahrawi Arab Democratic Republic (SADR) was proclaimed; a Saharan government in exile was formed in Algeria. Morocco severed its diplomatic relation with Algeria and the prospect of a general large-scale war between the two countries appeared to be a reality.

In April 1976 Morocco and Mauritania reached agreement on the division of the Saharan territory, of which the greater part containing most of the known mineral wealth was allotted to Morocco, which then set about absorbing the new territory as three new provinces of the Kingdom. The annexation of that area to Morocco was, and still is, very costly. Morocco is only able to keep control and security of the few scattered urban centers, but most of the region is still open to Polisario activities and raids. Their raids are successful in sabotaging the mining areas of Bou Craa in Morocco and Zouerate in Mauritania. The continuous war is causing heavy casualties on both sides, but it seems that due to the Polisario tactics of guerilla war, the loss of the Moroccan side is more than that of the Polisario. The problem was internationalized when the French air force, requested by Mauritania, bombed the Polisario after the Polisario attacked and caputured personnel working in the mining area. In the meantime, King Hassan made it clear that his forces would follow the Polisario fighters inside Algeria which was giving

them training grounds, bases, and protection. Algeria
announced that if the Moroccans would do that it meant a
declaration of war. The Orgainzation of African Unity
was not able to solve the problem since most of the
African coutries kept neutral and did not like to commit
themselves. From 1979 to 1982 the war swallowed more
than 25 percent of the Moroccan economy which had its
toll on Moroccan social health and educational programs.
The economic and financial pressure on the already
desert-poor country of Mauritainia was so enormous that
it lead to a coup d'etat. The leader of the coup, and
the new president of the country, Colonel Mustapha Ould
Salek, was willing to withdraw from the Sahara, but the
10,000 Moroccan troops stationed in Mauritania prevented
such a movement. President Houphouet-Boigny of Ivory
Coast, encouraged by France, proposed the creation of a
Saharan Republic in the sector occupied by Mauritania,
but all the parties, with the exception of Mauritania,
rejected the proposal.

Spain got involved in the problem not only as the
former colonial power and a party in the Madrid
tripartite agreement of 1975, but also because of its
political and economic interests. Spain was trying to
buy the friendship of Algeria to stop it from backing
and financing an independent movement in the Canary
Islands. It recognized the Polisario and supported the
World Court decision that gave the Saharans the right
for self-determination. At the same time, it was
cautious not to antagonize Morocco in order to safeguard
its fishing activities in Moroccan waters and to secure
the safety of its two enclosures of Melilla and Ceuta.

The OAU proposed that a committee of "wisemen"
formed by the heads of State of six African coutries,
Guinea, Ivory Coast, Mali, Nigeria, Sudan, and Tanzania
would mediate in the dispute. In July 1979 the OAU
summit conference passed a resolution calling for a
referendum on self-determination. In August of the same
year Mauritania, burdened with a huge budget deficit and
unable to stop the Polisario activities on its own,
withdrew from the war and signed a peace treaty with
Polisario and renounced its territorial claims in the
western Sahara. Morocco declared it as a province of
the country. The annexation of that part stretched the
Moroccan defense forces thin and gave more claims for
Polisario to attack and felt so confident to the extent
that the organization established another base in
Maruritania. Libya, a financial supporter of the
Polisario, proposed that Mauritania and western Sahara

would unit and form one republic, a proposal that Morocco rejected immediately.

In the meantime, international recognition of the Saharan Arab Democaratic Republic (SADR) was increasing. By the end of 1980, forty six countries recognized the government in exile. The U.N. passed two resolutions confirming the legitimacy of Polisario's struggle for independence and called for Morocco to end its occupation of the western Sahara. In July 1982 SADR applied for membership in OAU, 26 states out of the 50 members approved the admission of SADR. Morocco insisted that for membership two-thirds majority was needed and threatend to walk out of the organization if that government would be seated in the OAU. The decision was postponed and referred once agin to the committee of "wisemen." The committee recommended that a ceasefire should be established followed by a referendum to be supervised jointly by OAU and the U.N. King Hassan, in the summit conference of the OAU in July 1981, accepted the principle of a referendum, but each side, Polisario and Morocco, put conditions that they know in advance were not acceptable to the other. Morocco insisted that the referendum should be based on the last Spanish census in 1974 that enumerated only 74,000 inhabitants and refused to negotiate with Polisario saying that its members are Algerian mercenaries. Polisario stipulated that Morocco had to withdraw all its troops and its administrators before the poll could take place. The Saharan refugees in Algeria should be allowed to go back and participate in the referendum and an interim international administrator should be set up. The referendum did not take place and the war is still continuing. The situation worsened further when a Moroccan aircraft was shot down by what the Morocco claimed to be a Soviet-made SAM-6 (Surface to Air Missile). Morocco accused Mauritania of not only helping Polisario but also of taking part in the attack on Moroccan forces. Morocco asked the United States for increased military assistance; the U.S. responded postively to a "friendly moderate" Arab coutry by tripling its military aid.

In October 1981 at the OAU Council of Ministers held in Addis Abbaba, the SADR delegation was seated. Morocco walked out in protest, followed by representies of 18 other countries. It was the most serious crisis within the OAU. The problem was not solved until December 1983.

In August 1984 the Moroccan government ratified a treaty that was signed early in July, forming a unity with Libya. In fact, the treaty is no more than a wise endeavor by King Hassan to deprive the Polisario from the money, supplies, and political backing of Libya as well as to get the official recognition of Libya for the Moroccan annexation of the Spanish Sahara.

REFERENCES

[1] The updated and detailed study of the life and culture of prehistoric Egypt see, Hoffman, Michael. Egypt Before the Pharaohs.

[2] Gabrieli, Francesco. Mohamed and the Conquest of Islam.

[3] Hitti, Philip. Makers of Arab History.

[4] Hitti, Philip. Markers of Arab History.

[5] McNeill, William. A World History.

[6] Abu-Nasr, Jamil. A History of the Maghreb.

[7] Kinross, Lord. Between Two Seas, The Creation of the Suez Canal.

[8] Vatikotis, P.J. A modern History of Egypt.

[9] Waterbury, John. The Egypt of Nasser and Sadat.

[10] Dawisha, A.I. Egypt in the Arab World.

[11] U.S. Policy. Policy in the Middle East. U.S.A. Department of State, selected documents No. 4. 1976.

[12] Wright, John. Libya: A Modern History.

[13] Written also El Qaddafi or El Qazzafi.

[14] Garas, Felix. Bourguiba et la Naissance d'une Nation.

[15] For a detailed history of the French in Algeria see, Talbott, John. France in Algeria.

[16] Vatin, Jean-Claude. L'Algerie Politique, historie et Societe.

[17] Julien, Ch. History of North Africa from the Arab Conquest to 1880.

[18] Bovill, E.W. The Golden Trade of the Moors.

[19] Halstead, John. Rebirth of a Nation: The Origins and Rise of Moroccan Nationalism.

[20] Damis, John. Conflict in Northwest Africa. -see also: Thompson, Virginia and Adloff, Richard. The Western Saharans.

CHAPTER 7

GENERAL ECONOMIC FEATURES

Since the five countries of Mediterrranean Africa
show some resemblances and differences in both the
physical and cultural features, it is inevitable that
there are some general characteristics prevailing in the
economies of these countries in spite of the clear facts
that there are also wide differences concerning the
natural resources and the degrees of economic development in each of these countries.

The first of these characteristics is that the
economy of these countries can be described as dual
because two non-integrated sectors - the traditional and
the modern - exist side by side. A clear-cut line of
demarcation, however, is very difficult to draw between
the two sectors, particularly in agriculture.

Primarily the traditional sector consists of small
agricultural farms run by peasants, nomadic and
semi-nomadic communites which use primitive methods of
production. This sector also includes handicrafts,
small-scale trading, and a wide range of simple
services. The modern sector, on the other hand, includes
large-scale farms, mining, industry, construction,
transportation, and communication, all characterized by
the employment of more sophisticated, up-to-date
techniques. Modern banking and commercial undertakings
also belong to this sector.

The distinction between the modern and traditional
sectors is usually made on the basis that the
traditional sector uses undeveloped techniques, rather
primitive equipment with low per capita productivity, in
other words, it is of subsistance nature. In fact these
criteria may lead to over-simplification. In the case
of Egypt, it is difficult to include agriculture in the
traditional sector in spite of the fact that the
majority of land holdings are 50 acres or less due to
the land-reform rules. These land holdings are small
plots owned or rented by peasants who still use tools
that were in use thousands of years ago. The very high
yields of high quality that contribute to both exports
and domestic consumption are due to certain conditions,
such as excellent systems of irrigation, soils of high
fertility, well-arranged crop rotation systems, lavish
usage of various kinds of fertilizers and chemicals, and
considerable agricultural experience. Due to intensive

101

cultivation and high yields, the agricultural economists find it appropriate to include Egypt's agriculture in the modern sector.

New agriculture in Mediterranean Africa has been recently monetized in response to the needs of growing urban centers in and higher demand for agricultural products. The increase demand resulted from the rise in per capita income generated by the rapid development of oil production as in the case of Algeria and Libya, or more income from phosphates and other natural resources as in Morocco, or more income received from members of the families working abroad as the case of Morocco, Algeria, and Tunisia. The peasants and semi-nomads grow wheat, barley, and vegetables and the nomads raising livestock, sell their surplus in the village's markets or in the urban centers for cash. The development of modern transportation system has contributed to that modification.

Traditional handicrafts also play a fairly important role in the economics of all these countries with the exception of Libya; leather products, wood work, silver and copper works, homemade rugs, handmade tapestry, and many other varieties are produced. (The market for these handicarfts is shifting due to an increasing supply of cheap, imported or domestic manufactured goods.) More is now producd for tourists and exports than for local consumption, hence necessitation modernization of designs, equipment, techniques, and marketing procedures.

The different forms of small-scale trading and various services contribute significantly to both employment and GNP. Most of the labor engaged in these tertiary activities are not registered and do not pay taxes. They are, therefore, omitted from national estimates of labor force statistics.

The type of agriculture which belongs to the modern sector consists of large estates, owned privately, by the state, or sometimes by large cooperatives. These estates usually occupy the best lands which formerly belonged to the the European settlers in Morocco, Algeria, Tunisia, and Libya; in Egypt they belonged to the royal family and the rich land owners. After the political and institutional changes, the ownership of a large proportion of these areas was "nationalized."

In Algeria, one fourth (the most productive) of the total arable land belonged to the French settlers, after

102

independence the national government took over the foreign-owned land. Modern agriculture now constitutes the basis of the Algerian socialist economy; during the 1970's and early 1980's the modern sector of Algerian agriculture produced 65% of the total agricultural out put.

In Tunisia the government in 1963 nationalized 1,120,000 acres that belonged to French settlers; it also took over 900,000 acres that belonged to other foreigners (mostly Italians) and native rich land owners (that has cooperated with the Frnech authority). Although the government redistributed that land among landless farmers, the modern methods of farming, under government supervison, are followed. It is estimated that these lands, that constitute less than one fourth of the total arable land, are responsible for 51% of the agricultural production in Tunisia.

In Morocco about 70% of the exported citrus fruit and fresh vegetables are produced on large land holdings that were once owned by former French settlers or owned presently by rich farmers. Those large holdings are the last affected by changing climatic conditions since most of the irrigation projects are serving these lands.

In Libya practically all the arable land (1.4% of the total area of the country was in the hands of Italian settlers, but after independence no foreigners were allowed to own any agriclutural land. Because of the hard environmental conditions, the government is pouring large sums of money into irrigation projects and land reclamation to increase agricultural production.

The second of these characteristics is the relatively limited size of the national markets. The main reason being the very low income of the nearly 60% of the population participating in the traditional sector. The purchasing power is so low that the possiblitiy of expanding the markets is slim. It should be noted that most of the individual income is spent to buy basic needs, especially food. This pattern of consumption does not encourage the industrial and the service sectors of the economy to grow. Although Libya has the highest per capita income in the region, it should be noted that its total population at the end of 1982 did not exceed 3,100,000 and its labor force at that time was only 800,000 which does not make a large market. Another factor that further limits the markets is the wide gap between the very rich minority that can afford spending and prefer to buy imported goods, and

103

the poor large majority that can hardly live. Egypt has
the largest of all Mediterranean Africa national
markets. In 1981/82 Egypt's market was almost as big as
the combined Moroccan and Algerian markets. This is due
mainly to the rapid rate of industrialization, the
expansion of administrative services and the
condiderable increase in the per acre and per capita
agricultural prodcution. The 44.6 million living in
Egypt of whom 47% are urban and the steady growth of the
middle class since the late 1950's helped in expanding
the national market. Easy transportation, a more
integrated ecomomy and more developed educational
systems contributed to expanding its market. However it
should be noted that due to the relatively low per
capita income, which in 1982 was equal to 870 American
dollars, the size of the market is still limited
compared to European markets. (PCI increased during the
late 1970's and early 1980's due to reopening the Suez
Canal and more oil production.)

The limited size of the markets has been
responsible, to some extent, for the small share of
industry in economic activities and most of the industry
is externally oriented (exports an in some cases
transfers of profits). Egypt is exporting most of its
steel and aluminum production, Algeria and Libya export
their petrochemicals, and Morocco exports most of its
processed phosphates.

Although all these countries, with the exception of
Libya, are trying to encourage foreign investments, it
is difficult for such limited-sized markets to attract
these investments. This difficulty is aggravated by the
low productivity of labor which leads to high costs of
production.

The third of these characteristics is the balance
of payments. With the exception of the two large oil
producing countries Libya and Algeria, the other
countries Egypt, Tunisia, and Morocco have trade
deficits.

Egypt's deficit in 1979 was 1,398,400,000 Egyptian
pounds and it jumped to 4,924,000,000 in 1981. The
exchange rate in 1982 was US $1 = LE 0.82.

Tunisia's deficit in 1979 was 430,044.000 Tunisian
dinars, and in 1981 it jumped to 673.608,000. The
exchange rate was US $1 = 2.025 TD.

Morocco's deficit in 1979 was 7,106,000,000 dirhams and in 1981 it jumped to 10,052,000,000 dirhams. The exchange rate in 1981 was US $1 = 5.172 MD.

In the three cases of Egypt, Tunisia, and Morocco, food imports were leading items. Egypt's food imports in 1981 valued 2,051.6 million LE; the total imports valued 6,187.5 million. Tunisia food imports in the same year reached 113.4 million TD; total imports valued 1,907.4 million TD. Morocco's food imports valued in that year 4,613 million MD while the total imports valued 22,455 million. The three countries also subsidiize food prices. These facts may look contradictory in countries where the majority of its population are rural and their main economic activity is farming. The explanations for these large food imports in such agricultural coutries are: The rapid increase in population is not matched by increase in agricultural production. The recent relative increase in per capita income among most of the population has resulted in demand for more consumer goods, especially food. Limitation of arable land, climatic difficulties, unreliable rainfall, soil problems, and traditional methods of agriculture, are formidable factors facing food production.

When the governments tried to reduce the food subsidies in order to improve their budgets, violent demonstrations took place in the streets of the capitals and large cities, casualties resulted and/or curfews were imposed.

Libya, one of the very rich oil producing and exporting countries, has a large visible surplus in its balance of payments. However, although not published and kept as a top state secret, it spends most of its surplus in buying weaponry and supporting foreign political activities. The surplus in 1979 was 1,357.1 million Libyan Dinars and in 1981 was 4,483 million. The rate of exhange in 1981 was US $1 = 0.296 LD. Libya, like the other countries of Mediterranean Africa, imported large amounts of food in 1980. The latest published figures showed that the value of food imports was 338,638,000 LD, the total imports valued 2,006,200,000. The per capita value of imports is high considering that the population is 3 million. Libya is investing heavily in agriculture. Only 1.4% of the total country is arable and less thatn 0.1% is irrigated. Primitive agricultural methods make increasing food production difficult.

105

Besides the huge food imports, all these countries are investing heavily in imported machinery for factories, durable producing goods, raw materials and transport equipment. These investments show the determination of those countries to develop themselves economically, to be less dependent on industrialized countries, and to create more jobs for a fast increasing population. While imported food bills are high in all the five countries, the bills for the imports of machinery, transport equipment and other materials for industrialization were the largest in the tables of imports in all of them. In 1980 the value of such imports amounted to 34% of the value of the total imports in Egypt, 42% in Libya, 27% in Tunisia, 41% in Algeria, and 25% in Morocco[1].

All these countries with the exception of Morocco are oil exporting countries, even Tunisia, a member of the OPEC who has the smallest produciton, oil is the most important item of its exports. Morocco has huge depostis of phosphates processing a small portion while exporting most of it as raw material.

Another feature of the foreign trade of the five countries that does not show on the import tables is the huge imports of weaponry of various kinds and for different reasons. Whatever may be the reasons for such imports, the investments involved in them deprive the ecomomic and social devolopment from valuable, badly needed resources.

Egypt, since the creation of Israel in 1948, keeps large armed forces and was engaged in four wars against Israel. In 1964 it sent to north Yemen (Republic of Yemen) more that 50,000 soldiers to back the revolution; these forces remained there until 1967. The British-French-Israeli invasion of Egypt in 1956, that followed the nationalization of the Suez Canal in part, forced Egypt to believe that it had no alternative but to continue to maintain and modernize its armed forces to defend itself against any possible aggression, in spite of the formidable economic and social problems. Its great and very important strategic location has through history made it a target of the Great Powers. Another factor that is forcing Egypt to invest heavily in arms and build arms is the very fluid and changeable political situation in the Middle East in general and in the Arab World especially. After the Camp David peace treaty with Israel in 1978, it was thought that Egypt would be partly relieved from the huge investments in importing arms. Libya, the western heavily armed neighbor, and the rest of the Arab world once strong allies, turned out to be bitter adversaries. Libya's insistance on a united Arab policy, anti-American policy, and direct confrontations against Israel forces Egypt to keep large forces on its western boundary lines.

Prior to 1978, Egypt was depending on the Soviet Union to equip its armed forces as the United Staes in 1953-54 refused to sell arms to Egypt becuase of the Israeli-Egyptiona War. Following the Camp David peace treaty, Egypt is importing most of its arms from the United States and also from France, West Gernamny, Italy, Canada, and also from the People's Republic of China. Egypt is also building a huge arms industry.

Libya with large oil revenues is building heavily-equipped armed forces and Libya's per capita investment in arming itself is thought to be among the highest in the world. The reasons for such huge investments in importing arms are its expansionist policy in Saharan Africa, its suspicion of Egypt's intention, thinking (wrongly) that it may be invaded by Egypt, because of its oppostion to the Egyption foreign policies and that Egypt may try to get the oil fields of Libya in order to solve its economic problems. Libya also claims that it is buying these arms to counter the Israeli armed forces although so far none of the Libyan troops or planes have fought against Israel. Libya also says it is arming itself because it does not trust the American "Imperialist" policy that is trying to put all Mediterranean Africa into its sphere of political influence.

Although Tunisia is a small country without expansion ambitions, it is also spending relatively largely on arms. Tunisia's reason for buying arms is its suspicion of its heavily armed neighbor Libya and its very recent activities in Tunisian national affairs. Tunisai is not hiding its fears that Libya may try to impose a political unity against the Tunisian wishes. The main suppliers of arms are the United States, France, and Italy.

Algeria, that won its independence after bitter, armed struggle against the former colonial power France has a strong army. After independence, the Algerian armed forces were involved in boundary skirmishes with the western neighbor, Morocco. Now Algeria is backing the Polisario struggle to gain control of former Spanish Sahara. Most of the army equipment is bought from the

Soviet Union, but its source of navy units is the United Kingdom. Lately Morocco bought transport aircrafts from the United States.

Morocco, in trying to hold a strong grip on former Spanish Sahara, has no other choice but to keep large armed forces. The fierce resistance of the Polisario which, backed by Algerian and Libyan help, is forcing Morocco to invest heavily in armament. In the Arab-Israeli war of 1967, Morocco sent a token symbolic force to the Syrian battle front. Morocco's main suppliers are France and Italy, but lately the United States became involved in suppling it with arms.

Another feature of the economic geography of Mediterranean Africa is the low per capita income, with the exception of Libya. In spite of their natural resources, important geographic and strategic location, and warm, sunny climates favored by tourist industry, if compared with European countries of the same size of smaller with the same or less population, we find that both the GNP and the per capita income are inferior. This indicates that these countries are not making full use of their resources, along with the failure of these countries to control their population growth rate are the contributing factors to the low per capita income. It must be taken into consideration that all the countries, even Eygpt, have just emerged from one or another form of colonizaiton that imposed on them economic policies that certainly served the colonial powers. It should not be denied that they are struggling hard to improve their economics and they are learning through trial and error.

Egypt's per capita income in 1982 was equivalent to US $809, which is a great improvement from $500 reported in 1979. The increase is due to more oil production and exports, and opening and modernizing the Suez Canal.

Libya's per capita income in 1980 reached $8,640; it was the year Libya exported more oil at the highest price. In 1982 due to reduced oil production and lower prices due to less oil demand, the per capita income dropped to $8,500. Although this figure is the highest in the region, it is far less than developed European countries in 1982 that have no oil resources.

Tunisia's per capita income in 1982 was recored as $875. Tunisia's economic figures show large flucuations from one year to another. The main source of export is oil, and its price and demand were down in 1979. The other exports are phosphate and olive oil, and the prices of both are depressed in the world market due to less demand and competition from other countries. The share of agriculture in the GNP varies from 17% to 14% depending on weather conditions. Tunisia's economic future is not very promising, as its oil reserves are limited and expected to dry before the end of the century. In the same time, the rate of population growth is more than 2.6%.

Morocco reported an estimated per capita of $900 in 1982. Since Morocco's economy is dependent upon both phosphate (It has almost two-thirds of the noncommunist world reserves) and on agriculture, its economy and its GNP varies from year to year, depending on world demand and prices for phospates and on climatic fluctuations, which have noticeable effects on agricultural outputs.

Another feature of the economics of the countries of the region is that all of them, again with the exception of Libya, are in debt. In order to pay for the imported machinery and raw materials for industrialization, to build a modern system of transportation and communication, to import food, and to maintain large armed forces they have to borrow. Borrowing is from international sources. Since as mentioned the per capita income is low and the cost of living after inflation in relation to personal income is high, there are no substantial national savings that these governments can depend on.

Egypt's foreign debts in 1983 were 13,600 million dollars, equal to 42% of the GNP, and the debt service payments accounted for more than 17% of export earnings. These debts do not include national debts or ourtright grants. In spite of the large magnitude of this amount, Egypt has been able to maintain its payment on time. Most of the debts are to the United States, France, Japan, West Germany and the World Bank.

Tunisian total foreign debt in 1981 was 2,970 million dollars, it is 40% of GNP and the debt service payments were 11.9% of the total exports. It is expected during the economic plan period of 1982-1986 that the debt will reach 3,200 million dollars. The main lending countries are U.S.A., France, Saudi Arabia, Qatter and the World Bank.

Algeria's international debt reached 17,800 million in 1981, about 38% of GNP, and the debt service payments was more than 27% of the value of all exports.

Mainlenders were the World Bank, United States, France, West Germany, Austria, Saudi Arabia and Iraq.

Another general feature in these countries of Mediterranean Africa is that its population, contrary to what the economic indications may show, is eating well. The daily per capita caloric supply in Egypt is 2,760 representing 118% of the requirement. In Libya it is 2,985 calories, with 122%; in Tunisia it is 2,674 with 119%. In Algeria it is 2,502 with 103%, and in Morocco it is 2,534 with 107%.

During the last twenty years these countries made impressieve progress in supplying most of the population with safe water. Egypt, until the early 1950's, had no access to safe water in most of its villages. By 1982 most of the country's rural population had safe water and it is reported that 80% of the total population had no water problems. Libya's population also had safe water, Tunisia had 76% safe water, Algeria 77% and Morocco 78%. All of those that did not have safe water were either living in remote areas or in small hamlets. It is expected that by the turn of the century all the population of those countries will have access to safe water.

In the field of health services these countries show some differences. In Egypt in 1982 there was one physician for every 1,101 people, which is a great improvement, compared to 1960 when the ratio was one physician for every 2410 people. Egyptian medical schools are graduating adequate numbers of physicians, but because of higher wages abroad, a considerable number of them are working abroad, especially in the Eastern Arab countries or in Libya.

Libya, due to its wealth, has the highest number of physicians, per capita; one for 895 persons. Most of the physicians working there are Arabs, especialy Egyptions. In 1960 it was 1/6,580. (Tunisia is reporting one physician for every 3,580; in 1960 it was 1/1,030.) Are they worse off now??

In Algeria it is 1/5,330 which was the same for the nation in 1960. It is clear that it is a low ration for a country with rich oil production. This stagnation resulted, in part, from the exodus of most French physicians after independence.

In Morocco the ration is really low, it is 1/11,040; in 1960 it was better with 1/9,410 again most

110

of the French physicans left and the higher education was not able to fill the gap fast enough.

REFERENCES

[1]World Book Statistics, 1984.

CHAPTER 8

EGYPT

Egypt is located in northeastern Africa, its area is about 386,900 square miles with almost geometric boundaries that separate it from Libya in the west, Sudan in the south and Israel in the northeast. It has two sea fronts, in the north the Mediterranean Sea and in the east the Red Sea with its two arms, the Gulf of Suez and the Gulf of Aqaba.

Egypt has been described by Herodotus, the ancient Greek historian, as the gift of the Nile. The description is very true, any physical or human geography map shows that the country is an elongated oasis along the Nile valley and its delta and on both sides there is a barren, harsh, dry desert, a reminder of what Egypt would be like without its lifeline of water.

Egypt also is the product of intensive hard work and an excellent strategic location. Since the upper Paleolithic (10,000 - 20,000 years ago), man started to move from the drying Steppe of the Sahara to the valley. There he developed agriculture and was in continuous hard labor to drain marshes, claim the land for agriculture, build canals and banks, try to tame the river, and develop an irrigaiton system. All these efforts had to be organized through an advanced political and social system that led to the establishment of the state of Egypt as a united political unity by King Menes (3400 B.C.). The success of this system was the economic basis of Egyptian civilization.

Egypt was protected for centuries (indeed millennium) by desert and distance. To the west there is the endless Sahara Desert, to the east the Red Sea and the Red Sea Mountains and the Eastern Desert. To the northeast the Sinai Peninsula never offered an easy crossing. To the north it was open to the Mediterranean Sea but otherwise inaccessible to overland contact. To the south, the Nile is interrupted by a series of cataracts. The ancient Egyptians had themselves a natural fortress, and in their comparative isolation they converted security into progrss. The Nile was then and remains to this day the main artery for unity, association, and trade. This national protection enabled the country to grow economically, politically, and culturally.

113

Egypt, of all the countries of the world, has kept its unity, political image and geographical personality for such a long history. Since it was established as a political state around 3400 B.C. to the time being, its entity has never been shattered.

Recently, in the Middle East, Egypt is not only the largest in terms of population but also, by most measures, the most influential. Its nearest rival, Turkey, has since the early twenties altered its attentions, orientation, and energies to Europe and the West. In Africa, Egypt has no Arab or Islamic competition to mask its status. In fact Egypt is Africa's second most populous state, after Nigeria. Egypt alone is spatially, culturally, ad ideologically is the heart of the Arab world.

The strategic location is clearly a primary element in Egypt's eminence. The country's position in the southeastern point of the Mediterranean Sea made it in direct contact with the Levant countreis as well as with Eruope in general and the countries of southern Europe in particular. This location gave it protection in the ealry stages of ancient history, prevented the isolation of the country and its culture during its medieval and modern history. Indeed the continuous seepage of European ideas through trade, cultural contact, and even wars was the main factor in the revival of contemporary Egypt.

The Red Sea front offered an easy connection between Egypt and Arabia and East Africa. The ancient Egyptions built a canal that connected the Nile with the head of the Suez Gulf. Queen Hatshebsot recorded the trip of her ships that sailed to east Africa (Punt) on her temple in Luxor. The same canal was rebuilt during the Arab conquest and was used to carry the grains to Arabia.

The Sinai Peninsula, that was always a part of Egypt since the Pharaoeic history, served as a land bridge between Africa and Asia. The Egyptian influence was felt in the Middle East during all ages of history as well as most of those who invaded Egypt came on this land bridge.

In modern history that strategic location of Egypt was the focus of the Great Powers. Napoleon invaded Egypt to cut the short transportation line of the British Empire to the Far East.

114

Building the Suez Canal and opening it for navigation in 1869 was a turning point in world history and the histroy of Egypt. The canal is 107 miles long, it joins the Mediterranean and Red Seas between Port Said and Suez. It offers the shortest route between Europe and South and East Asia as well as between Europe and East Africa. The canal was built by foreign interests and with foreign capital and Egyptian cheap labor, many of whom died during construction. Originally Egypt owned 44% of the shares and the company was considered an Egyptian company registeried in Cairo. Since the day it was opened for navigation, the British who considered it as the main artery of the Imperial Sea transportation line, were trying to pick a chance to put their hands on the canal and on Egypt. The chance came when the corrupted, debt-ridden government of Egypt was compelled to sell its share to Britain in 1875. In 1881 Britian occupied Egypt. Although Egypt became offically independent in 1922 and another treaty of "friendship" was signed in 1936, the British influence remained paramount, the Suez Canal was operated by foreigners and the British kept a base in the Canal Zone. In 1956 Egypt nationalized the Suez Canal. The miscalculated and strategically disastrous invasion of Egypt by Britain and France in Octover 1956 gave Egypt the chance to get rid of the British and to gain real unquestionable independence.

The location of Egypt was instrumental in granting the national movement in Algeria victory. Egypt was the country that funneled assistance, arms, and ammunition to the nationalists whose movement was crowned by indepndence. It was that Egyptioan help to Algeria that provoked France and led her to participste in the British-French-Israeli invasion of Egypt in 1956.

To the south is the Sudan, the twin country that shares Egypt in the usage of the Nile water. For some time the Sudanese looked at Egypt with suspicion as a colonial country. In 1953 Egypt announced that it would not oppose the independence of Sudan which became a reality in 1956. The water agreement between Egypt and Sudan of 1966 put the friendly relationship between the two countries on solid ground.

The events of wars in the Middle East since the Second World War have proved that the enemy can reach Egypt in few minutes; the deserts, the Mediterranean and the Red Sea are not offering as much protection as they did before the development of civilization. From another view, the location of Egypt close to the Persian

115

Gulf, where large resources of oil and natural gas are located and are very important to the western industrial powers and Japan, is making it an important country in defending the region and keeping the flow of that oil to world markets. This explains the new military cooperation between the United States and Egypt. It is clear, too, that that location meant that Egypt always was either conquered by foreign countries or, even during the periods of independence, was ruled by foreign dynasties. Since 1952 Egypt has been ruled by Egyptians.

There are four main regions in Egypt: 1. The Nile Valley and the Delta, 2. The Eastern Desert, 3. The Sinai Peninsula, and 4. The Western Desert.

THE NILE VALLEY AND THE DELTA

The Nile Valley and the Delta extend in Egypt from the southern boundary line of the country north of Wadi Halfa to the Mediterranean. It is a distance of about 900 miles. The valley is flanked on both eastern and western sides by cliffs of sandstone and granite until it reaches the First Cataract about 4 miles north of Aswan. North of the cataract the valley broadens and the flat strip of cultivable land, extending between the river and the cliffs that bound its valley on either side, gradually increases in width northward. Near Isna, the sandstone cliffs give place to limestone, and at Qena, the river makes a great bend bounded with limestone cliffs rising to heights of more than 1200 feet above the river level. Near Asyut the cliffs on the western side of the valley become much lower than those on the eastern side of the valley and continue so until it reaches Cairo, where they diverge from each other, leaving in between a triangular lowland, the famous Nile Delta.

Throughout its entire course, the Nile in Egypt tends to occupy the eastern side of the valley, so that the cultivable lands on the west side of the river are generally much wider than those on the east side. In fact, in some places, the river almost washes the eastern cliffs. Consequently, most of the towns and villages as well as most of the main road and railroad are located on the western side of the valley.

About seven miles north of Cairo, the river branches to the western Damietta branch; it is about 130 miles long and the eastern Rosetta branch is almost 126 miles long. Both branches empty into the Mediterranean. The Delta extends about 100 miles from south to north.

116

117

Its greatest width is about 155 miles, between Alexandria and Port Said. It covers an area of about 10,000 square miles. Toward the seaward border there is a considerable amount of salt-marsh and four extensive lagoons, Lake Maryut, Lake Idku, Lake Burullus, and the largest of them, Lake Manzala. After building the High Dam at Aswan and depriving the Delta as well as the Valley from the silt that was building the Delta, its shores are showing signs of being eroded by the Mediterranean waves and its southern current.

The Faiyum Depression, which lies in the western desert and is connected and irrigated by a narrow channel, is about 500 square miles. Although the connecting channel, Bahr Yusef, is doubtless a natural stream, it has been carefully remade and controlled by the hand of man. The depression extends about 50 miles form east to west and some 37 miles from north to south. The lowest part of that depresion is occupied by a shallow brackish lake called Birket Qarun (Lake Maurice) which is about 150 feet below sea level. Its floor slopes downward to the lake in a norhtwesternly direction for a level of about 75 feet above the sea. Archeological excavations prove that the lake was of greater dimensions in prehistoric times.

The whole region may be subdivided into four subregions: Upper Egypt, Middle Egypt, Lower Egypt, nd El Faiyum Oasis.

Upper Egypt: There is a general agreement that the part of the valley known as Upper Eygpt extends from the Egyptian-Sudanese boundary line north of Wadi Halfa northward to Luxor (old Thebes) where the river starts its large bend known as Qena Bend. The average width of the valley is less than two miles and in some parts the width of cultivated land is less than 200 yards. In Fact, the cultivated land in this part of the valley consists of a succession of irrigated basins marked off from one another by those points where the two clifflike walls of the valley approach close to one another. This part of Egypt in general and the Luxor (Thebes) basin in particular was the illuminating center of the known world in the time of ancient civilizations. The incredible richness in ruins of temples, palaces, obelisks, and towns is lasting evidence of ancient glories. Here, at the head of the First Cataract and just north of the city of Aswan, the old Aswan Dam was built. A dike of resistant igneous rock that traverses the valley was used as a foundation for the masonry. The dam was completed in 1902 and was raised two times

which increased the capacity of the reservoir to 176,500
millin feet. Building that dam started an agricultural
revolution in Egypt. Perennial irrigation was
introduced, the crop area of the country was doubled,
most of the cultivated land in lower and middle Egypt is
used for two and even three crops a year instead of the
ancient basin irrigation which prevailed since
prehistoric times.

The dam did not only revolutionize the agriculture
system, but it also ignited a strong movement of modern
industrialization. It is used for hydroelectric power
production that is utilized in modern chemical industry,
mainly the badly-needed nitrogenous fertilizers. After
building the High Aswan Dam, the old dam is used only
for power production. Another important irrigation
project in that region is the Esna (Isna) barrage which
was completed in 1933 and helped perennial irrigation.

The greatest project in all the country and one of
the largest in the world is the High Aswan Dam (El Sadd
El Aali). The dam was built with Soviet technical and
financial aid. It is located about 5 miles south of the
old dam. The waters of the Nile are held back in a huge
lake, Nubia Lake^I, that extends southward beyond Kosha
in northern Sudan, a distance of more than 310 miles and
averages 14 miles in width. It is the world's second
largest man-made lake after Lake Kariba in South Africa,
held by a dam 364 feet high, the top of which carries a
2.7 mile long highway. A diversion tunnel on the east
bank channels the Nile's waters through six spillway
tunnels to a downstream hydroelectric power station
housing twelve generators with a total capacity of
10,000,000,000 kilowatt hours yearly (although it was
lately reported that not all this electricity was
developed). Lake Nubia stores 130,000 milion cubic
yards of water for perennial irrigation and land
reclamation. The first filling of water behind the dam
was in 1964 and completely engulfed the Sudanese border
town of Wadi Halfa. The dam and its subsidiary works
cost in the region of $800 million. It is estimated
that by 1974 revenue from that dam exceeded the cost of
its construction. The project was started in 1960 and
was completed in 1970. The benefits of the dam are:
1. About 1.2 million acres are added to the
   irrigated land of Egypt; about 500,000
   acres are converted from basin to perennial
   irrigation. Thus the dam practically
   increased the irrigated land by 25 percent.

2. Crop yields, especially rice, have increased as a result of more available water.

3. The dam has diminished the risk of high flood as well as the risk of low water seasons.

4. The power from the dam has meant a five-fold increase in Egypt's power potential^2. The need for fossil fuels in industry has been reduced by 2.5 million tons annually. Transmission lines carry the power from the dam site Cairo and further north.

5. Fishing activities that started on a limited scale on Nubia Lake are increasing and developing on a modern basis to partly fill a large gap in the protein diet of the population. Navigation between Aswan and Wadi Halfa (the northern terminus of the Sudan Railway running to Khartoum) has improved; there are steamers for regular service all year around.

6. Aswan, the old frontier and tourist town, grew to be a center for chemical industry, and a growing fish industry.

Some 500,000 inhabitants of Egyptian Nubia south of Aswan, displaced by the rising water of the lake have been resettled in the Kom Ombo Basin. The government built for them 75 new townships and reclaimed 25,000 acres of new cropland.

Not all the effects of the High Dam have been positive, however. The availability of more water for irrigation that is not matched by expanding the drainage system led to the rise of the level of groundwater and an infertility. The deposition of silt in Lake Nubia which previously used to build up the soil and renew its fertility and built the delta, deprived the soil for natural fertilazation and led to the erosion of the delta shore.

About 18 miles north of Aswan the sandstone cliffs receed, marking the entrance to Wadi Kom Ombo (Vally-Plane). The width of the valley at the Nile front is about 15 miles, after which the sandstone cliffs rise forming Gebel es-Silsila that delimits again the northern edge of Wadi Kom Ombo^3.

The valley is graben-structured depression bounded by a major northwest-southeast fault to the north and a hinge line to the south. Two important wadis run in the valley, Wadi Shait and Wadi Kharit, both rise from the crest of the Red Sea Mountains in the east. The floor of the valley is covered mostly by Pleistocene and Holocene deposits of mud, clay, and silt. The modern Nile deposits exist only as a narrow strip along the river.

The Kom Ombo region was obscure during the early history, but it played a significant role as a frontier during and after the New Kingdom. There are few records before the fifteenth century B.C. when Queen Hatshepsat (1503-1482 B.C.) quarried sandstone and Thutmosis III (1482-50 B.C.) built a now-lost temple on the site of Ombos. Large-scale quarrying activities were continued on both banks of the river well into the Twentieth Dynasty (1200-1085 B.C.) providing building stone for Thebes and other cities of Upper Egypt.

In Ptolemaic times, Ombos replaced Aswan as the nome capital of the southern most province of Egypt and occupied a key position at the head of the caravan route to the Red Sea port of Berenice, via Appollones in Wadi El-Gemal. Between 180 B.C. and 30 B.C., an attractive temple was built to adorn the new metropolis and was jointly dedicated to Haroeris and Sobek. During the Coptic era Ombos played a very minor role in the history of the country. Between the 8th and 15th centuries, upper Egyptians, Nubians, and Beduinis clashed repeatedly in the shatter zone, and trade was the only economic pursuit of any stability. Daraw emerged as a significant market town; at the head of the Eastern Desert caravan route from Berber in the Sudan, camel herds destined for Middle and Lower Egypt, were watered and pastured here before being driven further north to Farshut. Pilgrims en route to Mecca followed another caravan trail from Daraw over Bir Quleib and Bir Abu Hashim to the former Red Sea port of Aidhab. The impoverished sedentary population was either displaced or absorbed by infiltrating beduins. By the end of the 18th century the agricultural lands along the river were largely occupied by former Ababda from the Eastern desert.

The contemporary role of Kom Ombo began in 1903 with the foundation of the Wadi Kom Ombo Company by a group of international financiers. Making use of the Aswan Reservoir waters and of steam-driven, high-pressure pumps, the company developed the undulation

121

Pleistocene silt Plain (which lies about 50 feet above modern flood level north and east of Ombos) into a great commercial sugar and cotton enterprise. By 1914 over 23,000 acres had been put under cultivation and some 20,000 colonists, mostly impoverished Lower and Middle Egyptians, settled on the virgin lands. Further expansion of cropland to a total of over 29,000 acres was made in the 1920's. The second raising of the Aswan Dam led to the relocation, after 1933, of some Nubian groups form El-Diwan to Dar-Es Salan, near Daraw. By 1947 the new market and administrative center of Kom Ombo, two miles northeast of ancient Ombos, had a population of over 40,000. The remaining high pleistocene silts on the northern, eastern, and southern peripheries of the plain (totaling and area of 25,000 acres) were claimed between 1961 and 1964 as part of the final irrigation project. Fifty thousand Nubians evacuated from the area of Lake Nubia, formed by the High Dam, were resettled on these newly owned lands during 1963-64.

North of Kom Ombo the two cliffs approach each other again. Teh river continues its trip northeward in its narrow valley. The valley gets a little wider on the west side at Idfu and Isna, two rural administration towns in upper Egypt. The Isna barrages were built in 1908 to improve basin irrigation, its function changed after the High Dam was built. It is now used for perennial irrigation. The barrage is showing symptoms of aging and has to be replaced or reinforced.

Advancing northward on the western bank is Armant, known for its sugar factory. Luxor (Thebes), in the middle of a basin on the eastern bank, was the capital of Egypt for centuries during the glory of its former famous history. It is one of the most important world tourist centers; thousands of tourists, scholars, archeologists and students visit the town each year to see, study, and admire the many temples, palaces, and tombs left by the ancient Egyptians.

North of Luxor the river makes its famous bend, Qena Bend. The towns of Qus, Qift, and Qena on the eastern side of the bend are rural towns and market places for agricultural production. They were also old towns that flourished during ancient history; they were located at the junctions between the valley and the roads that followed the dry valleys (wadis) to the gold mines in Eastern desert. Qift (coptos) was the seat of a bishopric and an important religion center during the Coptic history. Qos, located in the region of sugarcane

122

production, is now a center for paper industry using the
bagasse of the canes as the raw material. At the
western end of the bend and on the western side of the
river is Naga Hamadi. It is growing as an industrial
center. A factory was built for aluminum production,
depending on the electricity transmitted from the High
Dam at Aswan. The factory is located at the edge of the
western desert, thus saving the fertile land of the
valley for agriculture. Naga Hmadi is also well known
for sugar production, depending on the lush sugarcane
fields in this part of the country. Naga Hamadi barrage
was built in 1930; it supplies two canals which irrigate
115,000 acres on the east bank and 315,000 on the west
bank. The railroad and the main road that connects
Cairo with Aswan run on the west bank, crosses the river
at Naga Hamadi, and run on the east bank until they
reach Aswan. Naga Hamadi is also at the railroad and
road connection to the Kharga Oasis in the Western
Desert.

Middle Egypt: This region can be considered the beating
heart of Egypt. It extends northward to the head of the
Delta. The river resumes its trip northward after the
Quena bend and the east-west direction of the river
comes to an end. The valley gets wider with an average
width of 10 miles. The walls of the plateau that define
the valley become lower in altitude in a downstrean
direction. The soil is of high fertility; agricultue is
intensive; chemicals, fertilizers, pesticides and
herbicids are used lavishly; and the crops are
diversified. Crops include cotton, sugarcane, wheat,
maize, sorgham, bersim (Egyptian clover used as fodder
and considered and important crop in the crop rotation);
Lentils, beans, and other pulses are very important as
crops, the government is encouraging their cultivation,
since they are improtant in the Egyptian diet. Sesame
and other oil seeds are important for the production of
cooking oil as are onions for home consumption and
export; they are also grown on a considerable area. The
agricultural output per acre is very high as is also the
quality of the production. The region is dotted by
small and large villages as well as with tens of small
and large towns. As everywhere in Egypt, the
archeological sites and the monuments are numerous. In
all Egypt generally and in Middle Egypt especially, the
very modern and the very old, in culture, technology,
architect and even traditions, exist side by side.

This part of the valley starts near Dandara where
the ancient town of Abydos and its temple were located.
Northward Girga is located; the signs of modernization

has been introduced to this small market town in the form of a modern sugar refinery factory and a paper factory depending on the bagasse as a raw material. North of Girga is Sohag, the administrative center of that province. On the eastern bank of the river is Akhmim well known since the medieval ages by its cottage industry that produces carpets, rugs and textiles. The government is encouraging this type of production. Asyut is the largest and most populous town in Middle Egypt before reaching Cairo. It is an important administrative center as well as a market place. Its reputation for cottage industries, especially for the production of rugs and textiles, goes back to the medieval ages. The town was also known during the ancient history as one of the important religion centers, and since the Coptic era to the time being, it served as a seat for the Asyut Bishopnic, one of the very important Coptic monasteries is located near the town. The area of the Asyut province is dotted with many archaeological sites that belong to different civilization states. The excavations at Der Tasa and El Badari revealed the history of the epochs of neolithistic and predynastic Egypt. Tell-el-Amarna (Akhetaton) was the center of the religious revolution led by the young King Tutankhamun. The famous Tell-el-Amarna letters (tablest) written to Egypt by the petty kings of ancient Canan, Phoenicia and Syria give valuable historical information. Asyut is the home of the famous Univeristy of Asyut, an institute well known for higher education and research.

Just north of Asyut, at Asyut Barrages, starts Bahr Yousef, originally a branch of the Nile, dredged and rebuilt to carry water to Middle Egypt and the Fayun Oasis. The valley extends northward without any signs of any physical or cultural change. El-Minya and Beni Suwef are two administrative centers and Abu Qurqas is known for its sugar production, the plant has been recently modernized and Al Bahnasa is known for its monuments that go back to the ancient history.

Approaching Cairo, the norhtern most section of the valley gets relatively wider. On the western side of the valley there are the pyramids of Meidum, Dahshur, Saqara and the famous pyramids of Giza; thousands of tourists visit those famous areas yearly. On the eastern side at El-Maadi the excavation recovered a lot of materials related to prehistoric ages. (Maadi neolithic civilization). El-Tabbin, once a small village near Helwan, became the site of the iron and steel industry. The huge cement factory is located north of Helwan at Maassra.

Cairo, the capital of Egypt is located at the head of the valley and just south of the point where the river branches to form the famous Delta. Egypt, during its long histroy, chose different sites for their capitals. First, it was Memphis (on the western side of the valley just south of modern Cairo). Then Thebes in upper Egypt. Averis in the eastern part of the Delta (modern small town of San-el-Hagar) was the capital during the first foreign invasion by the Hyksos and it was known as Ramses during the age of the modern kingdom of ancient Egypt. Alexandria became the capital during Greko Roman eras as well as during the Byzantine Empire. The Arabs chose a site, located now in the southern part of Cairo (Messr el qadyma, El Fusstat) to be their capital. Cairo (Al Qahirah) was built by the Fatimides who invaded Egypt during the early fourteenth century, and it became the capital of the country up to the time being. Cairo as a capital is rationally situated. It is easily connected with the Delta and Mediterranean towns as well as with all the locations in the valley by roads, railroads and waterways. Metropolitan Cairo has approximately 8 million inhabitants and the city's rapid growth of recent decades, especially after World War II, continued unabated. It is considered one of the ten largest urban centers in the world. It is the largest in Africa, the Middle East and in the Mediterranean basin. It has all the problems of a large city that grew beyond its capacity, problems of being over-crowded, lack of adequate housing, problems of sanitation, health, traffic congestion and above all, education for its huge numbers.

Cairo is a city of immense contrasts. Along the Nile and in downtown there are elegant hotel-skyscrapers, huge office and government buildings, residential buildings that look European in general and Parisian in particular. Beyond these marvelous builings there are the depressing ghettos, that were once residential areas for middle class but neglect and rules of rent controls turned them to slums. There are many old mosques built during medieval ages as well as many others of modern architecture, churches of the Coptic era (some of them are underground), and modern cathedrals. Saladin Citadel, a reminder of that legend of the crusaders era, is built on the Moqattam hills east of the town. Cairo is still a cosmopolitan center. It is the cultural center of the Middle East and of the

Arab World, with great museums and universites that make
it the mecca of those who seek higher education. It is
city known for its botanical and zoological gardens,
national libraries, national theaters and symphony
orchestras. Although Cairo is primarily a center of
government and administration, it is also the main
political center of the Arab countries and an important
minaret in the Islamic world.

Cairo is also an industrial city where different
modern industries with large investments employing large
numbers of labor are located (textiles, food processing,
iron and steel, assembly plants, tools and furniture).
Countless numbers of small handicraft industries exist
in the old districts of the city.

The Delta: About 8 miles north of Cairo the river
branches and forms its famous Delta. For a long
time, only the area nearest the tributaries was under
agriculture. The main part of the Delta was flood-prone,
sandy, marshy and the soil had high salinity. The river
had seven branches running northward to the
Mediterranean. Modern irrigation engineering turned the
Delta to a very fertile productive region with dense
population settling in many cities and hundreds of
different size villages. A system of barrages,
irrigation canals, drainage channels and covered
drainage pipes were built to control the river,
cultivate most of the land and maintain its fertility.
The most important of these barrages are Mohammed Ali
barrages built at the head of the delta on both branches
of the river (the only two existing branches). It is
the first major modern irrigation project built in
Egypt; it was completed in 1861. When these barrages
became too old to function well, other barrages were
built on the same site in 1942. Other important
barrages were built on the eastern branch (Damietta) at
Zefta. Other barrages were built at the mouth of
Rosetta and at the mouth of Damietta, to keep the salty
water of the Mediterranean out of the branches and to
help irrigate the northern part of the Delta. There are
three major irrigating canals that take the water from
the two braches to feed secondary and field canals. One
of the canals irrigate the western side for the Delta,
the second serves the middle part, and the third serves
the eastern region. The Ismailia Canal that takes water
directly from the Nile north of Cairo was built with the
original purpose of supplying the Suez Canal Zone and
its cities with fresh water. That canal is also used to
help irrigate the eastern part of the Delta and now
supplies the Sinai Peninsula with fresh water that is

126

carried under the Suez Canal. The Mahmoudya Canal takes
from the Rosetta branch and supplies Alexandria on the
Mediterranean Sea with fresh water. The canal helps,
too, in irrigating that northwestern part of the Delta,
and is very important as a waterway in linking
Alexandria with Cairo.

The drainage canals run northward to empty into the
lakes and the Mediterranean Sea. Since there the level
of the Delta is almost at sea-level, huge electric pumps
were installed at the outlets of these canals to lift
the drained water to the sea.

The water from the High Dam enables Egypt to
reclaim about one million acres in the Delta for
agriculture. Most of the land that will be reclaimed is
marshy area, parts of the lakes and some land that
flanks the Delta. Relatively large areas on both sides
of the Delta are in the process of being reclaimed. In
fact, the land is fertile land that was built by the
deposition of the river but has been neglected, and the
sands of the desert covered it⁴. Agriculture in the
Delta, as it is in all Egypt, is an intensive type of
agriculture and of mixed crops. However, the type of
soil and marketing conditions create a certain degree of
specialization . In the northern areas, near the lakes
and marshes where soil salinity is relatively high, rice
is an important crop. In eastern and western areas
where the texture of the soil is lighter, citrus fruits
and fresh vegetables, especially potatoes (mostly for
export), are more important. The southern part of the
Delta (close to Cairo) as well as close to the large
cities (Alexandria, Tanta and El Mansura) are areas for
vegetables and fresh milk. The central part of the
Delta is well known for its long-staple cotton.

The western desert approaches the western region of
the Delta, especially in its southern part. This is the
region where the new administrative province (El-Tahrir
Province) has been established. Its area has been
almost entirly reclaimed from the desert⁵. New
irrigation canals, pipes and sprayers (very modern for
Egypt) were installed and new villages were built. The
cost of reclamation far exceeded the returns; however,
it shows the determination of the country to expand its
agricultural area to face the problem of the increasing
population. Northward on the western side is the
province of Behera with Damanhur as its administrative
center. The government is trying to establish handcraft
industries in the town, especially handmade rugs. Old
factories, for extracting oil from sesame and ground

127

nuts, were modernized and are increasing their production. Two industrial towns, Kafr El Dauwar and El Baida, are located in that province. Their textile production, dependent on the finest of long-staple cotton, has an excellent reputation in the world market. In fact, most of their production is for export. There is an extensive program to reclaim some parts of Lake Idku and Lake Maryut to expand rice cultivation.

The middle part of the Delta between the Damietta and Rosetta branches is very densely populated, especially in its southern part, in the two provinces of El Menoufya and El Gharbya. Shebin El Kom, the rural and administrative center of El Menoufya province, is becoming a center of optics and electronic industries. Tanta, the largest city in the region and the capital of Gharbya, is expanding its food processing and chemical industry. Mahala-El-Kubra is the main center of the textile industries; its huge factories have been modernized and the production of cotton and wool fabrics is for both export and home consumption. Talkha, thanks to the nearby newly discovered natural gas, became a center of chemical and fertilizer industries. Kafr El Shiek, the capital of the northern province that carries its name is just a rural and agricultural market town.

The eastern area of the Delta extends from the Damietta branch to the Suez Canal zone. The eastern desert approaches it in the south, while the Manzala Lake, the largest of the Delta Lakes, is in the north. The southern province (Qalubbya) is well known for its fresh vegetables, milk, poultry and fruit production, and most of it is marketed in the very densely populated metropolitan Cairo. Banha is the capital of that province. Since it is located in the shadow of Cairo, it did not have a chance to grow as a large or industrial city. The only industry it has is cotton ginning. Zagazig is the administrative center of Sharquia province. Besides its importance as a market for agricultural production, it expanded and modernized its cotton ginning, cooking oil and soap factories. The town is now one of the centers of higher learing in Egypt, after establishing a large university. The eastern part of that province - Sharqia - is belived to have been the "land of Goshen" where the Hebrews lived during their stay in Egypt before their exodus to the "promised land". This area is now included in a large program of land reclamation, not only with the purpose of increasing the cultivated land in the country but also to supply the Suez Canal towns with their needs of agricultural products and to strengthen the hinterland of the canal both militarily and economically. Daqahlya is the northern province in that region of the Delta. El Mansura is its capital, the largest town in the region. It is an administrative center, market place, home for a large university, and famous for its history during the Crusades. Other smaller towns in the area are Mit Ghamr, Dikirnis and El Simbillawein: all are rural towns known for cotton ginning and food processing.

There has been a controversial debate going on for some years concerning the future of the northern lakes of the Delta. Some economists believe that reclaiming these lakes for agriculture should be accelerated and completed as soon as possible. Their point of view is saying that the country has to expand its agricultural area as much as it can in the shortest possible time to increase its food production, especially grains and meat, and to cut down the huge bills for importing food. This idea is strenghtened by the fact that reclamation of these lakes is easier and costs less than reclaiming the desert land. Other economists say that the lakes should stay as they are since they are very good fishing grounds in a country that has little meat production and is not yet ready for high seas fishing. So far the land that has been reclaimed from the lakes, especially Lakes Menzala, Maryut and Idku, are productive and the cost in relation to the return is reasonable.

The most important city along the Delta coast is Alexandria. It is the second city in Egypt and its main port. It handles most of the imports and exports of the country. The government is engaged in a large project to expand and modernize the harbor and its facilities. Alexandria is a main center of industry. Textiles, chemicals, petro-chemicals, car assembly, ship building, cement: all are important and modern industries in and around the town. A new steel mill has been built west of Alexandria at El Dikheila. The city is well connected with all parts of Egypt by roads, railroads and waterways. An oil pipeline, extending from Suez in the Gulf of Suez to Alexandria (on the Mediterranean) SUEMED, increased the business and economic activities in the city. Alexandria's population in 1980 was over 2.5 million. The city was built in 332 B.C. by Alexander the Great. It became the capital of the country until the Arab invasion in 642 A.D. During the Greek era it was the main center of Hellinic learning with a magnificent library. The city was second only to Rome during the Roman history. It became a main theological center and the seat of the Coptic Patriarch (during the Christian era). After the Arab invasion and

the choosing of their capital to be south of modern
Cairo (El Fustat), Alexandria went into a lengthy
decline. When Napoleon invaded Egypt in 1798, it was
estimated that the population of the town was less than
13,000. Alexandria made a huge but gradual recovery
during the 19th century, especially after linking it
with Cairo by a road and a railroad and after the
opening of the Suez Canal. In the interwar period
(1920-1940) the city made another big jump by becoming
an important industrial and finanacial center; since
World War II it has been growing steadily and became
another center of higher education after establishing
its important university. The city is also an important
tourist center, especially for those interested in the
Greek-Roman history and its monuments. Because of its
location on the Mediterranean and its less hot summers,
compared to the interior, it became a major summer
resort.

East of Alexandria is Abu Qir Bay, the site of the
famous "Nile Maritime Battle", where the British navy
destroyed the French convoy that carried Napoleon's army
to Egypt. The Abu Qir area is now known for its
production of gas which is piped to Alexandria. There
are also black sand dunes close to the shore, from which
some radioactive materials are extracted.

Rosetta (Rasheed) is located at the mouth of
Rosetta branch. It was an important port and a fishing
town. Rosetta lost its importance because of the
deposition of the Nile silt, and it is not suitable as a
port for modern ships. The town gained back some of its
importance after an important paper factory was built.
The paper industry uses the rice straw as raw material;
rice is the main crop in this northern part of the
Delta. Idfina, just south of Rosetta, is well-known for
its food processing and canning industry.

Damietta, at the mouth of the Damietta branch, was
the main port of the country during the Islamic Era.
It lost its importance as a port because of silting of
the river. Now the government is building a port about
15 miles west of the mouth of the river. It is designed
to handle about 12 million tons of cargo yearly. The
town is a prosperous center for some industries,
especially furniture, shoes and leather works, dairy
prodcuts, textiles and a variety of handcrafts. It is
also a summer resort.

The Suez Canal Zone: The Suez Canal is a vital
international waterway[6]. The canal that operated

130

without any interruption since it was opened in 1869, served world trade and expanded east-west relationships on a large scale unitl 1956. The British and the French, who operated the canal, reaped huge incomes through collecting tolls from the ships using the canal and deprived Egypt, the real owner of the waterway, from any income. The canal was closed for the first time during the French-British-Israeli invasion of 1956 that followed the nationalization of the canal. The closure led not only to stopping the shipments of oil from the Persian Gulf to Europe, which caused economic chaos, but also to the termination of the British and French influence in Egypt, the Middle East and in most of the world. Since the world cannot afford the closure of the canal for a long period, the world community, through the World Bank and the United States, helped Egypt to reopen the canal and resume international navigation as soon as the hostilities came to an end and the invading armies retreated. Unforutuantely the canal was closed for the second time in 1967 as a result of the Arab-Israeli war and the Israeli occupation of the Sinai Peninsula and the eastern bank of the canal. That second closure lasted for a long time, and the canal was not opened for navigation until July 1975. The closure for such a long time had a drastic effect on Egypt and the industrial countries; it also affected the world navigation pattern, especially for oil as well as the engineering of building oil tankers. Egypt lost the huge revenues that she used to get from the canal since it was nationalized and started to get subsides from the Arab rich oil countries. That was humiliating for the Egyptians as people full of pride. The three main cities of the canal Port Said, Ismailiya and Suez, especially the last two, were evacuated under continuous heavy bombardment from the Israeli forces, and their residents lived as refugees in other cities of Egypt, especially Cairo. The Egyptian industries in the whole canal zone, especially the petrochemicals, chemicals and gypsum were completely destroyed. The closeure of the canal lead the oil tankers carrying oil from the Persian Gulf, to travel the long seaway around Africa to reach Europe, which further raised the price of oil and caused more world inflation. It also considerably affected the trade between Europe, in general, and South Asia and the Far East. The long trip the oil tankers made arourd Africa and the long time it takes and the expenses involved encouraged the engineers and tanker builders to build giant tankers. The average capacity of the tankers before the closure of the canal was around 50,000 tons, and the canal allowed the passage of almost all world tankers. After the closure, the capacity of the tankers went up to beyond 300,000 tons, and some of these had the capacity of 500,000 tons. When the canal was cleaned of the obstacles and reopened, with the help of the Americans in 1975, it was already obsolete. Egypt has to embark on a large scale program for widening and deepening the canal and its navigation facilities. It also set an ambitious program to rebuild the cities and their industries. After several projects, mostly with Japanese financial and technical help, the canal now has the depth of 53 feet, and its maximum width is 1,095 feet, and its minimum width is 643.3 feet. The average transit time is 15 hours. It enables the passage of vessels of 150,000 tons fully laden, 200,000 tons partly-loaded and 370,000 tons unloaded. A bypass was built at Port Said. The improvements helped also to increase the number of ships that cross the canal to be 90 ships per day.

There is another project to build another canal parallel to the existing one to make each used for one-way direction. This last project was supposed to be completed by 1995. However, that last project has been slowed down and its future is not certain yet, not because any financial or technical problems, but because the oil and gas production of the North Sea, the completion of the oil and gas pipelines from U.S.S.R. to western Europe, and the great increase of oil production from countries located west of the Suez Canal (especially Nigeria and Mexico) made the European countries less dependent on the oil from the Persian Gulf, all of which may decrease the return from such an expensive project. It is hoped that the new Saudi pipeline that crosses the peninsula and ends at Yenbo on the Red Sea may increase the traffic in the canal. Another project is to build three tunnels to traverse the canal. One of them, Ahmed Hamdi Tunnel, has been completed and is already in use.

The cities of the Canal Zone were rebuilt, and the industries were restored. In the two cities of Suez and Ismailiya, new residential districts with highrise apartment buildings were erected. Schools, hospitals and government offices were reopened. The government compensated the house owners whose buildings were destroyed during wartime and gave them generous subsidies to repair the damage. A new univeristy was built in Ismailiya, and a Canal Research Center was established. The petrochemical industries, oil refineries, and chemical industries were resettled on a more modern basis in Suez. Suez now has a population of more than 200,000 inhabitants, and Ismailiya has 150,000 inhabitiants. The city and important port of Port Said at the Mediterranean junction of the canal now has a population of about 300,000 inhabitants. The city was the least damaged of the canal cities during the war, because it was naturally protected from the big Israeli guns that were located in Sinai by the marshy area of the northeastern extension of the Manzala Lake. Nevertheless, Port Said had a good share of the money allocated for the reconstruction of the canal zone. The port has been enlarged and equipped with modern facilities, new storage areas to serve transit cargo, a tax-free zone with different industries especially textiles, clothes, and appliances to be exported or reexported. Fishing industries were encouraged and modernized.

The Faiyum Depression is morphologically part of the Western Desert, but it owes its existence, fertility and prosperity to Bahr Yousef which takes water from the Nile to irrigate that depression. Overlooking the depression from the northwest is Gebel Qatrani, an escarpment of limestone. Most of the geologists agree with Stanford and Arkel who suggested that the depresson is the result of wind erosion that took place during the lower Pleistocene Period[7]. Caton Thompson and E.W. Gardener suggested that the high terraces above the level of Lake Qarrun (Maurice) that represent former lake beaches are the result of fluctuation of the level of the Tethys Sea (that preceeded the Mediterranean) during the Pleistocene, and the size of the lake was much larger during the Paleolithic and Meolithic ages. These terraces contain many of the remains and flint and stone tools of these prehistoric civilizations. The depression also forms one administrative unit, the Faiyum Province. That region can be named the fruit gardens of Egypt. More fruit is grown in that region than any other part of Egypt. Grapes, figs, all kinds of citrus fruits, apricots and mangoes, all are of high quality. Rice is one of the main crops, especially in the low lands close to the lake where soil salinity is relatively high. Other crops are olives, maize, sorgham, wheat, barley and cotton. The region is also well-known for its poultry production. The administrative center is El Faiyum (Madint El Faiyum); other rural and market towns are Sinnuris, Itssa and Fidimin. The population of the province now exceeds 1.2 million inhabitants. The main industries in the region are fruit canning, textiles and leather.

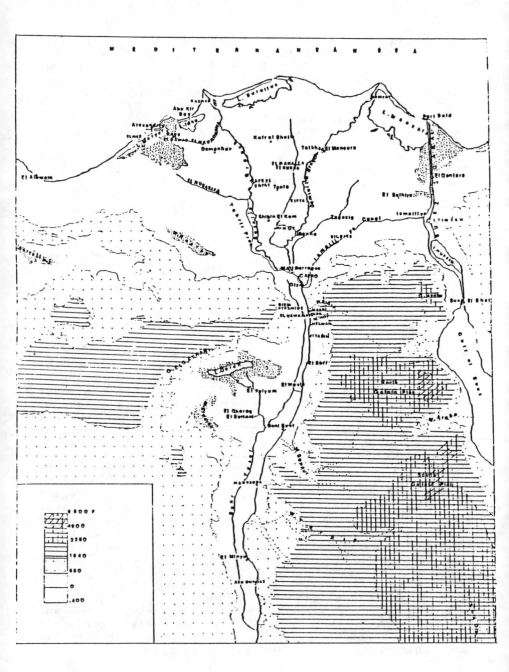

The Eastern Desert: Extending from the Nile Valley the Gulf of Suez and the Red Sea, the Eastern Desert consists essentially of a backbone of high and rugged mountains running parallel to the coast. The mountains are built of igneous and metamorphic rocks. The highest peak of those mountains is Gebel Shayeb (7280 feet). To the north of the mountains are the limestone plateaux of South Galala (4880 feet), North Galala (4245 feet) and Gebel Ataqa (290 feet), separated from one another by broad wadis (dry valleys). To the west of the mountains is a plateau built in the north of limestone, and in the south of sandstone that extends, as the mountains themselves, further south in the Sudan.

The Eastern Desert is disected by wadis either running eastward to the Red Sea and the Suez Gulf (and those are very short wadis because the mountains are very close to the coast) or running to the Nile Valley. The most important of these wadis are Tarfa, El Assyuti, Qena, Shait, Kharit, Hammamat and Alaqi. As it was mentioned before, all these mountains were formed during the Pluvial Age.

Although it is an arid region and understandably there are extensive waterless area, many of these valleys have water wells and some vegetation. This is due to the fact that the mountains are high enough to get some rain, irregular in amount and season. In few seasons these wadis are flooded and carry their water, which becomes yellowish by the desert sand, to the Nile and the Red Sea.

Belonging to the same geographical region are some islands in the Red Sea. The important ones are: Ashrefi, Tawila, Shadwan, Safage and St. John's. Most of these islands are small, flat and built of coral reefs.

Near the coast of the Red Sea and the Suez Gulf, there are many coral reefs that make navigation along the coast very dangerous. The Eastern Desert was the gold mining area of the ancient Egyptions. Now the expenses of getting any gold make it uneconomical, even though the prices are very high. The desert has phosphate deposits that are mined economically from Quser, Safaga, along the Red Sea and Sibaiya near Isna close to the valley. Iron ore is in the eastern part of the Aswan area. The most important is oil which is produced from Ras-Gharib, Gemsa and Ghardaga. Off shore oil production (Al Morgan oil field), where the Gulf of Suez joins the Red Sea, is very important.

135

There is no agriculture of any importance due to the lack of water and the poor soil. The total population in the region does not exceed 75,000 inhabitants, including some 15,000 in Ras Gharib and Ghardega. There are some 10,000 nomads mostly of Bisharyeen and Ababda origin, mostly in the southwest.

A new air base and military communication center has been built with the cooperation of the Americans on the small peninsula of Ras Banas. It is supposed to help in defending the oil fields and navigation in the Persian Gulf.

Two important Coptic monasteries were built during the fifth century; they are in the northen part of the Easten Desert. One of those is Deir Mari Bolos, known as Deir Anba Baula (Monastery of St. Paul). It is located on the eastern slopes of the southern Galala Plateau. The other monastery is known as Deir El Qaddis Antonious (Monastery of St. Anthony), on the northwestern slopes of the same plateau, but located close to a tributary of Wadi Araba. Both monasteries are known for their historical contributions for the spiritual and monastic life of Christianity, and still have a large number of monks and are visited yearly by a large number of pilgrims and tourists.

Sinai Peninsula: The Sinai Peninsula extends from the Mediterranean in the north to Ras Muhammed on the Red Sea in the south. To the west is the Suez Canal and the Gulf of Suez, and to the east the Gulf of Aqaba and its northeeastern part emerges to the Negev Desert (Negeb) in Asia. The core of the peninsula, situated in the south, is built of igneous and metmorphic mountains that slope to three directions: to the Gulf of Suez west, to the Gulf of Aqaba east and northward to the Mediterranean. The mountains have the highest peaks in Egypt including Gebel Katherina (8800 feet), Gebel Um Shomer (8525 feet) and Gebel Musa (Moses) (7616 feet). This mountainous core is dissected with deep wadis and the total region has very rugged relief. The higher part of the limestone plateau, which flanks the igneous core to the north, is called Gebel El-Tih. The southern part of it is the Egma (Igma) Plateau. The central part of the plateau surface forms a fairly open region, draining to the Mediterranean by numerous affluents of Wadi El-Arish (the river of Egypt). The eastern and western edges of this pateau are dissected by many deep wadis draining to the Gulfs of Suez and Aqaba. In such rocky rugged areas, the wadis and the gaps between the

136

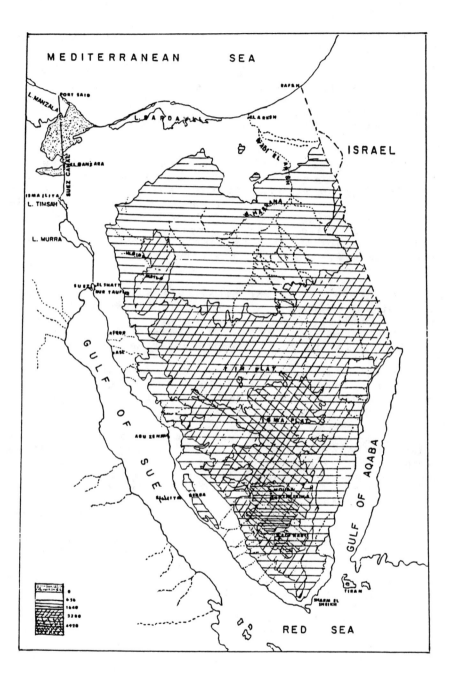

MEDITERRANEAN   SEA

ISRAEL

GULF OF SUEZ

GULF OF AQABA

RED   SEA

137

hills form very important passes, such as Mitla (Mamer Mitla) and Giddi (Mamer Giddi).

In the northern parts of the peninsula, the general northward slop of the plateau surface is broken by some hills. The most important of them are Gebel Maghara, Gebel Yelleg and Gebel Halal. Along the coast there are some coastal sand dunes and Lake El Bardawil (Sabakhet El Barduwil).

The peninsula, that has been since the dawn of history an integrated part of Egypt, always had its distinctive position. It has been crossed back and forth by armies either from Egypt or from the Middle East. Its limited number of inhabitants (estimated to be 250,000) have different geographical orientation; while the majority of them that are located in the west are oriented toward Egypt, the inhabitants of the eastern reaches are oriented toward Arabia.

Gold and copper was mined by the ancient Egyptians from Sinai. Now oil is the most important product from the peninsula. The most important oil wells are in Sudr, Asl, Ras Matamara and Bilayim. Off-shore wells in the Suez Gulf are yielding more oil than those on shore.

Manganese is mined from Um Bugma and there are limited resources of coal in Gebel Mahgara. Light, concentrated uranium has been discovered and may be used in the furture.

Agriculture is for substistence and is limited to small areas along the coastal plain, and most of it is either close to the feet of the sand dunes that serve as reservoirs for the limited amount of winter rain or is on the floor of the wadis, especially in the south where some wells and springs exist. The main crops are barley, olives and melons and date palms. The Egyptain government, in order to encourage the beduins to settle and to increase the settlements so Sinai would no longer be a "no man's land", has embarked on an ambitious program to expand agriculture based on irrigation by piping Nile water beneath the Suez Canal to the Peninsula. The program is also aiming to introduce other crops such as figs, almonds, and citrus fruits. The government tried in the early sixties to help expand agricultue by building a dam across Wadi El-Arish, but it was not very successful because the reservoir behind the dam lost most of its capcity in a few years due to the large silting of the desert sand in the reservoir.

138

Some fishing activities are taking place along the coast, especially on the Mediterranean and in the Lake Bardawil.

The government is also trying to promote the tourist industry. It could be a successful effort and a source of good revenue if the efforts are organized and well financed.

St. Katherine Monastery on Gebel Katherina (a Greek Orthodox Monastery) was built duirng the era of the Byzantine Empire, and it is the destination of many pilgrims and tourists.

El Arish is the administrative center of the north and El Tur is the main town in the south.

The Western Desert: The region extends westward for the Nile to the borders of Libya whre it emerges with the Libyan Desert. It is a part of the Sahara that extends to the Atlantic shores, and it makes up about two-thirds of the total area of Egypt. The region is basically a plateau with vast flat expanses of rocky ground, numerous deep desert depressions and large areas covered with drifting sand and mobile sand dunes called the seas of sand.

The western desert attains its greatest height in the southwest where the mountain mass, Gebel Uweinat, is located. The mountain itself is located in Libya and Sudan, but its norhteastern slopes are within the country. The soutwestern part of the desert forms the sandstone plateau known as the Gilf El-Kebir. This plateau slopes gradually to the depressions that contain the Oases of Dakhla and Kharga. Following these oases to the north and east is a limestone plateau in which the oases of Farafra, Siwa and Bahariya are situated and where the great Qattara depression and the other depressions of Wadi El Rayan, Wadi El Natroun and the Faiyum depression are formed. The northern edge of the Farafra oasis and the Qattara depression is an escarpment that marks the southern end of another plateau that extends norhtward to the Mediterranean.

An important feature of the Western Desert is the nature and distribution of its water resources. Along the narrow northern coastal plain there are wells and cisterns fed by local rainfall. At the piedmont of Gebel Uweinat (the extreme southwest) there are some springs fed by the occasional rain that falls on the mountain. The vast area in between is rainless. The

139

Faiyum depression, as was mentioned before, owes its existence to the water supply it gets from the Nile. The oases of Siwa, Bahariya, Dakhla and Kharga owe their habitability to artesian supplies. All the oases, as well as the scattered wells, are situated in great depressions where the ground water supplies can rise to the surface; but the vast intervening parts have no water at all.

Considering the formation of the depressions and oases, all geologists agree that the main reason, if there would be any other reason, for their formation is wind erosion, and the depth is determined by the ground water level which forms a base level for wind action. Large quantities of the sandy constituents of the formation thus removed have been blown by the wind southeastward (the direction of the prevailing wind most of the time) and have been deposited in the form of great chains of sand dunes.

The most important areas for human habitation in these vast expanses of sand and rock are the oases where the gound water supports agriculture and sedentary population. The most populated of all these oases is the Kharga; it is estimated that of the toatal of 200,000 inhabitants in the Western Desert, Kharga has about 20,000. All the other oases are losing some of their population as most of the younger generation moves to the cities of the valley seeking employment. The main crops of the subsistence agriculture are barley, olives, sorghum and date palm trees. The governement is drilling some water wells and clearing or deepening the older ones. There is a project under study to pipe the Nile water from Nubia Lake to both the Kharga and Dakhla Oases and use sprinkling methods to avoid the problems of drainage. The project would increase dramatically the area under cultivation in Egypt and may lead to independency in grain and food production. It is estimated that about 800,000 acres can be reclaimed.

The coastal plain also has some limited agriculture based on the limited winter rainfall and on the water wells at the feet of the coastal sand dunes. The government established two extension centers in Fuka and Ras El Hikma to enocurage the cultivation of fig trees, almond, olives, barley and green fodder. The most effective method of agriculture in that narrow coastal strip of land is dry agricluture.

Most of the population along the caost, especially west of Mersa Matruh, are beloning to Awlad Ali, a tribe

140

of beduins, most of them are living in Libya. Some limited heards of sheep, camels and goats are raised by these beduins, and their animals find good markets in the valley.

Bahariya Oases has rich iron ore resources that are shipped to the main steel mill in Helwan. The Qattara depresion is an extensive waste land (more than 7,000 square miles). Its floor, that drops to 435 feet below sea level, is covered with fine loose sand and some salty marshes. It served as a defensive area during World War II when the Germans tried to capture Egypt since even the modern machines of war could not cross that depression. The famous battle of Alamein took place in the bottleneck between the depression and the Mediterranean. The cemetery of those who were killed in that war is visited by many relatives and tourists, and it is a reminder of the events and sacrifices of that war.

There is another ambitious project in the Western Desert. The project is to construct a channel or install pipes that would carry water from the Mediterranean to the deep Qattara depression to be used primarily to generate hydroelectric power that is badly needed in the valley and delta. The area also would have a resort that encourages tourist industry. One of the difficulties of that project, which is still under study, is the effect of the lake that would be formed in the depression and the impact of its humidity on agriculture in the delta.

Another project is to build two nuclear reactors which will be provided by the Americans to generate power and to be used in experiments to desalinate the sea water and to supply electricity to the Delta. One of the reactors will be built west of Alexandria and the second near Alemein.

Oil production on a commerical scale has started in Alamein, Umbaraka and Aba Ghardeq.

Wadi El Natrun, west of the Delta, is known for its procdution of nitrates. The wadi has world fame, it is known in the history of Christianity as Baryet Sheheit (the wilderness of Sheheit). The monastic life in Christianity and the first monaserties were built here. There are still three very important monsateries crowded with a new generation of highly educated pious monks; they are Deir Makarius, Deir El Suriani and Deir El Baramus. The monasteries are the destination of

141

tourists, pilgrims, visitors and many theologians.

There are two administrative centers in the Western Desert. Mersa Matruth in the north is a summer resort on the rail line between Alexandria and Libya, and Kharga is the administrative center of the southern region of the desert (El Wadi El Gedeed).

ECONOMY

The factors that affect the Egyptian economy are: the resources of the country, the population, and the national and international political situation. The economic history of Egypt and the present economic conditions are the result of the interaction and the dynamic motion of these three factors.

The natural resources of this country are limited. The main resource, of course, is the Nile and the land, as was mentioned before. The Nile is the soul of Egypt which made it different from the deserts surrounding it. It gave Egypt its fertile soil and was the main creator of its civilization and is the life giver of the country. Since immemorial times the Egyptians tried to discover its resources, tame it and use each droplet of its water by builing the very expensive, excellent system of irrigation. However, the amount of water that the river can supply is limited, and its use is also limited mostly to the valley and its delta which makes only about 3.3% of the total area. That 3.3% under cutivation is about 5.8 million acres. It is almost the same as during the ancient history. Although the High Dam added to the area about 1.2 million acres, that added area roughly compensated for the land lost to urban and rural expansion. The modern irrigation projects doubled the crop area since, thanks to the availability of water all year, the land is put under two and sometimes three crops. The lavish use of chemicals, the introduction and expansion of commercial crops such as rice, cotton and sugarcane, and the diversification of crops, especially the increasing area under vegetables and fruits, all have been agricultural improvements which increased the agricultural product-ivity, but it never matched the very high growth rate of population.

Mineral resources of Egypt are limited. Although the country is a net exporter of oil, these exports are limited by a relatively limited production and a growing consumption due to the lack of other fuels. Egypt is no match in oil production or exports to its neighbor Libya or to Algeria, another county in the region, Other minerals produced and exported on a limited scale are phosphates and manganese. Iron ore production is also on a small scale, and all of it is used locally. In conclusion, minerals will not play a major part in the economic development of the country.

Another of the main resources of Egypt is the Suez Canal. After a long time of being deprived of its income. Egypt got back its canal and its income. It was operated successfully from 1957 to 1967. The closure of the canal from 1967 to 1975 meant the loss of the revenues. The reopening of the canal and the several projcts of modernizing it have revived the canal as an important world waterway; however, if the revenues will be a factor in improving the financial and economic conditions in Egypt,it is left to the future to tell.

The climate and history of Egypt is making it an important tourist center. The warm, dry winters and the monuments, museums, historical mosques and churches that present the different stages of civilization, make Egypt the destination of various goups of tourists, scholars, students, archeologists and pilgrims from all over the world. If more attention is paid to the tourist industry, it would be a main source of revenue and foreign exchange.

The main factor that has a tremendous impact on the economy of Egypt is its population. With population estimated at the end of 1983 to be more than 45.5 million, and a cultivated area of 5.8 million acries, the density is 7.8 persons per acre represeting one of the highest man/land ratios in the world. The growth rate of the population of the period 1977 - 1982 averaged 2.31% per year, which adds about one million people yearly. Such a huge increase and excessive pressure on limeted arable land and on a country with limited resources, is the main reason for poverty among the Egyptians. If the population growth rate would even drop to 0%, which is very unlikely even in a hundred years, the country is still both very densely and overpopulated. The hope for raising the per capita income in Egypt lies in not only bringing the natural popuation growth to 0%, but also in developing to the maximum both the limited natural resources and the huge human resources; and, the three of them demand huge edcuational efforts.

The international political situation affected the economy of Egypt in several ways; when Egypt was occupied by the British, the British forced the country to follow the rule of free trade, and thus made it rather impossible to start any industrializaiton; the sole benefactor of such condition was the British industry, which made Egypt a market for its industry and a farm to produce the cotton needed for the Lancashire textile produciton. That same political situation deprived Egypt from the Suez Canal income. The Egptian-Israeli War that lasted from 1948 until the return of the Sinai peninsula in 1982 has drained the country financially, deprived it from the capital badly needed to invest in the economy and social service, and was the main reason for the huge debts that the country has to serve and pay back.

The stagnant economy of the sixties and seventies led to unemployment and masked underemployment on a large scale, coupled by the unreasonable government policy of the sixties which deprived the people from seeking employment abroad further complicated the problem. As soon as movement of people and labor was allowed in the early seventies, many persons, professionals, skilled and unskilled labor, left Egypt to better opportunities and much better paid jobs abroad, especially in Libya and the eastern Arab countries. Many of the qualified personnel have also immigrated to the west and to Australia. In the fiscal year 1982-83, Egyptians working abroad sent home somewhere in the region of 2,500 million dollars. Unfortuantely for the government, much of the income from foreign remittances avoids the official banking system because there are practically two exchange rates for foreign currency, the offical one and the free market.

As the feudal system and British colonization crippled the economic growth until the end of the fifties, the policy which was based on soicalist planning of the sixties tended to degenerate into the redistribution of poverty with immense coercion. Socialism cannot be built on emotions and good intentions and not taking into consideration developing the productive forces.

As soon as the Camp David Peace Treaty in 1979 took place, the economic situation started to sowly improve. Reopening the Suez Canal in 1975 accelerated the progress, and the return of the last section of Sinai in

144

1982 restored the confidence in a long lasting peace, and the economic picture became brighter.

Although the rich Arab oil countries withdrew the financial aid to Egypt, the economy did not suffer more, because the United States offered financial and economic aid of loans on soft terms. The western countries and Japan, also eager to promote peace, offered soft term loans. The improvements in the Suez Canal increased the number and capacity and tonnage of the ships using it. In 1982, 22,545 ships used the canal with a tonnage of 363,538,000. The revenues reached 1,000 million dollars with 956 million being derived from transit tolls and 44 million from services to ships in transit. It is expected that by the end of 1984 the revenues will exceed 1,500 million dollars. In fact, the canal is the main earner of foreign exchange.

In June and July of 1984 there was an attempt of mysterious origin to disrupt the navigation in the canal and the Red Sea. Several ships of different national- ities were damaged by sea mines in both the Gulf of Suez, just 15 miles south of the canal, and in the Red Sea. Although the navigation was not disrupted the international communities were alarmed. Mine sweepers, airplanes and helicopters belonging to Egypt United Kngdom, U.S.A., France, Holland, Italy and the U.S.S.R. were used to discover the mines. By the end of August it was declared that the seaway was clean and no mines were discovered. The Egyptian government accused Libya indirectly and took the steps allowed by international law to check suspicous ships to ensure the safety of navigation in the canal.

The return of Sinai meant not only the return of its minerals and oil to Egypt, but also it gave confidence to the foregn oil company to invest in oil exploration and production. In 1982 oil production reached 675,00 barrels per day. Oil is the second earner of foreign exchange after the canal.

This improvement in the economy has been reflected in per capita income which was 500 dollars in 1979. In 1981 it jumped to 860 dollars. It is noticed that in spite of that increase, Egypt is still in the category of these low-middle income countries.

AGRICULTURE

Agriculture was the main source of GNP (GDP) in Egypt. Agricultural products, especially cotton and rice, were the main exported commodities. Most of the population of Egypt was rural, and subsequently agricutlure employed more labor than all the other sectors of the economy combined. Most of the investments were in land, and most of the trade and business were directly or indirectly involved in agricultural prodcuts. Even manufacturing activities such as cotton ginning, textiles, sugar, and food processing were directly dependent on agriculture. In the 1940's agriculture contributed to 50% of theGNP, and in the 1950's it contributed 35%. By the late 50's, 62% of the population was rural and 58% of the labor force was directly engaged in agruculture. In the 1950's the value of agriculture exports represented 70% of the total exports.

The economic profile started to change in the beginning of the 60's, and that change accelerated during the late 70's. This change was due to the discovery of oil on a larger scale, the introduction and development of industry, especially of iron and steel, petrochemicals and chemicals in general, the modernization of the older industries especially textile and sugar, and the return of the Suez Canal. In 1980 the share of agriculture in the GNP was 21% only, and it employed less than 40% of the labor force. With the introduction of mechanization in agriculture and the lack of opportunities that had driven the population from the country to the already overcrowed cities, the rural population dropped to 56%. Considering the exports, in 1978 the agrucultural sector accounted for approximately 60% of the total exports: in 1979 it was 50%, and in 1982 it dropped to its lowest level, it accounted for less than 45%.

Due to the intensive type of agriculture and the very limited area, the average annual increase in agricultural production during he 1970's was limited to 3%. That limited increase was outstripped by population growth and more demand for food, as a result of relative increase in the per capita income. That unbalanced situation led to a huge increase in food imports, especilly grains. In 1960 the country imported 3,877,000 metric tons of grains, and in 1980 7,287,000 metric tons, besides 1,855,000 that was given Egypt as an economic aid from the west, especially the United States. In other words the deficit in grain production

reached 9,142,000 metric tons. The only grain that
Egypt exports is rice. Although the area under rice
production was expanding and the productivity is getting
higher, the growing consumption has decreasecd the
amount and value of rice exports to almost one third.
In 1966 exports of rice valued 71 million Egyptian
pounds, and in 1980 it valued 24.6. To face that severe
problem the government economic policy toward
agriculture represented extreme contradicting ideas. In
the early 1950's the government embarked on the
ambitious program of reclaiming desert land (Tahrir
Province). It was very expensive compared to the
returns. Instead of correcting the situation by trying
to reclaim lands in the Delta which would cost less, the
government went to the other extreme of paying no
attention at all to expanding the arable area. This was
reflected by diminishing stress on agriculture in
government plans.

The price the country is paying for that faulty
policy is huge and will continue for sometime. The
government not only had to increase food imports in
general and grains in particular, but it also had to
subsidize many food items, especially flour and bread,
to make them available for the people at a cheap price.
When the government tried to reduce the subsidies in
order to improve fiscal conditions, demonstrations and
riots took to the streets and discontent was expressed
in the media (although it was controlled by the
government), and the cabinet ministers who were favoring
reducing the subsidies resigned.

In 1981 the government reconsidered its agricultual
policy and announced a new plan for land reclamation.
The plan is to reclaim 2.4 million acres at a rate of
126,000 acres per year over the next 20 years. The
largest planned development is to take place in the
Behera province along the Nuberiya irrigating canal
where, in the first phase, 20,200 acres will be
irrigated and drained. Some of the land will be
distributed among landless families; each family will be
allocated 5 acres, and there are also plans to create a
large estate farm. The total cost of the scheme is
estimated at 193 million dollars of which the
International Development Association (IDA) has pledged
an 80 million dollar loan.

A second major agricultural reclamation project is
in progress in the northern Tahrir province and a third
is in Sharqia in the eastern region of the Delta.

Nearly 75% of agricultural income comes from field crops; the remainder is derived from fruit, vegetables, livestock, poultry and diary products. The main summer crops are cotton, rice, maize and sorghum, an in winter the chief crops are wheat, beans and clover. While there is selfsufficiency in fruit and vegetables and even some surplus of both to export, it is with the basic grains (especially wheat) that these shortages are encountered. Egypt, as mentioned before, produces only 38% of its wheat consumption and 80% of its maize requirement.

The following table shows the area and the production of the main grains.

	Area (1,000 acres)					Production (1,000 tons) Average				
	1969-71	78	79	80	81	69-71	78	79	80	81
Maize	1,268	1,594	1,582	1,600	1,428	2,370	3,177	2;938	3,231	2,700
Wheat	1,102	1,170	1,168	1,114	1,170	1,509	1,943	1,865	1,796	1,850
Sorgham	1,850	2,280	2,280	2,330	2,230	615	582	550	600	580
Rice	974	870	978	816	924	2,566	2,358	2,517	2,350	2,500

Although the production of both maize and sorgham is enough as cereals, the country still has to import both to use them as animal feed.

Rice is an important crop. Its area is mostly in the northern part of the Delta and in the lowlands of the Faiyum province since it tolerates high saline soil. Rice enters the crop rotation in the reclaimed soil of the Delta. It is now as important as fruits and vegetables in the agricultural sector as a foreign currency earner. It is hoped that its role in exports may increase with more land reclamation.

Another high-yielding crop and very important to industry is sugar cane. It is nurtured by an expanding sugar industry, supplying the bulk of national require- ments. It is grown mostly in upper Egypt, especially in the provinces of Aswan, Qena, Sohag and on a smaller scale in Minya. In 1981 the production of sugar reached 679,000 tons compared to 564,000 in 1971. The increase is due to cultivation of higher yielding species and modernization of the factories, not to the expansion in the area, since the land suitable to its production is limited. It is planned to increase sugar production by growing sugar beets in the sandy soil on the reclaimed land that flanks the Delta. The sugar cane bagasse is the raw material for a growing paper industry.

Egypt produces many kinds of fruits and vegetables that do not only cover home consumption, but there is a big surplus to export. Those products are earning as much of foreign exchange as rice, and there are good potentialities for expanding their area, their role in diversification of agriculture, and their role in exports. The government is encouraging every effort to expand the area of fruits, especially citrus fruits. It has already allotted special areas along the Mediterranean, along the Suez Canal and in the Tahrir Province for citrus fruits. In 1981 fruit exports earned more than 40.8 million dollars. The production of bananas, which was declining since 1960, made a fast comeback. In 1982 the production reached 137,000 tons compared to 57,000 in 1962. Grapes are also exported now in considerable amounts to the Arab coutries, and they are a base for an expanding wine industry based in Alexandria. Onions and potatoes are the most improtant exported vegetables, although recently other varieties were encouraged to be exported. The climate of Egypt, which allows two and in some cases three crops of vegetables, is giving the country a golden chance to expand their production.

Poultry production has been tripled during the last fifteen years. The government is offering loans at very low interest rates to those involved in the production, the amount of imported poultry has been decreased, and it is hoped that by the end of 1985 the production will cover the consumption.

In order to reduce the deficiency in dairy and meat production, more effort has been made to increase and improve the quality of livestock. Egypt is facing formidable difficulties considering the problem: it has no pasture, and the maize and sorghum, which would be used as animal feed is just enough to feed the people. There is only so much land to spare for livestock farming and above all for the increasing number of population. All are factors that contribute to the little success in increasing meat or dairy production. Egypt is a net importer of meat and cheese and will

149

remain importing for some time, at least until the end
of the century.

Cotton was the main crop in Egypt, and the main
exported commodity. Cotton production started early in
the 19th century. It expanded during the American Civil
War, and when the British occupied the country they
turned it into a cotton farm to support the textile
industry in England. Cotton is not the main exported
commondity now nor the largest foreign exchange earner,
although it ranks first considering those matters among
agricultural products only. The future of cotton in
Egypt does not look promising. The exports are
decreasing due to depressed international markets and
stiff competition from synthetics. The expenses of
growing cotton are now higher and the government's
policy is that of monopolizing the national market and
the international trade: the government is the only
buyer from the farmer and the only exporter, and
therefore it fixes the prices. All of these are factors
discouraging the farmer from growing cotton. In fact,
if it were not for the rules that impose the production
of cotton on farmers, its area would be decreased
considerably since the return from fruits, vegetables,
and horticulture is better than the return from cotton.

In spite of all these factors and in spite of he
decrease of the acreage under cotton production, Egypt
is still producing about one-third of the world crop of
long staple cotton. This is due to the government's
rule of imposing the growing of it in certain areas and
to the intensive use of chemicals under government
supervision, especially of insecticides and fertilizers.
In 1968-69 the area under cotton was 2 million; in
1978-79 it was 1.26 million; in 1980-81 it was 1.24
million; in 1981-82 it was 1.1, and in 1982-83 it was
1.06 million acres. The average production for these
years was around 1.55 million bales per season (each
bale is 720 lbs.).

Another factor that contributed to the decline of
cotton exports is a successful economic policy of using
more cotton for the domestic textile industry. It is
reported that in 1982 it used more than 30% of the crop
compared to 19.8% in 1972 and 15% in 1962.

Land Reform: Until 1952 when the revolution ousted the
monarchy, most of the agricultural land of Egypt was
owned by a few people who were of the royal family or
feudalists. Forty percent of the land was owned by less
than one percent of the landowners, and since most of

150

the investments were in agriculture the value of the land was very high, so that only the very rich landowners could afford it. This situation made more than 2 million families own less than one acre each per family, and more than 1.5 million families in the rural areas were landless. Those families were working as cheap farm labor or as tenants or share croppers. During the late 1940's and in 1950 the proposals for land reform that were introduced in the parliament, which was controlled by the landowners, were rejected. The idea of the urgency for land reform rules was an important factor that encouraged the revolution. Immediately after the revolution, land reform rules were imposed. A limit of 200 acres was imposed on individual ownership of land. This limit was lowered in 1961 to 100 acres and again to 50 acres in 1969. The primary aim of this reform was the destruction fo the feudal power of the old politicians, an aim that was easily achieved. By 1975 the reform rules had their efffect in creating an equity in land ownership. Only 12.5% of the total cultivated land was held by owners of 50 acres. In fact, the rules have further results through rent control. Most of the 50 acres that were owned by an individual were rented, and the government fixed the rent and the owner was not allowed to dislodge the tenant. The rent particularly did not exceed 20% of the income of the land. The land reform rules became successful by introducing the agricultural cooperative system which helped the farmers to cultivate the land by using modern systems of agriculture. However, cooperatives were open to corruption, and in the process of dispossessing the large landowners and promoting cooperatives, the authorities unwittingly helped to eliminate many highly efficient, medium-sized farmers.

The land reform rules achieved their political goals. They created a kind of social justice in land ownership, but they proved that the problem of agriculture in Egypt was not the problem of land distribution as much as it is of land scarcity and overpopulation.

If the government tackled the projects of land reclamation and the population problem with the same vigor and with as much energy as it tackled the land reform rules, social justice and economic equity would be achieved as the political goals were reached. However, other indirect results of the land rules were the substantial rise in the standard of living in the rural areas. Most of the 15,000 villages now have fresh

running water and electricity, social services and
schools, and there is more demand for consumer goods.

MANUFACTURING INDUSTRY

Manufacturing started early in the 19th century,
but unfortuantely it was short lived since it was built
to serve the expansionist policy of Mohammed Ali; as
soon as that policy came to an end, the industries that
developed fast, declined fast. The British occupation
never encouraged any industrialization. However, the
foundations of modern industry were actually laid in the
thirties when new tariffs were adopted, foreign trade
policy changed, and initiatives were taken by some
foreign investors and a limited number of Egyptians and
Misr Bank (Egypt's Bank) with its affiliates in
establising large-scale industries. To protect the
development of national industries, high customs duties
were imposed on competitive import goods such as cotton
fabrics, cement, sugar, alcohaol, cigarettes and soap.

World War II gave a chance for the existing
industries to grow and new industries to be established.
Steel and steel products based on scrap steel were
established on a limited scale north of Cairo
(Mustorod), with petrochemicals and fertilizers in Suez.

After the 1952 revolution, the government put
particular emphasis on the speeding of industrialization. Various measures were designed to foster this.
Foreign trade policies became strongly protectionist,
import duties on machinery and basic raw materials which
the country did not produce were sharply reduced or even
abolished, whereas they were raised on competitive
manufactured goods an all non-essential commodities.
These measures were strengthened by various systems of
import control. Import licensing, which aimed at
reducing or preventing the import of goods that could be
produced domestiically, left room for raw materials and
capital goods needed to hasten industrialization.

Further measures were taken in 1962 when the
government nationalized all major industries, and the
ministry of industry, directly or indirectly, was in
full control of industry and industrial planning. The
private sector was abolished and foreign investments
were Egyptianized. In 1975 the economic and industrial
policies were subjected to major change. While the
heavy industries and other major industries remained in

the hands of the government, the private sector was
encouraged to participate in industry and foreign
investments were invited to invest, and were given all
guarantees against Egyptianization.

Now modern industry is based on solid ground, and
its future looks brighter, although there are still
severe obstacles facing it. Large investments needed
are not available and the national savings are not
enough. The lack of large domestic market to encourage
more production is another difficulty. Another obstacle
is the inability, so far, of the Egyptian products to
compete in the world market. It is hoped the last
obstacle can be dealt with through better management,
reduction in waste, and by more experience. The
peaceful atmosphere in Egypt that prevailed after 1975
has encouraged foreign investment to participate in
industry and encouraged foreign countries and financial
institutions to lend money to Egypt.

The share of industry in GNP in 1981 reached 18
percent, the highest ever. 1,459,000 of the labor force
was employed in manufacturing and mining, 83,200 in
electricity, gas, and water, and 426,000 in
construction, totaling 19 percent of employed labor.

Textiles still account for about one-third of the
total output of the manufacturing industry. The three
large factories of Mahala El Kubra, Kafr El Dawar, and
El Byda have been modernized. Their cotton textiles are
of high quality and are successful in competing in the
world market. Other centers of textiles are Alexandria,
Cairo, and Port Said. Wool textiles are gaining root
and are covering the domestic market requirements.
Textile exports in 1981 valued 633.6 million dollars of
the total exports which valued 2,263.0 million.

After modernizing the old sugar factories and
adding a new refining factory at Girga in upper Egypt,
sugar prodcution reached the high record of 680,000 tons
in 1981 as compared to 564,000 in 1971. It covered the
domestic requirement and left a surplus for export that
valued 18.7 million dollars. Progress was also made in
canned foood, wine, beer and cooking fats. Paper
production, which is in great need for an expanding
education and culture, has been expanded, and developed;
in 1981 it reached 125,000 tons from the two paper
factories in Rashid and Qos. If it is taken into
consideration that in that same year of 1981 the value
for imported paper and paper products jumped to 127.7
million dollars, it can be seen that Eygpt has to expand

further its paper industry; especially, as it was mentioned before, since the raw material needed to increase the production is available in abundance.

The revolutionary government made it a national policy to establish heavy industry based on iron and steel production. For the government, steel production meant achieving an important factor in economic creating independence, creating jobs, increasing the GNP, and above all a symbol for success and determination. The large iron and steel mill was built in Helwan, south of Cairo. There are many questions about whether Helwan was the right site for the mill, since iron ore is shipped from Aswan or Bahariya Oasis, manganese from Sanai, and cooking coal from West Germany. The mill was built by financial and technical aid from the Soviet Union. The production started in 1957 with a capacity of 50,000 tons. The two projects to increase the production were completed, the first in 1973 that increased the production to 1.5 million tons per year and the second in 1982 that increased it to two million tons per year, making Egypt second only to the Republic of South Africa in steel production on the African continent.

Another steel mill was established in 1982 outside Alexandria. This joint venture is to operate the Dikheila steel works being built by the Japanese. Production is due to start in 1986 with a capacity of 350,000 tons per year, which is to rise to 723,000 tons at full capacity. A new port is also to be built at El Dikheila, and the World Bank is lending 132 million dollars to help finance it .

Other heavy industries include sponge iron plates and a steel pipe plant that was built using 13 million dollars as a loan from U.S.A. and 180 million from Japan. A steel reinforcing bar plant has been built by the financial and technical aid of Japan, which amounted to 88 million dollars; its production is badly needed to help the construction industry.

In 1975 Egypt started aluminum production. The aluminum complex is built at Naga-Hammadi in upper Egypt with Russian financial and technical aid. It is using the hydroelectric power generated from the High Dam and imported Australian ad Guinean bauxite. The production started with a capacity of 40,000 tons and reached 170,000 tons. The site of the complex was correctly chosen; it is close to the power source, the most important cost in aluminum production; it is not in Cairo or Alexandria, where the huge industrial concenteration is located; it is helping to spread the industry to relatively less-developed areas in the country; and above all, it is built on the plateau and is not taking any land from agriculture.

Fertilizer production, which is badly needed in Eygpt, is receiving good attention from the government. The hydroelectric power generated from the old Aswan Dam is entirely used by the chemical plant located at Aswan for the production of nitrogeneous fertilizers. It has the capacity of 500,000 tons yearly, and there are plans to expand it to prodcue 700,000 tons.

Two other plants producing phosphate fertilizers are at Suez and Kafr El Zaiyat (in Beheira province) with a combined capacity of 119,000 tons.

Another large plant is built at Talkha. Its cost was 130 million dollars; 88 million was in foreign loans. The plant has a capacity of 570,000 tons of urea fertilizer per year using gas from the Abu Madi field as its feedstock.

Other chemicals produced, as reported in 1981, are: sulfuric acid, 35,000 tons; caustic soda, 44,000 tons; ethyl alcohol, 260,000 hectolitres, and coke-oven coke that reached 3.1 million tons.

The severe deficiency in chemicals is in the field of pesticides and herbicides that are badly needed for agricluture. The country is importing most of its requirements inspite of its impressive progress in chemical industries. The value of imports in 1982 was 470 million dollars.

Within the field of the motor industry, a truck and diesel engine plant is to be built by Ford of the U.S.A. That company also enlarged and increased its capacity of its assembly plant in Alexandria. American Motors built a Jeep plant, but so far all of its production is sold to the armed forces. It is reported that the production in 1982 reached 18,000 passenger cars and 3,000 commercial vehicles. Michelin Tire Company is investing 81 million dolalrs in a tire company in Alexandria.

Another industry that expanded fast is the cement industry, the old plant at Tura, just south of Cairo, has been expanded with French financial and technical aid. Three other plants were built in Alexandria, Ismaila and Asyut. Although the industry produced a record 3.5 million tons in 1982, it is still not able to

155

cover the national needs due to a huge surge in the construction industry.

The armament industry has also received government emphasis. It is not only producing light arms, but plans are underway to produce the first Egyptian-made tank in 1985. It is also receiving French technical aid to produce air-to-air and surface-to-air missiles.

A shipyard for building boats and ships of up to 12,000 tons has been built in Alexandria by the technical and financial help of the Soviet Union. No figures are available regarding the production. After opening the Suez Canal, the shipbuilding an repair industry has been restored and expanded in Port Said.

The fast industrial expansion and the extension of electric power to all of Egypt's villages has not only consumed all the sources of thermal electricity and hydroelectric power generated from both the old Aswan Dam and the High Dam, but it created a power shortage. The problem will be eased by using nuclear power. The American Westinghouse Company is building Egypt's first nuclear power station at Sidi-Kareer, west of Alexandria. Egypt and the U.S.A. signed an agreement in 1981 to build another two nuclear power stations. France has agreed to offer loans and technical aid to build another five nuclear power station. The total capacity of the eight staionis will total 9,600 MW which will supply about 20 percent of the power needed by 1990. The Federal Republic of Germany is building a plant for the production of nuclear fuel using the domestic uranium deposits in the Eastern Desert about 300 miles southeast of Cairo.

Another project that has been in the planning stage for decades is the Qattara Depression Project to generate hydorelectric power by flooding the depression with water from the Mediterranean. The Federal Republic of Germany is financing and helping in the study. The project may cost around 2,600 million dollars.

The mineral resources of Egypt, as was mentioned before, are limited. The production of phosphates is of significant importance. It is supplying a growing industry of fertilizers, and there is a large surplus to be exported. It is produced from Abu Tartur in the Western Desert, Bir El Beida, Umm Haweitat and El Subeiya in the Eastern Desert and near El Tur in Sinai. The production in 1982 reached 680,000 tons.

Manganese is mined in Umm Bugma in Sinai, and the ore was discovered in Hammata and Wadi Araba in the Eastern Desert. It is reported that the production in 1983 reached 8,000 tons of pure metal.

Iron ore is mined in both Aswan and Boaharia Oasis. In 1983 the production of the metal content in the ore reached two million tons. All of it is used in the domestic production of iron and steel.

Oil is of utmost importance to Egypt. Although the produciton is relatively limited if compared with Libya or even Algeria, it is the largest earner of foreign exchange, beside its covering all the domestic requirements.

Oil was first discovered in Egypt in the early 1920's in Gemsa on the Red Sea and in the 1930's in Ghardaka (Ghardhqa). The license for exploration, production, refining and marketing was given to the British Company (Anglo-Egyptian oil fields) in return for 15 percent of the net profits was given to the Egyptian government. The production enabled Egypt to cover its relatively limited domestic consumption during the interwar period and during World War II. After the war, oil was produced from the Sinai Peninsula in Sudr, Asal, Bilaiyim and form Ras Gharib along the Red Sea. Those new areas covered the continually increasing consumption and left a limited surplus to be exported. The revolutionary government nationalized the Anglo-Egyptian oil company and other smaller companies and established the gvoernment company (Misr Oil Company). The loss of Sinai after the Arab-Israeli War of 1967 did not mean only the loss of the major producing wells, but also turned Egypt into an importer of oil in a time when foreign exchange was rare; that was a major factor for crippling the economy of the country from 1967 to the middle of the 1970's.

The return of Sinai to Egypt and the Camp David Agreement, as well as the loosening of the oil nationalization policy and the more liberal economic policy, enormously affected the oil production and made Egypt an oil exporting country.

In 1974 oil exports made only 4 percent of Egypt's export revenues; in 1980 they made 58 percent. Production of crude oil at the end of 1980 was averaging 600,000 barrels per day, and the oil revenues reached 1,500 million U.S. dollars. In 1982 the production reached 670,000 barrels per day, and the revenues were

1,670 million U.S. dollars. However, after domestic consumption, that substantially increased due to industrial expansion and remarkable social development, this left only 200,000 barrels per day available for export. In fact, rising domestic demand for hydrocarbons, growing by an estimated 30 percent each year, is evidently restricting oil exports. That in itself is a clear sign that the country is growing economically and socially after long years of stagnation, although it is decreasing direct foreign exchange earnings.

The great increase in oil production is due to the return of Sinai oil fields in 1979 and the increase in explorations, oil concession agreements, and finds especially in the Gulf of Suez. In 1983 the proven oil reserves were estimated to be 3,146.6 million barrels and the revenues for 1983/84 reached $2,400 million. Egypt is still expanding both its exploration and finding activities as well as its production. It is estimated that by the closing of the 1980's the country will be producing 85 percent above the level of 1983/84.

The main producing areas in Sinai are Belayim, Alma and Sudr. In the Gulf of Suez the main producing fields are Morgan, Ramadan and July. In the Eastern Desert, Ras Gharib, the area around Gemsa Bay, and West Bakr are of considerable importance. It is believed that the Western Desert could be an overlap of the giant Libyan oil producing fields. This belief is justified by the discovery and production of oil in Alamein and Razzaq. In 1983/84 more finds in the Western Desert were reported, but commericial production has not yet started.

The oil companies that are exploring and producing in cooperation with the Egyptian Petroleum Authority (EGPA) are of different nationalities: American, British, West Germam, French, Japanese, Swiss, Italian and Brazilian. The business relationship between the EGPA and the companies is on a production sharing basis.

Pipelines to feed the refineries in Mustard near Cairo, Mex, and Amiriyah near Alexandria and Tanta in the Delta, are extending from Ras Shuqair export terminal to the offshore Gulf of Suez oil field.

Gas reserves were estimated in 1981 to be around 86 m.c.u.m. The producing gas fields are at Abu Madi in the northeastern part of the Delta, Abu Kir in the northwest part near Alexandria, and Abu Gharadeq in the

158

Western Desert. Gas production is not only used for fuel, but also in developing chemical and heavy industry.

FOREIGN TRADE

The foreign trade deficit has persisted without interruption since 1938. According to International Monatary Fund (IMF), the visible trade deficit in 1972 was $357 million. In 1982 it jumped to $4,476 million. That deficit was recorded in spite of the relatively large increae in oil and petroleum products and exports. Although the government is trying hard to reduce imports especially "luxury" items and keeps a constant vigil on external payment, the pressure of the constantly increasing population on limited resources is not helping in reducing the deficit in the balance of payment. It is very probable that the problem will persist in the near future, and without changing the pattern of imports and exports, there would be no solution to that problem for a long time. The main imported items responsible for that situation are a very high and increasing bill for food imports, especially flour, wheat and corn; and also due to an expanding economy especially in the area of industrialization. The country is importing machinery, raw materials, a variety of unfinshed products and transport equipment.

The imports of arms and military equipment for defense purposes are doubtlessly adding to the imbalance of payments. The decline of exports, especialy of agricultural items mainly cotton, due to its depressed cost in the world market and more cotton consumption at home, is reducing its export values. The income from crude oil and petroleum exports is not growing with the expected rate due to increasing local consumption and a glut in the world oil market. The agricultural projects of reclaiming more land, improving the yields especially of wheat, maize, and sorghum and expanding the area under rice cultivation, may lead to reducing the food imports. It is also expected that new oil findings and increasing the petroleum exports combined with checking home consumption would be a key to reducing those huge deficits in the balance of payments. It was announced lately that Egypt will produce military armaments which will help in reducing military imports. Above all the high growth rate of the population is the main threat to the Egyptian economy, to the per capita income, and to the standard of living among Egyptians.

159

With all the problems of cotton, either from its high cost of production and the very limited return the farmer gets from it due to the fixed price the government pays for it (the government is the sole buyer and exporter of cotton), or problems from the depressed world market prices because of increased world production and synthetic fabrics competition, it is still and will be for the near future the main agricultural commodity exported.

Rice, which always has a good world market, is an important item in the exports. Although its production increased after building the High Dam the exports are declining due to continuous increase in home consumption. It is expected that both production and exports will increase as soon as the projects of reclaiming more land for agriculture are complete, especially in the norhtern part of the Delta, where rice will be an important crop used in the process of crop rotation for improving the fertility and decreasing the salinity of the soil.

Fresh fruits and vegetables are gaining more importance as exports. The increase in production coupled with improving the quality made these items, especially citrus fruits, potatoes and onions, very competitive in the world market especially in Western European countires. The foreign markets for these items is practically unlimited and the warm climate of Egypt is helping to produce them early in their seasons.

Oil and petroleum products have jumped to be not only the main exports of Egypt, but also to be the main foreign exchange earners. In 1981 these items made 54 percent of the value of all exports. In 1983 it made 57 percent, and it is very likely that this trend will be greatly increased in the next few years due to more findings, on the condition that home consumption will be bridled.

The ranking of countries that trade with Egypt has changed considerably during the last decade. From the middle sixties until 1976, over half the exports went to the countries of Eastern Europe especially the Soviet Union, to pay off debts. In 1977 the share of these countries in Egyptian exports dropped to less than 50 percent but the U.S.S.R. remained Egypt's largest export market. The considerable change in export markets started in 1979 when Italy ranked first with 27.5 prcent of the total exports, putting the U.S.S.R. in second place. In 1980 Italy stayed in first place followed by

160

the U.S.A., the Netherlands, Switzerland and the
U.S.S.R., respectively. In 1981 Italy was still the
largest market for the exports followed by Japan,
Greece, the Netherlands, the U.S.S.R. and the U.S.A.

Most of the imports were coming from the Western
countries with the U.S.A. in the first rank while all of
the Eastern European countries' share of the imports was
only 15 percent. In 1979 the U.S.A. was still the
largest source of the country's imports, followed by
West Germany, Italy, France and the United Kingdom;
these five countries supplied Egypt with 51.2 percent of
all its imported goods. In 1981 the U.S.A. was still
the main supplier of the imports followed by Greece,
West Germany, Japan and the United Kingdom.

As a result of that continuous deficit in the
balance of payments for so long a time and the huge
loans that are borrowed to modernize the country and
develop its economy, the foreign debts became huge. It
was estimated that the foreign debt reached 17,000
million dollars at the end of 1983. Debt service
payments accounted for about 17 percent of total export
earnings in that year. That hard financial situation is
placing a further burden on an economy which is not in
good shape. In spite of the magnitude of the debt and
its service, Egypt has been able to maintain its
payments on time.

TRANSPORT

Egypt is not only the gift of the Nile, but the
river was and remains to this day the country's highway
of trade and transportation. River transport is being
improved and expanded; more sailing boats and barges are
sailing on the river to relieve the load on roads and
railways. The Nile and its branches are navigable all
year from Aswan to the Mediterranean. Regular transort
connects Egypt with the Sudan by boats sailing on Lake
Nubia from Aswan to Wadi Halfa, a border town in Sudan.
The major irrigation canals are also used for
transportation all year especially Ismailiya, Mahmudiya
and Nubaria canals in the Delta and Bahr Youssef in
Upper Egypt. The length of these waterways is about
2,1000 miles, of which one-half is the Nile and the rest
are canals.

The railway system is well developed in Egypt,
although it needs modernization. There is a railroad
that connects Cairo with all the towns in the valley

161

until Aswan. It runs on the western side of the Nile to Naga Hamadi and then crosses the river to run on the eastern side. The Delta is also covered with a good net of railroads; lines connect Cairo with Alexandria as well as with the Suez Canal towns and the heart and nothern towns of the Delta. The railroad that was used to connect Egypt with Palestine running across the Sinai Peninsula was destroyed when Israel occupied Sinai in 1967, but it was replaced with a good road. There is also a railroad tht runs along the Mediterranean coast from Alexandria westward to the small border town of El Salum, connecting Egypt with Libya. A narrow gauge extension connects the valley at Naga Hamadi ith the El Kharga oasis in the Western Desert. The length of these railroads is more than 2,700 miles. Modernization is being undertaken using foreign loans totaling 165 million dollars; it is projected that by the end of 1985 all the locomotives in the country will be replaced and more than 1000 miles of the railway will be repaired.

Cairo, in order to solve its local congested transportation system, is building the first section of its subway system. A French consortium won a contract to build the subway that connects the northern suburbs with the southern suburbs and to supply the system with 52 electric trains.

The road system is also well developed; all the main urban centers are connected with good roads. The government started in 1979 to pay good attention to building more roads to connect the villages and the countrysides with the main towns, and is allocating more money for the maintenance of these roads. Other new roads have been built to connect the Aswan industrial area with the Red Sea ports of Oaser, Ras Benas and Safaga. Another road is connecting the towns on the Red Sea shore, and Sinai peninsula is now almost surrounded by new, well-built roads. In the Western Desert a road was built along the shore extending to Libya and an extension from it is reaching the Siwa Oasis as well as a road from Cairo to Baheriya Oasis.

The Mediterranean and Red Sea ports have been expanded and modernized to meet the expanding foreign trade and the increasing volume of goods. Port Said which became a free trade zone has been enlarged. Suez and Ismailia have been revived and their capacities expanded to cope with the increasing traffic passing through the improved and enlarged Suez Canal. New ports are built in Dekheila west of Aexandria that also include new shipyards able to build ships of tonnages up to 12,000 tons. A new port will be built just west of the old city of Damietta.

Egypt Air, the state airline, is a successful venture that recorded in 1983 a profit of 36 million dollars and carried more than 2.6 million passengers. It operates a network of domestic routes between the big towns and to the tourist's sites as well as international routes that connect Egypt with western Europe, U.S.A., North Africa, Sudan and the Middle East.

POPULATION

Unlike all other African countries Egypt has no racial, tribal or linguistic problems. Most Egyptians are of the south Mediterranean type. Thanks to the limited ecumenical area along the Nile and its delta, and as a result of the easy transportation offered by the navigable river and its branches, the Egyptians enjoy a great degree of homogeneity. All the people speak Arabic. The Coptic language, that was developed from the ancient hieroglyphic language and was the national language of Egypt, has been replaced by Arabic; it is the language of the Arab conquerors and the Quoran. The Coptic language is used only in the Coptic church as the language of the litergy and the church is trying to revive it as a spoken language among the Christians. There are some inhabitants in the oases of the Western Desert an others in the southern part of the Eastern Desert that still retain a kind of Hametic language and some Nubians that still speak cushite languages; they are all bilingual and speak the Arabic language. That is the result of the spread of schooling in these areas and because most of the men among those groups are employed in the Valley. The majority of the population are Sunni Moslems. There is also about 6 to 7 million Christians (the government never published any reliable statistics about their number) mostly of the Coptic Orthodox Church. The relationship between the Moslems and Christians has been peaceful, especailly when politics do not interfere. The main complaints of the Christians are that they are disriminated against in leading government positions and that the Islamic rules that govern family relationships (especially divorce and inheritance) are imposed on them; also they are complaining that rules that were established during the Ottoman rule concerning building churches are still standing. But in all parts of Egypt freedom of religion and worship is the rule.

163

More important than the composition of population is its growth. It has shown a remarkable rise in the last century and a half. Incidentally, Egypt is the only country in Africa that has adequate and accurate population statistics that cover considerable time. The French mission of Napoleon Bonaparte in 1880 estimated the number in the whole country to be slightly under two and a half million people. In 1821 Mohamed Ali estimated it to be 2,540,000. The development of agriculture accompanied with improved irrigation systems led to more increase in population. In 1846 the number was 4.5 million, in 1882 nearly 7 million, and in 1900 it was almost 10 million. Building the Aswan Dam and the introduction of perennial irrigation that led to doubling the crop area increased the population to 14.2 million in 1927 and to 19.1 million in 1947. The introduction and fast expansion of modern industry, the building of the Aswan High Dam, the improved free medical services and the decline in the infant mortality rate that is not matched by a decline in the birth rate led to more growth in population. In 1960 the number was 25,000,000; in 1982 the number jumped to 44,673,000, and it is estimated that at the end of 1985 it will be about 48 million with a density of over 127 per square mile; and if we take into consideration that the real inhabited area is less than 3.5% of the total area of the country, the density will be above 2,200 per square mile which makes it among the highest if not the highest in the world.

Although all the valley and the delta are very densely populated by any standard, the very northern part of the delta, due to relatively high salinety of the soil and the southern provinces of Aswan and Qena in upper Egypt, due to the basin type of irrigation (the two provinces have just turned to perennial irrigation in the 1970's), have less density compared to the rest of the inhabited areas. Starting with the 1940's the rural-urban population patterns began to change. Now over 46% of the population is urbanized, compared with 32% in 1940 and 38% in 1960. That case is due to the fact that there is less agricultural land available to meet even the basic needs of the growing rural population and to the modernization of agriculture especially using more machinery and chemicals; both factors led to migration from the countryside to the towns. It may be argued if the industrial development in the towns contributed to that migration movement. The following tables show the population in each governorate and in the principal towns of the country, as in the last census of 1976.

164

AREA, POPULATION AND DENSITY

Area (sq km)	997,738.5
Population (census results)	
30 May 1966	30,075,853
22-23 November 1976	
Males	18,647,289
Females	17,978,915
Total	36,626,204
Population (official estimates at mid-year)	
1980	42,289,000
1981	43,465,000
1982	44,673,000
Density (per sq km) 1982	44.7

CIVILIAN LABOUR FORCE ('000 employed)

	1979	1980	1981
Agriculture, forestry and fishing	4,002.0	4,151.9	4,006.4
Mining and quarrying	22.8	19.9	20.7
Manufacturing			
Electricity, gas and water	65.7	83.2	69.5
Construction	448.5	425.6	515.2
Commerce	918.4	884.3	848.1
Transport, storage and communications	488.4	503.3	552.3
Finance and insurance	116.8	126.8	131.1
Social and personal services	1,820.5	1,981.8	2,046.1
Other	608.3	719.2	751.0
Total	10,023.5	10,335.0	10,517.9

GOVERNORATES

Governorate	Area (sq km)	Capital
Cairo	214.2	Cairo
Alexandria	2,679.4	Alexandria
Port Said	72.1	Port Said
Ismailia	1,441.6	Isma'ilia
Suez	17,840.4	Suez
Damietta	589.2	Damietta
Dakahlia	3,470.9	Mansura
Sharkia	4,179.6	Zagazig
Kalyubia	1,001.1	Benha
Kafr el-Sheikh	3,437.1	Kafr el-Sheikh
Gharbia	1,942.2	Tanta
Menufia	1,532.1	Shibin el-Kom
Behera	10,129.5	Damanhur
Giza	85,153.2	Giza
Beni Suef	1,321.7	Beni Suef
Fayum	1,827.2	Fayum
Menia	2,261.7	Menia
Asyut	1,553.0	Asyut
Suhag	1,547.2	Suhag
Kena	1,850.7	Kena
Aswan	678.5	Aswan
Red Sea	203,685.0	n.a.
New Valley	376,505.0	n.a.
Matrih		n.a.
		n.a.

166

El Qahira (Cairo, the capital)	5,074,016	Asyut	
El Iskandariyah (Alexandria)	2,317,705	Zagazig	
		El Suqeis (Suez)	
El Giza	1,230,446	Damanhur	
Shubra-El Khema	394,223	El Faiyum	
El Mahalla el Kubra	292,114	El Minya (Menia)	
Tanta	283,240	Kafr-El Dwar	
Bur Sa'id (Port Said)	262,760	Isma'ilia	
El Mansura	259,387	Aswan	
		Beni Suef	

Greater Cairo (November 1976): 6,808,318, (July 1979): (1984): c 10,000,000.

There is also about 1.7 million Egyptian nationals abroad, most of them are working in the eastern Arab countries and Libya. Some highly educated Egyptians are living in the western countries and Australia (there is no acurate esitmate for their number).

The structure of population by age shows the same characteristics of developing countries. Infants of one year old and less make 15.4% of the population; children whose age is between one and five years make 13.6%, and those between five years and ten years make 11%; those between ten years and 15 years make 11.3%, and the rest make 48.7%[18].

The birth rate between 1973 and 1983 averaged 35.9 per thousand, while the death rate averaged 11.0 per thousand, and the natural increase rate was 24.9 per thousand. That means there is more than a one million increase in population every nine months, and the population will reach 53 million by the year 1990 and 64 million by the end of the century (2,000).

Also as it was mentioned before that, due to better and free medical services and considerably better diet, the life expectancy at birth jumped from 46 in 1960 to 57 in 1981, the infant mortality rate dropped from 128 per thousand in 1960 to 110 in 1981, and the children's death rate (between 5 and one year) from 33 in 1960 to 16 in 1981.

These growing numbers dealing with the increase of population are really alarming, especially in the light of the grim facts that both natural and cultural resources of Egypt are very limited, and even developing them to their upper limit will not be adequate to meet the basic needs of such growing numbers in population. These cold facts have encouraged the government to introduce different methods intended to slow the growth rate of population.

A "Supreme Council for Population and Family Planning" (it changed to "Family Planning Board"), a government agency, was established in 1966. Another private association "The Egyptian Family Planning Association" was formed by conscientious citizens to help the government agency in its effort to reduce the growth rate of population. A family planning policy was introduced. Family clinics staffed by physicains, nurses and social workers were established, the number of government general hospitals was largely increased, and contraceptive medicines were given for free on

168

demand. These efforts to reduce the birth rate and to spread the awaremess for the urgent need for family planning conceived limited results for several reasons:
1. The resistance of the conservateive segments of the population for these new "Western Ideas" that interfere to change the natural process.
2. The wide spread of illiteracy and semi-illiteracy that led to misunderstanding and misinterpretations of these programs.
3. The indifference of many of the religions, educational and political leaders to the population policies.
4. The lack of a concentrated media efforts and educational programs to create an awareness among the population.
5. Lack of funds, bureaucratic red tape and lack of enthusiasm among the economic planners are hard obstacles jeopardizing the implementation of the family planning policies.

As a conclusion for the family planning policy it can be said that its success is slow; the more the country rids itself fomr illiteracy and fake conservatism, the more successful the implementation policy will be. Official figures show that in 1981 only 17% of the married women are using contraceptives; although it is a low percentage, it is still an improvement compared to the year 1970 when only 9% of them were using that method.

In spite of that serious problem, the quality of life among the majority of Egyptians has improved to a great extent. It was metioned before that life expectancy has been prolonged, i.e., infant and child mortality rate has dropped. Both were results of extending free medical services. As a result of modernized agriculture and introducing the land reform rules, many of those who were landless peasants became land owners with incentives to produce more and increase their income. The great increase in industrial ourput, oil and mineralproduction and services increased the GNP and the per capita income. All resulted in improving living conditions; the World Bank reports that in the year 1980 the daily per capita calorie supply was 2,972 calories representing 117% of the healthy requirement.

In 1960 the number of population per physician was 2,550. It was reduced in 1980 to 970, and thanks to a larger number of graduated, well-trained physicians every year that number will be reduced more. The trouble facing the medical services is that the money allocated to building and maintaining hospitals and clinics is not adequate enough to match the needs of the growing population. It is not the problem of availability of medical personnnel. In fact there are many physicians that chose to work abroad especially in the Arab countries for better income and the availability of better facilities. Others are working in the western countries especally in England, France, United States and Canada.

One of the major problems facing Egypt to develop its cultural human resources is education. Ironiclly enough, Cairo was an important center of education and cultural illumination for centuries. The Alazhar Mosque that was established by the Fatamide Dynasty in the medieval ages has been the center of Islamic and Arabic language studies. In the late 1950's, the Alazhar University added modern higher education to the traditional religious studies. That university does not admit Christian students. In the 1830's Mohamed Ali, in order to modernize the country, introduced modern education. The higher schools of medicine, pharmacy, engineering and veterinarians were staffed mostly by French teachers. These schools continued without iterruption until they became faculties of Cairo Univerisity. Mohamed Ali was also wise enough to send many young Egyptians to be educated in Europe, especially in France. Secondary and elementary schools were also established, and the ministry of education was established to supervise education in the country. In 1873 the first girl's school was opened.

The financial difficulities that started in 1876 and the British occupation crippled the educational development. The number of schooled and educated people was limited. Illiteracy spread and became a social epidemic that hindered development. After World War I, with the emergence of a middle class that started to expand and with the rise of a strong national movement, more schools were opened and other schools of higher education were established-such as a higher school of agriculture, a higher school of commerce and several teachers schools. In 1922 Cairo University was opened. In 1950 elementary schooling became free and compulsory and secondary schools were for free. In 1955, all higher eduction was free and several universities were added. Nevertheless, the number of schools are not adequate enough to handle all the children that are eligible to go to school, especially in some rural areas that are far from large villages.

170

REFERENCES

[1] Lake Aswan or Lake Nasser

[2] The original estimate was that the increase would be eight-fold.

[3] Karl Butzer and Carl Hansen. <u>Desert and River in Nubia,</u> gives excellent information about the geological structure and the land formation of the Kom Ombo region.

[4] Mountjoy, A.B. Egypt Cultivates Her Desets; Geographical Magazine, XLIV (1972, pp. 241-250).

[5] Ibid

[6] Kirnoss, Lord. Between Two Seas. The Creation of the Suez Canal.

[7] Ball, John. Contributions to the Geography of Egypt.

[8] Egyptian Government Official Statistics Book.

CHAPTER 9

LIBYA

"The Socialist People's Libyan Arab Jamahiriya" is the new name that became in use after the change of the constitution in March 1977. Unlike Egypt that kept its geographic personality and political unity since the beginning of history, Libya's unity and its present political boundary lines were the result of Italian colonization. The northern shores of Libya are washed by the Mediterranean Sea. To the east it shares a long boundary line with Egypt. Sudan is located in the southeast. West of the country there is Tunisia and Algeria, and it is bounded on the south by the states of Niger and Chad.

The international boundary lines of Libya are almost geometrical lines. This is due to the desert nature of the country, the lack of physical features to be used as bases for separation and absence of major cultural differences, especilly its frontiers that are practically uninhabited except for very few isolated oasises.

Libya is a large desert country that has an area of 685,524 square miles. It comprises three regions: Tripolitania in the northwest with an area 11,100 square miles, Cyrenaica in the east with an area of 35,200 square miles and Fezzan in the southwest with an area of 22,200 square miles. The government changed the names of these regions in 1969. Tripolitania became the Western provinces, Cyrenaica was renamed the Eastern provinces and Fezzan is now known as the Southern provinces.

Although all of Libya is a part of the wide plateau of north Africa, known generally as Lower Africa, that extends from the Atlantic Ocean in the west to the Red Sea in the east, each of its regions still has its topographic features that gives each of them a rather distinctive individuality.

The Western provinces (Tripolitania) have a long shoreline that stretches from the boundary line with Tunisia to the east of Birumm Elgaranigh on the Gulf of Sirte. Nested along the seacoast between lagoons (sabkhas) and the sands of the coastal sand dunes are oasis dotted with villages of different sizes. Their existence is possible because of large numbers of

172

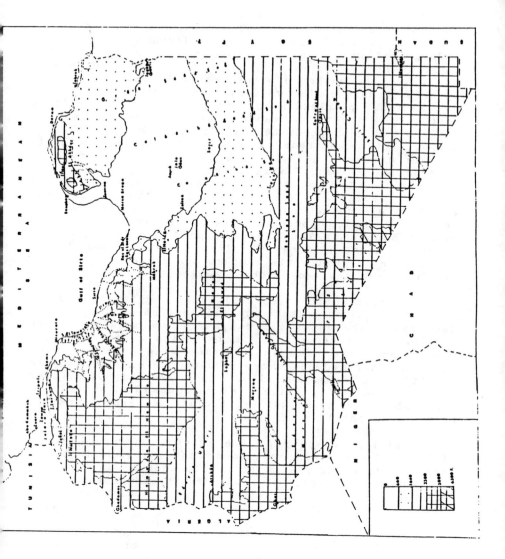

173

shallow wells dug at the feet of the dunes that trap and store the winter rain. It is believed also that some underground water, mostly close to the surface, feeds these wells. Since the amount of rain decreases eastward, the number of those oasis becomes less. The important oasis of the western section of the caost are: Zwara (the population of that oases are entirely Berbers), Tripoli the capital of the country and the largest and most populated, Elajilal, Sabrata, Ezzawia, Zanzur, Tajura and Khoms. Misurata is the largest oasis in the middle section. Other oasis on the coastal section are Zilten, Tawargha and Elgaddahya. The last two are located west to the large lagoon known as Sebkhet Tawargha. In the eastern section, where the rainfall along the coast is less than four inches, the desert conditions become harder, the number of these coastal oasis is less and the distance between each other is more. Sirte, Elsultan, Elawegia and Birumm Elgaranigh, although all of them are of small size, are the important oasises of that section.

Cultivation in these oasises is subsistent. Dates are the main crop. There are millions of palms, but the quality of the dates is too poor to command an export market. Other crops are citrus fruits, figs, apricots and grapes (the area under grape vineyards has been reduced after independence, because Libya is an Islamic country that does not allow wine production). Other crops are almonds, olives, different kinds of melons, vegetables, wheat and barley, but all of these crops are produced in small quantities.

Immediately south of the coastal oasis there are plains. The western section is named the Jeffara, an area of sandy steppes. The middle section is known as the Dufen, an area of semi-desert condition where periodic pasture is possible in the winter time. The eastenr section of that plain is a part of the Sirte Desert.

The Jeffara extends westward in southern Tunisia and gets very narrow eastward near Khoms, it is either too sandy or too dry (its western half has less than eight inches of rain per year) for reliable cultivation. Until the late 1970's, it was an area of semi nomads who used to grow cereals (especially barley) along the wadis (dry valleys) and on the muddy depressions into which water seeped at times. The revolutionary government of Libya, in its effort to expand the area under agriculture and increase agricultural productivity, has increased the usage of ground water. Deeper aquifers

174

are now being tapped by bore holes with mechanical pumps. Increased pumping has resulted in a lowering of the water table and infiltration of sea water.

There are no perennial rivers in Libya since there is no adequate rain and there is no river that crosses the country; however, there is a large number of wadis that testify to the erosive effect of torrential rain that may fall infrequently. The most important of those wadis that cross the northern part of Tripolitania is Wadi Zemzem. In the winter season, if filled, it may reach the Tawargha marshes (Sebekhet Tawargha). It runs straight and, like its tributaries to the south, carries their combined waters in times of flood to the Gulf of Sirte, after crossing wide desert and semi steppe areas. The two main tributaries are Wadi Bey el Kebir and Wadi Tamerel Mgenes. Thamd is another wadi that crosses the Sirte desert in east Tripolitania, and it my also reach the gulf if it is filled in the winter time. The more impressive wadis with steep, rocky walls have been proved to be the result of powerful water action during the pluvial age.

These coastal plains are the main region for nomadic and semi nomadic grazing. The Libyan government is pouring large investments into that region to reclaim land for agriculture and to turn the bedouins to sedentary livestock farmers. The difficulties facing these efforts are several:

1. The soil in most of the cases is sandy with a very low humid holding capacity or eroded by the wind since it does not have a protective vegetative cover.

2. As mentioned before, drilling deep water wells and using modern pumps has lowered the level of ground water and may threaten the present areas under agriculture.

3. Building dams for water storage may not be suitable for that region since torrential rain may carry a lot of loose sand to the reservoir, reducing its capacity.

4. Another major problem is the drift of the population to the towns and the decrease of the labor force involved in agriculture. This is coupled by the lack of trained technicians and administrators and poor education among the farming communities.

175

South of these coastal plains is the escarpment of the plateau of North Africa. It present itself in the form of cliffs and low hills; all the escarpment in general is named the Jebel (mountain). Only south of the Jeffara does it carry certain names: Jebel Nefousa, Jebel Garian or Jebel Tarhuna, that approaches the Mediterranean Sea just south of Khoms. Evidences of former volcanic activity, such as sheets of lava and old craters, exist everywhere in the Jebel. It is also serrated by dry water courses; in places it may reach 2500 feet in height but falls eastward, especailly in east Tripolitania where the height of that escarpment does not exceed 10,000 feet.

On the western section of the heights of the Jebel, mainly south of Jeffara, altitude has resulted in increased precipitation (up to twelve inches) and some dry farming is possible in a land with stunted Mediterranean plants. That is the area known locally as the "Dahr" (the back). On the southern slopes of the Dahr, semi nomadism is widespread and esparto grass collection is a minor industry. Southward down the Dahr, the steppe merges into desert.

South of the Dahr is an upland desert plateau. Its western part forms the Hamada Elhamra, a rocky, red desert which has been swept clear of sand particles by wind action. Jebel Essoda (the Black Mountain), a massive black volcanic cover, is located in the central part of the plateau. The eastern part is known as Alharuj Alaswad; it is an impressive extensive volcanic field formed during the Quaternary. The area is covered by black basalt sand and volcanic rock.

After more than 200 miles southward the plateau gives place to a series of east-west running depressions where ground water and, hence, oasis are found. These depressions make up the region of Fezzan (the southern province) which is just a collection of oasis on a fairly large scale, interspersed with areas of desert. There are several of these oasis of different sizes with water wells yielding different amounts. The largest of them is Sebha, the capital of the region. Ghat, Murzuq and Ghadames were famous as stations for the caravanees. In the very southern part of Fezzan the land rises considerably to form the mountains of the central Sahara.

The eastern regions known as Cyrenaica (Barqa) comprised three topographic divisons: The Jebel Elakhdar and Marmarica, the Sirte Desert Basin and the southern Plateau. The Jebel Elakhdar region is a relatively highland region formed of several steps. The lowest step extending along the shoreline is Elsahel. It is a narrow discontinuous coastal palin that runs from the Gulf of Sitra to the Gulf of Salum in Egypt. It is so narrow that in some palces it is only a few yards wide. It reaches its maximum width (about 12 miles) near Benghezi, the capital of the region. Because of its broken nature, the main roads must keep inland. On this narrow coastal plain there are many salt pans, fed by seepage from the Mediterranean. Numerous brackish marshes are formed during the rainy winter season and dry out in the summer season. That explains why agriculture is limited to a very few patches.

The second step is forming in the west a flat and relatively high plain (terrace) known as the plain of Elmarj. In the east that step is formed of several ridges that are disected by water courses running from the interior uplands. The Elmarj area is under intensive agriculture while in the east, the few wadis that are covered by some scrub and coarse grass in the winter season are under nomadic goat and sheep grazing.

The third step is what forms the proper Jebel Elakhdar (the Green mountain). It is a high plateau, broad in the west and narrow in the east. It reaches its utmost height in the area named Elhamrin. That plateau has more rain than any other part of Cyrenaica. It gets about 12 inches in the winter time, although the rainfall may vary from one locality to another and may reach 20 inches, it is not very reliable. The Jebel is an area of steppe grass, dense scrub and remnants of natural woodland. The government is trying hard to upgrade the livestock industry as well as to reclaim a good part of the area for agriculture.

South of the crest of the Jebel, there are several deep wais that run southward. These wadis were formed during the pluvial age and now either dry or carry some water for short periods during the winter rainy season. At the piedmont of the Jebel is an area of shallow basins filled with alluvium-playas, separated by low ridges or hills. The largest of those playas is the Baltet Elzulaq, whch has severl wadis draining into it.

The region east of Jebel Elakhdar and extending to Egypt is named Marmarica. The coastal area, as was mentioned before, represents the first step that forms the narrowest coastal plain of all--Cyrenaica. The other steps are not represented. Instead, there is a

177

succession of north-facing escarpments rising in a series of shallow steps. Tobruk and Bardia are the main towns along that coast. Both were known during World War II when the German and British forces exchanged their hands on them. Tobruk gained more importance and grew in size after it became the terminal of an oil pipeline that extends from the Serir oil field.

South of that northern region of Cyrenaica, the land falls in elevation, producing an extensive lowland in which few oases are located. The most important of them are Ojila (Aujila), Jabo and Jeghbub.

The second topographic region of Cyrenaica is the Sirte Basin. It is a desert basin occupying a major part of that Eastern Province. Beside the coastal sand dunes, the basin is dominated in its western part by the Calansho Serir, a huge reg area of gravel and masses of stones. In the east there is the vast Calansho Sand Sea. It covers several thousand square miles of mobile sand dunes that may reach hundreds of feet in height.

In that desert region lie the major oil fileds and oil reserves of Libya. The fields are close to the coast. There are no mountain barriers that would have obstructed building the pipelines or constructing the exporting ports. Ajedabya, Marada and Jabo were oases that supported limited numbers of population. Oil production has transformed the whole region, not only by the oil installations themselves but also by service roads, settlements, petrochemical industries and other related developments. On the Gulf of Sirte new ports have been built: Essidra, Marsa Elbrega and Zuetina. The port of Tobruk on the Mediterranean Sea has been enlarged after building the pipeline that extends from the Serir oil field. The new oil findings, offshore on the continental shelf in the Gulf of Sirte, will let the Libyan oil flow for a long time to come, even more than the most optimistic prediction hold.

The Sirte Basin gradually rises southward to the third region, the plateau that extends westward into Fezzan and eastward into Egypt and reaches its highest section in the south at the peidmont of the Tibesti massif. The plateau is covered in the north by the Reviana Sand Sea and in the south by the two regs known as Serir Tibesti and Serir Chiapo. There are some oases, the most important of them is the Kufra group. The Kufra Oases is the site of a large agricultural project aiming to expand the area under irrigation from ground water to increase grain and livestock production.

The desert landscape of Libya is identical with the desert sceneries that prevail in all parts of the great Sahara. Hamades, Ergs, Regs, Mesas, Wadis and Oases are all phenomenae of all countries of North Africa. Hamadas are flat rocky parts of the Sahara that have been swept by the wind and cleared from most of the sand. Examples of hamadas in Libya are the Hamadas El Hamra (The Red Hamada) south of the Dahr in Tripolitania and Hamada Zegher in the northwestern part of Fezzan. Ergs (Ramla or Edeyen or Idehan) are large expanses covered with sand and sand dunes. Examples of such ergs: the Edeyin Ubari, Edeyin Murzaq and Ramlet Elwigh in Fezzan. In east Cyrenaica, the Calansho sand sea is a very large erg. It extends into the Western Desert of Egypt where it is known as the Great Sand Sea. In southern Cyrenaica there is the Rebiana Sand Sea. The area of the Sahara that is covered by sand, contrary to popular conception, does not exceed 15% of the total area. Sand seas have different landscapes. Barchans may dominate in certain areas. They are large cresent-shaped hills of sand trending northeast to southwest in response to the north easterly winds that prevail most of the time in the region. These dunes travel slowly across the landscape by the removal of sand from rear to front. In other areas of the ergs, seif dunes may cover the area. They are elongated hills lined in the direction of the wind and apt to change their course due to change of the wind direction. These sand dunes are a serious threat to the oases and the nearby agricultual areas. The governments, in order to minimize their dangerous effects, are trying to fix them either by spraying them with a thin layer of oil or plastic, as Libya is doing, or by growing some euclyptus trees on them or by making a fence of these trees between the sown land and the dunes. Regs are large areas from which the wind has removed all the fine particles and has left only gravel and coarse sand. Regs may be known as serir or tenere. Because they have a firm surface, they are crossed easily by vehichles. The important regs in Fezzan are Serir Elgattusa and Serir Tibesti. In Cyrenaica there are two large regs: Calansho Serir in the west and Serir Chiapo in the southeast. The wadis are water courses that may carry some water during more strong storms but are empty and dry most of the time. All indications show that these wadis, anywhere in that vast Sahara, were formed during the Quatrenary Pluvial Age.

In fact most of the geomorphologists believe that water played a greater role in forming desert landforms than wind and insolation. Many of land formations of

179

the Sahara are explicable in terms of the action of
running water. The formation of large and sometimes
deep wadis, the large alluvial fans which are formed at
the base of escarpments, the playas as well as the
parallel retreat of slopes and the formation of
extensive prediplains, can only have been caused by
extensive water activities that took place during the
Pluvial Age.

CLIMATE

Libya, a Saharan country, has a climate
characterised by aridity and a wide variety in
temperatures. The only areas that receive adequate
amounts of rain for agriculture are : the western
coastal area, western Jebel and the Dahr of Tripolitania
and the Jebel Elakhdar of Cyrenica. Although the
average is about 15 inches (all of it is in the winter
season), the amount varies widely from one year to
another and may be uneven. The amount may jump to about
20-25 inches and usually every four or five years there
is a drought and sometimes there may be two successive
dry seasons. The rest of the coastal area receives less
than five inches and southward from the Mediterranean
coast the amount falls to a fraction of an inch.
However, winter storms in the north and summer storms in
the south may bring torrential and damaging amounts of
rain in a few hours and unexpectedly. Although Tripoli
has a January average of about 54°F, and the maximum may
reach 80° - 84°F if the Ghibi desert winds blow from the
south, and the minimum may go down to 25°F if the area
is subject to northerly or westerly winds. The same
conditions prevail also in the Jebel Elakhdar especially
in its higher area. In fact frost, snow and some days
of icy conditions are not abnormal in the winter season.
In summer all the country is hot and the areas with
maximum temperatures are in Fezzan and southern
Cyrenaica where figures of over 120°F are not uncommon.
The Ghibli winds, like the Khamesin of Egypt, is a
special feature of the Libyan climatic elements. It is
a hot, dry wind from the south that can raise the
temperatures in the north by 60° - 75° in a few hours.
It carries huge laods of sand and may blow at any time
of the year, but spring and fall are its most usual
seasons. It has a considerable damaging effect on the
growing crops.

ECONOMY

Libya is a desert country that has been transformed

(like the oil producing countries of the desert peninsula of Arabia) by the discovery and production of oil in the 1950's. Before the findings and exportation of oil, agriculture and nomadic grazing were the basis of a rather poor economy. The national revenue then generated from that limited economy, covered less than fifty percent of the government's ordinary expenditure. It was the economic aid and financial subsidies from the United Kingdom and the United States that used to cover the country's budget deficits and help in limited economic development.[1] These financial aids were given in return for permission to both countries to maintain military bases in Libya. The U.K. granted Libya one million sterling pounds annually for economic development an a further annual 2.75 million pounds to meet budgetary deficits. The U.S.A. had an agreement with Libya in 1954 that granted the country forty million dollars over twenty years. That amount was later substantialy increased. Libya also at that time had economic treaties with Italy and France that helped to relieve some of its financial problems. In fact the critical problem for Libya was to ensure that enough funds from abroad should be available to meet the normal expenses of the government and to pay only for the very essential development projects.

It is clear that the physical and climatic conditions of such a desert country imposed tough restrictions on agriculture, livestock production, trade an doubtless, on its foreign policy. The huge income from oil production has changed totally the whole economic, cultural and political image of Libya.

Between 1962 and 1963 the GNP increased from 163 million Libyan Dinars to 909 million. Since 1968, the country's GNP, according to offical figures, rose to LD 3,534 million in 1974, to LD 5,829 million in 1978 and in 1981 it exceeded LD 7,000 million and oil exports were 99% of the total exports. Since then, however, due to economic and political factors, the oil revenues started to shrink. The global oil glut and reduction in oil prices, especially in the open market, are two important factors. A third factor is the loss of the American market. In March 11982, the United States, in response to the worsening relation with Libya, banned imports of Libyan oil. The U.S.A. was an important importer of Libyan oil. Decreasing oil revenues have

AGRICULTURE

In spite of the fact that most of Libya is a desert

181

region due to the lack of adequate rainfall and absence
of any rivers, agriculture was the main activity of the
population and the main source of revenue for both the
citizens and the government before oil discovery. The
Italians, after occupying Libya, took over the best of
the arable land along the coast mainly between Tripoli
and Misurata and between Benghazi and Derna. The
indigenous population were confined to the drier areas
and the oases. They were involved mainly in shifting
agriculture of grain, especially barley, nomadic grazing
with herds of sheep and goats, sedentary cultivation,
was only in the oasis. Under any condition the native
farms were very small with poor productivity due to
their arid conditions and of course of subsistance
nature.

The Italians, who wanted to put their roots deep in
Libya in order to make it a jumping area to Egypt in the
east and Tunisia in the west, invested heavily in
agriculture. Large sums were also spent on roads and
water supplies. The land under arable cultivation was
more than doubled. Wheat gained more importance;
olives, citrus fruits, almonds and vegetables were grown
commercially.

During the Second World War, fighting in Libya
caused great destruction for agriculture, although the
relatively good, arable land still remained mostly in
Italian hands. The lack of funds led to deteriorating
agriucltural activity, and food production diminished.

The oil revenues gave direct backing to agricultural development. In the late 1960's the government
gave financial aid for native farmers who wanted to buy
the farms of the Italians that were still living in the
country. In 1970 the revolutionary government
confiscated almost all the land that was owned by the
Italians including more than 74,000 acres of cultivated
land, and distributed it among Libyan farmers. The
government, in its efforts to develop the economics of
the country, gave high priority to the agricultural
sector. Government credits for seeds, fertilizer and
machinery were granted to the farmers. Large sums of
money have been invested in reclaiming land and
irrigation projects. In spite of all of these efforts
and the great expenditure that agriculture has received
since 1969, its contribution to GNP declined in real
terms from 2.3% in 1975 to 1.9% in 1980. The proportion
of the working population employed in agriculture that
was around 50% in 1969 dropped to less than 19% in 1980.
The 1980-1985 plan envisages that the proportion will

182

decline to 16.8% At present, only a tiny proportion of the total area of the country is cultivable. Of this, a high percentage is used for grazing. Only 1.4% is arable, and only 0.19% is irrigated.

In 1973 the government allocated LD 700 million over the ten year period 1973-1983 to improve agriculture. The Three-year Plan, as revised in February 1975, provided LD 498 m. plus LD 977 m. for integral developments. In 1975, agriculture absorbed 21% of total budget expenditure while in 1976 it had shot up to a corresponding 30%. In the 1978 financial year, the agricultural sector was allocated 18.9% of budgeted development expenditure and 14.6% of overall budget spending. In 1976-1980 Development Plan LD 1,600 m., or 21% of expenditure, was alLocated to agriculture, whereas in the 1981-1985 Plan, the estimated expenditure on agriculture was LD 3,000 m. representing about 20% of the total.

Understandably the irrigation projects absorb a major part of the agricultural budget since water in a mostly desert country is the most critical problem facing agriculture. The most important projects are: the Kufra Oasis Project to irrigate 20,000 acres, the Tawurgha Project to use 6.000 acres, The Serir Project, the Jebel Elakhdar Project, the Jefara Plan Project, and the Wadi Qattera irrigation project (near Benghazi). In 1976 the Wadi Jarof Dam was completed and went into operation. All the projects are fully integrate, providing for the establishment of farms, rural roads, irrigation and drainage facilities; and in some of these projects the introduction of agri-industries. It is hoped that all these irrigation projects, the intensive use of fertilizers and training the farmers will help in reducing the large fluctuations of output.

The agricultural development showed some success in the first three years of implementing the 1973-1978 Plan. Total food stuff production increased in each of the three years from 1973 to 1976 when output, in aggregate, surpassed the previous records of 1970. However, overall agricultural production did not match the large investments that have been poured in that sector. In fact in spite of the harsh, dry desert environment, the Libyan government is doing it's best to promote cultivation and has not spared money or effort trying to overcome some of the environmental problems. One of the successful projects is that of the Kufra Oasis project. By the end of 1973 more than 100 wells were drilled and about 25 miles of roads were

183

constructed. The area under agricultural production reached about 6,400 acres and the sheep farms in that area raised more than 22,000 sheep. The government reported that the oasis produced 12,561 metric tons of wheat, 444 tons of barley and 45,8000 bales of animal feed. There may be some exaggeration in these numbers to show the success of the project and to justify the huge investment, but in the same sense they reflect the desire to improve agriculture. In 1983 the Wadi Qatara project in Barqa started irrigating about 1,050 acres. The most important agricultural irrigation project is the one in which construction will be made by a Korean Company at the cost of 3,300 million American dollars. The project is to drill 270 wells in the southeastern desert where there is an undergound reservoir. The wells will yield daily 4 million cubic meters of fresh water that will be carried in a 1,300 mile pipe to the coastal area of Barqa near Benghazi. The water will irrigate about 360,00 acres and will provide grazing land for more than 2 million sheep and 200,000 cattle.

The government is continuing to further land development and agricultural reform. It has an agreement with Poland to open up new farms in the Eastern Provinces (Cyrenica). In 1978, about 1,000 farms that had been owned by politicians were sold to farmers at a subsidized price. Another development in the late 1970's, that was expensive but shows the determination of the government to increase the country's agricultural output, was the introduction of hydroponic farming. It is only practical in oil-rich economies.

Animal husbandry is the basis of farming in Libya and will remain so even when irrigation and reclamation measures take effect, since meat and dairy products are in increasing demand as a result of the higher standard of living that Libyans enjoy in their oil-rich country. Recently, breeding of cattle for dairy produce has been expanded. Milk production reached about 117,000 tons in 1982, 63,000 tons in cows's milk, 39,000 tons sheep's milk and 15,000 goats' milk. Livestock is being imported on an increasing scale from different sources. In 1981 the number of cattle was 132,000, sheep 4,200,000, goats, 1,300,000, and camels 132,000. All of these numbers show a significant increase compared with the numbers in 1970. Fodder is manufactured now in Sebha, Zilten and Zawia. A successful way for increasing meat production was the introduction and expansion of chicken farms that do not need large space or special climatic condition. In 1981 the number of chicken reached 8.5 million compared to 5.1 in 1979.

Cereal production, as was mentioned before, is subject to wide fluctuation from one year to another. The yields are entirely dependent on climatic conditions, especially the amount and timing of rainfall. Barley, which is the staple diet of most of the population, is an important cereal. In 1982, the department of agriculture reported that barley production reached only 89,500 metric tons compared to 121,000 in 1981, 71,000 in 1980 an 100,000 in 1979. The record production of 184,000 was in 1976. Wheat production reached 108,600 metric tons in 1982 compared to 123,000 in 1981, 150,000 in 1980 (which was a record year) and 110,000 in 1979.

Dates are produced in the oasis and only the coastal belt. In 1980 it was reported that the production was only 87,000 tons compared to 97,000 in 1979. Other fruits that the government is expanding its production in are citrus fruits, grapes, almonds, figs and apples. Citrus fruit production in 1981 was 91,000 tons compared to 60,000 in 1980 and 48,000 in 1979. Grape production (not for wine production) reached 17,000 tons in 1981. Almonds recorded 14,500 tons compared to 5,500 in 1979. Other products are potatoes, tomatoes and ground nuts. Good attention was given to olive production in 1981. The production exceeded 155,000 tons.

Agriculture contibutions for the GNP in 1976 was 2.1% and 1.5% in 1977, and inspite of all efforts the country has to import no less than 80% of its food consumption. The 1976-80 development plan projected an annual growth of 15.8% in agricultural output so that the country would be self-sufficient in vegetables and dariy products and would be able to also produce 92% of its fruit needs an 75% of its meat requirements. However, these targets were too optimistic and even in 1983 were far from being achieved.

The Libyan Mediterranean waters are rich in fish, especially sardines and tunny. The government, in order to expand and make good use of these rich fishing areas, has built the Zilten fishing port. It was completed and started to operate in 1983 at a cost of 16.8 million dollars. The port is designed to be used by forty trawlers and provides storage for 200 tons of fish together with refrigeration facilities for up to 20 tons of fish per day.

185

OIL INDUSTRY

Exploration for oil started after independence. When oil findings on commericial scales were confirmed in 1957, the Libyan government set up a petroleum commission empowered to grant oil concessions on a 50-50 profit-sharing basis. It should be noted that the conditions of the consessions were identical to those applied in all other oil producing countries in the Middle East. One of the conditions of the Libyan concessions stated that parts of each concession would be handed back to the government after a given period. The commission granted several concesions first to American and British oil companies then later French, Italian and other foreign companies. By 1971, before the dispute with the British-Petroleum Company arose, 21 companies from 11 foreign countries held concession rights.

Production and exportation on a large scale stared in 1957. In 1962 the epxorts were 20,000 barrels per day, and when the Suez Canal was closed, as a result of the Arab-Israeli War of 1967, Libya became the forth largest exporter in the world. In 1970 the exports jumped to 1.3 million barrels per day. Production, exportation and oil revenues reached their peak in 1980 when exports totaled 1.8 million barrels per day, and the revenues were in the range of 23,000 million dollars.

Oil exports go through five terminals connected to the various fields by pipelines. The first terminal was built and started to operate in 1961 at Mersa Brega on the Gulf of Sirte; that terminal is connected with the Bir Zelten producing fields by a 200 mile long pipeline. At Mersa Berhga teminal an oil refinery and a gas liquifaction plant were built. The fields of Hofra are connected with two terminals: one is a Ras Elsidr, to the west of Mersa Berga, and the other is at Ras Lanouf, east of Ras Elsidr. The forth terminal is at Mersa Elhariga, near Tobruk. It exports the oil from Sarir through a pipe that extends about 330 miles. The fifth teminal that exports the production of the Augila oil fields is located at Zuetina. The Nafoora oil field is served by the termnial at Ras Lanouf. It is being planned to have a sixth terminal built to serve the west of the country. It will connect the western oil wells near the boundary line with Algeria with the refinery at Zawia.

The very strong national feelings that swept the countries of the Middle East and North Africa during the 1950's and 1960's and the struggle against what the population of these countries considered as western exploitation and economic colonization affected the conditions and the policies of the oil concessions in these countries. In July 1971 the members of the OPEC's Twenty Fifth Conference in Vienna declared that the oil producing countries have the right to participate in all aspects of oil operations in their own lands Libya's President Maammer Algaddafi, who was facinated by Egypt's success in nationalizing the Suez Canal and other foreign investments, lost no time in announcing that Libya would not be satisfied with nothing less than an immediate 51% share. Libya in reaching its goal followed a clever policy. It never negotiated with the companies as a group, but used to target each company alone and impose its demands on it. In December 1971 Libya nationalized all British Petroleum's 50% share of the Serir oil field. Libya, in hitting the British company hard, stated the excuse that Britain failed to stop the Iranian invasion of the Tumbs and Abu Musa Islands in the Persina Gulf (Arabian Gulf). British Petroleum (BP) tried to resist its takeover by suing the Italian importers and refineries that bought its exported oil. The Italian court dismissed the suit. After that judgment Libya felt confident that it would have no difficulty in exporting its oil. In June 1973 Libya nationalized the other 50% of the Serir oil which was owned by the American private company, Nelson Bunker Hunt, that was the partner with BP. In fact the nationalization of Bunker Hunt was a warning to the other companies to respond to Libyan demands. In August of the same year, Occidental faced with the threat of loosing the most vital source of oil it has outside the United States, announced its acceptance of the Libyan government's acquiring 51% of the company's assets at book value. Just five days after Occidental yielded, three other companies, Continental, Marathon and Amerada Hess, accepted a majority takeover on similar terms. In September, Gelsenberg, a German company in partnership with Mobil and W.R. Grace (another relatively small company in partnership with Esso), accepted the Libyan takeover of 51% of its ownership at book value. However, the large producers: Shell, Mobil, Esso, Texaco and Atlantic Richfield, joined in resisting any sort of arrangement with the Libyan government that might have jeopardized their participation agreements in other oil producing areas, especially in the countires of the Persian Gulf. After months of inconclusive negotiations the Libyan government in Februaary 1974

nationalized all the assets of Shell, Texaco and
Atlantic Richfield. At last in April 1974 Esso accepted
the Libyan takeover of 51% of their assests. When Mobil
and Esso withdrew from their concessions in November
1981, the Libyan government established the National Oil
Corportation to run both operations.

Libya's oil prodcution, which increased at a fast
rate during the late 1960's and 1970's as a result of
the closure of the Suez Canal, closeness of Libyan oil
terminals to the European and American markets, and
increase in world consumption and demand, has dropped
considerably during the 1980's as a result of more world
production espeically from the North Sea, the Soviet
Union, Mexico and Nigeria. The huge production of these
areas led to world oil glut and consequently a drop in
Libya's oil prices and revenues. That was coupled by
the United States boycott of Libyan oil and the quota
system that OPEC tried to impose on its members. All
these factors combined led to the decline of oil
exports. In a way that reduction in oil exports and
revenues may not be as bad for Libya as it may show, no
doubt it will keep the oil reserves of Libya for a
longer time, and it will impose on Libya a more
reasonable and responsible expenditure policy especially
concerning expenditures on its foreign policies.

Following the 51% takeover and the nationalization
policies, production fell from 1,597 million metric tons
in 1970 to 71.5 metric tons in 1975. In 1976, however,
output increased to reach 93.5 million tons under the
influence of more rising demand. This increase in
output continued in 1977 when production jumped to 100
million tons, but the output declined by 3.4 in 1978.
During 1979 and 1980, Libya, like all the oil exporting
countries and as a result of more demand for oil,
followed an aggresive pricing policy. In January 1979
it raised the price 28% to 30 dollars per barrel. In
February it hiked it up to $34.50, and in May brought
the price to $36.12 per barrel. The oil revenues totaled
about 23,000 millin dollars in 1980. Early in 1981 the
production started to slide down to an average of
650,000 barrels per day, and in July of that year the
spot price fell down to $33.00 per barrel, although the
official posted price was higher.

During 1982 OPEC, in order to gain control on world
oil prices, allocated quota production for its members.
Libya production ceiling was 750,000 barrels per day,
but its real production averaged more than 1,000,000
barrels per day. But, the spot price was as much as

188

$4.00 per barrel below the official posted price. The oil revenues that peaked in 1980 fell down to 15,000 m. in 1981 and to about $14,000 in 1982. In March 1983 OPEC gave Libya a quota of 1.1 m. barrels per day, but all indications showed that Libya was producing more than its quota. Oil revenues during 1983 were around $11,000 m. inspite of the slight rise of production, due to the lower prices on the spot market. The $11,000 m. of 1983 looks to be a realistic number for both 1984 and 1985.

At present the foreign companies, Continental, Marathon and Amerada, are responsible for over one-third of total crude oil production, while the national oil company production, including the production from the fully nationalized fields, accounts for only 21% of overall production. The national Oil Company is intending to increase its prodcution since it has rarely produced at more than half the rate of its oil fields since nationalization. The rest of the production is coming from fields operated by the relatively smaller companies.

The National Oil Company and the other foreign compaines are participating together in extensive exploration activities in both the Western Province (Tripolitania) and in the Southern Province (Fezzan) as well as in the Sirte Basin where most of the commericially producing areas are located. The purpose of these exploration activities is not only to discover more oil an natural gas, but also to evaluate and access the oil wealth and reserves of the country. Exploration in areas off the Tripolitiania coast has poven to be very fruitful; a number of rich oil and gas fields were discovered - Miskar, Ashtart and Isis. The largest Libyan offshore oil field, El-Bouri oil filed, was discovered about 60 miles on the continental shelf north of the port of Zuara. The National Oil Company announced that it will spend 2,000 million dollars in 1984 and 1985 on developing that rich oil field. Libya has now 1,692 oil producing wells of which 248 are flowing and 1,244 are on various forms of artifical lift. Natural gas reserves are estimated at 674,000 million cubic meters. Oil reserves were estimated in 1979 at that year rate of production to last for 34 years. However, new discoveries especially offshore, the increase in the number of exploratory wells, and the expansion of exploration to include Fezzan (which looks to be very promising after the reported finds of oil in the Mourzouk region), made Libya a country with huge reserves that may last well beyond the middle years of the twenty first century.

Because of the location of Libya, close to Europe, it is now the second largest supplier of petroleum to the European contries as a whole, after Saudi Arabia. Most of its exports go to the countries of the European community. Because of the strong economic and technological ties between Libya and eastern Europe, a large amount of Liyan oil is exported to these countries, especially Yugoslavia and Poland in exchange for tankers and machinery. Austria, Switzerland, Greece and Spain have trade agreements with Libya to import Libyan oil and oil products in exchange for manufactured goods. The controversial cooperation agreement is with the Soviet Union who is supplying Libya with arms, ammunition and technical assistance in exchange for oil. The U.S.S.R. is well-known for its huge oil production and exports.[3] It is probable that the U.S.S.R. is reexporting the Libyan oil to its allies and friends and other countries for political and strategic reasons.

Libya, however, would prefer to refine and process most of its oil rather than export it in its crude state. Six oil refineries have been built, and three more will be completed and will start operating before 1986. It is expected that the total refining capacity of the nine plants will be in the neighborhood of one million barrels per day. These refineries are located at Mersa Brega, Zawia, Misurata, Tobruk Ras Lanouf and Saipem. Libya is also investing in a refinery at Kiper in Yugoslavia on the Gulf of Trieste at the head of the Adriateic Sea. Mersa Brega is the largest center for petrochemical industry. In 1977 the National Oil Company completed the construction of an ammonia plant and an ethanol plant at Mersa Brega, each with a capacity of 1,000 tons per day. The two plants started to operate late in that year. Two other plants were completed and are operating at full capacity in the same area: one for the production of ammonia, and the other for the production of urea, each with a capacity of 1,000 tons per day. The two plants are located near the liquefied natural gas plant at Mersa Brega. These new plants necessitate the development an improvements of the port facilities. Ras Lanouf also became an important petrochemical industrial center. An ethylene plant with a capacity of 1,750 tons per day. Other petrochemical plants to be built and to start operating in 1986 and 1987 are: a high-density polyethylene plant with a capacity of 80,000 tons per year, a 60,000 tons per year polyethlene plant, a butadiena unit with a

capacity of 60,000 tons per year and an ethylene glycol
plant with a yearly capacity of 58,000 tons. These
plants will turn Ras Lanouf and Abu Kammash to large
chemical centers.

In order to satisfy the patriotic national
aspirations and to reduce its dependency on foreign
tankers, Libya's Grand National Maritime Transport
Company now owns 13 tankers. The company (GNMTC) has
also eight cargo vessels and two passenger ships.

INDUSTRY

Manufacturing activities that are dealing with
local agricultural products and such traditional crafts
as carpet weaving, shoemaking, leather working and
tanning have showed considerable progress. The
government also has established other modern light
industries, whose products are needed in the national
market, and have decreased imports. These industries
also have shown considerable progress. These new
factories produce diversified articles such as cement,
prefabricated construction materials, glass, cables,
pharmaceuticals and synthetic and woolen textiles.
Industrial production of both the traditional and the
modern light sectors during 1979 and the early 1980's
rose with an average rate of 14%.

In the middle an late 1970's several factories
started operating: a ready made clothing factory in
Derna, another new tannery and a tire factory were
opened at Tajura, a canning factory is now operating at
Zawia, and carbon paper factories in Tripoli, a
hypodermic syringe plant, a soap factory and a blanket
factory (at a cost of $35 million) started production,
also a glass factory is operating in Tripoli. Two
organic fertilizer plants were built: one in Benghazi,
and the other in Tripoli. A steel frame factory with a
capacity of 35,000 tons per year was opened in 1978.
Electric equipment and refrigeration plants are
scheduled to start production by the end of 1985. That
type of light industry that is planned mostly for the
national markets was allocated LD 1,200 million in the
1981-1985 Plan.

While the government is supporting such smaller
projects, it's giving more attention and allocating more
resources to heavy industry and infrastructure
development. The authority that is responsible for

191

industrial development and industrial planning in the country is the "General Public Organization for Industrialization". Libya as a socialist country is not allowing private enterprises to get involved in large industrial projects.

Libya as an oil rich country no doubt has the financial ability to develop such expensive heavy industries. The oil revenues, even after the decrease in exports and the decline of oil prices, have the surplus in the budget to finance huge industrial projects, can buy the technical assistance and can hire technicians, consultants, experts and expertise.

Energy needed is in abundance and of high quality, oil and oil products to generate thermal electricity is available at different locations. The lack of coal as a raw material needed for steel prodcution can be compensated for by the eventual production of petroleum coke and imports, especially the industrial sites are located at the coast.

Iron ore was discovered in Libya at Wadi Shatti, in southern Libya in 1974. The geological survey estimates that the reserves are more than 700 million tons. In 1973 Libya occupied the Aozou strip in northern Chad, although there is no legal foundation for that annexation, the Libyan troops are there, and it is clear that Libya would not be interested in occupying another desert area unless it is rich in minerals. In fact the area is known to be rich in both uranium and iron ore, and there is not even a slight indication that Libya will give it back.

The main problems that are facing heavy industry in Libya are: the shortage of trained labor force and the marketing possibilities appear to be limited. By the end of 1982 the population was estimated to be 3,244,000 of who 569,000 were foreigners. The total number of the labor force was estimated to be 800,000; 230,000 of those were foreigners. The majority of those were Egyptian, Tunisians and Algerians. There were some Turks and Sudanese. Libya is recruiting large numbers from the Islamic population of the Philippines, Bangladesh, Pakistan and Indonesia. The United Nations is forecasting that by 1190 there will be about 740 foreign workers in Libya. This number does not include engineers, administrators or technocrats. The labor shortage may be temporary, especially in such an Islamic country where large families are preferred and better living conditions encourage more births and reduce death

192

rates. Technical schooling should be encouraged to train skilled labor.

The real difficulty that is facing heavy industrialization in Libya is the limited marketing possibilities. With a total population of less than 3.5 million, the national market cannot absorb the large scale produciton of modern automated plants. That, beside the fact that even in the national market, the Libyan products will face the foreign competition, and if the government would try to protect its own market by high tariffs, it would invite retaliating activities that may hurt the entire Libyan economy. Looking at the international markets, it would be hard for the Libyan industry to compete with such countries as Germany, Japan and many others without introducing huge financial subsidies that might make it a heavy burden on the country's economy. However, in 1979 the government announced a master plan for heavy industry.

In 1981 the General Public Organization for industrialization started awarding contracts for the Misurata steel works; the first phase will cost $3,500 million. The plant will have an annual capacity of 1.2 million metric tons of steel by the end of 1986. A 600 mile railroad is to be built to connect the steel complex with the iron ore mines in the south. Work for developing the port and improving its facilities has already begun, and a town to house 20,000 people in the first phase is being built. It will be expanded after to accomodate 40,000 inhabitants.

Libya and Yugoslavia are cooperating in a joint project of building an aluminum smelter complex at Zuwara, 80 miles west of Tripoli. The complex will cost $1,250 million and will produce 120,000 metric tons of aluminum yearly. It is also planned to build a larger port and a petroleum coke plant in Zuwara.

Besides the petrochemical production in Mersa Brega and Ras Lanouf, a $1,000 million fertilizer complex at Sirte is being planned. The complex, which is expected to start production by the end of 1987, will produce 2,600 tons of ammonia per day, 1,740 tons of urea per day, 300 tons of ammonium sulphate per day, 1,000 tons of nitrogen per day and 500 tons of sulphuric acid per day.

The remarkable urban development, the infrastruc-ture expenditure and the every active construction work have given rise to a rapidly increasing demand for

cement. It is imported now in large quanities inspite
of the fact that there is some domestic production. The
government has embarked on an ambitious program to
produce more of the country's cement consumption
locally. The existing plant at Khoms has been expanded,
and a new plant that will cost $150 million has already
started prodcution. Three other new plants are being
built at Derna, Souk Elkhamis and Benghazi. It is
estimated that the combined production of all these
plants will reach 4 million tons per year.

INTERNATIONAL TRADE

Oil is the main item in the external trade. It is
the only commodity of large value that is exported, and
its revenues are the main resources for paying for all
imported goods and other expenditures. Before oil
production, the country's exports were only agricultural
products, and the imports were manufactured goods. In
1960, just before exporting oil, imports were valued at
LD 60.4 million (LD 21 million were accounted for by the
petroleum companies) and exports at 4.0 million. If the
petroleum companies imports account is subtracted from
the total value of imports, there is still an adverse
balance of LD 45.4 million. Oil was discovered and
first exported late in 1961. It started a revolution in
the external trade, in imports and exports, and in
Libya's international trade relationship. In 1969
imports totaled LD 241.3 million and exports LD 937.9
million, of which LD 937.5 million were the value of
exported oil. Oil exports showed steady increase during
the 1970's. They rose from LD 2,109.5 million in 1974
to LD 4,419.2 in 1979, representing 99% of the total
exports. The minute proportion of the reaning exports
were mainly hides, ground nuts, almonds, metal scrap and
reexports. Imports are chemicals, machinery, motor
vehicles, clothings, textiles, timber, cement and
building materials and a wide variety of luxury consumer
goods. In addition, foodstuffs have to be imported,
especially sugar, tea, coffeee, wheat and flour
(especially in years of drought) and live animals. The
percentage of total imports that is accounted for by
foodstuffs and live aminals is increasing annually,
rising from 15% in 1979 to 19% in 1981, reflecting the
rising of higher living standards and the higher per
capita income among most of the population. Although
the value of imports increased by more than 500% between
1971 an 1979 from LD 250.4 million to LD 1,572 million;
whereas over the same period exports grew by 400% only,
there was a significant mathematical surplus in the

balance of payment during each of those years. The decline in oil production that was coupled by another decline in oil prices on both the open world market and even as posted by OPEC is reflected in trade figures since 1979. Between 1979 and 1981 imports rose by 58%, whereas in 1981 exports were worth only 97% of their 1979 value.

Since 1962 Libya has had a considerable trade surplus. In 1971 the surplus recorded LD 712.1 million, in 1976 it reached LD 1,570.45 million in 1978, it jumped to a new record in 1979 to reaach LD 3,189.6 million and another record in 1981 whcih was LD 4,483 million. Since that record was reached, the oil prices started to drop, and there was considerable cut backs in production and exports that may suggest that Libya may not enjoy such huge surpluses, at least during the 1980's.

Although Libya has so far enjoyed a trade surplus, it also has experienced a large deficit on invisibles (money paid for services and transfer payments). These invisible deficits increased from $1,450 million in 1973 to $2,265 million in 1977. In the early 1980's, when the trade surplus was reduced, the deficit on invisibles pushed the current account into deficits. In 1980 the current account showed a surplus of $8,240 million, but in 1981 there was a deficit of $2,978 million. In the years from 1982 to 1984 the current account appears to have been also in deficit. The main reasons for those invisible deficits are the aid payments to countries, political parties and revolutionary activities that are backed by the Libyan political regime and above all for the considerable arms purchases. In fact the deficit in the current account forced the government to make barter agreements with India in 1984 to take crude oil in payment of $200 million owed to Indian companies operating in Libya. In the same year, Libya made a similar agreement with Turkey for the payment of $700 million.

The western and Mediterranean European countries are the best customers for Libya's oil and oil products. That is because of the closeness of Libya to those oil thirsty European countries, and also because tankers carrying the Persian Gulf oil. The United States was a good customer to Libyan high grade oil in 1982. It imported 25% of all of Libya's oil exports. In fact the western European countries and the U.S.A. together accounted for 90% of all Libya's oil exports. However, in 1982, due to the deterioration of the political

195

relationship between the United States and Libya, the
U.S.A. banned all oil imports from Libya, and early in
1986, it severed all economic relations with Libya. The
United Kingdom was a good customer of Libya's oil until
the North Sea oil fields were developed, and it turned
from an oil importing country to one of the major
exporting countries.

The oil exports that started to decline in the
1980's have not only reduced the total value of imports,
but also the patterns of the major suppliers. The
U.S.A., who was a major supplier of imports, totaled $31
million in 1981, dropped abruptly to less than $300 in
1982 and in 1984, was of no significant value. The
major supppliers in 1984 were Japan, Italy, Yugoslavia,
Turkey and Spain.

POPULATION AND URBAN DEVELOPMENT

The population of the Caucasien Mediterranean
group, however is the long-continued traffic in Black
slaves (which unfortunately did not come to an end
before the 1940's) has left a visible influence on some
of the Libyan population especially in the southern
oases.[4] Originally the Libyan population was Berbers.
The establishment of Greek colonies during the seventh
century B.C. onwards had little or no ethnic effect on
the population since most of these colonies were mostly
contained city states that did not deal or mix with the
indigenous population. During the second century A.D.,
most of the population living in the coastal areas
adopted christianity. They were followers of the
Coptic Church of Egypt. Druring the tenth century
strong immigration movemnts of Moslem and Arabic
speaking groups in several waves have changed the ethnic
compostion of almost the total population who converted
to be Moslems and adopted the Arabic language as a
native language.[6] However, a few Berber elements still
survive in the south and the west of the country. Until
the late 1970's there were few Roman Catholics (mostly
the Italian residents), but after the revolution and the
departure of the Italians there are no more Catholics.[7]

The 1964 census estimated that the population of
Libya was 1,564,369; in 1973 it jumped to 2,249,237; and
in 1982 it recorded 3,224,000. Of that population 32%
are urbanized. Tripoli (the capital has 481,295
inhabitants followed by Benghazi with 219,317
inhabitants). Other towns are Misurata, Azzawiya,
Elbeida, Agedabia, Derna, Sheba, Tobruk (Tubruq), El

196

Marj and Zilten. Each has a population of less than
43,000 but more than 21,000. Of the total population
mentioned, about 570,000 are foreigners living in Libya
for employment. They represent 18% of its inhabitants.
The largest foreign gourp is the Egyptian, estimated to
be 174,158 people. Most of the other foreigners are
Tunisians, Algerians, Turks, Palestinians and a few
Sudanese. Some other Islamic elements from the
Phillipines, Bangladesh and Pakistan are starting to
drift to Libya as a result for more demand for labor.

The steady increase in the population coupled with
higher per capita income led to more demand for housing,
schools, hospitals, easier transportation and better
means of communication. Building new industries
necessitated enlarging the old towns or building new
ones. Tripoli, Benghazi, Tubrouq, Azzawiya and Khoms
were enlarged, Ras Lanouf Abu Kammash and Sirte
practically were nonexisting as towns before the
industrial development. Misurata, Zuwara and the other
towns were just small oases of little significance. In
all these towns and in other rural communites new
districts were established and large apartment complexes
were built with schools and hospitals as well as water,
sewage facilites and power stations.

Infrastructure expendirute has put great emphasis
on generating electricty. During the 1976-1980 period
about $3,195 million was spent on electricty projects.
Installed generating capacity rose from 879 MW in 1975
to 1,700 MW in 1979. The 1980-1985 plan is expected to
increase capacity to 3,878 MW. In the middle of 1985 it
seemed the target of that generating capacity was not
reached because there were delays in power station
construction due to lack of finance. It was planned
that the increase would include some use of nuclear
power, but the agreement on nuclear technology with
India to help in building the nuclear reactor ran into
difficulties. Although it was reported that a nuclear
power station would be built on the Gulf of Sirte by the
help of the Soviet Union, no progress has been made.

Water shortage for growing towns and industries is
a continuing problem. To solve that problem two plans
were set in 1982 to supply Tripoli with its water needs:
one for building a 462,000 cubic meter per day
desalination plant, and the other to build another
desalination plant west of Tripoli at Janzour to supply
the town with another extra 150,000 cubic meters per
day. Those are beside the major plans for drilling 270
wells in the regions of Tazerbo in the Southern Desert

197

and Serir in the Southeastern Desert whose water will be piped to the coastal region between Sirte an Benghazi to supply water for domestic-industrial use and for irrigation. Another power and water complex at Zuetina (Azweitna) is scheduled to be completed in 1987 and will have a capacity of 20,000 cubic meters per day of water and a power capacity of 720 MW.

As a result of increasing business an urbanization, Libya had to expand, develop and update its telecommunication network. Nippon Electric, a Japanese company, was awarded a contract to install a microwave network in 1976. Since that time Libya is constantly developing its telemcommunication system. In 1979, a 480-line, 970 mile telephone cable was opened between Tripoli and Marseille (France) that provided Libya with more international telephone links.

The constant increasing volume of imports led to a large-scale expansion of the two main ports, Tripoli ad Benghazi. The ports of Tubruq, Derna an Misurata were reconstructed.

The only main road that had been constructed before the oil revenues started to pour in was the coastal road from the Egyptian boundary line in the east to the the Tunisian boundary line in the west. It was built first by the Italians, then rebuilt by the British during and after their Libyan campaign. Now, thanks to the oil money and keen interest in linking all parts of such a vast desert country together, a good net of roads was built. Desert roads tie Sebha and Mirzuk in the southwest with the main coastal road in the north, Mirzuk in the southwest with the main coastal road in the north. The oases of Ghat and Ghadames have now easy accessiblity with Tripoli, Kufra Oasis and the oil producing areas of the Sirte Basin, Serir and Jaghbub as well are served with good roads that connect them with the northern towns.

There were plans to build a railroad system in Libya. The plan that was made in 1982 was to build a railroad from Tripoli to Ras Ajdir on the Tunisian border; another railroad was to be built from Tripoli to Misurate in the east and to Sebha in the south, and the third railroad was to connect Benghazi with Agedabia and Tubruq. However, in the light of the new financial situation, most of these projects had to be postponed, and the only project which is to be completed is the railroad that connects Tripoli with Ras Ajdir. The

People's Republic of China has reached an agreement with the Libyan government to build it.

Libya is a rich country with large oil reserves of high-grade oil and natural gas. But the Libyans know that these resources, although large, are not renewable. They may last for another four or five or at the most six more decades. The country now, even with the relative decline of exported oil, has a high income, and the people have high per capita income. The country has to prepare its economy for that coming time when the oil wells will dry up. Better financial planning, especially by reducing the invisible deficits that offset the trade surplus, is necessary.

The following tables show some of the geographichal aspects of contemporary Libya.

AREA AND POPULATION

AREA, POPULATION AND DENSITY

Area (sq km)	1,775,500[*]
Population (census results)	
31 July 1964	1,564,369
31 July 1973	
Males	1,191,853
Females	1,057,384
Total	2,249,237
Population (offficial estimates at mid year)	
1980	2,974,000
1981	3,096,000
1982	3,224,000
Density (per sq km) 1982	1.8

[*]685,524 sq miles.

POPULATION BY MOHAFDA (DISTRICT) (1973 census)

Tripoli	707,438	Gharian	154,297
Benghazi	332,333	Jebel Akhdar	132,366
Zawi. (Zavia)	244,456	Derna	122,984
Misurata	178,129	Sebha	111,303
Khoms	160,882	Kalig	105,049

PRINCIPLE TOWNS (population at 1973 census)

Tripoli (capital)	481,295	Derna	30,241
Benghazi	219,317	Sebha	28,714
Misurata	42,815	Tubruq (Tobruk)	28,061
Az-Zawia (Azzawiya)	39,382	El Marj	25,166
El-Beida	31,796	Zeleiten (Zliten)	21,340
Agedabia	31,047		

PRINCIPAL TRADING PARTNERS (US $m.)

Imports c.i.f.	1979	1980	1981
France	439	458	526
Germany, Federal Republic	761	903	882
Greece	157	137	165
Italy	1,402	2,002	2,535
Japan	474	511	640
Netherlands	91	127	177
Romania	75	52	122
Spain	148	298	248
Turkey	52	53	191
United Kingdom	365	472	582
USA	284	426	524
Yugoslavia	67	82	130
TOTAL (incl. others)	5,311	6,776	8,382

Exports f.o.b.	1979	1980	1981
Bahamas	552	1,097	144
Brazil	40	178	319
France	946	604	569
Germany, Federal Republic	2,375	2,764	1,604
Greece	273	722	784
Italy	2,896	4,061	3,713
Japan	74	297	328
Netherlands	519	371	432
Romania	315	427	315
Spain	845	1,079	1,037
Turkey	. 304	699	796
United Kingdom	172	35	72
USA	5,543	7,765	4,268
Yugoslavia	128	275	286
TOTAL (incl. others)	16,076	21,919	15,576

EDUCATION

(1981/82)

State schools	Schools	Students	Teachers
Primary	2,679	718,124	39,214
Preparatory	1,240	229,294	19,359
Secondary	189	57,120	4,532
Teacher training	106	27,853	2,477
Technical	72	16,936	1,449

EMPLOYMENT (official estimates, '000 persons)

	1976	1977	1978
Agriculture, forestry and fishing	141.2	144.9	147.9
Mining and quarrying	18.5	19.2	20.4
Manufacturing	37.4	41.7	47.4
Electricity, gas and water	13.9	14.7	15.8
Construction	167.8	171.4	164.3
Trade, restaurants and hotels	52.0	52.3	47.5
Transport, storage and communications	57.9	63.1	67.5
Financing, insurance, real estate and business services	8.1	8.5	9.1
Community, social and personal services	175.8	185.9	191.2
Activities not adequately defined	60.1	63.3	62.1
TOTAL	732.7	765.0	773.2

AGRICULTURE

PRINCIPLE CROPS ('000 metric tons)

	1979	1980	1981
Barley	100	71	121
Wheat	110	140	123
Olives	100	161	155
Citrus fruits	48	60	91
Groundnuts (in shell)	13*	13*	13*
Almonds	5.5	5.3	14.5
Tomatoes	198	206	168
Dates	98	87	n.a.
Potatoes	90	103	97
Grapes	16	15	17

* FAO estimate.

MINING

	1979	1980	1981
Crude petroleum ('000 metric tons)	100,879	88,324	55,120
Natural gas (million cu m)	23,470	18,552	n.a.

INDUSTRY
(Value of output in LD'000 - Large establishments only)

	1976	1977	1978
Food manufacturing	32,541	33,289	35,578
Beverage industries	6,744	3,198	3,480
Tobacco manufactures	33,065	31,109	33,405
Chemical and products	14,458	9,703	10,342
Textiles	5,459	2,082	2.020
Cement and products	14,629	8,157	12,004
Fabricated metal products	3,704	226	473
TOTAL (incl. others)	127,079	98,760	106,519

EXTERNAL TRADE

SELECTED COMMODITIES (LD'000)

Imports c.i.f.	1979	1980	1981
Food and live animals	238,067	338,638	404,575
Beverages and tobacco	7,517	10,711	12,169
Mineral fuels, lubricants, etc.	10,363	13,062	24,769
/nimal and vegetable oils and fats	17,591	37,062	33,008
ι rude materials (inedible)			
except fuels	29,366	36,910	39,127
Cremicals	64,149	107.760	111,435
Basic manufactures	366,710	484,473	591,765
Machinery and transport equipment	668,248	762,194	946,731
Miscellaneous manufactured articles	170,401	214,831	317,828
TOTAL (incl. others)	1,572,410	2,006,200	2,481,407

Exports f.o.b.	1979	1980	1981
Crude petroleum	4,419,237	6,486,378	4,592,718
TOTAL (incl. others)*	4,761,960	6,489,190	4,611,175

*
Including re-exports

203

REFERENCES

[1] Owen, Roger.   Libya, A Brief Political and Economic Survey.

[2] Waddas, Frank.   The Libyan Oil Industry.

[3] Allen, J.A. Libya: The Experience of Oil

CHAPTER 10

TUNISIA

Tunisia is the smallest of the northwestern African
countries (Mahgreb) in both area and population. Its
territory is about 63,200 square miles; its population
was 6,726,100 in 1982, and the census of 1984 indicated
that they marked almost 7,000,000 with overall density
of 111 per square mile and a natural growth rate of
2.65%.

Tunisia comprises three main physical regions: the
mountainous humid north , the semi arid central plateau
and the southern dry desert region. The mountainous
north is formed of two of the Atlas mountain chains.
The northern chain is the Tell Atlas known in Tunisian
mostly as the Kroumirie Mountains. That chain is less
in altitude compared to its height in Morocco and
Algeria. It reaches elevation of 3,000 feet in a few
places and declines toward the east before reaching the
Bizerte Plain. The southern chain is the High Tell,
Dorsale. (It is considered a south eastern extension of
the Saharan Atlas.) It is known in Tunisia as the
Tebessa Mountains. It reaches its utmost height of
5,066 feet in Tunisia at Mount Chambi (Sha'nabi) in the
western part of the country. The chain gets lower in
altitude eastward and terminates in the Cap Bon
Peninsula.

Those two chains of mountains do not form hard
barriers that separate the different parts of the
country as they do in Morocco and Algeria. In fact,
surface communications are well developed, penetrating
most of the inhabited parts of the country along
networks of 1,500 miles of railroads and more than
12,000 miles or roads. That physiographic structure
that enabled the country to build that relatively good
system of transportation is responsible for the ethnic
and cultural homogenity in the country and its strong
national unity.

Between the two mountain chains is the important
Medjerda (Majardah) River Basin. The river is the only
perennially flowing river in Tunisia. The valley has
most of the country's best cultivated land and the most
important irrigation projects. Flooding has been a
serious problem in the valley; however, the government
is implementing a major irrigation and flood pervention
project.

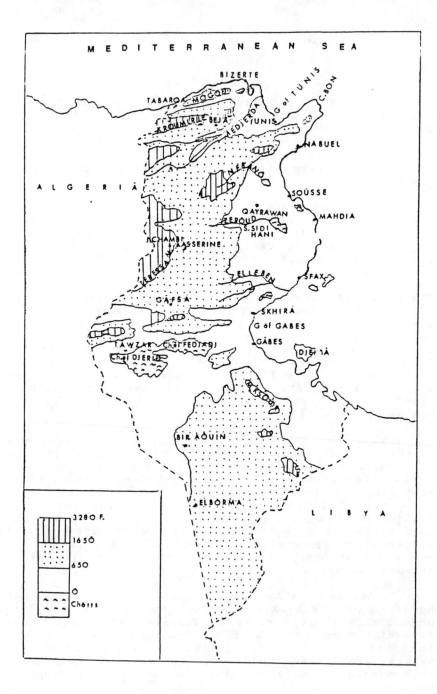

MEDITERRANEAN SEA

BIZERTE

TABARQA
MOGOD
KROUMIRIE
BEJA
MEDJERDA
G of TUNIS
TUNIS
C BON
NABUEL
ALGERIA
N FANOU
SOÛSSE
QAYRAWAN
ZEROUD
S. SIDI HANI
MAHDIA
KCHAMBI
KASSERINE
TEFESSA
ELLEBEN
SFAX
GAFSA
SKHIRA
G of GABES
TAWZAR
Chott FEDJADJ
GABES
Chott DJERID
DJERBA

BIR AOUIN

ELBORMA
LIBYA

|||| 3280 F.
∴∴ 1650
∴∴ 650
◌ 0
∼∼∼ Chotts

South of the mountain chains is the central
Tunisian semi arid plateau. It is an extensive platform
sloping gradually toward the east coast. Its western
part, known and the High Steppe, is formed of alluvial
basins rimmed by low mountain. In the east the
mountains give way first to the Low Steppe, which is a
mountaneous gravel-covered plateau, and ultimately to
the flat coastal plain of the Sahel. Some watercourses
cross the Steppes, but they only run after torrential
rain usually fans out and evaporates in salt flats
(sebkhas) before reaching the sea.

The central plateau gives way southward to a broad
depression occupied by two large seasonal salt lakes
(shotts). The largest of those is Shatt-El-Djerid. It
lies at 54 feet below sea-level and is normally covered
by a salt crust. It extends from close to the
Mediterranean coast in the east to almost the Algerian
boundary line in the west. It is adjoined on the
northwest by the Shott El Rharsa which lies at 70 feet
below sea level. South of the shotts the country
extends for over 200 miles in the Sahara. Rocky,
flat-topped mountains, the Monts des Ksour, separate a
falt plain known as the Djeffara, which borders the
coast south of Gabes, from a sandy lowland which is
partly covered by the sand dunes of the Great Eastern
Erg.

The coastal plain strip that extends from the
Bizerta Plain in the north and extends southward along
the Mediterranean Sea to the town of Gabes is known as
the Sahel. The soil is mainly loamy or sandy and the
region has long sustained a dense population inspite of
the sabkhas and the lakes along the coast.

The shape of the Mediterranean coast and the
location of Tunisia at the eastern end of the Atlas
chain endows it with an east as well as a north coast,
so that marine influence affects a substantial part of
the country. The northern mountainous region is the
wettest part of Tunisia. It lies exposed to the
rain-delivering, low-pressure cells of the Mediterranean
winters. The northern slopes of the Kroumirie Mountains
receive as much as 45 inches of rain during the winter
season that starts in September and ends in April or
early May. These slopes are the wettest areas in north
Africa. The least accessible parts of these slopes are
covered with forests in which cork oak and evergreen oak
predominate. The rainfall decreases quickly southward.
The valley of the Majardah River receives an average of
25 inches. The Tebessa Mountains (Tell-Dorsale) get

only 15 inches. That southern range froms the
transition from the relatively humid north to the
semi-arid and arid south where the rainfall declines to
less than 10 incles at the plateau and to less than 5
inches on the Tunisian Sahara. With the exception of
the northern slopes of the Kroumirie Mountains, lower
rainfall, severe exploitation of the forests and
overgrazing combine to replace forest with meager scrub
growth. Large areas of the Steppes are covered only
with clumps of esparto grass which are collected and
exported for high quality paper manufacture. In the
south where desert conditions prevail, not only is the
rainfall below 5 inches, but it occurs only at rare
intervals. Extremes of temperature and wind are
characteristic and vegetation is completely absent over
extensive areas. That desert region, as expected,
supports only a sparce nomadic population, except where
ground water is available as in the oasis of Tozeur on
the northern rim of Shott El Djerid which is famous for
high quality date production.

ECONOMIC DEVELOPMENT

Tunisia, the smallest country in Mediterranean
Africa, has very little of the oil-rich Sahara lands
that made Libya, to the east, a very rich country or
sustain and help develop Algeria to its west. In fact
when Tunisia became independent in 1956, the prospects
of economic development were limited, since at that time
the natural resources of the country were phosphates and
limited amounts of lead and the agricultural land of the
north is always under the mercy of climatic conditions.

From 1957 to 1970 the economic development was
rather slow. The GNP rose only with a rate of 2.6% and
the international debt was increasing. In fact there
would have not been any rise if it was not for the flow
of oil from El Borma and Douleb oil fileds in 1964 and
1963 respectively.

During the period of 1973-1976 the Tunisain economy
grew with a fairly impressive rate of 7.2%. This rate
of growth was due to high price for oil, phosphates and
olive oil. However, in 1977-1978 because of sharp
declines in world demand for the three of these most
important Tunisian export commodities, coupled with poor
agricultural outputs due to unfavorable climatic
conditions the growth rate was only 4%. That condition
led to growing unemployment and rapid increase in the

rate of inflation that caused social unrest and a series
of strikes.

The two years of 1979 to 1980 the Tunisain economy
had the highest performance since the country got
independence. It rose with a rate of 16% and the per
capita income reached the equivalent of more than $1,200
compared to $280 in 1965. In 1981 the growth rate
dropped sharply to 5%, and in 1982 it went down to just
0.3%. In 1983 the economy was making significant
recovery; the GNP increased 4.5%; the total GNP at
national market prices was TD (Tunisiain Dinars) 3,270
million. The economic forecast for the years 1984-85 is
predicting a modest growth of around 4%. Tunisia, like
all developing countries, is loaded with a heavy burden
of international debts. In 1970 the debts were $541
million; in 1981 it jumped to 3,171 million, which is
equivalent to 38% of the GNP. The interest to serve the
debt in 1981 was $204 million. It is 6.1% of the GNP
and equal to 13.9% of the value of the total export.

AGRICULTURE

The total population of Tunisia was estimated in
1982 at approximately 6,726,000; of those, about
5,405,000 are rural population making about 80.4% of the
inhabitants. Also the total labor force in the same
year was 1,674,000. Those that were in the different
agricultural sector were estimated at 601,700. That
makes about 35.9% of all the labor force. It is also
estimated that about two-thirds of the total area of the
country is suitable for farming. In spite of all these
facts, agriculture is not faring well. While the GNP in
the period from 1970 to 1981 was growing with a rate of
7.3%, agriculture was growing only 4.1 % compared with
services that were growing at a rate of 7.5% and
industry at 9.3% and manufacturing at 11.7%. The
contribution of agriculture to the GNP (in constant
prices) fell from 533 million Tunisian Dinars in 1981 to
TD 480 million in 1982 and to TD 483 in 1983. The food
account deficit which was TD 110 million in 1982 nearly
doubled in 1983, when it reached TD 203 millin due to
lower exports and abrupt increase in imports. In fact,
the imports of grain are rising yearly because the local
production, although increasing, cannot keep pace with
the growth rate of population which is averaging 2.65%
yearly. Wheat production, which was about 869,000
metric tons in 1980, jumped to about 1,000,000 in 1983.
Barley, which was 296,000 metric tons, increased to
300,000 metric tons in 1980. At the same time, the

values of imported wheat increased from TD 62,795,000 in 1980 to 91,113,000 in 1982 and in 1983 reached TD 124 million. The government, in order to keep the prices of food within the reach of the people with limited income, is subsidizing food, which is putting a considerable financial burden on the budget. Several governmental attempts to reduce the subsidies led to violence, political and social unrest and street demonstrations, the last of which was in early 1985.

The Tunisian government, aware of the seriousness of problems facing agriculture, has been trying to solve the problems. The problems are both physical and political, and the government is tackling both sides. The hardest of the physical obstacles is climate, especially the rainfall. The northern region is receiving relatively adequate amounts of rainfall that average more than 20 inches. South of the Tell Mountains the Sahel region is receiving about 15 inches and the Steppe region has about 10 inches, and in both cases the rainfall is insufficient for the regular agriculture of grains without irrigation. The southern region that comprises about one-third of the country is a part of the Sahara, and agriculture is restricted to the few oasis in the region. Even in the norhtern region, where the precipitation is adequate in amount on the average, the rainfall is subject to extreme yearly fluctuation in amount as well as the suitable time of rainfall. In some years the rainfall may come too late or may end too early. It may be suitably distributed during the agricultural season, or it may come as sudden floods and end abruptly. To correct the situation the government has embarked on a program to build irrigation projects with the aim not only to restore the needed water for crops, but also to reclaim more land for agriculture. The French settlers started building dams in the Medjerda River Valley to control floods. Since the early 1970's the government has made some progress in building irrigation dams. The World Bank is supervising the overall plan for a massive water development program that includes building several dams for irrigation and flood control. Among these are the Bou Heurtma Dam in Jendouba, that will irrigate 40,000 acres, which is financed by the Federal Republic of Germany,; the Sidi Salem Dam, which was completed in 1982 and irrigates about 30,000 acres; the Nefta project in the south; and Sidi Sa'ad Dam near Kairouan, that was also completed in 1982 and irrigates about 8,600 acres. A study is undertaken to access the potentialities of the underground water resources in the Sahara. The reclamation program is intending to drain the swamps of the Medjerda Delta and the lagoons of the Sahel region in order to turn it into agricultural areas mainly for cereal crops. In fact work has already started to reclaim a part of the delta and Sebkhet Sidi El Hani. The reclamation will not only add more land for cereal production, but will help improve the health situation by easing the malaria disease.

No doubt that irrigation and flood prevention projects are badly needed to improve agriculture and to develop it in order to achieve self-sufficiency in Tunisia, but these expensive projects should be supported by wise agricultural management policies as well as land ownerhsip and land tenure policies. Since Tunisia got its independece, the government is trying to develop such policies. From 1960 until 1969 the foundation of the Tunisian agrarian reform program lay in the formation of collective "agricultural units'. Each of these units comprise 1,000 acres, atleast, to be managed as collectives in order to use land expropriated from French Settlers and to consolidate small peasant holdings to avoid fragmentation of agricultural land that had prevented the use and application of modern cultivation methods. The system was managed through credits provided by the Agricultural Bank. By the end of 1968 there were more than 225 state cooperatives and about three hundred more were being put together. However, that collectivization method was not popular among the farmers, opposed by many economists and politicians and the foreign aid donors (espeically the World Bank), were not pleased with its results. The system did not increase productivity, and wide spread corruption in the cooperatives was reported as well as poor performance, heavy debts and misappropration of state funds.

In 1970 the state system of collectivization was dismantled, and the large estates that were owned or managed by the government or privately owned were broken down and split among landless or small farmers or private cooperatives. The Ministry of Agriculture has stepped up its efforts to modernize agriculture and to stimulate output, including the provision of funds for mechanization, a reduction in taxes and the introduction of subsidies for purchases of fertilizers, pesticides and seed. The government also has embarked on an ambitious program to prevent soil erosion.

It was reported that by the end of 1975 approximately one-half of the total cultivated area of 18 million acres was privately owned. A further 4.2

211

million acres were managed by cooperative farm groups and the remainder was farmed by state and religious institutions. In order to support small land holdings and to improve farming methods, the government established a "supervised credits scheme" whereby small and medium-sized farms could be given supervised short-term credits to improve farming. In fact that last scheme is fulfilling its purpose as well as encouraging diversifying crops.

In planning for a sound agricultural policy, the Tunisian government is trying to reach three goals. The first is to achieve self-sufficiency, not only to be independent in food production by also to save on expensive food imports, which the country can ill afford, and to cut on governmental food subsidies that are overburdening the country's budget. The second is to develop rural areas and encourage a good segment of the population to stay in the countryside and rural communites instead of migrating the urban areas and creating urban problems as they are doing in the rest of the north Arfican countries. And the third is to create a kind of social equity in land ownership by prohibiting land ownership for more than 150 acres, while encouraging small and medium-size ownership without jeopardizing using modern methods of agriculture and also prohibiting fragmentation of land less than 10 acres. In order to make that policy a reality, the government has allocated the necessary funds in the state's budget. Investments in the agricultural sector of the economy in the 1982-1966 development plan has risen to 19% of the total economic investments - some TD 1,550 million - from 12.9% in the previous plan of 1978-82.

The government took another important side step to develop agriculture by establishing two financial institutions: the "Agence de Promotion des Investise-ments Agricoles" (APIA) was established in 1982 to channel funds into productive projects, especially the development of new cash crops, and the "Banque Nationale de Developpement Agricole" (BNDA) was created to ease investments in this sector.

There are five agricultural regions in Tunisia: the mountainous north with its narrow coastal plane and large fertile valleys, especially the Medjerda River Valley where cereals and a large variety of fruits and vegetables are grown; the norhteast that includes the Medjerda Delta, Cap Bon and Bizerta Plains where the citrus fruits are the most important production and also

the soil is suitable for sugar beets and almonds; the
Sahel, along the east coast, where olives grow; the
center (the Steppe) where there's pasture and raising of
sheep and goats; and the desert south which is a part of
the Sahara and agriculture is confined to the oasis
where dates are prolific.

In the northern mountainous and valley region
cereals are grown, and the most important cereal crop is
wheat. The government is trying to increase wheat
production hoping to be able to be self-sufficient in
the near future. The ministry of agriculture guarantees
the price to the grower and even pays transport costs of
merchants. The ministry, in order to maximize the output
per acre, is encouraging the spread of the Mexican dwarf
wheat that is know for its high productivity and
relative ability to stand drought conditions. This
variety now accounts for about 15% of the country's
output. Barley is the second important cereal crop. It
is mostly consumed in the central and southern parts of
the country. The production is subject to climatic
fluctuations, especially the rainfall; in 1982 wheat
production reached about one million metric tons and the
barley was about 300,000; in 1983 the production of both
was about 920,000 metric tons, a drop of about 30%. It
is hoped that more irrigation projects will not only
increase production but will prevent yearly fluctuation
and stabilize it.

Olives and olive oil are among the high items on
both the production and export tables. The main region
for olive production is the Sahel region. The size of
the harvest varies considerably, mostly due to the two
year flowering cycle of the tree. Production of olive
oil was about 150,000 metric tons in 1984 and almost
double the production of 1981 which fell to a ten year
low of 80,000 tons. Tunisia is considered the world's
fourth largest exporter of olive oil. The amount and
value of exports does not depend only on olive
production but also on world prices and the production
of the other large Mediterranean producers, especially
Spain and Italy. In 1984 the value of exports reached
TD 57.2 million. It was TD 25 million in 1983 and TD
56.9 million in 1982.

Grapes are mostly produced in the northeast
especially around Bizerta and Tunis. The production has
been slipping since the French settlers started to leave
the country in 1984. The production was estimated to be
less than 98,000 metric tons in 1984. It was 135,000
metric tons in 1980. The same for wine production that

213

reached a peak of almost 2 million litres in 1963. In 1983 it was about 560,000 litres. Tunisia, like Maghreb, is not prohibiting the drinking or production of wine although it is a Moslem country.

Citrus fruit production, mostly in the north and northeast, was 145,000 metric tons in 1984. It was 198,000 in 1981. Date production, considered a high quality, fluctuates between 40,000 and 60,000 metric tons per year. The main areas of production are in the south, especially the oasis of Tozeur, Gafsa and Mefta. Most of the date variety known as Deglat en Nour is exported; the exports are about 7,000 tons per year.

Sugar beet became an important crop in the 1960's when the government encouraged the production to try to decrease sugar imports. The production reached 104,000 tons in 1982; however, the government decided to limit the production in 1983 to about 70,000 tons, since the sugar refineries capacities were not able to handle the increasing production. The Beja refinery has a limited capacity of 1,850 tons of sugar per year. A new refinery at Ben Bechir in Jendouba started production in 1983 with a capacity of about 40,000 tons of sugar per year. In 1984 sugar imports totaled LD 23 million compared to TD 41 million in 1981.

New crops produced as a result of the diversification policy and mostly to be exported, especially to France and the European Common Market, include apricots, almonds, tomatoes, melons, onions, artichoke and peppers. The island of Djerba offshore of the southeastern coast is known for vegetable and grape production as well as for its olive groves and for its tourist industry.

The ministry of agriculture is sparing no effort to improve the quality of cattle in the country in order to increase meat and dairy product's outputs. Different French and Swiss breeds are imported as well as Spanish sheep to improve wool production. The main area for cattle is the north an northeast where the number of cattle was estimated to be about 600,000 heads in 1984. The main area for sheep is the Steppe of the plateau, and the number of sheep was estimated to be around 4.5 million heads and the number of goats 559,000. The chicken farming (as the case in all Mediterranean African countries) is increasing to meet the increasing demand and is a way to solve the meat production problems. Poultry meat production reached almost 43,000 tons in 1984.

The government, with the help of financial foreign aid mainly from the World Bank and technical help especially from Spain and France, has increased its fishing activities and improved its techniques. The fish catch has almost tripled in the last 3 decades. In 1984 it reached 68,000 tons compared to 22,500 tons in 1953. The main center of the fishing industry is the port of Sfax on the southeastern coast. The industry employs directly about 23,000 men. Fresh fish are now among the exports of Tunisia.

MINERAL WEALTH

Inspite of the fact that Tunisia is not a mineral rich country, minerals are still the most important foreign exchange earner. Mining and quarrying are employing more than 24,000 persons. Minerals produced in Tunisia are the base of a developing chemical industry.

Oil is the country's main source of export earnings. The export value of oil and oil products was TD 565 million in 1983 compared with TD 557 million in 1982. Revenues from oil exports reached their peak in 1980 when they recorded TD 665 million.

In 1982 oil reserves in Tunisia were estimated at 1,690 million barrels. Since 1970 oil production was more than 4 million tons per year. In 1980 it reached a peak level of 5,627,000 tons, but it fell to 5,400,000 tons in 1981 and to 5,100,000 in 1982. Because of increased production from the new Ashtart field in 1983, production rose again to 5,600,000 tons. In the late 1960's it was estimated that Tunisia's oil reserves will decline fast, and by the mid 1980's it would be a net importer; however, the new offshore findings have pushed that date to the mid 1190's.

Exploration for oil has been carried out in Tunisia since it was discovered in Algeria across the Algerian-Tunisian boundary line. The Italian company Ente Nazionale Idrocarburi (ENI) in 1964 discovered oil at El Borma, in southern Tunisia close to the Algerian oil field. In 1970 recoverable reserves were estimated at 53,000 tons. The Tunisian government took a 50% share in the El Borma operating company when oil was found.

In 1968 the second oil field in the country came into operation at Douleb, 130 miles north of El Borma.

215

This field is operated by a joint French-Tunisian company, the Societe de Recherches et D'Exploitations des Petroles en Tunisie (SEREPT), together with Societe National Elf Aquitaine.

Other oil fields include Tamesmida, near the Algerian border, southwest of Douleb. It started to operate in 1969. The Bihrat and Sidi al-Itayem both began producing in 1972.

Important new discoveries offshore at Ashtart, east of Sfax in the Gulf of Gabes, now account for about 50% of the country's total output. The field is operated jointly with Elf Erap and Aquitaine-Tunisie. A dispute with Libya over demarcation of territoral waters in the Gulf of Gabes, where promising findings of oil have been made, was settled in 1982. A ruling by the International Court of Justice delimited the two countries offshore territorial waters around a boundary approximately 26° east from the land border to latitude $34^{\circ}10'30"$ north, where it deviates 52° east.

In 1979 Compagnie Francaise des Petroles (CFP) - totally won an exploration concession covering about 4,100 square miles in the central part of the country, and in April 1980 AMOCO (American Oil Company) won an exploration permit for about 6,200 square miles in southern Tunisia. By the beginning of 1981 three more onshore permits had been granted - to EAT, in a joint ventrue with Entreprise Tunisienne d'Activites Petrol-ieres (ETAP- 6,600 sqaure miles southeast of Djerba); to Total Exploration Tunisie, in a joint venture with ETAP - 1,879 sqaure miles in the Cap Bon-Kelibia region, and to Occidental of Tunisia - 2,900 square miles close to Bizerta.

New Tunisian oil fields include Makhrouga, Larich and Debbech, all in the south. They are developed by the Societe d'Exploitation des Permis du Sud (SODEPS) and ETAP. The Tazerke field is in the Gulf of Hammamet. It is operated by Shell, AGIP and ETAP. The largest of all the new fields is the offshore field in the Gulf of Gabes, the Isis oil field. It is operated by Shell, Amoco, AGIP and CFP.

The main pipeline that carries the Tunisian oil from its fields to the Mediterranean is the major pipeline that extends from Zarzaitine and Edjelehin in Algeria to the terminals at La Skhirra on the Gulf of Gabes. All the Tunisian oil fields are connected with that pipeline with other "spur" pipelines.

Tunisia's only oil refinery is located at Bizerta.
It has a capacity of 1.8 million tons per year. In most
of the time since the refinery was built it was
operating at almost full capacity. However, the oil
products consumption in the country was rising. In 1984
it was estimated to be 3 million tons. The country was
forced to import about 50% of its needs of refined oil
products. There is a plan to increase the capacity of
the refinery to 6.5 million tons, but the money needed
for expansion was not allocated in the budget of 1984-85
fiscal year.

Tunisia became a member of the Organization of Arab
Petroleum Exporting Countries in March 1982. Libya was
objecting to Tunisia's admission, but it withdrew its
objection after solving the mutual boundary problem of
the territorial waters.

Tunisia also has natural gas reserves estimated at
80,000 million cubic meters. Most of the country's gas
production comes from El Borma Field. Output of both
natural and manufactured gas was 441 million cubic
meters in 1983, a drop from the 449 miillion cubic
meters that was produced in 1982. An important source
of natural gas is liftings by Societe Tunisienne
d'Electricite et du Gaz (STEG) from the Trans-
Mediterranean pipeline. The 1680 miles of pipeline,
that crosses Tunisia, was built in 1981 for the main
purpose of supplying Italy with Algerian natural gas.

Tunisia is considered the world's fourth largest
producer of calcium phosphates. Phosphates and
phosphatic fertilizers are the country's second
important export. In 1982 it was 4.7 million, and in
1983 it recorded almost 6 million tons. In fact the
investments in phosphates' industry are planned to
increase the production to 7 million tons before the end
of 1987. The policy is not only to develop new
resources but also to manufacture highly profitable
fertilizers and phosphoric acid. Calcium phosphates are
mined mainly from six deposits in the central part of
the country: Metlaoui, Redeyef, Moulares, M'Dilla,
Kalaat Djerda and Ainkerma.

More than 60% of the production is exported to
Western markets, especaily France, Federal Germany and
Italy, while the balance goes to Eastern European
coutries and China.

Almost 73% of the total phosphate output is
exported as phosphate rocks, although exports of triple

superphosphate (TSP) and phosphoric acid has increased substantially during the last four years. In 1983 triple superphosphate production reached 633,000 tons while phosphoric acid rose to 620,000 tons. The industrial plan for which substantial investments are allocated, when completed, will enable Tuinisia to manufacture most of its production of calcium phosphate and to export it as fertlizers. In 1981 two companies, one is French and the other is Japanese, got a contract for a new plant at Gabes Fertilizer complex for the production of 70,000 tons of sulphuric acid and 40,000 tons of phosphoric acid. The plant was completed and started production in 1983. The plan includes building in the same complex a plant of the production of ammonioum nitrate with a capacity of 1,000 tons per day and three more plants at Gafsa: one for the production of triple superphosphate with a 400,000 per year capacity; another plant to produce 150,000 tons of phosphoric acid annually, and the third plant for the production of sulphuric acid with a capacity of 450,000 tons per year. A new company with a 49% Kuwaiti shareholding has been established to develop and use the phosphate reserves that are located at Sra Quertane in the norhtwestern part of the country. The production will start in 1986 and could reach 700,000 tons per year in 1989.

Zinc is mined in the northwestrn part of the country near Tabarka and in the western part west of Kasserine. Output of zinc concentrates totalled 15,500 tons in 1983 compared with 15,200 in 1982. The Societe Tunisienne d'Espansion Minere is announcing a plan to increase production to 21,000 tons by 1986.

Lead concentrates production in 1983 was only 10,400 tons down from 15,000 in 1982. The drop was mainly due to depressed world market prices due to economic depressions of that year. The production is expected to increase only by about 2,000 tons in 1986. Lead is mined mainly near Zaghowen and Sidi Sa'ad in the northeast.

Tunisia has limited resources of iron ore estimated to be around 25,000,000 tons. The ore is at Djerissa and Tamera. The production has declined fast since independence. France was the main importer. It is now getting its ore needs for the European Common Market countries. In 1955 the production was above one million tons. In 1981 it was 400,000 tons, and in 1983 it dropped further to reach a record low of about 300,000 tons.

In 1984 a French company completed building and equipping a uranium purification plant that is able to produce 100 tons of green cake uranium per year. Some of it is planned to be used in a reactor that would be producing electricity.

Salt is produced from the salty water near the lagoons, and along the shores, production runs between 320,000 - 35,000 tons per year. Most of it is exported to Japan, France and Federal Germany.

INDUSTRY

Tunisia's dependency on oil and phosphate exports has not prevented the establishment of a developing and thriving industrial sector. This has grown from the traditional artisan activities such as copper works, leather, handmade rugs and textiles, and the creation of "downstream" industries based on the country's reserves of phosphate. According to Tunisian leading officals and the economic plans, the industrial sector of the economy should expand and develop further because of the prospects of reduced oil production and exports and the need to create new labor intensive outlets to combat the growing and severe problem of unemployment.

Tunisia, like most of the young developing countries, has difficulties in builidng up its industries as fast as their ambitions aspire. This is mainly due to lack of investments, technological dependency on foreign countries and the strong ties between the agribusiness and food processing industries and agriculture that its production is dependent on climatic fluctuations.

During the period of 1973-76 plan, the industrial sector grew by 7.4% instead of the 10.2% planned, although the plan allocated 32% of the total investment for developing industry. In 1977 there was another setback when that sector's growth rate was only 4.2% due to a sharp fall in agribusiness and the food processing industries. However, apart from a zero rate of growth in the textile industries, the sector's performance improved in 1978 with a 10.6% growth rate. In 1982 the growth rate of the manufacturing industry fell to only 3% but rose again in 1983 to about 8.9%. In the 1982-86 development plan, the manufacturing industry was allocated 19.5% of total investment (TD 1,600 million) compared with 18% (TD 8167) during the previous plan. Mechanical and electromechanical industries are to

219

receive the major part of this investment: 24%, compared
with 13.2% in the 1977-81 plan. The share of total
exports which is accounted for by manufactured goods is
due to an increase from 40% in 1981 to 57% in 1986.

During the first decade after independence,
manufacturing tended to concentrate on processing raw
materials, especially foodstuffs, and its aim was to
satisfy the local consumption in order to reduce
imports. The situation changed with the introduction of
the development plan of 1973-76. The government is
encouraging the establishment of export-oriented
industries under a 1973 investment law. It offers
competitive conditions for foreign companies which
produce export goods only.

Tunis, the capital of the country is not only the
largest town with almost 50% of the total urban
population, but also more than 50% of the industry is
located in it. In 1981 the government introudced
legislation to promote decentralization. Now other
industrial centers are growing such as Sousse, Gabe,
Bizerta, Gafsa, Sfax, Beja and Kasserine. The
decentralization policy worked well. It spread
prosperity to rural communites that were loosing their
population and were suffering from poverty and
unemployment problems. It is also helping to reduce
urban problems in the already crowded Tunis. The policy
of encouraging export-oriented industry, although it is
still in its childhood, is already starting to pay some
dividends; exports of clothing and accessories jumped
from TD 2.2 million in 1980 to 8.2 million in 1982.
Phosphoric acid exports recorded TD 58.5 million in 1982
compared to TD 40 million in 1980.

Textiles and food processing are the two major
sectors of manufacturing in Tunisia; in 1982 both
accounted For about 50% of the industrial production.
Sugar is produced at Ben Bechir and Beja, but the
country is importing sugar because while consumption is
increasing, the factories do not have the capacity to
handle all the sugar beets that could be grown in
Tunisia. Olive oil production is in Sousse Bizerta
Kasserine and Sfax. Wine and raisins are produced
mainly in Tunis and Bizerta. Beer production is in
Tunis, and the production is on the increase as well
with cigarettes and vegetable canning. Carpets and rugs
using domestic wool are handwoven at Kairouan and have
good markets in Western Europe, especially in France and
Germany. Textiles, depending on synthetic fibers and on

imported raw cotton and cotton yarn as well as clothing, are located in Tunis. A new fish canning factory started production at Sfax in 1984. Leather goods for exports and shoes for local use are produced for the national market, produced in small factories and handmade in the main towns.

A cellulose factory and paper pulp is located at Kasserrine. It is using the locally grown esparto grass. Wood works, furniture, glass, paint, varnish and batteries are also manufactured in Tunis, Bizerte and Beja, and ceramics are made at Nabeul.

The metallurgical industry is growing steadily. It is depending on the iron ore produced in Djerissa and Tamera. The iron and steel complex (Fouladh Steel) is located near Bizerta at Menzel Bourguiba. It has an annual capacity of 175,000 tons of iron bars, wire and small sections. The capacity will be increased to 400,000 by the end of 1986. A new steel mill with a capacity of 100,000 tons annually will start production in 1986. It is being built at Bizerta. Iron and steel are now among the important exports of Tunisia.

Mechanical industries have had good attention and encouragement from the government. The government-owned STIA vehicle assembly plant at Sousse produces Peugeot cars, buses and trucks. Under an agreement signed in 1983 with the French Company, the plant is assembling 15,000 vehicles per year. The American General Motors Company and the German Volkswagonwerk Company also have made similar deals to produce cars in Tunisia. Production of farm machinery started in 1983 with an output of 2,200 tractors, 6,000 diesel engines, 100 combine harvesters and 700 small farm machines per year. The investments in that project totaled $120 million. Tires are produced in Menzel Bourguiba. There are plans to increase the production to cover the national market needs.

Sfax and Gabes are the centers of the young but fast booming chemical industries. The principal activity within this sector is the procesing of phosphate rock into phosphatic fertilizers and phospheric acid instead of exporting most of it as raw material. The chemical plant at Gabes is owned by the government, and the plant at Sfax is partly owned by the government. Other chemical industries are the production of paint, glue, detergent and soap; most of them are located in Tunis and Bizerta.

221

By the end of 1986, two plants for the production
of wet lime will start production, each with a capacity
of 650 metric tons per day. The plants are to be built
at Thala and Mezuna in the south.

The urban expansion and industrial developments
have led to a spur in the construction industry and an
increase in cement production. In 1983 cement
production was more than 2.5 million tons compared to
1.8 million in 1982. More expansion in the industry is
planned by the help of French and Japanese companies.
The industry is located at Enifida and Oum El-Khelil. A
new plant at Ferianna (near Kasserine) started producing
white cement in 1984. It has a capacity of 100,000 tons
per year.

There are 18 power stations in Tunisa. Most of
them are producing thermal electricity. Hydroelectric
power is of less importance since there is only one
perennial river with limited discharge (Medjerde).
Production in 1982 reached the record of 3,173.5 million
K W h; in 1980 it was 2,797.2 million K W h). Tunisia
is planning to enter the nuclear era by building a
nuclear reactor for the production of electricity at a
cost of TD 15 million. It will be located at Gabes.
The reactor is expected to have a capacity of 50 MW and
to produce more than 20,000 cubic meters of desalinated
water per day. Both power and water are badly needed
for social, urban and industrial development.

The Tunisian economy is served by a modern system
of road and rail communication that the country
inherited from the French Colonial era. The transport
system covers most of the populated areas. The length
of railroads is more than 1,500 miles, and the roads
cover more than 10,000 miles. A new railroad is built
connecting Gafsa with Gabes. Tunisia is doing its best
to maintain, upgrade and keep the efficiency of its
transport system. Tunis, the capital, is building city
railway roads of about 20 miles. There are five
airports serving both national and international air
transportation. Tunis has two airports, and three are
in Djerba (important for tourism) at Monastir and at
Tozeur.

Tunisia made impressive progress in the field of
navigation. The Compagnie Tunisienne de Navigation
started to operate in 1971 and now has a fleet of 31
vessels with an aggregate capacity of 463,000 deadweight
tons. By 1981 the Tunisian fleet carried more than 30%
of the country's foreign trade. Since 1980 work started

to modernize and expand port facilities at Tunis-La Goulette and Sfax ports. In 1984 work started to expand the port of Gabes. Under the 1982-86 development plan new ports are to be built at Cap Ferrat to serve the planned oil refinery, and at Zarzis near Djerba to handle potassium and salt exports.

TOURISM

Tourism is a main source of national income for Tunisia. There are good prospects for tourism, and the government is trying to encourage that sector of the economy. Tunisia is not a great archeological center nor is it as dry and sunny as Egypt. It still has some archeological sites belonging to the ancient history of Crthage, the Roman and Islamic Empires. It has Mediterranean warm winters as well as good summer resorts along the waterfront. Tourism is an industry which is very sensitive to political stability and good services offered by the host country, and Tunsia is trying to achieve both.

Between 1961 and 1972 total tourist arrivals grew at a rate of 30% annually. From 1972 to 1976 tourism was the largest foreign currency earner (before it gave up its place to oil exports). The number of tourists has fluctuated from one year to another, depending on the national condition of Tunisia and on the economic prosperity of the tourists' countries. In 1980 the number was 1.6 milion. In 1981 it was 2.2 million, and in 1983 it ws 1.44 million. Tourism receipts rose from TD 340 million in 1982 to TD 388 million in 1983. France was and still is the main country of origin of tourists followed by Federal Germany, Algeria and the United Kingdom. The four main centers for tourists are: Hammamet, Sousse, Djerba and Tunis. The 1982-86 development plan is expecting to build more hotels, especially at Mahdia (known for its sunny, warm winters), and the number of tourists by the end of 1986 is expected to reach a record of 2.2 million.

INTERNATIONAL TRADE

Tunisia, like all developing countries, has a chronic and serious trade deficit that is decreasing its ability to develop economically. The seriousness is that the country, although doing its best to encourage exports and devaluate its currency, is still not able to limit the deficit. It is growing from one year to

223

another. In 1981 the deficit was TD 632 million; in
1982 it climbed to TD 820 million, and in 1983 it
recorded TD 846 million. The ratio of exports to
imports is ranging between 59% to 64% yearly. The main
problem with the Tunsian exports is that it's heavily
dependent on minerals and agricultural products. The
price for minerals has always been determined by
international economic conditions, and the agriuclutural
products are always subject to climatic changes that
affect the crops.

However, the deficit in the trade balance is offset
to some extent by earnings from tourism and remittance
sent home by Tunisians working abroad. Unfortunately
the host countries for Tunisian workers in Western
Europe, especially France, have now a serious problem of
unemployment, and they are encouraging the Tunisians to
go back home, and tourism is subject to conditions
beyond the control of the Tunisian government.

Oil and oil products are the main source of export
earnings. In 1983 they provided TD 565 million up from
TD 557 million in 1982. Natural phosphates earnings
were TD 262 million in 1983 compared to TD 107 million
in 1982. Textiles provided TD 246 million in 1983, a
jump from TD 216 million in 1982. Other major
agricultural products exported include fresh fruits and
vegetables, olive oil and wine, which recorded high
earnings. All these high export earnings show the
struggle and determination of the country to increase
its exports to try to reduce the wide gap in trade
deficit.

Tunisia's main imports are machinery, needed for
industrialization, crude oil (grades not produced
locally) and oil products (since the only refinery at
Bizerta does not yet have the capacity to cover the
local consumption) wheat, vegetable oils or fats to
satisfy the needs of the constantly increasing population, especially in years of unsuitable climatic
conditions and failure of crops. Raw cotton and cotton
yarn are imported for the production of textiles and
clothings that make a good portion of exported goods.
Other imported goods include electric equipment,
vehicles and timber. In 1983 imports of capital and
durable goods totaled TD 540 million. Food import costs
jumped to TD 287 million compared to TD 184 in 1982.
Semi-finished goods costs were TD 460 million and energy
imports reached a record of TD 235 million in 1983
compared to TD 221 million in 1982.

The countries of the European Economic Community
(EEC) are responsible for most of the foreign trade with
Tunisia. These countries account for about 60% of the
imports and also for around 60% of the exports. France
is the largest importer of Tunisian goods. In 1983 its
imports totaled TD 297 million worth of products.
Italy's imports were worth about TD 200 million, and
Federal Germany imported Tunisian goods worth TD 145
million. The United States is also a very important
purchaser of Tunisia's products. In 1983 it ranked
second after France, buying goods worth TD 249 million.
France is also the largest exporter to Tunisia. In 1983
French goods sold to Tunisia valued TD 536 million.
Federal Germany ranked second; its exports were worth TD
536 million. The USA was third (TD 194 million), and
Spain ranked fourth by selling to Tunisia goods that
valued about TD 97.3 million.

The EEC-Tunisian mutual trade relations, as
expected, are not always running smoothly. Tunisia
benefited from abolishing the import levy on its olive
oil and lowering tariffs on all of its agricultural
products imported by the EEC countries. At the same
time a quota was imposed by the EEC on its textiles and
clothing exports. When Spain and Portugal joined the
EEC, Tunisia became very anxious about the economic
consequences resulting from this new membership. Spain
and Portugal are large producers and exporters of olive
oil and have the same agricultural products that Tunisia
is exporting to the EEC countries.

Tunisia has a modern banking system sophisticated
enough to back the economic development and the
financial needs of the country. Besides the Banque
Centrale de Tunisia, the government owned bank and the
sole bank of issue of Tunisia national currency, the
Tunisian Dinar. There are some commercial investment
banks owned jointly by Tunisians, Arabs and rich oil
producing Arab governments. The Tunisian banks combined
together and are providing about one-third of the total
capital invested in the 1982-86 development plan, which
is estimated to be TD 8,360 million.

In spite of the complaints about inflation and the
constantly rising cost of living, the national savings
in 1983 represented 21% of the gross national products
(GNP). Investments in the same year reached TD 1,625
million which is about 29% of the GNP. The rise in the
national savings means that the dependency on foreign
loans for development has been reduced.

225

The strong and peaceful relation between Tunisia and Western European countries had helped its financial situation. These countries are providing Tunisia with generous loans for relatively low interest rates that stretches for relativley long periods. Thanks to the influence of these loans, foreign reserves (excluding gold) were $417.2 million at the end of the fiscal year 1983-84. The World Bank Group is another important provider for loans; other lenders are Kuwait and Saudi Arabia. The country's foreign debt is increasing substantially. In 1976 it was $1,508 million dollars. By the end of 1982-83 it will reach more than $3,500 million. The debt services ratio rose from 6.6% of current receipts in 1974 to 11.9% by the end of 1986. So far Tunisia was able to meet its foreign debt obligations.

The Tunisian government is trying hard to develop the country by setting economic, social and financial development plans. Its first three-year plan was that of 1962-64 and then a successive four-year plan (1965-68). The last plan is that of 1982-86. The main difficulty facing the planners is the high rate of population growth that does not only consume most of the fruits of the economic development but also leads to more consumption for food and more expenditure on services resulting in consistant budget and foreign trade deficits. That means also that a good portion of the development expenditure has to be financed by foreign aid. Foreign aid financed about 40% of the plans during the 1960's and the early 1970's; however, more exports of oil, the average growth rate of GNP by about 6%, the increase in the per capita income and the concentration on establishing job oriented industries led to an increase in the national savings that allowed the planners to depend on these savings to finance between 75% to 84% of the development expeditures. Tunisia has been depending on oil exports for economic growth, but the time is certainly coming soon when the oil resources will be depleted and Tunisia will become a net importer of oil and the country has to plan for economic growth without relying on oil revenues.

During the 1977-81 plan, exports grew with a fast rate that averaged 14.6% per year, while imports increaed at a relatively slower rate of 8.9%. The 1982-86 plan marks the adjustment of the economy away from oil dependency. The planners goal is to achieve a GNP growth rate of 6.6% yearly by investing more in the engineering sectors of industry, giving a freer hand to the private enterprises and following a more liberal

226

policy to encourage small industries and free economy instead of giving preference for cooperatives and government owned sectors. More money is allocated for agriculture to decrease food imports and for labor-intensive manufacturing to reduce the 13% of unemployment and even for a higher rate of underemployment. The government is planning to create about 54,000 jobs yearly. So far by the end of 1984 only 40,000 jobs were created per year.

The total expenditure in the recent economic plan will be TD 8,200 million which is about 31% of GNP. The investment sources are: TD 2,710 million from government funds, TD 2,070 million from the private sector and 1,670 million from national savings. The plan is to limit growth in imports to 4% and in consumption to 6.8% and restrict the rise in the deficit in the balance of payments to 8.6%. With all these provisions borrowing requirements from foreign sources to meet planned expenditures will reach the neighborhood of TD 3,500 million and major foreign companies and foreign investments are invited and encouraged to particiapte in the development plan to invest in every sector of the economy.

POPULATION

The last official estimate for population in 1982 shows that the total number of Tunisians is 6,726,100, and the estimated number for 1984 is 7,000,000. In 1975 it was 5,572,193, an increase of 1,153,900 in 7 years. That makes the population growth rate 2.65% which is above the world average and too high for the Tunisian economy to raise the living and social standards of the inhabitants. The density of populatin is 111 per square mile, but if we take into consideration that the ecumenical area is only 42,113 square miles, the density rises to 159.7 per square mile. As expected the major towns and even the rural population are concentrated along the coastal plain where there is more rain and more water. The number of males was 3,376,000 and females was 3,350,000. The birth rate was 32.9 per thousand, and the death rate was 11.1 per thousand (not all deaths were reported, especially in the relatively remote areas). Tunisia's population age structrue is like all the other developing countries; 3,354,000 of the inhabitants are less than 25 years, which makes 50% of the population. The labor force was estimated to be 1,576,900; of that force 1,235,000 are male and 341,900 are females. About 598,400 are working in the primary

227

activites of the economy (agriculure, mining, fishing and forestry). Another 368,000 are working in the secondary activities (industry, manufacturing and construction), and about 610,500 are active in the tertiary activites (services).

Tunisia lay directly in the path of the Arab invasion. In fact, it can be considered the eastern door of the Maghreb countries. Arabization of the Berber popualtion is almost complete; less than 1% of the total population still speak the Berber language, and they live in the interior remote hills. Arabic is the offical language, but due to a long time of French political, social and cultural influence (from 1881 to 1956), French has come to play a dominant role in education, the daily press and in government circles. This linguistic uniformity forms a strong element in Tunisia's national cohesivenes.

Just as the country got its independence, the European settlers numbered more than 250,000; about 60% of them were French and the others were Italians, Greeks and about 85,000 were Jews (originally Italian and native Tunisaian Jews). Half of those settlers were living in Tunis, the capital. Less than 40,000 Europeans are now Tunisian residents, and most of the Jewish population have left the country.

Islam is the religion of the country, and the constitution of 1956 recognizes Islam as the state religion, with the introduction of certain reforms, especially the abolition of polygamy. Christians and Jews are less than 40,000.

The government is doing an impressive job in the field of education, trying to abolish illiteracy that was spreading among most of the population during the French control of the country. In the development plan of 1977-81, spending on education absorbed almost one-third of the budget. In the latest plan of 1982-86, although spending on education was relatively restricted, it still will increase by 14.2%. The offical statistics of the ministry of education shows that in the school year of 1983-84 there were 1,201,645 pupils enrolled in 3,074 primary schools; 378,349 pupils enrolled in 326 secondary schools, and the University of Tunis had 29,573 students and a teaching staff of 4,105 instructors.

Tunisia is paying remarkable attention to public health. In 1982 expenditure on public health will rise

20% to reach TD 823.2 million, following a rise of 8% in 1981. The health conditions improvement in the country resulted in the steady decline of the death rate, especially among infants; the death rate in 1960 was 21 per thousand; in 1982 it was about 11.1 per thousand; child mortality rate dropped from 36 per thousand to about 18.7 per thousand for the same years. One of the problems that face the ministry of public health in Tunisia is the lack of trained medical staff. Before independence the number of physicians was 10,030. After most of the European doctors left their number drop sharply to 3,690 in 1981.

The improvement in economic conditions was reflected in health conditions. In 1970 the per capita income was $290, and the per capita daily calorie supply was only 2,190. It was inadequte, representing only 90% of the health requirements. In 1981 the per capita income rose to $1,420 and the daily calorie supply rose to 2,790; that represents 116% of the requirements. Life expectancy also improved. In 1960 it was 48 years, and in 1981 it rose to 61 years.

Tunisia made condsiderable progress since it became an independent country, but it has along way to go to take a good place among the developed countries of the world. Since its natural resources are limited and event oil reserves are expected to be depleted before the end of the century; it has to depend on its human and cultural resources. The main human problem facing the country is the high growth rate of its population. The government is encouraging family planning, but the goverment efforts have to be matched by the residents conviction of the importance of small sized families, not only for the total economy of the country but for their own welfare.

229

STATISTICAL SURVEY

Area and Population

Area, Population and Density	
Area (sq km)	163,610*
Population (census results)	
3 May 1966	4,533,351+
8 May 1975	
Males	2,811,201
Females	2,760,992
Total	5,572,193
Population (official estimates at mid-year)	
1980	6,392,000
1981	6,565,000
1982	6,726,100
Density (per sq km) 1982	41.1

*63,170 sq miles.
+Excluding adjustment for undernumeration, estimated to have been 4.0%.

Economically Active Population
(Labour Force Survey, '000 persons, 1980)

	Males	Females	Total
Agriculture, forestry and fishing	438.5	113.2	551.7
Mining and energy	45.0	1.7	46.7
Industry and manufacturing	153.8	146.1	299.9
Construction	156.6	1.5	158.1
Transport, and communications	66.3	3.7	70.0
Trade, banking and insurance	111.1	8.7	119.8
Other services	214.6	57.0	271.6
Activities not adequately described	49.1	10.0	59.1
Total	1,235.0	341.9	1,576.9

Source: Institut National de la Statistique.

Principal Communes (population at 1975 census)

Tunis (capital)	550,404	Kairouan	54,546
Sfax (Safaqis)	171,297	Gafsa	42,225
Djerba	70,217	Gabes	40,585
Sousse	69,530	Beja	39,226
Bizerte (Bizerta)	62,856		

Agriculture

Principal Crops ('000 metric tons)

	1980	1981	1982
Wheat	869	963	1,000*
Barley	296	270	300*
Potatoes	120	140	140+
Olives	735	462+	410+
Tomatoes	280	380*	380+
Chillies and peppers	115	124	125+
Dry onions	22	23	23+
Watermelons	195*	195*	197+
Melons	85*	85*	86+
Grapes	135	120*	10(*
Dates	53	50*	5?
Sugar beet	73	101	104 *
Apricots	26	21	30
Oranges	92	141	93
Tangerines, mandarins, clementines, and satsumas	30	34	33
Lemons and limes	18	23	20*
Almonds	37	35*	38
Tobacco leaves	4	4*	5+

* Unofficial figure.   + FAO estimate
Source: FAO, Production Yearbook.

Livestock ('000 head)

	1980	1981	1982
Horses*	50	52	52
Asses*	205	205	206*
Cattle*	599	589	600*
Camels*	170	173	173
Sheep	4,967*	4,635	4,500*
Goats	900*	804*	800
Chickens	13,100*	13,700*	14,000

* FAO estimates.
Source: FAO, Production Yearbook.

Forestry

Roundwood Removals ('000 cu m, excluding back)

	1980	1981	1982
Sawlogs, veneer logs and logs for sleepers	6*	6*	6*
Pitprops (mine timber)	1*	1*	1*
Pulpwood	34*	34*	34*
Other industrial wood	75*	76*	78*
Fuel wood	2,391*	2,447*	2,515*
Total	2,507*	2,564*	2,634*

* FAO estimate.
Source: FAO, Yearbook of Forest Products.

Fishing

('000 metric tons, live weight)

	1980	1981	1982
Total catch	60.2	57.5	62.8

Source: Banque Centrale de Tunisie, quaoting Ministere de l'Agriculture (Dir·-ction de la Peche).

Mining

('000 Metric tons)

	1980	1981	1982
Iron ore*	390	396	274
Lead concentrates*	14.2	9.7	8.6
Calcium phosphate*	4,502	4,924	4,729
Zinc concentrates	16.3	14.1	15.2
Crude petroleum	5,627	5,407	5,146
Natural gas (million cu m)	354.9	388.1	422.8
Salt (unrefined)	316	430	407

Source: Institut National de la Statistique.

* Figures refer to the gross weight of ores and concentrates. The metal content (in '000 metric tons) was: Iron 211 in 1980, 211 in 1981; Lead 8.8 in 1980, 6.0 in 1981; Zinc 9.0 in 1980, 7.8 in 1981.

Industry

Selected Products

		1980	1981	1982
Superphosphates (16%)	'000 metric tons	66.3	61.2	39.9
Superphosphates (45%0	'000 metric tons	610.9	616.9	607.8
Phosphoric acid	'000 metric tons	474.5	453.0	506.2
Cement	'000 metric tons	1,751.9	1,751.9	1,833.8
Lead	'000 metric tons	19.2	17.5	15.1
Electric power (production by Societe Tunisienne d'Electricite et de Gaz)	million kWh	2,429.2	2,677.7	2,738.0
Electric power (other producers)	million kWh	368.0	342.3	435.5
Town gas	'000 cu m	25,056	25,300	26,500
Beer	'000 hl	322.8	323	357
Cigarettes	million	4,419	3,965	6,016
Wine	'000 hl	618	556	513
Olive oil	'000 metric tons	85	145	85
Semolina	'000 metric tons	325.1	340.3	350.1
Flour	'000 metric tons	376.8	402.6	419.6
Refined sugar	'000 metric tons	60.8	58.1	45.6
Crude steel	'000 metric tons	177.9	173.0	104.9
Lime	'000 metric tons	528.8	465.8	470.6
Petrol	'000 metric tons	160.6	174.3	187.2
Kerosene	'000 metric tons	115.2	122.8	118.5
Diesel oil	'000 metric tons	439.2	722.9	405.3
Fuel oil	'000 metric tons	617.4	623.9	532.3

Source: Institut National de la Statistique.

233

EXTERNAL TRADE

Principal Commodities ('000 dinars)

Imports	1980	1981	1982[*]
Wheat and meslin (unmilled)	62,795	54,400	91,113
Sugar (raw and refined)	30,569	41,300	24,022
Soybean oil	16,896	17,700	13,866
Crude petroleum	126,710	205,400	51,139
Petroleum products	131,226	n.a.	n.a.
Pharmaceutical products	24,429	28,200	35,173
Wood	32,194	23,600	39,295
Raw cotton, cotton yarn and fabrics	32,090	12,600[+]	11,200[+]
Plastics and products	34,542	35,000	38,784
Iron and steel	118,810	n.a.	157,543
Machinery (non-electric)	154,366	n.a.	276,338
Electric machinery	65,670	n.a.	97,689
Tractors	14,539	24,500	29,813
Road motor vehicles	1,738	89,900	n.a.
Aircraft and air equipment	557	n.a.	n.a.
Optical and scientific equipment	16,644	26,100	29,149
Total	1,427,400	1,907,379	2,008,054

[*] Provisional figures. [+] Raw cotton only.
Source: Institut National de la Statistique.

Exports	1980	1981	1982[*]
Fresh fruit	12,565	24,100	13,613
Olive oil	24,984	50,100	56,652
Wine	3,114	4,200	4,081
Natural phosphates	19,959	20,600	24,267
Cruse petroleum	449,978	624,800	492,937
Phosphoric acid	42,766	57,600	58,545
Superphosphates	40,314	54,100	48,468
Cotton fabrics	11,242	11,100	11,752
Clothing and accessories	108,039	119,800	152,997
Iron and steel	2,233	n.a.	8,192
Refined lead	5,004	3,900	4,455
Total	904,821	1.233,971	1,168,215

Principal Trading Partners ('000 dinars)

Imports	1980	1981	1982
Belgium/Luxembourg	38,566	43,700	51,007
Brazil	12,504	21,600	20,883
Canada	26,265	45,500	56,039
France	349,639	453,300	521,554
Germany, Federal Republic	141,970	171,700	231,270
Greece	77,512	96,100	66,385
Italy	219,452	274,000	296,950
Netherlands	34,279	56,500	101,990
Poland	8,874	49,100	18,921
Saudi Arabia	108,161	17,200	50,497
Spain	46,615	206,700	81,997
Sweden	15,254	60,700	21,407
USSR	11,270	26,300	10,584
United Kingdom	27,740	21,600	4,166
USA	79,770	34,800	157,284
Yugoslavia	9,352	140,700	18,901
Total (incl. others)	1,427,400	1,907,379	2,008,054

Source: Banque Centrale de Tunisie, quoting Institut National de la Statistique.

Exports	1980	1981	1982
Algeria	15,743	24,200	13,726
Belgium/Luxembourg	26,356	30,700	40,796
Brazil	739	3,800	n.a.
Bulgaria	2,413	2,900	6,229
Czechoslovakia	2,788	7,700	4,672
France	136,137	218,900	226,006
Germany, Federal Republic	114,413	100,700	121,709
Greece	163,907	100,100	31,716
Italy	142,603	254,200	189,530
Libya	7,432	54,500	45,704
Netherlands	39,938	24,400	27,774
Spain	3,914	4,500	14,157
Switzerland	2,258	29,700	10,700
Turkey	10,338	7,500	11,507
USSR	2,163	6,100	1,886
United Kingdom	12,770	214,700	3,042
USA	130,112	6,900	268,840
Total (incl. others)	904,821	1,233,971	1,168,215

TOURISM

Foreign Tourist Arrivals By Nationality ('000)

	1980	1981	1982
Algeria	422.5	896.5	155.8
Austria	35.7	40.0	32.6
Belgium	39.8	36.4	32.5
France	365.9	378.1	360.9
Germany, Federal Republic	307.0	327.9	299.0
Italy	68.2	71.6	64.7
Libya	4.2	13.5	88.0
Netherlands	39.8	36.4	33.9
Scandinavia	54.9	47.5	42.8
∪witzerland	38.7	41.1	45.6
United Kingdom	144.2	150.7	100.4
USA	9.6	10.3	10.3
Total (incl. others)	1,602.1	2,151.0	1,355.2

Tourist beds: 68,843 in 1979; 71,529 in 1980.
Tourist nights: 12,017,016 in 1979; 12,792,378 in 1980.
Tourist spending (million dinars): 219.2 in 1979; 259.7 in 1980.

Source: Office National du Tourisme, Tunis.

EDUCATION

Institutions		
Primary	2,937	3,074
Secondary	297	326
University of Tunis	1	1
Teachers		
Primary	30,186	33,546
Secondary	16,000	17,500
University of Tunis	4,600	4,106
Pupils		
Primary	1,142,060	1,201,645
Secondary	328,250	378,349
University of Tunis	29,640	29,573

Source: Ministere de l'Education Nationale.

236

CHAPTER 11

ALGERIA

Territorially, Algeria is the largest of the five countries that comprise North Africa. It is the second largest country in the continent, after Sudan. It has an area of 919,595 square miles and a 620 mile shoreline that is washed by Mediterranean waters. Tunisia and Libya are located on its eastern border. Morocco is on its western side and Mauritania, Mali and Niger are on its Saharan southern borders. So far its problem with Morocco over the Western Sahara is not yet solved. Another minor problem considering its boundary line, is with Tunisia over the southwestern Tunisian boundary lines.

The three countries of northwest Africa, Tunisia, Algeria and Morocco, are collectively called Al Maghreb Al Aqsa (the Far West), because of their location as Arabic speaking Islamic countries in the far western part of that cultural realm. They are also called Djeziret El Mahgreb (the Western Isle), in recognition of the Atlas region as an island lcoated between the Mediterranean Sea on the north and the great Sea of Sand of the Sahara in the south. The Arabic name for Algeria, El Djezair, may have been derived from the rocky islands along the coast line, which have constituted a danger to ships approaching the harbors.

From a generally geographical viewpoint, Algeria is made up of two parts: the north that comprises the Atlas region with its high chain of mountains, the plateaux, the coastal plain, the valleys (where most of the population live and which contain all the fertile farmland), and the cities and the ports, sometimes referred to as Algeria proper; and the south which is the desert region, a part of the western Sahara but has valuable oil, natural gas, and other minerals.

The geometrical boundary lines of Algeria, like those of Libya, Egypt, Tunisia, and Morocco, and other desert countries are due to the lack of physical or ethnic features and the lack of population in desert regions. The relatively large area of Algeria, especially its extension in the Sahara may be explained in the light of the fact that France, the former colonial power that drew and demarketed the boundary lines of Algeria, was considering it as a part of France itself; and since all the neighbors of Algeria, with the

238

exception of Libya, were under direct French control, France expanded the area of Algeria to its present boundary lines.

The Atlas Mountain System in Algeria, as well as its extension westward in Morocco and eastward in Tunisia, is a part of the great Alpine System that extends in Eruope and Asia. They came into existance during the third geological era, Tertiary. They consist of maritime sedimentary rock that were deposited beneath an ancestral Mediterranean Sea. These rocks were folded, fractured, and upfolded. Their rather young age makes them unstable and liable to severe earthquakes. El Asnasam was devastated two times, in 1954 and 1980.

The Atlas System in Algeria forms two major chains that extend generally from west to east, and in between them is a high plateau. Along the Mediterranean Sea coast, and separated from it only by a narrow and discontinuous coastal plain, is the northern chain, the Tell Atlas. It is a complex series of mountains and valleys. The several mountain ranges, massifs, and plateaux vary in height from 1,600 feet to 7,500 feet and are separated from one another by deep valleys and gorges that divide the region into self-contained topographic and economic units. Examples of such ranges and massifs are: Mts. des Traras, separated from the main Chain by the Tafna River: the Oran (Ouahran) massif, separated from the Mts. Du Tessale by the plain and Sebkha of Oran; the Mebtoub River, separates the Du Tessaa from the main chain. The Dahara chain, that runs along the coast, dissected by many small rivers that run to the sea, is separated from the Masif de L'Ourarsenis by the Cheliff River Valley, the highest peak in the Dahra is Djebel Bou Maad. In the central part of the Mititdja Plain that surrounds Algiers (El Djezair), the capital, is an enclosed basin that lies between the Tell Mountains and the sea. In the east the important chains anD massifs are the Grande KabyliE massif aNd Djurdjura chain, separtated from the Little Kabylie (Petite Kabylie) by the Soummam River. The Plain of Annaba (Bone) is another enclosed plain open to the sea and surrounded by the Tell Mountains.

South of the Tell Atlas is the High Plateaux of the Shotts[1]. They are extremely monotonous expansions of thick alluvium. Their name is derived from the presence of several saline mud flats, known as shotts, which are the result of internal drainage. The Plateaux, which have the average height of 3,100 feet and an average width of 90 miles, gradually narrow and fall in height

eastward to end in Shott el Hodna, a large enclosed
depression, its floor is only 1,200 feet above
sea-level. Other important basins in the plateaux are
Shott Gharbi and Shott ech Chergui on the western part,
and Zahrez Chergui, Zahrez Rharbi and Garaet et Tarf on
the central part. During rainy periods water
accumulates in these shottts to form extensive shallow
lakes which give way as the water is absorbed and
evaporated to saline mud flats and brackish swamps.
Some ridges project through the thick mantle of
alluvium, breaking the monotony of the level horizons.
The most important of these ridges in the western part
are Monts de Tlemcen, Monts de Daia, Djebel Antar, and
Djebel Alleg. In the east where the two Atlas chains,
the Tell and Saharan, approach each other so closely,
these ridges are numerous. In fact the Plateaux Region,
which is an important topographic feature of western
Algeria, is virtualy absent here.[2]

The Saharan Atlas are lower than the Tell Atlas and
appear to be in a more advance stage of erosion. Viewed
from the air they look buried in their own debris.
Those chains of mountains are also more broken than the
coastal chains and present no hard barrier to communication between the Shotts Plateaux and the Sahara.
They comprise several massifs and mountian chains such
as the Ksour, Amour, Auled Nail, Zuban, and Aures. The
Aures is the most spectacular chain in all the Algerian
mountain system and includes the highest peak in the
country, Djebel Chelia, which is 7,640 feet high. The
relief of the Aures is very bold, with narow gorges cut
between sheer cliffs surmounted by steep, bare slopes.
And to the east and north of the Hodna depression, its
ridges merge with the southern folds of the Tell Atlas.

South of the Saharan Atlas, the country extends for
over 950 miles into the heart of the western Sahara.
Structually, that vast desert, that extends across the
whole northern part of the continent, consists of a
resistant platform of geologically ancient rocks against
which the Atlas system were folded. Although most of
the relief is slight, there are some regional variations
in the desert surface. There are several plateaux, such
as Eglab, Tademait, and Tassilian-Ajjer, rising above
vast spreads of hamads, regs, and ergs. The most important of the hamads are: Hamada du Dra, Hamada Tounassine
in the west and Hamada de Tinrhert in the east. The
vastest expanses of mobile sand dunes that form the ergs
(seas of sands) are the Great West Erg (Grand Erg
Occidental) and the Great Eastern Erg (Grand Erg
Oriental) that extends in southern Tunisia and western

Libya. The Admer (Erg d-Admen) extends southward in the southern neighboring country of Niger. Erg Iabes separates the Tademait Plateau from the Eglab. The Gourara Reg and the Tanzrouft Reg are the vastest gravel expanses in the Sahara.

The great massif of Ahaggar (Hogggar) lies in the southeast and rises to an altitude of more than 9,570 feet. The erosion of its volcanic and other crystalline rocks has produced a lunar landscape of extreme ruggedness. Mount Asekram and Mout Tahat are the highest two peaks in the Ahagger. Southward form the Ahaggar the massisfs of Adrar des Iforas and Air extend across the Algerian boundary line into the southern neighboring countires of Mali and Niger.

Another important topographic feature of the Sahara is the huge desert depression, located southeast of the Saharan Atlas and extending eastward across the boundary line in neighboring Tunisia, where it is occupied by Shott Djerid and Shott el Rharsa. In Algeria the deeper part of the depression is occupied by several Shotts: the largest of them is Shott (Chott) Melrhir (it is about 100 feet below sea-level) and Shott Me Rounne, which lies southwest of Shott Melrhir.

Due to climatic conditions and the long, dry season that lasts for four months on the coastal plain and the northern slopes of the Tell Atlas, and as a result of low and uneven rainfall combined with high rates of evaporation especially during the hot, summer months, the rivers of the Tell are short and suffer large variations in flow. Most of these rivers dry out completely during the summer season and are only full for short periods following heavy winter rain. The longest semi-perennially flowing river is the Cheliff that rises in the High Shotts Plateaux and crosses the Tell Atlas to reach the Mediterranean east of Oran (Ouahran). There are no permanent rivers south of the Tell Atlas due to the prevalence of semi-arid and arid conditions. Any surface run-off following rain is carried by hundreds of temporary watercourses toward local depressions, such as the shotts or straight to desert where the water sinks in the sand, or it may form sebkha (small salty likes - like the shotts) such as Sebkha Mekerrhane, Sebkha Azzal Matri, and Sebkha de Tindouf. Many watercourses rise in the Ahaggar, due to its relatively high altitude and its ability to catch some moisture. Some of these watercourses are so deep and their floors are covered with alluvium, the geomorphologists believe beyond any doubt that they

241

formed during the pluvial phase of the Quaternary. Archaelogical studies, in particular those of flora, fauna, and cave-paintings, have revealed flourishing prehistoric periods.

Oases are important features of the Sahara; some of them have developed into substantial settlements, after the French succeeeded in drilling deeper artesian wells. Most of these oases lie along the foot of the Saharan Atlas such as Biskra, Tolga, Laghouat, Ain Safra, Figuig, and Colomb-Bechar. Other oases are located along underground watercourses such as Touggourt, Ouargla, El Golea, Timimoun, and Ain. There are some other oases in the valleys of Ahaggar mountains and around its slopes. The most important of them is Tamanrasset. Some of these oases are rather small in size with little economic significance or used as watering stations for the nomadic inhabitants whose camels manage to find sustenance from the meager stands of grass and bush scattered through this dry harsh environment.

There are some locations that had no importance at all until the findings and large-scale production of oil and natural gas. Typical are Hassi Messaoud, Hassi R'Mel, Hasi Keskessa, and Nezla. The oil production made these locations places of utmost economic importance for Algeria and the Algerians.

CLIMATE

In general there are three climatic regions in Algeria: the Mediterranean Region, that includes the coastal plain and the Tell Atlas; the Steppe Region (a transitional zone), on the Shotts High Platea; and the Desert Region, south of the Saharan Atlas.

"Mediterranean" type climatic conditions with wet, warm winters and hot, dry summers prevail in the north, but rainfall varies in amount from over 40 inches annually on some coastal mountains to less than 15 inches in areas located in rain shadow locations. In fact, the region's varied relief creates several and different local climates that differ widely in degrees of warmth and moisture. Skikda (Philipville) is receiving 32.9 inches, Annaba (Bone) 31.0 inches, Algeris 27.3 inches, Tiencen 21.5 inches, and Bou Sfer 15.5, all along the Mediterranean coast but receiving different amounts of rain. Most of the rain falls in the winter season when depressions associated with the

242

westerlies   pass   across   the   Mediterranean   most
frequently.   The   dry   season   lasts   from   three   to   four
months.

Towards   the   interior   on   the   High   Plateau   the   Ain
Aflou   is   receiving   13.4   inches,   Telergma   12.2   inches,
and   Lekreider   8.2   inches.   South   of   the   Saharan   Atlas
the   desert   conditions   prevail,   and   the   rainfall   becomes
of   little   or   no   economic   value.   Biskara   and   Laghouaton,
at   the   foot   of   the   chains,   receive   5.8   inches   and   6.7
inches,   respectively,   Colomb-Bishar   3.5   inches,   Elgolea
2.0   inches,   Tindoff   1.4   inches,   and   In   Saleh   0.9   inches.
However,   this   limited   amount   of   rainfall   is   very
irregular   and   often   torrential.   A   fall   of   one,   two,   or
even   three   inches   in   one   day   may   be   followed   by   several
years   of   absolute   drought.

The   winter   temperatures   are   warm   along   the
Mediterranean   coast,   but   on   the   Plateaux   they   go   down
below   the   freezing   points.   The   absolute   minimum
recorded   in   Skikda   is 35°F,   in   Algiers 32°F,   in   Telergma
22°F,   and   in   Aflou 18°F.   In   the   desert   extreme
temperatures   are   normal;   Laghouat   recorded 16°F   in
January   and 120° in   July.   Both   In   Slah   and   El   Golea,   in
the   heart   of   the   Algerian   Sahara,   recorded 25°F   in
January   and 121°F   in   July.   Even   Tamanrasset,   south   of
the   Tropic   of   Cancer,   recorded 20°F   in   January.

The   Chehili,   southerly,   sandy,   hot   wind   blowing
from   the   Sahara   (like   the   Khamasin   of   Egypt   and   the
Gibli   of   Libya)   scorches   the   coastal   area   for   about   25
days   every   summer,   and   its   frequency   increases   to   about
40   days   on   the   Plateau.   Its   effect   is   hard   on   crops   and
vegetation;   unable   to   withstand   the   intensity   of
transpiration,   they   may   wither   and   die   within   a   short
time.   The   Chehili   is   even   harder   in   the   Sahara   where
the   high   temperatures   are   combined   with   very   violent
sandstorms.

These   Sahara   conditions   are   quiet   in   contrast   with
the   Tell   Atlas   that   are   ice   capped,   and   their   higher
slopes   are   snow   covered   in   winter.   In   some   of   their
isolated   parts   that   escaped   deforestation,   there   are
relatively   thick   soils,   podzols   on   sandstones,   and   terra
rossa,   and   rendzinas   on   limestone.   They   support   forests
of   Aleppo   pines,   cork-oaks,   and   evergreen   oaks.
However,   the   lower,   more   accessible   slopes   are
over-grazed,   deforestated,   and   in   some   few   cases
over-cultivated,   have   eroded   soils,   or   have   thin   soil
and   are   partly   covered   with   scrub   growth   of   thuya,
juniper,   and   various   drought-resistant   shrubs.   Only   a

243

few remnants survive of the once dense and extensive forests of Atlas cedar, which have been exploited for timber and fuel since ancient times. Those are found mainly above 4,700 feet in the eastern Tell Atlas.

South of the Tell Atlas there is no woodland except in the higher and more moist parts of the Saharan Atlas, especially on the northern windward slopes. However, most of these areas have been destroyed by the depredations of nomadic flocks; consequently, bush vegetation of the maquis and garrigue is very common.

In the Steppe Region of the Shotts Plateau (where the rainfall is usually around 10 inches, the soils are thin, light-colored, and humus deficient, and the sparce vegetation is dominated by esparto grass and artemisias, with jujube-trees and dwarf palms along the wadis. On the uncultivable saline soils around the edges of the sebkhas and shotts, saltbush is common. The extensive waterways, which may on very rare occasions carry some surface water, mark the lines of underground streams, and sparse lines of vegetation growing on their beds. Long rooted shrubs and course wiry grasses offer some rough pastures for camels, and few areas (mostly the ergs) are completlty dispised by the desert nomads.

These hard desert conditions are reflected in the pattern into which the populations are divided into settled cultivators who live in the oases, dependent on permanent supplies of underground water; nomads, who make use of the sparse and temporary pasture, and the very new comers, who work in the oil and natural gas fields.

ECONOMY AND DEVELOPMENT

France colonized Algeria to make it a part of France. It followed a ruthless policy of expropriation and expulsion that deprived the natives form their land and drove them to areas that could not support them. As a result, tens of thousands of Europeans (not only French, but also some Italians, Spaniards, and Greeks) settled on the best of the Algerian farm land of the coastal plain and the Tell.³ Others came to the Algerian cities and in the process these cities witnessed another transformation. The crowded old ciites (medinas) with their narrow, winding lanes and alleys, and crowded bazars, could not accomodate the European influx, and; therefore, new modern towns, adjacent to the old, were built. Consequently, not only the modern commerical agriculture was in the hands of the European settlers, but also manufacturing activities, mining, business, trade, professions, and all aspects of the modern development econonmy. In fact, the part of Algeria that was really a part of France was the productive part, and the economic sector that became a part of the French economy was the developed sector, and the part of the population that enjoyed the same standard of French life were the European settlers.

The nationalists who led the country to independence discovered the economic plight of the country as soon as they got control of the government. Aside from their own struggle for power, their different ideologies, and the loss of more than one million Algerians during the war, they were faced by formidable economic problems. The European settlers, about one million, representing all the technicians, physicians, teachers skilled workers, landowners and business men, had left the country. Farms, factories, shops, offices, hospitals and schools had closed, leaving more than 70% of the population unemployed. Public buildings, records, farm and factory equipment had been destroyed, and the investments had been taken out.

Against this background of political, soical and economic difficulties, the country's natural and human resources enabled it to survive and to make good progress. The coastal plain, thanks to the efforts of the former French settlers, is very productive. Mineral resources are abundant and revenues from oil and natural gas exports are used to finance ambitious development plans. The Algerians, living abroad (mainly in France) and numbering almost one million, are helping the country indirectly, not only by decreasing the number of unemployed and relieving the country's budget from their problems, but by sending remittances to their families in Algeria. Real and honest efforts of the governments to improve the country's economy, inspite of the fact that many mistakes have been made, have achieved considerable success.[4]

Since independence, Algeria's government planned to build a socialist society through economic growth. They have nationalized all the foreign compaines or have taken controlling interest in them. The unoccupied land, that was deserted by the French settlers, was taken over. All banks, financial institutions, and insurance companies were also nationalized. In 1971 all the petroleum and natural gas companines were taken over

245

by the government. The newly introduced heavy
industries, engineering industries, chemicals,
petrochemical, and energy, were state run. However, in
order to increase productin and distribution of consumer
goods. The economic policy allows controlled expansion
of the "non-exploitative" private sector. This sector
is working mostly in consumer oriented light industries,
especially textiles, leather, food processing and retail
distrubution. More than 5,000 light industrial firms
are owned and run by the private sector. They employ
about 60,000 people.

In 1982 a new investment code was declared to
introduce a degree of liberalism and decentralization in
the economy that would help to improve efficiency and
increase productivity. Private savings and business in
"nonstrategic" fields like shops, bars restaurants,
housing, hotels, handcrafts and some light industries,
were encouraged. Private joint ventures "societes
mixtes" are given incentives through tax exemption;
however, the code made it clear that these joint
ventures should exist for only fifteen years, and the
government also has split up about 93 of the giant state
corporations into smaller untis. Some import procedures
were simplified and relaxed, while exports were given
more indirect subsidies.

During the 1970's the Algerian government, in order
to build up the country's economy and increase the GNP,
followed an economic and financial policy based on three
principles: revenues from hydrocarbon are the key to
development and progress; first priority was given to
heavy and engineering industries and chemicals and a
high degree of austerity, with storng ties placed on
imports of "luxury and consumer" goods. The first
Four-Year Plan sector, involving the hydrocarbon, iron
and steel, chemical, and engineering industries, had
around 34,000 million Algerian dinars invested. The
plan achieved a 9% annual growth rate. In the second
plan for 1974-77 the investments reached 110,000 (as a
result of the very high and abrupt rise in oil prices).
The heavy industry had the lion share with allocations
of 45.5% of the total expenditures; infrastructure got
14%, social services and housing combined got 13.3%,
while industry and construction provided 55.5%. The
investments in the 1980-84 Five-Year Plan were 400,600
million dinars. The concentration was still on
industry, but there was a shift in emphasis from heavy
industry to light industry, especially those that
produced food and consumer goods. However, more

246

investments were alocated for education, health services, housing and agriculture.

In 1984, President Chadli made it clear that heavy industry will not have the first priority in the following development plans: revitalizing agriculture and consumer oriented industries and manufacturing that would employ more people, will get most of the government's encouragement and attention. The per capita income by the end of the plan in 1984 reached a record high of about 1,500 American dollars or 7,500 dinars, second only to Libya in all North Africa.

The difficulty with the development plans of the 1970's and early 1980's was that inspite of the fact that it laid a strong foundation for industrialization and raised the GNP of the country, it failed to create enough jobs for an increasing population and a labor force of which 20% is unemployed, inspite of the fact that there are more than one million working abroad. These plans also did not give the deserved attention for agriculture and developing the rural parts of the country where 56% of the population live.

Although Algeria is rich in oil and natural gas and has a considerable wealth of minerals, it faces a hard uphill struggle just to preserve the economic staus quo, let alone improve the social and standard of living of most of the population and reduce the costly imports of food and other goods. The main reason is the same everywehre in the countries of North Africa and the rest of the developing world, the continuing high growth rate of population.

An important component of the Algerian economic policy is the diverisification of its revenue resources. In 1984 the government began to encourage the growth of nonhydrocarbon exports, especially agriculture produce, other minerals and manufactured goods. That accounted for only 2% of the total exports. In fact, Algeria is diverisfying its production and exports of the hydrocarbon, sales of refined oil prodcuts, condensates and natural gas, which has helped the country to overcome the slump of crude oil prices and the surplus of oil in world markets.

AGRICULTURE

Algeria is mainly an agricultural country; 56% of the population live in the rural areas of the country,

247

and more than 42% of the Algerian work force is employed in agrcirulture. However, agriculture accounts for only 7.0% to 7.5% of the GNP. From 1962, the year of independence, to 1970, the year of applying the first development plan, agriucultural output was falling by an annual average of 1.6% which was due to the departure of the Eruopean landowners. During the 1970's and the early 1980's the output decline was at a rate of 8.7% yearly, and that was due mainly to the negligence of agriculture in the successive development plans in favor of industry, especillay heavy industry. Although the allocation for agriculutural development in 1980-84 was doubled compared to its share in the 1974-77 plan, in relative terms these allocations dropped from 11% to about 5% of total investments in the plan. This negligence and decline was happening, inspite of the fact that all the Algerian development planners and economists were aware that food scarcity has been an acute problem and that the cost of importing food was climbing sharply every year. In 1969 the deficiency in food production was 27%, and in 1983 it rose to 77%. It is estimated that the 1985-89 plan will allocate about 20% of the total investment for agriculture. Giving more attention to agriculture is the government's aim to increase the selfsufficiency to about 80% by the year 2,000, to decrease the cost of food imports that reached more than 2,500 million American dollars annually since 1979. An important goal is to improve living conditions and to create more employment opportunities in the rural areas, not only to decrease unemployment and underemployment but to stem the continuous drift of population especially of the young people to the main cities. It is estimated that about 100,000 peasants migrate yearly to the towns seeking jobs. The World Bank estimates that the urban population is growing by 5.7% to 6.6% yearly since 1962.

In order to achieve these goals, investments alone will not be enough. The plan is to improve the rural environment, rural housing, and electrification, as well as direct agricultural services. As an incentive for the rural poulation to keep the earnings and wages of the farmers and farm workers in the countryside, the young people especially should be raised to be closely related to those of the their industrial counterparts.

The new plan is also initiating a major program for irrigation, building dams to store water, and to decrease flood destruction and drilling water wells to make better use of ground water.

To help apply these new ideas and enhance
agricultural development, a new bank was setup "Banque
d'Agricultue et Development Rurale" (BADR). The
specific job of the bank is to serve the rural sector
and to help in improving the output of farms, whether
socialist, state owned, or private. The bank started in
1982 by a heavy lending drive to farmers who liked to
get involved in poultry farming in order to make Algeria
self-sufficient in eggs and chickens.

The government took another two steps of some
significance. It relaxed price controls on agricultural
produce, allowing farmers to sell directly to markets or
private vendors and across province (wilaya) boundaries.
The government is also encouraging private, small-scale
farmers by supplying equipments, loans, seeds, and
fertilizers in order to increase prodcutivity.

More than 90% of the 920,000 square miles, which is
the total area of Algeria, is arid plateaux, mountains,
or desert supporting only scattered herds of sheep,
goats, or camels. The intensively cultivated land lies
almost exclusively in the plains of the Mediterranean
zone, especially the Mitidja Plain south of Algiers and
the Chelif Plain near Oran. These are about 18 million
acres of cultivable land representing less than 1.9
acres per rural inhabitant.

Modern commerical agriculture started in Algeria
when the Europeans started to immigrate to Algeria. The
French colonial authority did not only expel the natives
from the arable land but gave the Europeans all the
encouragement, facilites and subsidies that enabled them
to turn the land to highly productive farms that made
agriucltural produce the main source of GNP and the most
important exports. The settlers greatly extended
cultivation on these plains and the adjacent sloping
hillsides on which they built the famous terraces by
conquering two problems, malaria and drainage, by using
modern science and technologies. The plains are
normally separated from the Mediterranean Sea with
highland, and without well-organized drainage systems
they become waterlogged an a good environment for
malaria. The French government built some irrigation
projects as well as some dams that serve both irrigation
purposes as well as flood prevention. These projects
are irrigating about 525,000 acres or only 3% of the
cultivated land. The main dams in the western region
are: Beni Bahdal Dam, the Sherufa Dam, Sarno Dam, Bou
Hanifia Dam, and Fergoug Dam. In the central region:
The Fodda, Bakhadda, Hamiz Bakhadda, and Gharib Dams.

249

In the eastern region there are the Zardezas, the Dsob, and the Foum el Gueiss Dams. In the interior the Biskara, Foum el Guezra, and the Shott esh Shergui (Chott ech Cbergai) are irrigation projects depending on undergournd water pumped mechanically.

Unfortunately, the Algerian government did not try to expand the irrigated area or the building of any drainage systems or flood prevention dams. Lately it is hoped that more dams and irrigation projects will be built, since the new economic policy is giving "absolute priority" for agriculture.[5]

One of the socio-political aspects of agriuclture that the government gave it the highest priority since the day of independence, was the "Land Reform Policy". The policy was a practiced application for the principles of nationalism and socialism that the government had adopted. Between 1962 and 1966 the government expropriated all the lands that were owned by the French. These lands were turned into state farms managed and run by workers' committes (comites de gestion). These state farms accounted for 40% of the cultivable land in the county. The workers' committees that managed the land, under the supervision of the government, used the same modern agricultural and technical methods that the French used. The revenues from those farms are almost twice that of the traditional private sector, but they employ only 135,000 permanent workers and 100,000 seasonal workers, while the private sector provides a living for more than five million people. In 1972 the government took another step by distributing about 1.5 million acres, that were owned by Algerian large landowners, among 60,000 peasants. In 1979 a further step was taken by forcing absenteee landowners either to cultivate their land or to hand it over to peasant farmers. The new small landowners (or land-users) had to join an agricultural cooperative. By 1973 more than 6,000 cooperatives of various kinds have been set up in many rural areas. In 1980 another one million more acres, taken from large farm owners, were distributed among the peasants.

The government, in order to improve both agriculture and the rural environment, started in 1981 to redistribute livestock among herdsmen grazing their animals on 50 million acres of steppeland on the Shotts Plateau. It is reported that more than 175,000 breeds of cows have been redistrubuted. The government also began building "socialist villages". By the end of 1981, 340 of these villages were completed. The program was to build 1,700 villages that would have 140,000 peasant families.

One of the physical problem facing agriculture in Algeria is rainfall that varies from floods to droughts and their enormous effects on the crops, the economy and population. The government, in the 1985-89 plan, is allocating considerable investments to build several irrigation and flood control schemes that would decrease the effects of this problem. In fact since almost all the rivers and the watercourses in Algeria are seasonal and small, these projects are not very costly. The other physical problem is soil erosion, and this shoud be handled through educating the farmers and through the usage of more advanced technical methods in agriuclture. The main cultural problem facing crop improvement is to give more incentives to the farmers to produce more.

Wheat and barley are among the very important crops in Algeria and the most needed. They are grown on the coastal plain, especially in the areas of Steif, Annaba, Constantine, and Tianet. The production fluctuates considerably from 1.2 million to 1.7 million metric tons a year for the wheat, and from 700,000 to 800,000 metrics tons yearly for the barley. The fluctuation is largely due to the amount of rain and its timing. The yields are low compared to the European, American, or even the other countries of north Africa. The ministry of agriculture, aware of this fact, started in 1980 to introduce new seeds and increase fertilization. In 1982 the wheat prodcution was 1.2 million metric tons, compared to 1.51 metric tons in 1980, and barley, too, fell to 650,000 metric tons in 1982 from 800,000 in 1980. Grains, especially wheat and flour, are imported yearly mostly from France, Canada and the U.S.A.

Grapes are grown in the coastal areas as well as on the low slopes of the Tell Atlas where terraces were built. Although vines have been grown since ancient history for local consumptoin, it was the French settlers who expanded the area under grapes and introduced new wine producing species. Wines became the most important export at that time. Although wines still represent an important agricultural export, the government regards agricultural dependence on wine compatible with real political independence. It replaced the less productive vines with grains, dairy farming and forestry. In 1978 vines occupied 500,000 acres compared to less than 300,000 acres in 1982. However, in 1982-83 the government sought to increase wine production, especially of better quality since the prices in the world market are rising.

Olives are grown mainly in the western coastal areas and in the Kabyles where rainfall is relatively less and the soil is relatively thin. It is the nature of the olive tree that the crop fluctuates. In 1983 the crop hit the record of 160,000 metric tons compared to 90,000 metric tons in 1982 and 140,000 metric tons in 1980. Olive oil is still an important item of agricultural exports as well as of agricultural production. Olive oil production in 1983 reached a record high of 16,000 metric tons, recovering from a low of only 9,000 metric tons in 1982.

Sugar beets prodcution, mostly grown on state farms, has almost doubled in 1983. It reached 94,000 metric tons, a jump from 49,000 in 1980. Potatoes for home consumption are also increasing in both acreage and production, as well as a large variety of dried vegetables (pulses).

Citrus fruits are grown mostly on state farms and 70% of the crop is exported. Total production varies between 400,000 and 500,000 tons. Dates are mostly produced in the oases, and the production has an average of 200,000 tons, but most of it is for home consumption.

Tobacco is an important crop for industry. The production is about 2,500 tons, and the tobacco industry is employing about 13,000 workers.

Since 1980 the government is trying to increase meat and poultry production, but special attention is given to the production of poultry and eggs. It looks like the government is exclaiming its efforts in the 1985-89 plan to keep its promise of increasing food production.

Algeria has about 1.4 million head of cattle, moslty on the coastal plain. It has more than 8 million sheep and 2.9 million goats. Most of these are on the steep area of the Shotts Plateau. The 1985-89 development plan is to improve the quality by importing new breeds of animals to meet the requirments of a growing population of meat and dairy products. Large amounts of both are imported.

The new plan allocated more capital to increase the fishing fleet and to improve the fisheries. Total fish catch in 1982 was 64,000 tons. The effort is to increase it by 25%-30% by 1989.

Forests that were covering the Tell Atlas were eliminated from most of the region, and even during the last two decades the problem became more critical, not only for forests as a very important natural resource, but because the decline in the areas that were covered by forestry led to soil erosion and a loss of valuable cultivable land. The government, awaking to the serious problem, planned to reforestize about 1,200,000 acres in the 1980-84 development plan. The major forestry project that the Algerian government is trying to complete. is to grow a vast "green wall" of pines, cypresses and eucalyptus 12 miles wide, along 10,000 miles on the norhtern edge of the Sahara from the Tunisian to the Moroccan border. The main purpose is to stop the steady northward encroachment of the desert. Work began in 1975 and was supposed to be completed before the year 2,000. It involves about 100,000 acres as well as building reservoirs, drilling wells and constructing roads. The project is behind schedule and encounters numerous problems, especially it proved to be more expensive than was expected. Eventually the project will be completed and will be the first world experience applied on a large scale to arrest desertification.

HYDROCARBONS

The findings of hydrocarbons in Algeria has been a major factor in the determination of its political status and economic conditions. Petroleum was discovered and produced on commercial scale in 1958 at the time when Algerians were launching their war for independence. During the hard and long negotiations between the French governments and the nationalists, France tried to partition the country to Algeria proper that would be granted independence and to Sahara where the oil resources are existing, that would be under a form of French control. The nationalists opposed that movement, and the French tried again to put the Sahara under joint control, under a Franco-Algerian government. Again the French failed, and Algeria as a whole became independent. Since the first day of independence, the Algerian government tried to get control on its oil fields and oil production. The Algerians looked at the French control of the oil industry as a symbol and a part of the former French control and as economic colonization of Algeria.

253

The main producers of the Algerian petroleum before independence were the two French companies, Campagnie Francaise de Petroles (CFB) and Entreprise des Recherches et d'activities Petrolieres (ERAP). The American compaines of Phillips, Elwearth, and Shell were also participating in the production but on a smaller scale. In 1963 the government established its own company, Societe Nationale pour La Recherche, La Production, Le Transport, La Transformation et La Commercialisation des Hydrocarbures (SONATRACH). The company started by building a pipeline from Hassi Messaoud to a new terminal at Azrew on the coast. The pipeline started carrying oil in 1966.

In 1970 the negotiations between the American companies and the government failed to reach agreement. The companies' interests were nationalized, and SONATRACH took over those interests. Since the American share in the industry was relativley limited, the nationalization did not cause Algeria political or economic harm.

The problem was harder with the French companies, who were at the time responsible for most of the country's production and who were in a special position under the Algerian-French Agreement signed in Evia. However, a serious dispute about the prices erupted between the French companies and the government. The Algerians politically were very sensitive, picked the chance in 1971 and nationalized 51% of the French companies' assests. SONATRACH now directly controls all the Algerian oil industry. It is the largest, most complex, and economically most important state company in Algeria. The government under new laws allowed foreign companies to cooperate in the exploration and prodcution of oil, and by 1982 there were 15 foreign companies working in Algeria from the U.S.A. (Getty, Sun Oil, Amoco), France (Total, ERAP), Poland (copex), Spain (Hispanoil), Brazil (Petrobras), West Germany (Dominex, Shell) and others. In 1980 the government restructured the company and formed twelve units. SONATRACH is one of them. The specialized new units are for exploration, production, engineering, transport, marketing, exporting, refining and other subspecialities.

In 1959 Algeria produced 1.2 million metric tons, and the production increased to 25 million tons in both 1964 and 1965. The producing areas then were Hassi Messaoud in central Algeria and Edjeleh-Zarzaitine in Eastern Algeria, close to the Libyan boundary line. The limited capacity of the two pipelines Algeria has at that time limited oil production. One of the pipes extended from Hassi Messoud to Bejaia on the Algerian coast and the other from Edjeleh-Zarzaitine to El Skhirra (La Skhirra) across Tunisia on the Gulf of Gabes. The production increased sharply in 1966 when SONATRACH completed the construction of the third pipeline to Azrew with a capacity of 22 million tons annually. Since then more oil fields were discovered at Gassi Touil, Nezla, Rhourde el Baguel, Hoaud Berkaoui, Rhourde Nouss, Ouargla, Mesdar and El Borma. Recently more findings that contributed substantially to the production are at Hassi Kesskessa, Guellala, Tin Fouye and El Maharis. To transport the petroleum of these several fields, four other pipelines have been constructed, Mesdar-Skikda, Ohanet-Haoud el Mahra, Mesdar-Elborma and Beni Mansour-Algiers.

Oil production in 1977 reached 51.7 million tons (with a daily average of 1.11 millin barrels). It peaked up ot its record in 1978 when production reached 54.0 million tons. In 1980 the government, in order to conserve its petroleum resources, decided to cut production by 15%. Production of that year fell to 47.4 million tons, and in 1981 it was less than 40 million tons. Due to a glut in the world market and dwindling international demand, Algeria agreed with other countries (especially Japan) on an oil-for-goods exchange. In 1982 production fell again to 33.8 million tons, and in 1983 it reached its lowest level in the 1970's and the early 1980's, which was 31.3 million tons. In 1984, the production was almost around the same figure.

The Algerian oil is considered of high quality with low sulphur content. In 1970 the oil exports estimated the Algerian reserves to be around 8,000 million barrels. These relatively limited reserves might be the explanantion for the Algerian hard line price policy it was taking in the OPEC meetings (trying to get more from its production before it dries up). In 1980 Algerian oil was selling for $40 a barrel. However, due to depressed world demand and lower world prices, the government reduced the price gradually. In 1983 it was $31.5 per barrel. Algeria is feeling the tough competition of the other three countreis that are producing the same high quality oil: U.S.S.R., Nigeria and Libya.

The best customer for Algerian oil is the U.S.A., followed by France, Federal Germany, Italy and Japan.

Federal Germany, as well as the other European
countries, may reduce their purchase of Algerian oil,
since the gas and oil pipelines extended from U.S.S.R.
have been operating and since the U.S.S.R. may, for
political as well as economic reasons, reduce its oil
prices.

Algeria, like most of the oil exporting countries,
is trying to refine as much as it can from its crude oil
to sell it as oil refined products. It is following
this policy in order to make higher profits from the
value added and also to establish its own petrochemicals
and refinery industries, that creates more jobs for its
increasing labor force. Most of the expanison in oil
refining industries. That creates more jobs for its
increasing labor force. Most of the expansion in oil
refining was achieved from 1981 to 1983. By the end of
1983 the share of crude oil revenues (by value) was not
more than 26% of the total revenues from hydrocarbons.
There are now three large oil refineries in Algeria.
Hassi Mesaoud refinery has a capacity of .3 million tons
annually. Azrew refinery has a capacity of 2.5 millin
tons, and the refinery at Skikda is the largest of all
and has a capacity of about 15 million tons per year.

In 1979 revenues from hydrocarbons reached $9,300
million U.S. dollars, and in 1981 they reached the
record of $13,100 million. In 1982 and 1983 they were
less than $13,000 million. It was almost the same
figure for 1984.

As a result of industralization and more use of
electricity, the Algerian domestic consumption was
estimated to be more than 18 million tons of petroleum
equivalent. The Algerian government is in full control
of domestic allocations for the different sectors of the
economy as well as of fixing local prices.

While oil production from relativley limited
resources starts to dwindle, natural gas production and
exports form rich reserves are increasing and will
replace oil as Algeria's most valuable foreign exchange
earner. It is estimated that the proved recoverable gas
reserves are about 3,200,000 million cubic meters.
Algeria is the world's fourth largest country in gas
reserves, holding about 4% of the World's total in 1981.
In fact it is estimated that there are more than
3.000,000 million cubic meters as possible reserves.

Most of the known proved gas is in the area of
Hassi R'Mel. It has about 2,300,000 million cubic

meters. A Japanese consortium has completed in 1983 the building of a $250 million liquefied petroleum gas (LPG) plant with a capacity of 1.2 million tons per year. A pipeline from Hassi R'Mel to Arzew, Algiers and Oran was built and started to operate in 1961.

Unassociated natural gas has been discovered at In Amenas, Almar, Gassi Touil, Rhourde Nouss, Tin Fouya and In Saleh. In 1984 an Italian company got a contract to develop the Rhour de Nouss gas field. Other gas fields are in the process of being developed.

Gross natural gas production in 1980 totaling 42,500 milion cubic meters, of these 10,971 million cubic meters were liquefied for export. In 1983 the figure production was 89,900 million cubic meters; 15,600 million cubic meters were liquefied for export.

Sales of natural gas in 1984 to western European countries and the U.S.A. have increased to a large extent inspite of the fact that the U.S.S.R. natural gasline, that extends from northwest Siberia to western Europe, has been completed. Companies from the U.S.A., France, Italy, Germany, Spain and Yugoslavia have signed contracts to buy almost all the Algerian natural gas production. In fact France, after a meeting between Presidents Metterand of France and Chadli of Algeria, agreed to pay a higher price for Algerian natural gas of 5.1 American dollars per million BTU's (British Thermal Units). That was really the price of political goodwill and massive increase in the trade between the two countries.

In order to export natural gas, the country is investing heavily in building pipelines, liquefaction plants and tankers.

The First liquefication plant, the Camel Plant, was built at Arzew in 1964. This Arzew Plant was further expanded by building another plant, Arzew II. It started to operate in 1978 with a capacity of 10,500 million cubic meters per year. Arzew II Plant started production in 1981. In 1972 a plant was built at Skekda and the capacity of that plant is to be increased. The original program for building liquefaction plants included building two more plants at Arzew and a third one at Skikda, but the government decided not to build those last three plants, at least not in the near future, on the bases that the price it gets now for its natural gas is too low to justify the large investments needed to build such plants.

257

A 358 mile pipeline with a 40 inch diameter has been built from Hassi R'Mel to Skikda. It started to operate in 1972 with a capacity of 12,700 million cubic meters annually. A second to operate in 1972 with a capacity of 12,700 million cubic meters annually. A second pipeline extending from Hassi R'Mel to Arzew, with a 40 inch diameter, started to operate in 1978. Two other pipelines were built by an Italian company; one from Hasis R'Mel to Arzew, to increase the capacity of the liquefaction plant at Arzew (its diameter is 28 inches); the other is 91 miles, with a 48 inch diameter, was built from Hassi R'Mel across Tunisia to the Mediterranean coast opposite Sicily, completed in 1981, and operating in 1983 with a capacity of 12,500 million cubic meters. Its capacity will be doubled by the end of 1985. The cost of building the pipeline was $$2,500 million. There is also a possibility of building another pipeline directly to Sicily under the water across the Mediterranean. Another study was completed to build another pipeline to carry the Algerian gas to Spain and Europe. One option was to build it through north Morocco to Spain across the Strait of Gibraltar. The other was to build it directly to Spain under Mediterranean water. Both pipeline projects were shelved for the time being until the economic effect of the U.S.S.R. pipeline to western Europe becomes clear. The Algerian national shipping line (CNAN) owns seven liquefied natural gas tankers. Algeria could expand this fleet, but it prefers to follow the policy of wait and see, regarding the world market and world prices and their effect on its production.

MINERALS

Mining and mineral prodution is controlled by the government, and the mineral resources are diversified and rich. Revenues from mineral production depends on world demand, during the late 1970's and early 1980's the world economy was rather sluggish, production and revenues did not increase and in some cases were reduced.

Iron ore is mined at Quenza and Boukhadra in the east as well as at Beni-Saf in the west. It is mined also form Zaccar, Timezrit in the central part. The quality of the ore is good with metal content varying between 50% to 60%. The deposits at Ouenza represent 75% fo the total iron ore in the country. Production has fluctuated considerably during the last decade. In 1974 it reached 2.06 million metric tons (metal content), in 1980 fell down to 1.06 million metric tons, and in 1982 it rose to about 1.88 million tons).

Other deposits of the same good grade are in the area of Colomb Bichar-Kenadza and Ksiksou. In 1957, before finding oil, the production reached 153,000 tons, in 1983 the production was about 5,200 tons only.

Zinc deposits are in the west, and they are extensions of deposits of eastern Morocco. The main two producing areas are El-Abed and Oued Zounder. In 1972 the produciton was 17,000 metric tons (metal content.) In 1977 the production fell to 2,700 tons, but rose to 5,000 tons in 1979, and the World Bank has estimated the 1982 production to be around 21,600 tons which is so far a record prodcution.

Lead is mined from El-Abed where zinc is produced. Production in 1979 was just 2,400 tons. In 1980, production hit a low record of just 1,800 tons, but in 1982 it climbed to about 6,000 tons. The 1984-89 development plan included developing a zinc and lead mine at Kherzet-Youssef in Setif province (wilaya).

The largest deposits of phosphate in Algeria are at Djebel-Onk and Le Kouif, Tocqueville (Bordj-bou-Arreridj). The production is used to supply the Arzew fertilizer plant and to export the surplus. Most of the surplus is exported to France, Spain and Italy. In 1982 the production reached 982,000 metric tons.

Algeria is also producing mercury. The production in 1979 was 508 tons. In 1982 it reached a record of 893 tons. The production is at Ismail, where a new refinery was built. Copper production is standing at 200 tons yearly. Other mineral resources not developed yet are antimony, tungsten, and manganese. The government is planning for a massive exploration operation for minerals in south Algeria, especially in the Ahoggar mountains and the areas surrounding that massif. It is the least explored area in the country. Uranium and gold are expected to exist in large commercial quantities.

MANUFACTURING

The Algerian leaders, who wrote and interpreted the constitution of the new born republic in 1962, believed in "progress and socialism", and both ideas cannot be transfomed into real achievements without building and developing the industrial sector of the economy. Industralization became the cornerstone and the keynote of the government political, economic and financial

259

policies. The 1974-78 a development plan devoted to the manufacturing sector alone 43.5% of the total investment. In the 1980-84 plan that sector got 38.6% of the total allocations.

Industry before independence was limited to food processing, textiles, building materials, minerals and handcrafts.

When the French (who controlled the economy) left, it meant that the capital, the skill, the administration, at the demand had left. The industrialization process broke down and manufacturing activities had to restart again form the ashes. One of the difficulties facing the reestablishing of industry was the fear and reluctance of foreign capital and foreign companies to invest in Algeria because of the threat of nationalization or the taking over by the socialists and the politically very sensitive Algerian government.

In the 1960's and 1970's the young, inexperienced, independent government made use of the increasing oil revenues to build a huge industrial structure that concentrated on heavy industry. There was no doubt that there were serioius mistakes made in the areas of administration, technology, marketing and labor training, but no doubt also that through trial and error learning was very beneficiary, and in the 1980's the industry was reorganizing and restructuring itself which resulted in more productivity.

By the end of 1979 there were about 300 state-owned manufacturieng plants. The productivity was so low that the majority of these plants were operating at only 15%-25% of designed capacity. However, the liberalization of industry in the early 1980's, that emphasized productivity rather than expansion and efficiency rather than policization and introduced the principal of profit-sharing, has led to an increase in output and a decrease in the financial losses. The industry has also been restructured. The large state steel organization, Societe Nationale de Siderurgie (SNS), has been broken into smaller units,and the local administration got more authority as a result of the new decentrallization policy.

In line with the Algerian economic philosophy, the iron and steel industry received large investments. The plant was built at Annaba (El Hadjar complex) and started to operate in 1969. It has a capacity of 400,000 tons per year, but the production has never reached that figure, however the complex has been expanded by adding new steel rolling mills to raise the production to 1.8 million tons annually.

A new huge complex to be built is included in the 1985-89 development plan. An integrated steelworks, built at Jijel, is designed to have a capacity of 2 million tons yearly. The production will supply 4 rolling mills each with a capacity form 300,000 to 400,000 tons yearly. They will be located at Ballana, outside of Jijel. The project includes building a port; the World Bank has already committed 80 million dollars for the port and a railroad, which is already under construction by a French company. Another project, that is on the drawing boards, is that of bulding a steel works plant at La Macta in the west with a capacity of 10 million tons annually.

A large aluminum smelter at m'Sile, southeast of Algiers, is also being planned. It will have a capacity of 132,000 tons annualy. The smelter will supply a sheet and extrusion factory at Bordjbou Arreridj. The bauxite will be imported form Jamaica and Guinea. The needed petroleum coke and carbon for electrodes are already available as by-products from the local oil refineries.

A nitrogenous fertilizer palnt, using natural gas, started to operate in 1970. It has a capacity, if fully oeprated, of 800,000 tons yearly. At Arzew intermediate petrochemical products are also manufactured. A phosphate fertilizer plant at Annaba with a capacity of 550,000 tons yearly started producing in 1972. A new unit was added in 1982 to that plant, as well as at Arzew. Unfortunately while these additions were being built, none of the plants were operating at full capacity; however, it is expected that the new reorganization of the industry will increase the productivity and provide more exportable products.

A farm machinery complex was completed and started production in 1976. Also at Constantine there is a factory producing tractors and diesel engines. Algeria, in order to improve its transportation system and to serve the industrial development, has started building trucks; Berliet Company of France has built a truck assembly plant with a capacity of 10,000 units per year at Rouiba, outside Algiers; truck production started in 1979. In 1984 the Algerian government reached an agreement with the French company to expand the assembly plant and to build a mechanical factory to produce

261

mechanical parts and components. The plan was to raise the production to 11,000 units with 75% of the parts made in Algeria. In 1989 all the components will be Algerian made. The Italian (FIAT) and the French (Renault) have reached an agreement with the government to produce 200,000-250,000 private cars per year. The plan is to assemble imported parts, gradually increasing the contribution of locally-made components.

The Ministry of Industry, to establish the industry of heavy-duty tires for tractors and trucks, gave Michelin and Pirelli the contract to build a new tire factory that will be located near Algiers to supplement a smaller factory located there. Motorcycles, bicycles and small motors are produced at Guelma. Pumps and irrigation equipment are produced at Medea.

Industry is growing in other areas, such as paper production and textiles. Flat glass is produced with an annual production of 40,000 tons. Paint is produced in two new factories, one at Sig and the other at Souk Ahras, with a 40,000 ton capacity per year.

Building materials, especially cement production to meet the continous urban and industrial expansion, have increased. There are 6 cement works with a local design capacity of about 9 million tons, but the production has never reached even 50% of the capacity, and the country is still importing cement; although if the plants work at full capacity, the building industry will be selfsufficient. Three more cement works, at Ain Touta, Bouira, and Batre will start production in 1986 and 1987. The French Company of Creusot Lorie was hired to study the cement production and to suggest means to increase productivity.

The problem facing Algerian industry is not the lack of investments or labor. It is the bureaucracy, lack of incentives and centralization all combined, resulting in lack of productivity in all branches of industry. The new code of industry and the 1985-89 plan are concentrating on solving these problems.

INTERNATIONAL TRADE

Algeria is one of those oil rich countries that not only have large oil exports, but also the huge rise of the value of their oil during the 1970's has altered the deficits in their balance of international trade into a surplus. Since independence up to late 1973, the country had a consistent deficit in the visible trade account. Even the remittances, that came from the Algerians working abroad, and the foreign financial and economic aid did not change that situation, with the exception of a very small surplus recorded during 1967 and 1968 when the climatic conditions favored the agricultural products and exports on one hand, and the government policies of restricting the imports on the other.

In 1973 oil prices started to rise dramatically; and the balance of payments tilted fast to the positive side, and the pattern of trade changed almost completely. Before oil findings nearly all the Algerian exports were agricultural products, mainly wine, olive oil, and citrus fruits; and some minerals, mainly phosphates and iron ore. Since 1974 hydrocarbons account for about 98% of the total value of all exports. In 1980 the revenues from oil exports reached the record of 11,700 million American dollars, compared to $1,100 million in 1973. In 1983, it was 9,700 million, and it stayed almost the same in 1984. Inspite of all the efforts of the government to diversify its exports, oil, oil products and natural gas will remain for the foreseen future the main exports and the main earners of foreign currency. Other exports that are responsible for the 2% of revenues include tobacco, hides and skins, vegetables and dates, and also phosphates, lead, zinc and iron ore.

Machinery, other capital goods, raw materials and semifinished products have been responsible for the largest part of money allocated for imports. This is understood in the light of the economic ideology and government policies of industralization. In 1978 the cost of importing these items was nearly $4,500 million; in 1981 it reached $5,760 million, which accounted for more than 60% of the value of the total imports. The food imports are essential for Algeria, as a result of the government's negligence of agriculture, climatic fluctuations and the high growth rate of population. In 1978 imports cost a little above $1,000 million making 14.3% of the total imports in 1981. It reached $1,900 million, making 19.9% of the total imports. In 1983 food imports allocated $2,100 million. Most of the important food items are grains, especially wheat, flour, dairy products and meat. Unfortunately food shortage and food imports will continue at least for the foreseen future. Imports of consumer goods are under firm restriction, although the new economic policies of the early 1985's have relatively relaxed the ties on

these imports.   In 1980 consumer good imports totaled
only $800,000.   In 1982, they were allocated at
$970,000.

All   the   business   of   export   and   import   was
monopolized by the government. Through the government's
economic policy and as designed by the development
plans, certain sums of money were allocated to certain
imports in specific amounts and from certain countries.
It was also the same for exports.   The change of that
system started in 1982, and it is gradually becoming
more   liberal.   In 1982 the government allowed the
private sector to import some spare parts.   In 1983 more
items, that were not available through the state, were
allowed to be imported by individuals.   New rules to
encourage   exports   were   introduced   in   1984.   Now
agricultural   products,   surplus   manufactured   goods,
phosphates, textiles and leather works are exported by
the private sector.

France always has been the most important partner
in the Algerian foreign trade, inspite of the fact that
due to political disputes and disagreements in the
1970's, the share – not the rank – is imports of France
in that trade has decreased.   Before independence, when
Algeria was considered a part of France, 81% of the
Algerian exports went to France, and 82% of the Algerian
imports came from France.   However, in 1971, during the
period of the Franco–Algerian disputes concerning the
Algerian nationalization of the Freench interests in the
oil industry, the French share in Algerian exports was
only 12.7 and 24% of the imports.   In 1979 the political
and economic relations between the two countries started
to   improve   again,   and   this   was   reflected   on   the
international trade figures.   In 1980, France still was
in the first rank for exports and imports.   Imports from
France were of the value of AD 9,253 million, followed
by Federal Germany with AD 5,800 million.   Total imports
for   that year were AD 41,545 million.   For exports of
that year, France ranked second after the U.S.A. because
of the huge American imports of Algerian oil and natural
gas.   The share of France in Algerian exports was AD
7,630 million.   In 1982 new trade agreements between the
two countries, especially regarding oil and natural gas
prices, has immensely improved the trade relations.
Following France as an important partner are Federal
Germany, Italy, the U.S.A., and the United Kingdom.   The
U.S.S.R. and the eastern European countries are not
among the important traders with Algeria since the
petroleum is the only important item that is exported,
and the U.S.S.R. is a world major exporter and supplies

the eastern Europeans with their petroleum needs. In fact, if it was not for the arms and other military equipment acquired from the European communist countries, the trade relation with eastern Eurpoe would be of a insignificant scale. Most of the Algerian international trade is with the western countries in general, and especially with the EEC countries.

During the years of 1982 and 1983 there were some proposals and some exchange of ideas about strengthening the political and economic relations between the Maghreb countries. It remains to be seen that these proposals and political reproachment will increase the size and value of trade between these countries.

Although Algeria is a very strong supporter of Arab unity and Arab cause, and its constitution is making it clear that it is an Islamic country. None of the Arab or Islamic countries are among the important partners in Algerian foreign trade.

TRANSPORT

Algeria, like the other two countries of Maghreb, inherited a good transport system that was built by the French authorities. There is about 2,313 miles network of railways that are managed by the "Societe National des Transports Ferroviares" (SNTF), it is a government authority.

The main trunk railway crosses the country to join the railway system of Tunisia in the east and Morocco in the west. It runs on the coastal plain and avoids the mountain massifs. Extensions from the main trunk run to some main cities along the coast such as Anneba, Skikda, Bejaia, Beni Saf and Nemduos, and to the south to reach Tebessa, Biskara, Touggourt, Ouargla, Djelfa, Colomb-Bishar and Abadla. Most of the railway is of single track, and some of its parts are of narrow gauges.

The SNTF is launching an extensive project to modernize its railway system, doubling the track and building a second trunk. By 1990 about $11,000 million will be spent in doubling the length and freight capacity of the existing network. Another $3,000 million will be invested in buying new locomotives and other new equipment. A very ambitious project is the building of another trunk that will run on the High Plateaux from east to west, which will encourage creating new industrial centers. A new extension will run southward to the oil center of Hassi Messaoud and Ghardaia Oases. The railroads are taking only 15% of the freight now, but since it is 75% cheaper, compared to the road transport, it is estimated that after the new development it will be responsible for no less than 45% of the freight. Companies from Austria, France, West Germany, India, and China have already been contracted for these extensive projects.

However, the scale of the SNTF plan is expected to be reduced in favor of the improvement and expansion of the national road network,. There are 7,500 miles of main roads, 5,270 miles of national roads, and 8,568 miles of secondary roads; all are usable throughout the year. There are also 7,230 miles of desert tracks, most of these roads were built originally by the French authority. The main elements are: two east-west trunk highways, constructed for both strategic and economic reasons; main roads, linking the large towns; roads running south from the ports; mine tracks; and trans-Sahara tracks (buses, trucks, and cars are using these desert tracks). The road system needs maintenance and remodeling. In 1984 Canadian companies were contracted to build a network of maintenance centers for buses and trucks.

Algeria is a member of the Trans-Sahara Road Committee, organizing the building of the "Road of African Unity". The first stretch from Hassi Marroket to Ain Salah was opened in 1973. The second stretch to Tamanrasset was completed in 1978, and by 1983 it was a part of the third stretch, reaching about 60 miles south of that oasis.

Air transport, served by Air Algeria, is gaining more ground and becoming more popular. The domestic service has been passed to the newly-formed Air Inter Services, while Air Algeria is responsible for international flights.

Inspite of the growing importance of the ports of Bejaia, Arzew, Skikda and Oran (Ouahren) as terminals for the oil and gas pipelines and the establishing of new industries, especially petrochemicals, Algiers is still the main and largest port of the country. It now handles more than four million tons of exports annually, including Algeria's wines, olive oil, citrus fruits, iron ore and phosphates. It also handles about five million tons of imports, especially grains, machinery

266

and other unfinished goods needed for the growing industry.

POPULATION AND SOCIAL PROBLEMS

The estimated number of population in 1984 was about 21 million. There is also about one million Algerians working abroad, mostly in France. The great majority of the population live in the northern part of Algeria, especially along the Mediterranean coast where the capital of Algiers (El Djezair) is located. Greater Algeires has an estimated population of about 2 million. Most of the other large cities and towns are also located on that coastal plain. Some of them are separated from each other by mountain massifs or off-shots of the Tell Atlas but are connected by the trunk railroad or its extensions as well as by the main roads and the domestic airways. There was about one million European settlers who left the country after independence. The population is almost solely Muslim and of the Sunni sect. The constitution of the country is asserting that Algeria is an Islamic country.

The majority of the population are Arabic speaking people. However the Berber population, living mostly in the Kabyles, Aures, Miliana, Namemcha and the Tuareg of the Hoggar Mountains are estimated to form 20-25% of the total population. They speak different dialects of the Berber language and many of them, especially those of the Kabyles and Aures, are bilingual; they speak both the Berber and Arabic languages.

The Algerian constitution is also making it clear that the Arabic language is the official national language. This led to suppression of the Berber language and the negligence of the Berber culture. This official attitude towards the large linguistic minority angered the Berbers, who in 1979 protested and demonstrated against the official policy. The unrest centered mostly in the Kabyles, a region long regarded as having dangerously separatist intentions. Although some concessions have been made, including the creation of chairs in the Berber languages at the universities of Tizi-Ouzou and Algiers and the provision of Berber radio programs, the government made it clear that the Berber demands were considered as a serious threat to the national unity, and that they would never be taken slightly or tolerated. In 1981 the situation flared up again when proposals for a "cultural charter", making provisions for the Berber culture as a part of the country's national heritage, was not approved. Violence and demonstrations accompanied the arguments. The tension has relatively relaxed since the government announced the establishment of departments for the study of popular literature and dialects in several universities.

The government was criticized in 1979 that it was slow in replacing French with Arabic as a language of education, media and civil service. The ministry of education responded by hiring more teachers from the Arab countries, mostly froim Egypt, to speed up the Arabization process and to announce that all the official newspapers will be published only in Arabic.

The assertation of the constitution, that Arabic is the official language of Algeria, created a split among the students of the Algerian universities. In 1975 some of the students, who were devoted to the revolution and nationalism, clashed with other students who thought that priority should be given to Arabization and Arab unity. Boumedienne, then the president of the country, came out strongly in favor of the nationalist.

Also some Muslim fundamentalist in Algeria, as everywhere in most of the Islamic World, have interpreted that the constitution asserts Islam as the official religion of the country, that the country's laws should be derived from the Shariaa - the Qoranic law. This interpretation led to the emergence of extremistist religious parties. Their activities caused several disturbances in 1981 and 1982.

The density of population of 22.6 per square mile is realy misleading, since most of the population are concentrated on the coastal plain, especially in the cities. Algeria, like all the developing countries, has the problem of the huge growth rate of population. It is 3.2% which makes the number of inhabitants nearly doubled in only twenty years. Birth rate is estimated to be 47.4 per thousand, and death rate is 15.5 per thousand. However the infant mortality rate is still very high. It exceeds 100 per 1000 live births, and life expectancy is below 56 years. These conditions prevail in Algeria inspite of the introduction of modern medicine, improved sanitation and drinking water, and the defeat of killer diseases, such as malaria, cholera and typhus. Health conditions are better in the urban areas compared with rural areas where 56% of the population are still living inspite of the large exodus from the countryside to the big towns in search of jobs.

Another problem facing Algeria is that 60% of the population are less than 19 years old. This puts a lot of pressure on the government's budget to meet the needs of such a population, especially in education, health and social needs. The growth of the urban centers is going at the high rate of 5.7 annually. In fact it has been cut down slightly; in the period of 1960-1970, urban centers were growing at a rate of 6.6% Most of the growth is due to the drift of the young people from the villages to the towns. That huge rate of urban growth is facing the government with three essential problems: housing, health and education.

During the 1970's with the strong drive toward heavy industrialization, housing became a severe problem. While the urban population was growing with a rate of 6.6% yearly, the government neglected tackling the chronic housing shortage. The situation changed in 1980 when the government of President Chadli made housing an important item in the 1980-84 Development Plan. The plan was to build 450,000 homes, and it was estimated, too, that in 1982-83 the private sector, after relaxing the government restrictions build about 30,000 homes. Prefabricated building techniques and materials were used in building most of the homes in the development plans, and most of the contractors were from the western countries, especially France, Italy, Spain and Sweden. In 1983 Yugoslavia, Hungary and Romaina agreed to build 10,000 new homes in exchange for oil purchases. Most of these homes were built in new districts and were attached to schools, hospitals and training centers. These new homes have eased the chronic housing problem but did not solve it entirely.

After independence the Algerians faced a formidable health and hygenic problem; most of the physicians and medical staff were Europeans, and they left the country. The problem became compounded by the huge influence of the people from the countryside to the towns and the lack of adequate sanitation and drinking water as well as medicine and the spread of malnutrition. The government, aware of the seriousness of the situation, tried to reduce the impact of the problem. Since training physicians takes a long time, the government hired a large number of foreigners to fill the large gap in the medical staff. The hiring was on personal basis or contracts. Most of those who were hired were Egyptians, Palestinians and some Italians and French. In 1963 the number of the population per physician was 5,530. In 1980 the situation improved dramatically. The number was 2,650 per physician.. New hospitals were

built, and the older ones were re-equipped. Medication
is free, and it includes the required medicines. The
building of new homes with adequate sanitation and
running water and compulsary vaccinations helped very
much to improve the general health problem.. The
problem is still rather acute in the countryside.

Daily per capita calorie supply has also improved.
It jumped from less than 2,000 in 1965 to 2,433 in 1980.
Although the last figure is considered adequate, the
problem is the difference between the rural and urban
population and is between the employed and unemployed.

In the field of education the government is doing a
remarkable job, although there is still a long way to go
to reach acceptable results. During the French
colonization, education was rarely available for
Algerians and was expensive. Illiteracy was spreading
among all ages everywhere in the country, and the few
elementary and secondary schools in Algeria at that time
were following the French pattern of education, and
French was the language of education. Reforms were
introduced in 1973, not only to abolish illiteracy,
especially among the young, but also to adapt schooling
and education to economic, social and political needs
and to the ideology of the country. Algerians now
receive nine years of instruction in Arabic and in
varied skills required to satisfy the technical and
economic needs of the country. The French language
remains the important foreign language which all pupils
have to learn in the secondary schools, and nearly all
the educated Algerians speak French fluently. In 1983
the share of education in the country's budget amounted
to 16% and it is on the increase.

In 1980 more than 80% of the children of school age
were enrolled in schools. There were almost 3 million
pupils in the primary schools compared to 845,000 in
1962; in secondary schools there were 840,000 compared
to 48,500 in 1962. There are twelve main universities
and several technical colleges and teachers colleges.
Total enrollment in higher education in 1980 was 51,500
and several students studied abroad, especially in
France. Actual illiteracy, which was 82% in 1962, has
been reduced to 65% in 1980.

Inspite of the good intentions of the Algerian
government and the remarkable progress that has been
achieved in a relatively short time, Algeria has still a
long way to go to improve the quality and standard of
life for all its population, and it has to use the oil

boom to create more jobs and produce more food for a
very fast increasing population.

STATISTICAL SURVEY

Area and Population

Area, Population and Density

Area (sq km)[*]	2,381,741[*]
Population (census results)[+]	
4 April 1966	11,821,679
12 February 1977[‡]	16,948,000
Population (estimates at mid-year)[+]	
1978	17,580,000
1979	18,190,000
1980	18,666,000
Density (per sq km) 1980	7.8

[*]919,595 sq miles.
[+]Excluding Algerian nationals residing abroad, numbering 268,868 at the 1966 census and an estimated 828,000 at 1 January 1978.
[‡]Provisional.

272

Area and Population

Principal Towns (estimated population in 1977)

Algiers (El Djezair, capital)	1,800,000	Sidi-Bel-Abbes	158,000
Oran (Ouahran	500,000	Skikda	132,000
Constantine (Qacentina)	430,000	Batna	120,000
Annaba	340,000	Tlemcen (Tilimsen)	120,000
Tizi-Ouzou	230,000	El Asnam (Ech-Cheliff)	118,000
Blida (El Boulaida)	162,000	Boufarik	112,000
Setif (Stif)	160,000	Bejaia	108,000
		Medea (Lemdiyya)	106,000

Area and Population by Wilayas (Departments)*

	Area (sq km)	Population+
Adrar	422,498.0	167,557
El Asnam (Ech-Cheliff	8,676.7	967,460
Laghouat	112,052.0	290,085
Oum El Bouaghi (Oum el Bouagui)	8.123.0	455,044
Batna	14.881.5	648,228
Bejaia	3,444.2	602,294
Biskra (Beskra)	109,728.0	531,895
Bechar	306,)00.0	149,808
Blida (El Boulaida	3,703.8	975,785
Bouira	4,517.1	428,807
Tamanrasset (Tamenghest)	556,000.0	45,555
Tebessa (Tbessa)	16,574.5	375,442
Tlemcen (Tilimsen)	9,283.7	630,059
Tiaret (Tihert)	23,455.6	689,106
Tizi-Ouzou	3,756.3	934,374
Algiers (El Djezair)	785.7	2,091,798
Djelfa (El-Djelfa)	22,904.8	259,018
Jijel	3,704.5	538,901
Setif (Stif)	10,350.4	1,074,116
Saida	106,777.4	309,986
Skikda	4,748.3	547,347
Sidi-Bel-Abbes	11,648.2	547,807
Annaba	3,489.3	596,675
Guelma	8,624.4	603,591
Constantine (Qacentina)	3,561.7	756,341
Medea (Lemdiyya)	8,704.1	528,089
Mostaganem (Mestghanem)	7,023.6	806,606
M'Sila	19,824.6	438,737
Mascara (Mouaskar)	5,845.6	489,603

Ouargla (Wargla)	559,234.0	198,322
Oran (Ouahran)	1,820.0	846,332
Total	2,381,741.0	18,524,768

*In December 1983 an administrative reorganization created 17 new wilayas, bringing the total number to 48.

+(estimates at 1 Jan. 1980) Excluding Algerian nationals abroad, estimated to total 828,000 at 1 January 1978.

Employment (wage-earning employees at 1977 census)*

Agriculture	692,160
Processing industries	302,055
Hydrocarbons	48,489
Other industries	50,918
Construction and public works	345,816
Transport and communications	132,420
Trade	183,580
Administrative and community services	397,019
Other services	100,984
Unstated	83,532
Total	2,336,973

*Excluding nomads, students and members of the armed forces.
Source: Annuaire Statistique de l'Algerie, Ministere de la Planification et de l'Amenagement du Territoire, Algiers.

Agriculture

Principal Crops ('000 metric tons)

Wheat	1,511	1,400+	1,200+
Barley	794	750+	650*
Oats	110	100*	80*
Potatoes	591	600*	610*
Pulses	53	54*	56*
Sugar Beets	49	90*	92*
Onions (dry)	118	120*	123*
Tomatoes	182	185*	190*
Grapes	453*	400*	360*
Olives	140*	100*	90*
Oranges	281	230	250*
Tangerines and mandarins	129	116	130*
Dates	201	195	207*
Water-melons	173	173*	174*
Tobacco	3	3*	3*

*FAO estimates. +Unofficial figure.
Source: FAO, Production Yearbook.

Forestry

Roundwood Removals
(FAO estamates, '000 cu m, excluding bark)

	1980	1981	1982
Sawlogs, veneer logs and logs for sleepers	20	20	20
Pitprops (Mine timber)	1	1	1
Other industrial wood	184	190	196
Fuel wood	1,412	1,461	1,461
Total	1,617	1,672	1,678

Source: FAO, Yearbook of Forest Products.

Fishing

(FAO estimates, '000 metric tons, live weight)

	1980	1981	1982
European sardine (pilchard)	26.7	31.1	35.8
Other marine fishes	19.2	22.4	25.8
Marine crustaceans	2.2	2.5	2.9
Total catch	48.0	56.0	64.5

Source:FOA, Yearbook of Fishery Statistics.

Livestock ('000 head, year ending September)

	1980	1981*	1982*
Sheep	13,370	13,600	13,700
Goates	2,723	2,723	2,760
Cattle	1,355	1,370	1,390
Horses	131	132	134
Mules	205	206	206
Asses	506	523	540
Camels	149	149	150
Chickens	18,000	18,500	19,000

*FAO estimate
Source: FAO, production Yearbook

Livestock Products (FAO estimates, '000 metric tons)

	1980	1981	1982
Beef and veal	33	33	34
Mutton and lamb	65	66	67
Goats' meat	11	12	12
Poultry meat	46	47	48
Cows' milk	518	520	530
Sheep's milk	160	164	166
Goats' milk	135	138	140
Hen eggs	19.1	19.7	20.3
Wool (clean)	10.3	10.4	10.5

Source: FAO, Production Yearbook

MINING

	1979	1980	1981
Coal ('000 metric tons)	7	7	7
Iron ore:			
gross weight ('000 metric tons)	3,170	3,500	3,350‡
metal content ('000 metric tons)	1,713	1,892	1,881
Salt ('000 metric tons)*	165	170	170
Lead ore (metric tons)+	2,400	1,800	3,300
Zinc ore (metric tons)+	5,000	4,100	10,900
Copper ore (metric tons)+	200	200	200+
Mercury (metric tons)	508	842	862‡
Phosphate rock ('000 metric tons)	1,084	1,025	916
Crude petroleum ('000 metric tons)	53,698	47,417	39,530‡
Natural gas (terajoules)	607,643	759,140	505,200

*Estimates of US Bureau of Mines.
+Metal content of concentrates. ‡Estimate.
Source: UN, mainly Yearbook of Industrial Statistics.
1982: Lead ore (metal content) 6,000 (Source: World Metal Statistics);
Zinc ore (metal content) 21,600 (Source: World Metal Statistics); Crude
petroleum 43,670,000 metric tons; Natural gas 517,870 terajoules.

elected Products

live oil (crude)	'000 metric tons	13	19*	11*
argarine	'000 metric tons	12.9	13.4	14.6
lour	'000 metric tons	551	628	694
aw sugar*	'000 metric tons	15*	15	15*
ine	'000 hectolitres	2,710*	2,840*	2,700*
eer	'000 hectolitres	620	650	n.a.
igarettes+	metric tons	14,000	15,150	16,000
otton yarn (pure and mixed)	'000 metric tons	15.0	18.3	n.a.
oven cotton fabrics*	million sq metres	59	61	n.a.
ootwear (excl. rubber)	'000 pairs	11,286	13,268	14,533
itrogenous fertilizers (a)‡	'000 metric tons	42.2	20.7	23.8*
hosphate fertilizers (b)‡	'000 metric tons	96.6*	53.5*	30.8*
aphtha	'000 metric tons	489	1,810*	1,800*
otor spirit (petrol)	'000 metric tons	1,078	1,137	1,140
erosene*	'000 metric tons	270	45	50
et fuel*	'000 metric tons	350	370	380*
istillate fuel oils	'000 metric tons	2,130	3,645	3,650*
esidual fuel oils	'000 metric tons	1,792	2,759	2,800*
iquefied petroleum gas	'000 metric tons	806	896*	880*
ement	'000 metric tons	3,768	4,159	4,457
ig-iron	'000 metric tons	396	400	430
rude steel	'000 metric tons	416	534	550
elevision receivers	'000	58	75	119
uses and coaches (assembly)	number	464	652	577
orries (assembly)	number	6,151	6,464	5,625
lectric energy*	million kWh	6,116	7,123	7,170

Provisional or estimated figures. +Estimates by the US Dept. of Agriculture. Production, in terms of (a) nitrogen or (b) phosphoric acid, during 12 months ending 30 June of year stated. Phosphate fertilizers include ground rock phosphate.
ource: mainly UN, Yearbook of Industrial Statistics
982: Olive oil 9,000 metric tons; Wine 2,300,000 hectolitres (FAO estimate); Nitrogenous fertilizers 23,700 metric tons; Phosphate fertilizers 22,700 metric tons.

EXTERNAL TRADE

Principal Commodities (million AD)

Imports c.i.f.	1978	1979	1980
Food stuffs and tobacco	5,034	5,143	8,008
Energy and lubricants	514	632	1,009
Primary products and raw materials	1,475	1,651	2,304
Semi-finished products	7,927	7,964	15,026
Capital goods	14,066	12,130	10,981
Consumer goods	5,053	4,547	4,046
Total (incl. others)	34,439	32,378	41,545

Source: Secretariat d'Etat au Commerce Exterieur, Algiers.
Total imports (million AD): 48,637 in 1981; 49,384 in 1982.

Exports	1978	1979	1980
Foodstuffs and tobacco	583	430	496
Energy and lubricants	23,329	37,148	51,379
Primary products and raw materials	187	248	217
Semi-finished products	169	175	266
Total	24,283	38,011	52,428

Principal Trading Partners (million AD)[*]

Imports	1978	1979	1980
Belgium-Luxembourg	1,395.4	2,192.0	2,514
Brazil	825.4	245.4	418
Canada	837.6	937.3	1,161
France	6,142.7	5,971.1	9,253
Germany, Federal Republic	6,063.4	5,862.6	5,830
Italy	3,702.9	4,065.5	4,994
Japan	3,089.3	1,642.3	1,705
Netherlands	742.6	773.2	1,140
Poland	185.4	200.0	192
Romania	489.3	469.1	192
Spain	1,567.9	1,711.9	2,245
Sweden	425.7	411.8	488
Switzerland	748.3	686.1	751
USSR	293.4	153.9	252
United Kingdom	1,104.0	1,016.0[+]	1,499
USA	2,287.8	2,090.7	2,889

[*] Imports by country of production; exports by country of consignment.
[+] Provisional figures.
Source: Secretariat d'Etat au Commerce Exterieur, Algiers.

Exports	1978	1979	1980
Belgium-Luxembourg	305.5	400.7	567
Brazil	231.8	47.9	378
China, People's Republic	86.1	33.3	1
France	2,654.6	5,208.8	7,630
Germany, Federal Republic	3,340.0	4,354.0	5,811
Italy	1,757.2	2,313.7	2,091
Japan	131.2	150.9	1,411
Netherlands	470.9	1,090.2	2,993
Paraguay	121.2	200.0	n.a.
Romania	192.5	541.4	357
Senegal	84.5	98.1	n.a.
Spain	607.5	943.4	2,040
Sweden	26.0	137.1	72
Switzerland	72.8	217.5	60
USSR	227.8	220.1	359
United Kingdom	452.5	541.0[+]	975
USA	12,129.3	19,894.7	25,783

Administrative Budget ('000 AD)

Expenditure	1980	1981
Presidency	111,000	216,272
National defence	2,702,516	3,481,419
Foreign affairs	331,680	351,598
Light industry	130,081	128,954
Housing and construction	146,584	194,163
Finance	540,000	592,120
Home affairs	1,410,645	1,641,505
Commerce	55,925	67,079
Youth and sport	278,338	296,510
Information and culture	301,549	336,167
Ex-servicemen	1,280,260	1,764,240
Tourism	33,925	37,501
Agriculture	532,809	759,167
Health	1,564,100	2,044,200
Transport	187,066	203,888[*]
Justice	252,500	285,592
Employment and training	373,100	418,140
Religious affairs	143,200	219,639
Public works	435,034	479,108
Education	4,955,227	6,713,494
Higher education and scientific research	1,493,000	1,891,791
Heavy industry	65,638	63,630
Water	219,728	297,997
Energy and petrochemicals industries	164,779	169,448

Rural planning and development	78,243	92,808
Fisheries	9,175	n.a.
Forestry	160,208	n.a.
Total (inc. others)	27,775,837	36,195,250

*Including fisheries.

Equipment Budget ('000 AD)

Expenditure	1980	1981
Industry	630,000	1,240,000
Agriculture	1,217,000	1,170,000
Water	2,000,000	2,700,000
Tourism	150,000	190,000
Fisheries	80,000	70,000
Economic sub-structure	1,900,000	n.a.
Transport	500,000	500,000
Urban development	3,360,000	n.a.
Livestock distribution	50,000	n.a.
Education	3,500,000	4,800,000
Training	1,615,000	1,700,000
Social affairs	1,180,000	n.a.
Housing	2,350,000	3,050,000
Administrative structure	820,000	920,000
Total (incl. others)	23,122,000	31,593,000

Revenue (1981): 68,305m. dinars, of which 3,830m. is from direct
contributions, 7,492m. from business taxes, 46,180m. from petroleum.

REFERENCES

[1] Referred to sometimes as the High Plateau, or High Plains.

[2] Depois, Jean: L'Afrique du Nord.

[3] Lebjavui, Mohamed. Veritess su ta Revolution Algeriane.

[4] Lambotta, R. Algerie, Naissance D'une Socie'te Nouvelle.

[5] Balta, Paul and Claudine Rulleau. L'Algerie Des Algeriens.

CHAPTER 12

MOROCCO

Morocco, the Kingdom of Morocco, is in fact "El
Maghreb El Aksa"[1] the farthest west. The country
occupies the northwestern part of the continent of
Africa. It has two sea fronts; its northern shores are
washed by the Mediterranean Sea, and on its western side
lies the Atlantic Ocean. It fronts the Iberian
Peninsula across the Strait of Gibraltar less than 12
miles wide.

Morocco's location in the far northwestern region
of Africa and as the Arab world's western flank gave it
a distinctive geographical personality among the other
countries of North Africa. A larger proportion of its
20.5 million population, approximately 35% - 36%, are
non Arabized Berbers that took refuge in the Atlas
Mountains and are living in its valleys and on its
slopes. Morocco is so close to Spain that it became a
launching pad for the Moors incursions into Europe.
When the Morrish power declined, the Spaniards crossed
the Gibraltor Strait and occupied the Rif Region and
some other bridge heads. Although the Spanish political
influence disappeared, Ceuta and Melilla are still
retained and considered parts of Spain. The Moorish
territorial expansion was not only northward in Spain,
but it also extended southward into Black Africa.
Moroccan armies occupied the ancient state of Ghana and
reached the Senegal and Upper Niger Rivers. Morocco,
even today, reflects its old associations with Black
Africa. The trade connections established during the
period of expansion outlasted the Moorish empire..
Black Africans today inhabit many of Morocco's southern
oases, and others live in the country's traditional
cities further north, such as Rabat, Maknes and Fez. In
fact Morocco's claim in former Spanish Sahara and its
annexation of this region is based on that historical
reason of political expansion and cultural relict.
While all the Arab world and North Africa fell victim to
the Turkish colonization, Morocco was the only country
in North Africa and in the Arab World that succeeded in
escaping that Turkish domination.

The location of Morocco on the eastern shores of
the Atlantic and on the southern shores of the
Mediterranean and across the Strait of Gibraltor from
Europe made its harbors good nests for pirates.
Moroccan pirates used to pray on vessels returning from
the colonies loaded with goods and riches. It was only

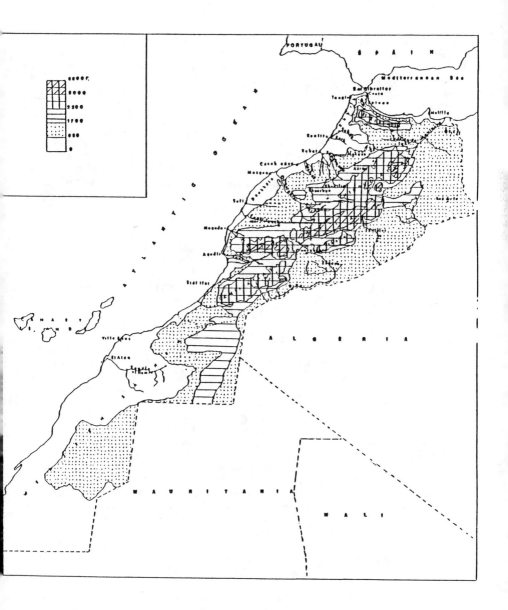

after immense pressure from strong colonial and maritime countries and even after wars that Morocco, in 1814, made it illegal to enslave the "Christians" captured in the process of piracy, and in 1817 stopped the acts of piracy that brought great wealth to the ruling dynasties.

The Moroccan terrain, beside the location, that preserved the Berber culture and language and prevented the Turks from annexing Morocco to their Empire, made it also very hard for the French to gain control over all the country. Although the French armies started to land in Morocco in 1907, it was not before 1937 that France had full control on the country.

That distinctive personality of Morocco is characterized by several physical and human features; it has two long sea fronts on both the Atlantic and Mediterranean with important fisheries, as well as a large population depending on farming and grazing. The high peaks of the Atlas, plateaux, deep valleys, coastal plains, Mediterranean climates, semi-arid and deserts, and winter snow covered peaks, all contribute to the complexity of its physical environment. Also cultural diversities; Islamic culture within a very modern European atmosphere, Berber language with different dialects, and Arbic language enlayed with several French and Spanish words. The constitution is making clear that Morocco is an Islamic country, but neither the government nor the people have tried to impose the Shariaa-Qoranic Law as a civil or criminal code. Although Islamic by constitution and by the reality that almost all of the population are Moslems, they have never been fans of Pan Islamism or Islamic unity. The country is a member of the Arab League but never was enthusiastic about the idea of Arab unity. In fact, it was always following a moderate and independent policy, even when the Arab-Israeli problem came to the foreground. Arabic is the language of the majority of the population, but they never tried to oppress the Berber languages nor discourage the usage of the French; in fact, French, the language of the former colonial

The constitution in its preamble is stressing that Morocco is a part of the Great Maghreb: Tunisia, Algeria and Morocco, and that it is an African state. It never mentioned, like the constitutions of the other north African countries, that it is an Arab country, although it is an active member of the Arab League. In fact Morocco had its hostility with its neighbor Algeria, with Libya, and even for sometime with Egypt during Abd El Nasser's presidency. It is a member of the Organization of African Unity (OAU), but it differed with many of the members of that organization on the problem of the former Spanish Sahara.

Morocco has its traditional and conservative routes, but it is opening it's doors wide to Western cultures. Even in education it has its very traditional religion schools as well as very modern universities, offering modern higher education. The Kingdom of Morocco is showing its strong unity within that large diversity. The wise leadership of its monarch is leading it on a long road toward development and modernization.

TOPOGRAPHY

The main topographic features in Morocco, like the other two countries of Africa Minor, Tunisia and Algeria, are the Atlas Mountains. However, in no other country are the Atlas so extensive and rugged, nor do they play such a significant role in the people's life as in Morocco. Although the huge tectonic activities that built these huge chains took place mainly during the tertiary era, the activities were so strong that some older Juressic folds and even Harcynian massifs have been reraised and rebuilt. The mountains are still unstable, and Morocco, like both Algeria and Tunisia, is liable to strong earthquakes, such as the very destructive one that destroyed the port of Agadir in 1960 where the number of casualties was very high.

In Morocco the Atlas Mountains form four main massifs: the Rif (Errif or Riff) Atlas, the Middle Atlas, the High Atlas, and the Anti Atlas. They are surrounded and partially separated by lowland plains and plateaux.

The Rif Atlas is a series of ranges and massifs rather than a continuous chain of highland. The mountains have precipitous slopes to the Mediterranean and reach heights of over 7,100 feet. Among the high peaks of these mountains are: Tidiguin, 8,110 feet; Chauen, 7,200 feet; and Yebel Buhasen, 5,300 feet. The mountains are forming such a rugged arc that functioned as a strong barrier to east-west communication. The mountains are the source of some short torrential rivers that mostly run to the Mediterranean through deep narrow valleys. The most important of these rivers are Kert-Igan, Guis, and Lau. Another river that rises from the western end of the Riff and runs through the Gharb (Rharb) coastal plain to the Atlantic is the Loukkos. Although all these rivers add to the physical complexity of the area and are useless for irrigation, they may be important for potential generating hydroelectric power. The coast is unhospitable and the valleys are narrow. These Berbers (Rifian) that live in the mountain villages of the Rif are practically isolated from their neighbours in the rest of Morocco. The main pass in these mountains is Bab Taza that is crossed by the main road that connects Melilla in northeastern Morocco with Tetuan, Ceuta, and Tangier in the far northwestern part of the country.

South of the Rif Mountains and separating them from the Middle Atlas is the Col of Taza, a narrow corridor that affords the only easy route between western Algeria and the Atlantic coast of Morocco. The Inaouene River, a main tributary of the Sebou River, runs in the corridor from east to west. The Moulouya River crosses its eastern end from north to south, heading north to the Mediterranean. The corridor can be considered as an eastward extension to the Sebou River Basin. Taza is the citadel guarding the corridor that becomes at that point just a narrow gorge of a mile and a half wide and 2,000 feet above sea level. Winter and early spring flooding of the corridor may be extensive and destructive, especially when the melted Atlas snows augment the rainfall.

The Middle Atlas (Moyan Atlas), a regularly folded chain, has summits that reach more than 10,000 feet, Djebe (Mot) Ayachi 12, 307 feet, Djebel Moussaow Salah 10,622 feet, and Djebel Masker 10,050 feet. Most of the chain consists of limestone plateau disected by river gorges and capped here and there by volcanic craters and lava flows. The middle Atlas forms a broad barrier between Atlantic Morocco and eastern Morocco. It also functions as a major hydrographic divide and is flanked by the basins of Morocco's principal rivers, the Oum er Rbia and Sebou that flow west to the Atlantic, and the Moulouya that flows northeast to the Mediterranean. The mountain system with its valleys and peaks are the home of some Berber tribes, the largest of them being the Amazigh who are semi-nomads that practice transhumance on a large scale beside depending on subsistance systems of agriculture in the valleys.

The southern extension of the Middle Atlas merges into the High Atlas. It is the most formidable of the mountain massifs and the highest. It rises to more than

12,000 feet. Djebel Toubkal reaches 13,663 feet, Djebel
Ighil to 13,352 feet, Djebel Azourki to 13,200 feet and
Djebel Siroua to 10,889 feet. The High Atlas extends in
a chain from southwest to northeast and has steep slopes
to both the Atlantic lowland to the north and the desert
plain of the Sahara and to the synclinal basin of Sous
to the south. The central part of the massif is built
of igneous resistant rocks that have been thrusted up
during the huge diastrophic movements that raised these
mountains. Beside these crystalized rocks, there are
also limestone and sandstone rocks that belong to the
Hercynian folding of the Palaezoic era. These rocks
have been eroded by earlier glaciation as well as by
present streams and snow and ice that cap these
mountains in the winter season. The erosion has formed
the high peaks and the steep-sided valleys and deep
gorges. Many of the high peaks are volcanic cones.
Through the winter season the snow covers the slope
above the 800 feet level. Yet there is no permanent
glaciers. The mountains are not easy to penetrate or to
cross. There is one good motor road that cuts across
the chain at Tizi-n-Test that leads from Marrakesh north
of the mountains to Taraudant south of them. There are
also numerous mountain tracks that cross the mountains
from west to east that make possible the exchange of
goods by pack animal between Atlantic and Saharan
Morocco. Eastward the chain loses height and continues
to form the Saharan Atlas; it comprises, as in Algeria,
a chain of massifs known as Djebel Tendrara, Djebel
Dough, and Djebel Grouz.

In between the Rif Atlas and the Saharan Atlas is
the eastern plateau of Morocco. It is an extension of
the Shotts Plateaux (Hauts Plateaux) of Algeria where
some high massifs rise above the plateaux levels and
where a lot of water courses run, filled with water
after rainy storms but dry most of the year. The most
important of these are the Az, the Charef, and the Guir.
The area is a steppe and semi arid region and considered
the domain of some nomadic tribes such as Beni Guil,
Oulad El Hadj, and El Snassena.

Nowhere better than in the High Atlas is shown the
juxta position of Mediterranean and Saharan conditions.
The westward and northwestward facing slopes are well
watered, and in their valleys fruit, olive, and grain
cultivation are the traditional economy of the Berber
population, and good portion of the land remains under a
canopy of forests. On the other hand the southeastern
flanks of the High Atlas, excluded from humid Atlantic
influences and exposed to discoating Saharan dry winds,

are distitute of tree growth and cultivation. Where not actually bare, they support only poor scrub.

The main Berber group that live on these mountains is the Chleuh. They are more sedentary than all the other Atlas dwellers. They live in the valleys in compact fortified villages. They played an important role in the history of the Maghreb lands.

The Anti Atlas is an upthrusted edge of the Saharan platform. It was uplifted during the Tertiary geological era when the High Atlas mountains were forming. It is lower in altitude compared to the massifs of the Atlas system. Its broad plateau surface has a nearly-uniform height of about 5,000 feet. It consists mostly of crystalline rocks, mainly schists and quartzites. It merges with the High Atlas, and the attachment is provided by the volcanic mass of Djebel Siroua that forms the watershed that separates the Sous River, running west to the Atlantic Ocean at Agdir from the upper Draa, which runs southeast towards the Sahara. The triangular groove, opening widely to the Atlantic, that separates the western extension of the High Atlas and the Anti-Atlas, respectively, is the Sous Valley, a depression resulting from the foundering and downfolding which were the counterpart of the Tertiary upfolding. On the southern side of the mountains barren slopes are trenched by gorges from which cultivated palm groves extend like green arms out into the desert. The most important of these gorges and watercourses, beside the Draa, are Todra, Ziz, Guir, and Dades. Dades is running in a valley that separates the eastern slopes of the High Atlas from Djebel Sarro, which is an extension of the Anti Atlas. It offers an important pass across the massifs, connecting the desert and semi desert region of eastern Morocco with Marrakesh, the most important town in the central part of the country on the western side. East of the Anti Atlas, as it is east of the High and Middle Atlas, there are some sparcely scattered oasis such as, Tagounit, Zagora, Toouz, and Akka located along the watercourses and the underground water channels.

Extending inland from the Atlantic coast is an area of coastal plain, relatively low and considered the heartland of Morocco and Moroccan economy. It is enclosed on the north by the Rif Atlas on the east and south by the Middle Atlas and High Atlas. It also includes the Sous Valley that is located between the High Atlas and the Anti Atlas. This important area comprises the Gharb (Rharb) plains that are located west of Rif Atlas. It is crossed by these small rivers:

Mharhar, Mehacen, and Harisa. The wide valley of the Sebou River is an important and productive part of that area, an important tributary of the Sebou is Oued Beth on which an irrigation project serving about 50,000 acres is located. Other important tributaries are: the Ouerrha and Inaouene. South of the Sebou and extending southward to the piedmont of the High Atlas is the Moroccan Plateau "Moroccan Meseta". It is an Archean platform, concealed for the greater part by horizontal strata of relatively recent sediments. The plateau rises from the Atlantic coastal plain gradually eastward where the crystalline rocks are uncovered. It is dissected by some rivers and watercourses that rise from the Middle Atlas and High Atlas but run mostly in the winter season and early spring. The most important of these rivers is Oumm er Rabia and its main tributaries El Abid and Tessaout; the Bou Regreg and its tributary the Grou flows to the Atlantic at Rabat; the Mellah empties just north of Casablanca (Dar el Baida) at Fedala, and the Tensift south of Safi. The Plateau has many irrigation projects, especially on Oum er Rabia where the Imfout Dam is located. Other important projects are the Beni Amir and Beni Moussa. On the Tensift River there is the important Haouz project. In the coastal regions of Abda and Doukkala the irrigation schemes are helping the good, fertile, black clay soil known as tir to be very productive. The other productive area is the cyncline forming the Sous Valley and drained by the Sous River and the Oued Massa. The irrigation projects here are responsible for the commercial grain products, especially wheat.

The newly-annexed territory known as Western Sahara (formerly Spanish Sahara) has mostly gentle relief. The coast is backed by a wide alluvial plain overlain in the south by extensive sand dunes aligned from northeast to southwest in the direction of the northeastern winds that prevail most of the year. These dunes extend inland over 160 miles. East of the coastal plain the land rises gradually to a plateau surface diversified by sandstone ridges that reach about 1,000 feet in height. In the northeast, close to the boundary line of the neighboring country Mauritania, there are isolated mountain ranges, such as the massif de la Guelta, that reach a height of 1,900 feet. Due to the desert climatic conditions that prevail in the region, there are no permanent streams, and the only watercourse of some importance is the Saguia El Hamra (Sekia el Hamra) that crosses the northernmost part of the region to reach the coast at El Aaiun.

CLIMATE AND VEGETATION

Morocco's climate is affected by the extensions and the heights of the Atlas mountains as well as by the Canaries cold current offshore of the Atlantic coast. Northern and central Morocco, west of the Atlas mountains experience Mediterranean type climate. Most of the southern half of the country extending to the Anti-Atlas is a semi arid region. South of the Anti-Atlas and east of the High Atlas desert conditions prevail. It is agreed in general that areas that receive 16 inches or more of rainfall are considered areas of Mediterranean climate, while areas between 16 inches and 4 inches are semi-arid regions and with less than 4 inches are deserts.

The northern and central region in general have warm, rainy winters and hot, dry summers. However, since the source of humidity is the westerlies that carry the humidity from the Atlantic Ocean, and since the season of these westerlies becomes shorter southward, the amount of rain and the length of the rainy season are less southward. In summer the whole country is under the effect of the dry north easterlies.

The northern slopes of the Rif Atlas and the western side of the Moroccan Mediterranean shore are the wettest in the country; nevertheless, the rain declines fast eastward. Tangier and Tetuan each receives 35 inches, while Melilla and Sidi Site to the east each receives 15.3 inches. Along the Atlantic Coast, Kenitra^2 has 23.9 inches, and the amount decreases southward. Rabat has 19.9 inches, Casablanca 15.9, Safi 12.9, and Agadir 8.6. South of the Anti Atlas the rainfall becomes scarce. Hassi Tan receives only 4.7 inches, marking the beginning of desert condtions that prevail southward. The upper Sebou Basin, open to the ocean, receives a good amount of rain. Fez has 22 inches, and Tazal (higher in altitude) has 24 inches with some seasons of destructive floods.

The Moroccan Meseta receives less rainfall in its western part, but the regions that lie in the shadow of the Atlas Mountains receive more. Sidi Slimane has 17.9 inches, while Meknes has 22.8 inches. The rainfall in the plateau decreases southward; Kasba Tadla has 16.1 inches, Nouasseur 14.8, Marrakech 9.4, and Ben Guerir has 8.7. East of the High Atlas, Medelt in the north has 9.0 inches, while Ouarzagate has 4.0 inches.

The Western Sahara experiences extreme desert conditions. Nowhere does average rainfall exceed 4 inches, and over most of the region it is less than 2 inches.

Snowfall is widespread on the Rif, Middle, and Great Atlas. The season lasts for two or three months. It is of particular benefit for the whole region, especially for the semi-arid regions such as the Valley of Sous. These regions are depending on the melted snows of the High Atlas for settled life.

Heavy falls of dew and dense fog are characteristic of the climate of the Atlantic coast of Morocco.

The cold Canaries current has its influence on the temperature of the coastal regions. In winter although the whole region is relatively warm with mean minimums in the winter season round 50°F, along the southern coast at Agadir, where the current approaches the coast, it is in the low 40's, and dropping below the freezing point is not abnormal. In the summer season the effect of the current shows as a reversal of what might be expected as the normal distribution of mean temperature along the coast. At Tangier, in the farthest north, the mean for August is 76°F, while for the same nomth at Rabat it is 73.5%F, and at Mogador, in the south, it's only 68°F. These relatively low temperatures are, from the standpoint of health, largely offset by the high relative humidity. Because of its drier atmosphere, the interior is preferred to the coastal areas.

During the summer, extremely hot, sandy and dry winds, known as Chergui or Sirocco, from the Sahara cross the mountains and sweep across the lowland, desicating all that lies in their path.

The main contrast in the vegetation of Morocco is between the mountains that support forests or open woodland, the surrounding lowlands, which when uncultivated are covered by scrubs of drought resistant bushes, and the desert areas, where vegetation is restricted to scattered patches of course grass that grow mostly in depressions.

In fact the natural vegetation has been altered to a great extent and in many areas actually destroyed by the collecting of firewood and overgrazing through many centuries. That did not only lead to deforestation but also to soil erosion and an arid appearance of many parts of the mountainsides. The forest of Mamora close

291

to Rabat is clear evidence that cork oak forest once covered most of the Atlantic lowland. The lowlands and the slower slopes of the mountains have been completely deforestated and just scrub species such as juniper, thuya, dwarf palm, and gonse are common. The middle and upper slopes of the mountains are often well-wooded, with evergreen oak dominant at the lower and cedar at the higher elevations.

The lowlands to the east and south of the Atlas Mountains support certain types of steppe and arid climate vegetation in which esparto grass (halfa) and the argan tree are conspicious.

ECONOMIC CONDITIONS

The economy of Morocco is the summation of three major important variables: the world prices and demand for phosphates and phosphatic products determine how much Morocco can get for its major exported items. The climatic conditions and fluctuations that affect agriculture (that sector of the economy in which 60% of the labor force and 60% of the Moroccan families are depending on for their livelihood) and agricultural products, are the second major item of exports. The social problem that plagues all the African countires and the rest of the third world, the high growth rate of population that does not only consume the increasing agricultural products but also reduces agricultural exports and is constantly increasing food imports. The summation of these variables is that the country is in deep international debt. Many of the very important economic projects that would help the economy are either postponed or curtailed, and the total financial situation, if not in critical condition, is at best disappointing.

The country's economy, that was showing relative prosperity and growing moderately during the 1960's, started to stagnate during the early 1970's, and since the mid 1970's it has been under increasing pressure. The financial situation in particular and the total economy in general in the early 1980's was in such bad shape that the country was not able to meet it's international debt obligations. The international financial institutions, in order to cooperate with Morocco, agreed to reschedule the repayment of the debts. In September, 1983 an agreement was concluded with the International Monetary Fund (IMF) and the major debtor countires to reschedule the debt of about 13,000 million American dollars. The main condition that the international financial institutions demanded from Morocco, in order to reschedule the debts, was to apply certain economic adjustments that included reduction of imports, government austerity measures, further cuts in commodity subsideis, and a revision of the country's original budget. Besides the dwindling income from phosphate and agricultural exports, the rising imports of foodstuff, the climatic fluctuations that hurt agriculture, and the unbridled high growth rate of population that created these economic difficulties, there is another factor that contributed heavily to that undesirable situation - the Saharan War. It is a very costly open war, and war of attrition inspite of the fact that annexing that territory is of a significant economic value for Morocco because of its large phosphate deposits.

The government was not able to fulfill all the conditions. The value of imports was not reduced. Although the imports of "luxury items" were decreased, the value of food imports is still on the rise. When the government tried to reduce the food subsidies, violent riots and huge demonstrations forced the authority to abandon its plan. The government put in to effect austerity measures in the country's budget, especilly cutting deep in social programs. Unfortunately, the country was struck by two successive years of drought that reduced the agricultural output and subsequently reduced the gross national product (GNP).

The austerity measures have shelved or delayed the implementation of some of the important plans projected in the 1980-86 development plan that were too ambitious for the present financial situation. Some other projects of economic importance that contributed to the development of natural resources were given priority, and the government was looking for external sources of finance to be invested in most of these projects.

Inspite of these conditions, there are two bright points that are reasons for optimism: 1. the Saharan War looks to be quieting down and may come to its end soon; and 2. beside the rich deposits of phosphates, Morocco has other minerals and relatively diversified sources of income that are not yet fully tapped.

The wise movement of King Hassan Altani of signing a "Unity" treaty with President Qaddafi (Gaddafi) of Libya led not only to pulling the rug out from under the Polisario by depriving that organization from the funds, arms, training grounds, and political backing, but also to get large sums of money estimated to be in hundreds of millions of dollars needed badly to be injected into the ailing Moroccan economy. The reproachment with Algeria, now headed by President Chadli and reviving the idea of the Greater Maghreb is removing the largest obstacle that is facing a peaceful solution (on the terms of Morocco) for the Saharan War.

Morocco's diversified natural resources give optimistic hope for the economic future of the country. Two-thirds of the world's known reserves of natural phosphates are in Morocco. There are many other minerals which are either not used yet or still are undeveloped such as copper, zinc, cobalt, antimony, fluorspar, phyrrhotite, chrome, manganese, coal and barytes. There is a good system of developed commercial agriculture based on relatively large areas of fertile soil. Although always under the threat of droughts or floods, there are good planned irrigation and flood control projects. Usage of ground water can reduce the effects of the natural hazards. Off the Atlantic coast there are rich fishing grounds that are nourished and constantly supplied by cool waters of the Canaries current; these fisheries are far from being fully used. Tourism is an important and growing industry that has great potential. Many European and American tourists are visiting the country every year for the many attractions that it has, and the number can be largely increased. The foreign exchange that the tourists bring to the country is badly needed.

The foreign debt in the early 1970's was limited. By 1976 it started to increase gradually, and since 1980 it climbed sharply to reach 13,000 million dollars at the end of 1983. In 1980 the IMF[3] granted Morocco a three year loan of about 1,000 dollars. It was the largest loan the IMF had ever granted to a developing country. The government failed to meet the conditions that the IMF attached to the loan and asked to reschedule the payments of the debt. In 1982 the IMF agreed and approved a $580 million finance package under stringent conditions that included a 4.5% annual increase in GNP, bringing down the inflation rate to less than 10% (in 1983 it was 12.5%, compared to 9% in 1980), and reducing both the budget deficit and the balance of payment deficit to acceptable levels.

Although some efforts have been made to meet those conditions, the deficit in the balance of payment soared high due to higher oil imports, successive two years of drought that reduced the outputs of agriculture and increased the value of food imports and less world demand and lower prices of the phosphates that the country exports. In August of 1983 Morocco made it clear that it cannot meet the debt obligation and asked for rescheduling the repayments for 1983/84 that were about 3,800 million dollars, especially after the Arab countries' financial aid to Morocco was cut sharply. Saudi Arabia alone provided about 1,000 million in aid in 1980 but had to cut it sharply because its income from oil had been reduced – due to the decline of world oil prices. In October 1983 the western European countries (Club of Paris), that are the main lenders, agreed to reschedule the debt for 1983/84, and new arrangements for the IMF debt were made. The World Bank also agreed to lend 150 million dollars to help the Moroccan exporters during the cutback on imports. Other separate agreements were made with foreign commercial banks to reschedule about 500 million dollars of debts.

All the banks and financial institutions in the country are either government owned or majority-Moroccan owned. Beside the regular functions of these banks, they used to give credits to start, encourage, or expand business, industry, and agriculture. Before the country's financial difficulties, credits were expanding by an annual average of 20%. Since the 1978-79 financial year, the expansion has dropped to less than 14% in order to control both the flow of money and spending, and to reduce the inflation rate.

AGRICULTURE

Agriculture has been the most important sector in Morocco's economy. Before the French colonization, agriculture was mostly a subsistance activity with little surplus to offer for international markets. The fluctuations of rainfall did not only affect the welfare and prosperity of the Moroccans, but in many cases it also affected the political structure and the change of the rulers and the dynasties that ruled the country. The situation changed rapidly after the foreign settlers entered the picture. Commercial agriculture and modern agricultural technology revolutionized the production. The success of the French farmers encouraged the rich Moroccan landlords to adopt the new methods. The French authorities also started to build flood control canals,

as well as irrigation projects. Since the 1930's and
until the early years of independence, the country used
to have a large surplus of wheat, citrus fruit, fresh
vegetables and wine that was exported mainly to France,
competing with the French production to the extent that
some measures to restrict the production were introduced
and were imposed especially on the native farmers.

Before independence the French settlers owned about
2.5 million acres divided into more than 6,000 farms.
Most of these farms were in the northwestern plains, the
Rharb (Gharb) and in the hinterlands of Rabat and
Casablanca. It is the most fertile land in the country,
and as in most of the colonized countries, was taken (or
bought) from the native owners who lacked the technology
to use it for commercial agriculture. The Moroccan
landlords who learned the new technology owned about 1.4
million acres. Most of the land that was owned by
foreigners was taken after independence and was given to
Moroccans. Beside the land for modern agriculture which
is about 4 million acres, there are about 11 milliion
under subsistance or traditional systems of agriculture.
However, large efforts are underway to modernize farming
through the extension of irrigation in the river valleys
of Moulouya in eastern Morocco, Sebou, Bou Regreg in the
hinterland of Rabat, Mellah and Umm er Rabie in the
hinterland of Casablanca as well as in the Sous Valley
and in the Rharb. The commercial banks and the Caisse
Nationale de Credit Agricole are financing the
agricultural projects and are giving credits to farmers
involved in commercial crops. The most important of the
irrigation projects include: 1. The Sidi Slimane
Scheme, under which about 85,000 acres are irrigated
from a dam at El Kansera on the Oued Beth. 2. The
Rharb Plain Scheme on the lower Sebou River that
included building flood control canals, irrigation dams,
and drainage canals that will irrigate about 500,000
acres of fertile land when completed. 3. The Haouz
Project, where nearly 300,000 acres are irrigated from a
dam on the Oued N'Fis. 4. The upper Tensift Project
that irrigates about 90,000 acres round and north of
Marrakech. 5. The Beni Amer Project that irrigates
about 90,000 acres. 6. The Beni Moussa Project that
irrigates 120,000 acres. The scheme uses the waters of
the Oued el Abid and works include a very high retaining
dam at Bin-el-Ouidane, a diversion dam at Ait Ouarda and
a tunnel to the Beni Moussa Plain. 7. The Abde
Doukkala Project, involving the Imfout Dam; it irrigates
400,000 acres. 8. The Triffa Project on the Moulouya
River in the northeastern region of Morocco; the project

involves several storage and diversion dams, and it irrigates about 85,000 acres.

There are other smaller projects on the Dra River as well as on the Dades and Ziz, and other indigenous systems are being improved like the smaller works in many areas. In fact, as a result of winter rain and melting of ice and snow that covers the higher slopes and peaks of the Atlas Mountains in the spring, there is much groundwater resources. The irrigation, drainage and flood control projects that are completed or would be under construction in the near future should raise the total irrigated area to more than two million acres of which somewhat over half will be under constant irrigation.

Agriculture is the cornerstone of the Moroccan economy. About 60% of the total population live in villages on the farm land, and more than 50% of the country's working force are engaged in the different sectors of agriculture. It is contributing from 11% to 13% to the country's GNP and agricultural products amount to 30% - 35% of the total value of all exports. In fact agriculture provides the means of livelihood of the majority of the population, supplies a high proportion of the country's food requirements and contributes substantially to the national income.

The purpose of the irrigation projects is not only to expand the area under plough and reduce the damaging effects of floods but also to decrease the destructive effects of droughts that do not only have the national economy and the welfare of the people at hand but lead to further social and political unrest. In 1977 the share of agriculture in GNP was only 13.9% compared to 19.3% in 1976. Again, because of the severe drought of 1981, grain production dropped by 50% from 4.5 million tons in 1980, while agricultural production in general fell by 25%. Although the production recovered in 1982, it fell again in both 1983 and 1984 due to the reoccurring of the drought.

Grains, especially soft and hard wheat followed by barley in the drier areas of the east and south and maise and millet as a summer crop in some irrigated areas, occupied most of the cultivated area. Morocco, that was once an exporter of wheat, especially during the lean years, has turned to be an importer of grains, all the time due to the unbridled increase in the growth rate of population. Citrus fruits especially oranges, grapes and wine, and great variety of fresh vegetables

297

especially potatoes, fresh tomatoes, olives and olive oil, dates and figs, all are important crops that do not only satisfy home consumption but are the main items of agricultural exports. Tobacco, cotton, and almonds are among the crops that find good foreign markets. Other crops are different kinds of pulses and spices. Tea cultivation has started in the Loukos River Basin in the Rharb. The government is encouraging the expansion of this crop in order to reduce tea imports that were increasing in recent years due to more consumption.. Sugarcane and sugar beets are also grown on an increasing scale to reduce sugar imports that are mainly from Brazil and Thailand. Production of raw sugar totaled 470,000 metric tons in 1984, which makes about 50% of the consumption. It is expected that by the end of 1986, the country will be able to produce 80% of its needs. That estimate sounds reasonable since sugarcane is cultivated on the irrigated lands that are less affected by droughts.

Livestock numbers have been generally declining, especially the number of cattle, and the quality of the herds is poor. There is about 12.6 million sheep and about 2.4 million cattle. The production of meat, milk, and dairy products, especially cheese, butter and fresh milk, falls far short of domestic demand. Imports of milk in 1983 climbed to about 20,000 metric tons, while butter imports in the same year cost the country more than 30 million American dollars. Most of the sheep and goat herds are in the hands of semisedentary farmers who practice transhumance. The government, in order to reduce imports of dairy products and milk, is trying to upgrade the quality of the herds by importing higher quality cattle and sheep.

A fruit processing industry has been developed, and it is expanding, exports of preserved fruit, jam and fruit juice now constitute and important part of the total exports and contribute substantially to the earnings.

Morocco is worried about the membership of Spain and Portugal in the European Economic Community (EEC) thinking that the new situation may affect its trade with the countries of the organization. The EEC imported more than 64% of Morocco's citrus fruits and fresh vegetables; however, these worries may be without foundation since the Moroccan products are primers. They ripen and reach the European market at least 5 to 7 weeks before the Spanish and Portuguese products.

Until rather recently Morocco has not fully used the rich and profitable fishing grounds that lie just offshore in the cool Canaries current of the Atlantic Ocean, and fishing boats from other countries, especially Spain and Portugal, took the catch. In recent years the Moroccan fishing industry has begun to take its share. A separate ministry of fisheries, formerly the responsibility of the ministry of commerce, was set up in 1981 and agreements were reached with both Spain and Portugal to limit their fishing activities in the Moroccan economic waters. The government also took advantage of the change in the international rules of economic water and extended it to 200 miles offshore. Safi and Agadir have become leading fishing ports with processing and canning plants. The catch is still modest; in 1984 it was about 400,000 tons, but the industry is growing. Most of the catch is sardines, herrings and anchovies that find good, foreign markets and supply the domestic market.

PHOSPHATES

If agriculture is considered the cornerstone of Morocco's economy, phosphate rock is the major earner of foreign exchange that is badly needed to develop the country. It is also the backbone and the main base of its modern industry. Morocco, after annexing the western Sahara region (formerly Spanish Sahara) became the country with the world's largest known reserves of phosphate rocks. It has about two-thirds of these reserves. The proved phosphate rock reserves are estimated to be about 10,600 million metric tons, but probable reserves are more than 78,000 million tons. There are an estimated 3,800 million cubic meters at Khouribga, 1,600 million cubic meters at Youssoufia, and more than 1,000 million cubic meters at Ben Guerir. Preliminary estimates for the reserves at Bou Craa in the western Sahara are more than 2,000 million cubic meters and may be in fact double this amount. The larger deposits consist of several regular, continuous, and horizontal layers of phosphate-bearing sand with a tribasic phosphate of lime content exceeding 75% in parts. The rock in most of the cases needs little processing before sale. Beside the high quality of the Moroccan phosphate, it has two other advantages; the layers can be mined mostly by strip methods or by underground mining which is not deep. Both methods make the production less expensive. The second advantage is that all these phosphate deposits are located on the

299

seaward side of the Atlas Mountains, not far from the coast which 'makes it easy to export the production. The rise in the prices of phosphate in the early 1970's from under $15 per ton to more than $60 increased the revenues of the country. Most of these revenues were reploughed in the industry or used for the development projects. New conversion and chemical plants were built. The ports of Casablanca and Safi as outlets for the exports were enlarged by the construction of new facilities at Essaouira and Eljadida.

Morocco is the world's third largest producer of phosphate rocks after the USA and the Soviet Union. It is also the bigest exporter. In 1983 the country produced 19.8 million tons compared with 17.1 million tons in 1982. The exports in 1983 that totaled 14.7 million tons were 5% higher than the exports of 1982; nevertheless, the value dropped by 3%, reflecting low world prices. The mineral development plan is to increase phosphate production considerably in the next 20 years. Total production capacity is now 29-30 million metric tons per year, but this should increase to 40 million tons before the end of the 1980's. The expansion will be mainly in the rich strip mining area at Khouribga. The new Ben Guerir area has an initial capacity of 3 million tons per year, and its production will be doubled by 1990. Another mine at Sidi Hajjaj will start producing in 1987 with an initial capacity of around 2.7 million tons per year. Morocco reached an agreement with the Soviet Union to develop a new mine at Meskala that will start producing in 1977/78. All its production will be shipped to the countries of eastern Europe (Members of the Council For Mutual Economic Assistance).

The government has invested substantially in the phosphate-processing and phosphate products with a view to increase exports of phosphate products that yeild higher returns than the raw rock. Some success in this direction has been achieved, and Morocco is finding ready markets for its phosphoric acid, but progress is relatively slow, not only because of the country's financial difficulties, but also because of the high costs involved in establihsing such industries.

Three phosphate-processing plants are already operating at Safi, and a fourth plant, Maroc Phosphore II, started production during 1982 with three sulphoric acid lines and three phosphoric acid lines. Moroc Chimie I produces phosphoric acid and fertilizers, Maroc Chimie II phosphoric acid, and Maroc Phosphore I, a

bigger plant, produces phosphoric acid and monoammonium
phosphate. Maroc Phosphore III and IV are under
construction and expected to be completed by the end of
1986. The plants will have six units, each producing
2,300 metric tons of sulphuric acid per day. The
success of the phosphate processing industry is proven
by the substantial increase in exports of phosphoric
acid and phosphoric fertilizers which rose in value by
42% in 1983 to about 400 million dollars, thus
compensating to a great extent for the loss in the value
of exports of phosphate rocks.

OTHER MINERALS

Morocco has a large variety of other minerals, but
none of them is on a large scale or tapped abundantly or
significantly contributes to export trade. Iron ore is
of limited amount but of relatively high quality. The
ore is magnetite and hematite in limestone, running
60%-65% iron. The phosphorous content is low. The
production varies between 62,700 tons to 78,000 tons of
metal content per annum. The main producing area is
about 10 miles south of the Spanish enclave of Melilla
at Uixan. Iron ore pellets are produced by the Soiete
d'Exploitation des Mines du Rif (SEFERIF) at Nador where
a steel mill has been built. Other producing areas are
Ait Amar and Khenifra. The ore is produced on a smaller
scale, if the market prices are suitable, at Beni
Slimane, Tifiet, and Dentara. The western Sahara has
proven to be not only very rich in phosphate rock but
also in iron ore. It is estimated that there are about
250 million tons of high quality ore in the barren hills
of the southern section of the region near the border of
Mauritania. Exports of iron ore have fallen sharply due
to the competition of Algeria and western African
countries and to the depressed world prices.

Production of lead ore fell to 145,000 tons in 1983
compared to 172,000 in 1980. The government is
expanding the capacity of the smelter at Oued Heimer
which is operated by the Societe des Mines de Zellidja.
The studeies have indicated that the areas of Bou Beker
and Touissit have high concentrated lead deposits. It
is estimated that each of the two areas have reserves of
lead of more than 900,000 tons.

Zinc is produced mainly in the Oujda area, but the
production fell to 14,000 tons in 1983 compared to
22,000 in 1982. Copper production in 1983 was about
69,000 tons showing a slight rise from 63,000 tons in

301

1982. It is produced from the area east of Marrakech and at El Kalaa des-Srarhna. Production of manganese fell from 94,000 tons in 1982 to 74,000 in 1983. The manganese deposits are in two main groups: at Bou Arafa and El Aioun the reserves are limited, an the other area is around Ouarzazate in the Draa Valley where further development depends on transport improvement. The manganese is carried now to Marrakesh across the Atlas Mountains by one of the world's lengthiest cableways.

Fluorspar and barytes production from the area of El Hammam, near Meknes, has increased. In 1983 a new barytes mine was opened at Zelmou with a production capacity of 100,000 tons annually.

Cobalt production from the area of Bou-Azzer has been upstepped after modernizing the mines and increasing world demand. Most of the production is exported to France. The ministry of Energy and Mines has shown lately a great interest in recovering uranium from the phosphate rock reserves. Exploration by the Bureau de Recherches et de Participations Minieres (BRPM) has revealed traces of uranium in the upper Mouloyuya Valley, east of Zeida, in the High Atlas and in the area of Bou Craa in the western Sahara. To this writing, there has been no uranium discovered, and it may take some time to produce uranium due to the financial difficulties of the country.

ENERGY RESOURCES

While Morocco is the richest country in Mediterranean Africa in phosphate production, and the third producer in the world, it is the poorest in north Africa concerning energy production. Its production of fossil fuels, coal, oil, and natural gas is almost negligible, and the country has to import large amounts to meet its consumption of these sources of energy. In fact one of the reasons for the country's financial difficulties is the high bill of imported oil.

Coal, in the form of anthracite, is produced at Djerada. Reserves are estimated to be in the neighborhood of 100 million tons. Production for 1983 was 751,100 tons, up from 735,000 in 1982. About 50% of the production is consumed for local usage. Morocco is increasing imports of bitumenous coal to replace oil

fired units in power stations, sugar industry, and
cement plants, in an attempt to reduce the imports high
bill for oil.

Because of the shortage in fossil fuel, Morocco is
depeding heavily on generating hydroelectricity using
its rivers and dams. In 1981 electricity production
reached 5,277 million kWh; more than 70% of it is
hydroelectric power. The most important hydroelectric
stations are located at Oued el Abid, Bir-el-Ouidane, El
Kansera, Lalla Takerkoust, Marakesh, Sidi Machou, Fes,
Kasba Zidania Meknes and Teruan. Understandably, there
are the usual difficulties associated with hydroelectric
power stations in semi-arid areas, mainly irregular
river flow and rapid silting of reservoirs. Thermal
stations are located at Casablanca, Tangiers, Oujda,
Safi, Sidi Kasem and El Jadida.

Oil production in Morocco is almost insignificant.
Total productin in 1983 totaled 17,736 metric tons. In
1978 it was 24,300 tons. The producing area is the Sidi
Ghalem field in the Rharb. Since the oil production is
so limited, Morocco is importing almost all its oil
needs. In 1983 imports of oil reached 4.7 million metric
tons. The cost of imports was also rising sharply and
fast. In 1983 it totaled the equivelant of
$822,393,000.

The government has expanded exploration efforts,
especially in the Atlantic continental shelf. The
American companies Phillips Petroleum and Getty, jointly
with British Petroleum and the Italian government owned
company AGIP, started exploring and drilling offshore
Cap Sim in 1978. The same companies have two other
offshore concessions at Simmow and off Tafrate and
Ksabi, east of Rabat. The French company EIF Aquitaine
and the Franco-Moroccan Societe Cherifienne des
Petroles, jointly are exploring in northern Morocco.
Their research is backed by a $50 million loan from the
World Bank. Inspite of all these concentrated efforts,
no oil on apprecieated commerical scales has been found
until the end of 1984. The ministry of minerals is
still planning to explore in the area of Essouira. The
World Bank supported the exploration in drilling of nine
exploratory wells by a loan of $75.2 million, approved
in 1983.

More successful and promising efforts are those to
extract oil from the relativley large and extensive
depostis of oil shale at Timahdid in the Atlas
Mountains. The American Company, Occidental Petroleum,

is cooperating with the Moroccan government in developing these deposits. It is expected that about three million tons of oil per year will be produced.

The government in order to cut down on import bills of energy is thinking, as a last resort, of depending on nuclear energy by building a nuclear power station near Casablanca; however, until the end of 1984, no discussion had been made. Since Morocco, like the other two countries of the Atlas region, is subject to severe earthquakes that may endanger the safety of nuclear stations; no decision on this matter is expected soon.

INDUSTRY

Morocco, like all developing countries is trying to industrialize its economy as much as it can and as fast as possible to acheive three main goals. The country wants to rid itself from the dependency on agriculture which is subject to climatic fluctuations and the phosphate exports. Industrialization will lead to reducing the high bill of imported goods and creating more badly needed jobs for a fast growing population. In fact the future political and social stability of the country will depend on the availability of jobs.

There is a large variety of industries; some of them are very modern requiring huge investments such as steel production, phosphate processing, chemicals, and oil refining. There are traditional such as carpets and rugs, leather and copper works mostly owned by private small business and other groups of light industries such as fruit and vegetable canning, fish and textiles. Although Morocco has made impressive progress in industrialization in comparison with the era of colonization, there is still a long way to go to improve and expand this sector of the economy.

One of the most important industrial projects is the Nador steel rod and bar mill. It was built by Davy Loewy, a British Company, at a cost of 75 million sterling pounds. The plant started operating in 1984 with a capacity of 420,000 metric tons per year. To facilitate building the plant, the British government gave an outright grant of 13.5 million sterling pounds to finance purchasig the equipment and machinery from the United Kingdom. Another loan that totaled 38 million sterling pounds was guaranteed by the UK's export Credits Gurarantee Department (ECGD) from Morgan Grenfell & Company to Morocco's steel company, Societe Nationale de Siderurgie (SONSAID).

Another important industry is petrochemicals. Morocco's biggest oil refinery is at Mohammedia. It has a capacity of five million metric tons annually. Another oil refinery is at Sidi Kacem with a capacity of 2 million metric tons, and one is still under consideration in the area of Jorf Lasfer. It is an area rich in phosphate, where a phosphate-processing plan is also proposed. There are still negotiations going on with Arab oil producing countries to finance the expensive projects, but no agreement has been reached yet. The government is trying to expand the existing refineries to increase their capacity as well as to build new refineries to reduce the imports of petroleum extracts and products. In fact, the capacity of the two operating refineries is now about 7 million metric tons. In 1975 Morocco produced 3.9 million metric tons only.

Metal industries are established to make use of the mineral deposits. A lead smelter with a 700,000 ton capacity per year is located at Meknes, and a 30,000 ton per year copper smelter is at Agadir. A plant for the production of about 500,000 tons of sodium carbonate from salt rock is at Mohammedia.

Morocco produced 16,200 private cars in 1983 compared to 15,500 cars in 1982. The French car manufactures, Citroen, is a joint venture with the government, each owns 50% and have two assembly lines in Casablanca and Tanier. The company is also producing spare parts and components. Another company producing cars is the state owned Societe Morecaine de Constructions Automobiles (SOMACA) which assembles Fiat and Renault cars.

Cement production has increased steadily, and in 1983 it totaled 3.8 million tons; that almost covered the country's consumption. The largest of the cement plants is located south of Casablanca with a capacity of 1.2 million tons. The two other plants are at Meknes and Agadir.

The textile industry has recieved considerable government encouragement and has expanded in recent years. It is important for the country because it requires only relatively low investment, and it is labor-intensive that offers more jobs for men and women

305

of different ages. Textile factories for wool and
cotton are located in Casablanca, Rabat, Meknes and Fes.
New factories are set up in Tansift and Oued Zem. In
Ben Guerir a wool textile plant as well as a synthetic
fiber plant started production in 1980. The textile
industry had hard economic times, mainly in 1977 because
a large proportion of the production was exported to
western European countries while the EEC imposed stiff
quotas on textile imports. In 1980 the problem was
solved after an agreement was reached with the EEC
allowing more flexible limits. Exports of textile goods
totaled the equivalent of 180 million dollars in 1983.

Sugar production and sugar refining is growing
fast, and the government has not spared any effort to
expand this industry in order to cut down on sugar
imports. There are now 18 sugar refineries in the
county. The latest of them was built in Zamamra. Total
production is supposed to reach 1.1.7 million tons per
year by the end of 1985, compared with about 370,000
tons in 1978. However, even with this high increase of
production, there will still be a gap of 20% between
production and consumption that has to be filled by
imports.

Other food and beverage industries include wine,
beer, and fruit and vegetable processing and canning.
Beer and wine production has been introduced by the
former French settlers. The industry is still strong
because the larger part of the production is exported
and the Islamic rules in Morocco, unlike most of the
other Islamic countries, do not prohibit consumption of
both beverages. Fruit and vegetable processing is
planned in the agriucltural areas of the Loukkos, Tadia,
Doukkala, and Lower Moulaouya and date packing in
Ouarzazate. Most of the production is mainly for
export.

Carpets and rugs, leather ware and copper trays and
many small industries, mostly dependent on talent and
hand methods and mostly for export and tourists, are
making considerable progress.

In order to encourage industralization, the
government changed the investment code in 1983. The new
code allows full ownership of foreign companies
registered in Morocco. The code is also easing
repatriation of profits and simplifying investment
procedures.

Two government owned financial institutions are responsible for encouraging industry in Morocco. They are the BNDE, that finances large projects, and the Caisse de Depot et de Gestion, that finances small local industries.

One of the major difficultues facing the industrial planners in Morocco is the immense concentration of industries in the Casablanca metropolitan area. The huge city was just a small village in the beginning of the century and now mushroomed into not only the cheif port of the country, handling 70% of the country's trade, but also the largest economic and industrial center. It attracts migrants from all over the county, especially from the overpopulated mountain massifs. Its several contrasting zones of modern and indigenous housing, and its slums, pose great problems to the planners. Industries are overlocalized in Casablanca. They include industries based not only on the national resources, such as flour milling, canning, carpets, leather works or the manufacture of cement and superphosphate, but also on imported raw materials such as textiles, sugar refining and chemicals. It has almost 45% of the country's industries and about 40% of its active labor force.

TRANSPORTATION SYSTEMS

Inspite of topographic complexity of the country, the infrastructure system is good. Morocco, as both Tunisia and Algeria, inherited from the French colonial era well built systems of railroads and roads, and the government is doing its best to maintain and modernize them. Railways and roads are well developed in the west and north regions of the country where most of the economic activities are located and most of the population are living. The railroad, that crosses the country from east to west and joins it with the Algerian railroad system, takes advantage of the Taza corridor to reach the old towns of Fes and Meknes and reaches the Atlantic to connect the main Atlantic ports of Tangier Rabat and Casablanca. Another railroad is extending from Casablanca eastward to reach Khowribge and Kasba for strategic reasons, is in the east and connects Skikda (Philippevile) with Bou Arafa and crosses the boundary line to reach Colomb-Bechar in Algeria. Two important railway projects have been shelved as a result of financial difficulties: the Marrakesh-El Aaiun railway and the Taourirt-Beni Enzarin project to the north. Maintenance of the existing system is high priority, hundreds of new locomotives, passenger coaches and phosphate wagons were bought recently. Track renewal and installing new equipment are always taking place. The railways are state owned and operated by the Office National des Chemins de Fer Marocains (ONCFM). It is reported that in 1984 the railways carried about 4.5 million metric tons of freight which will increase to reach 10 million per year by th end of 1985. Railways cover about 1,060 miles of which 106 miles are double track and 450 miles are electrified.

The road system of Morocco is well developed. It consists of 35,200 miles of roads of which 45% of them are paved and well maintained. The new road that connects Rabat with Casablanca has been completed. Other roads and tracks are being built now in the Western Sahara for military and strategic reasons; however, the new roads will help develop the phosphate and iron ore resources of the region.

There are seven well developed ports in Morocco; Casablanca is the largest and busiest of all of them. However, the ports of Mohammedia, Tangier, Agadir Kenitra (Mina Hassan El Tani), an Safi are very active, and their facilities are overloaded. A new port, Nador, where the new steel mill is located, was built by a Romanian firm, and the new port of Jorf Lasfer was inaugurated in 1982. More than 60% of the cargo that is handled by these ports is phosphates and phosphate products.

Air transport is served nationally and internationally by Royal Air Maroc. It was formed in 1953. The government owned 90% of the authority and it is expanding; its activities reach the U.S.A., Western European capitals, and most of the Arab countries and the countries of west Africa. In 1983 Royal Air Maroc served about 1.3 million passengers. There are several commerical air fields in the country, eight of them are of international standards. The largest of them are the airports of Casablanca, Rabat and Tangier.

INTERNATIONAL TRADE

The major factor contributing to the Moroccan financial difficultires is thedeficit in its interantional trade. The country's main source of foreign revenues are: income from exports of phosphate rock and phosphate products, income form exports of agricultural products, receipts from tourism and remittances from Moroccans working abroad. The country's expenditures are mainly on imports of capital equipment and machinery, food and oil. Morocco, like all the developing countries has had trade deficits since its first years of independence. However, since 1976 the deficit has widened as export earnings have increased by a smaller pace compared to soaring costs of oil and capital equipments. In 1983 the government became aware of the seriousness of the problem and took firm measures to narrow the wide import/export gap by reducing budget expenditure and restricting imports, especially on luxury items. These measures reduced the trade deficit from a record 13,550 million Moroccan dirhamsin 1982 to 10,867 million in 1983, giving a 58% ratio of exports to imports. The high cost of energy imports is the major reason for the high bill of imports. In 1983 imports totalled 25,591 million dirhams. Energy costs accounted for 48% of that amount. The cost of food imports, especially during years of drought, is another reason for the deficit in the balance of payments. In 1983 it reached 3,796 million dirhams. Exports also have been rising but at a slower rate. In 1983 the value of exports reached 14,724 million dirhams compared to 12,440 million dirhams in 1982. In fact, the amount of exported phosphate was at a higher rate, but the prices in the world market for phosphates and most of the other raw materials were depressed. In 1983 exports of phosphate rock fell to 2,997 million dirhams compared to 3,445 million in 1982, despite higher sales and more production. Exports of other minerals including iron, copper, lead and zinc performed better; although they fell by 9% in volume, they rose by 24% in value to 794 million dirhams.

Manufacturing output in 1983 rose by 4%, a remarkable growth compared to that of 1982 which was 0%, and the manufacturing sector contributed 16% to the GNP. The agricultural sector contribution to the GNP depends on suitable climatic conditions. In 1982 agricultural production led to a 6& increase in the GNP, following a 1.3% fall in 1981 due to the severe drought of that year. However, the production failed again in 1983, and the increase was only 2%.

Total debt service in 1983/84 was 3,800 million American dollars of which 1,600 million was interest and $2,200 million was repayment of principal.

France is Morocco's traditional and main trading partner. Moroccan exports to France in 1982 totalled 2,981 million dirhams, while imports reached

6,420million dirhams. Saudi Arabia followed by Iraq have so far been the main oil suppliers of crude oil, but it is expected, after the announced "Union" with Libya, that oil imports from Libya may increase. Spain, U.S.A., Federal Germany and Spain are also important foreign trade partners. The EEC countries are the most important group trading with Morocco especially for buying its agricultural products, including the citrus fruit and fresh vegetables. Morocco is very worried that the new membership of Spain and Portugal in the EEC will have a negative affect on its share of the European markets and is negotiating hard with the countries involved to prevent such a situation. Tangiers, that was once an international, political zone and now is a Moroccan free tradeport is a source of smuggling illegal imported goods that the government is estimating to be worth more than 4,000 million dirhams per year and adding to the trade deficit. The government is trying hard to close that illegal window.

DEVELOPMENT PLANS

Morocco's last three development plans give good pictures for the trends in the country's economy as well as the social aspirations of its people. The ministry of planning is the responsible authority to outline these plans in cooperation with the other ministeries. It is responsible, too, to supervise the executions of these plans.

In 1973-77 development plan investments were 50,000 million dirhams of which 35,000 million were provided by the government and 15,000 million came from a private sector and foreign investors. The government is encouraging the private sector to participate in the plan by offering the investors tax holidays. It also gave foreign investors the incentive of the right to repatriate all their profits. The growth rate of the GNP during each of that year averaged 6.8%.

In 1976, when the effects of the Saharan War were starting to show their pressure on the economy and as a result of applying some austerity measures to combat the deteriorating financial situation in the country, the government announced that the following development plan would span only three years, and the total investments would be 37,000 million dirhams. The growth rate of the GNP during each of the three years of that plan was limited to 3% only. Figures about that plan show that 16% of the investments were for industry, another 16%

310

was directed for rural development and hydroelectric schemes, 9% for energy and 50% divided between transport, communication, infrastructure, education, soical problems, tourism and urban and rural development.

The total investments for Morocco's development plan of 1980-85 is 111,000 million dirhams, of which 68% is provided directly by the government or indirectly through governement owned agencies and finacial institutions. A very good feature of the plan concerning the industrial sector is its encouragement for medium and small size industries that do not require huge capital and can be established by the private sector and can be set up in a short time. This type of industry has also the advantage of employing more labor and can be distributed evenly throughout the country to offer more economic opportunities instead of concentrating the industry in Casablanca.

POPULATION

The major problem which Morocco is facing is not stemming from economic or regional planning, which is rather sound, nor from the economic growth, which is the government in cooperation with the private sector are trying to develop, as fast as possible, nor from the Saharan War, which although is very costly, looks to be winding down, but it is the unbridled growth rate of its population that is running 3.1% yearly. It is one of the highest in the world. This high rate is not only consuming all the fruits of development and economic expansion, but also is causing the large deficit in the balance of payment by forcing the government to import more food and consumer goods, to spend more in social services, especially in the areas of education and health; and that is the main reason for urban problems as well as the deteriorating standard of living among the masses of population and the increase in unemployment that leads to soical and political unrest. The main reasons behind this high growth rate are the lack of education among the adults, the traditional way of life among most of the people who prefer the social way of extended families, interpreting the Islamic religion (which is the religion of 99% of the population both Berbers and Arabic speaking population), and lack of sound extension health and population education in the country.

311

In 1971 the total population numbered 13.5 million. In mid 1981 that number jumped to 20.4 million with an annual increase of 3.1%. Continuing with the situation means that Morocco's population will double every twenty years and is expected to reach at the close of the century, by the year 2,000, about 40 million people. The drastic feature that is revealed by the demographic statistics is that the growth rate is accelerating. From 1960 to 1970, the growth rate was 2.6%, from 1970 to 1980 it jumped to 3.1%, and from 1980 - 2000 it will reach 3.5%. The curde birth rate in 1981 was 46 per thousand, again one of the highest in the world. This means that 50% of the population are under 16 years old, thus not only marginally productive, but they need huge expenditures on food, health services and education. Other depressing statistics characteristic of underdeveloped countries are: an infant mortality rate ashigh as 15 per thousand, life expectancy at birth, barley over 50 years, and daily per capita calorie supply is about 110%; however, that percentage is rather misleading due to the fact that the wealth is not that evenly distributed among the population. In fact, more than 50% of the population are undernourished with a calorie intake of 2,180 daily, well under the F.A.O. minimum of 2,360.

The average per capita income in 1982 was 860 American dollars, but the average is misleading. Again there are the very rich, while most of the population are living on an average income far less than that.

In the field of health services, there is more deterioration compared agoinst the French Colonial Period. (The same for Algeria and Tunisia.) In 1960 there was one physicain per 9,410 persons, and in 1980 the ratio became 1/11,200.

In the field of education, the government is making apprecialted efforts and pouring considerable investment to raise the present rate of adult literacy. That is now as low as 28%. In fact since the year of independence, the government started to tackle a number of educational problems such as: a youthful, fast grwoig population, urgent need for skilled labor and top level employees, and great diversity of education methods between French, Spainsh, traditional Moslem and Moroccan government schools. The government spends now about 25% of its budget on education. The number of children enrolled in primary schools as percentage of the age group jumped form 47% in 1960 t 76% in 1982 (about 2,331,000 children). The percentage of the boys is about 75% of the age group, and the girls is 58%. Instruction in primary schools is in both Arabic and French. Secondary schools provide education for about 825,000 pupils or about 24% of the age group. About 24% of the age group. About 25% of the enrollment is in technical schools. Most fo the instructors are Moroccans, but there is also 4,100 foreign instructors; most of them are from France and a few are Egyptians and Palestineans. In the field of higher education there are about 115,000 students. Besides the traditional and famous Islamic University of Al Quarawiyin at Fez (Fes), there are three other universities at Rabat, Fez and Casablanca, and several other higher technical institutes and teacher-training colleges. Recently more attention has been givn to girls' education, and an increasing number of coeducation schools have been established, especialy in the big towns, and their number is growing.

Merely 50% of the population are in the working age; 52% of them are working in agriculture and fishing; 21% are in industry and mining, and 27% are in the services sector. However, many of those are unemployed or at best underemployed. In fact in 1982 only 26% of the population was economically active.

The most densely populated area is the coastal area that extends from the Rif mountain slopes and Mediterranean coast to the coastal lowlands along the Atlantic. The focus of the area extends from Kenitra (Mina Al Hassan El Tani), north of Rabat, southward to Casablanca. The density in this coastal area is from 150-250 per square mile. The Atlas region has a denisty of 50-150 per square mile. The country's most sparsely populated area between the Dra River and the boundary line with the western Sahara has less than two persons per square mile. The western Sahara region's population has less than one person per square mile.

The French transformation of Morocco set in motion a process of urbanization that is accelerating unabated, and the drift to the towns, especially to Casablanca, is still continuing. In 1982 the urban population was 8.7 million. In 1971 it was 5.4 million, a rise of 3.3 million in only eleven years. The rural population increased in the sme period by only 1.7 million, rising from 10 million to 11.7 million. As a result of this migration movement, there is now in Morocco a dozen towns, each with more than 100,000 inhabitants. The fasterst growing of all is Casablanca. Rabat with 450,000 inhabitants is the capital of Morocco. Other

313

large cities are: Marrakesh, Fes, Meknes, and Tangier. Each of these cities has its old quarters (medina), its bidonville, and the modern sector, a structure that will mark Morocco's cities for many years to come.

At the time of independence there was about 450,000 Eruopeans in Morocco. About 90,000 of them were Spaniards in the former Spanish zone, and about 50 thousand in the former international zone of Tangier. Most of them have left. In 1982 the French population in Morocco was less than 62 thousand, mostly teachers, technicians and engineers. There is also less than 30,000 Moroccan Jews. The Jews of Morocco were forming a prosperous community of 200,000 people. Most of them immigrated to Israel.

There is also about 300,000 Moroccans working abroad. They are pushed by unemployment at home. Most of them are in western Europe, especially France, Belgium and West Germany. Recently some Moroccan's are drifting to Libya.

Morocco has great economic potentialites. Irrigated land can be expanded, industry, fishing and tourism can draw more earnings. However, these potentialities would not become realities as long as the population explosion is taking place. In fact without a national population policy the standard of living would be deteriorating, and the great efforts of the government would be fruitless.

Area and Population

AREA, POPULATION AND DENSITY

Area (sq km)	458,730*
Population (census results)	
20 July 1971	
Males	7,669,957
Females	7,651,253
Total	15,321,210
September 1982	20,419,555
Density (per sq km) 1982	44.5

*177,117 sq miles.

PRINCIPAL TOWNS (population at 1971 census)

Rabat (capital)*	435,510	Tanger (Tangier)	185,850
Casablanca	1,371,330	Oujda	155,800
Marrakech (Marrakech	330,400	Tetouan	137,080
Fes (Fez)	321,460	Kenitra	135,960
Meknes	244,520	Safi	129,100

*Including Sale.

ECONOMICALLY ACTIVE POPULATION (1971 census)*

Agriculture, hunting, forestry and fishing	1,988,060
Mining and quarrying	44,540
Manufacturing	369,264
Electricity, gas and water	10,810
Construction	171,695
Trade, restaurants and hotels	289,082
Transport, storage and communications	100,425
Financing, insurance, real estate and business services	5,602
Community, social and personal services	501,728
Activities not adequately described	155,412
Total in employment	3,636,618
Unemployed	343,900
Total labour force	3,980,518
Females	605,15

*Figures are based on a 10% sample tabulation of census returns. The figure
for females excludes unreported family helpers in agriculture.

315

ADMINISTRATIVE DISTRICTS (1 July 1979)*

	Area (sq km)	Population (estimates)	Density (per sq km)
Provinces:			
Agadir	17,460	933,300	53.5
Al-Hocima	3,550	306,400	86.3
Azizal	110,050	395,500	39.4
Beni Mellal	7,075	572,600	80.9
Boujdour	100,120	n.a.	n.a.
Boulemaine	14,395	127,800	8.9
Chaouen	4,350	300,200	69.0
El Aaiun	39,360	n.a.	n.a.
El Jadida	6,000	703,200	117.2
El Kellaa Srarhna	10,070	559,100	55.5
Essaouira	6,335	456,300	72.0
Essmara	61,760	n.a.	n.a.
Fes	5,400	744,900	137.9
Figuig	55,990	107,800	1.9
Kemisset	8,305	427,700	51.5
Kenitra	8,805	1,192,200	135.4
Khenifra	11,115	299,100	26.9
Khouribga	4,250	424,800	100.0
Marrakech	14,755	1,224,100	83.0
Meknes	8,510	774,100	91.0
Nador	6,130	609,400	99.4
Ouarzazate	46,460	587,900	12.7
Oujda	20,700	769,100	37.2
Rachidia	59,585	405,000	6.8
Safi	7,285	652,200	89.5
Settat	9,750	694,100	71.2
Tanger	1.195	377,600	316.0
Tan-Tan	17,295	26,500	1.5
Taounate	5,585	560,800	100.4
Tata	25,925	106,100	4.1
Taza	15,020	618,000	41.1
Tetouan	6,025	682,100	113.2
Tiznit	6,960	336,400	48.3
Prefectures:			
Casablanca	1,615	2,357,200	1,459.6
Rabat-Sale	1,275	865,100	678.5
Total	659,970	19,470,000	42.4

AGRICULTURE

PRINCIPAL CROPS ('000 metric tons)

	1980	1981	1982
Wheat	1,811	892	1,824
Barley	2,212	1,039	1,190
Maize	333	90	315
Olives	277	145	250
Dates	75	65	65
Pulses	248	92	231
Tomatoes	400	370	385
Oranges	757	685	695
Tangerines	267	280	294
Potatoes	543	396	539
Sugar beet	2,241	2,107	2,300
Seed cotton	17	15	15
Grapes	200	210	210

FORESTRY

ROUNDWOOD REMOVALS ('000 cu m)

	1980	1981	1982
Sawlogs and veneer logs	48	67	68
Pitprops (mine timber)	28	37	33
Pulpwood	201	208	241
Other industrial wood	125	65	218
Fuel wood	1,150	1,078	1,107
Total	1,552	1,455	1,667

FISHING

('000 metric tons, live weight)

	1980	1981	1982
Jack and horse mackerels	20.1	17.5	14.1
European sardine (polchard)	211.9	243.7	169.6
European anchovy	9.5	22.2	19.4
Chub mackerel	24.2	21.0	56.9
Molluscs	12.9	25.2	36.1
Total catch (incl. others)	329.9	390.2	361.7

317

LIVESTOCK ('000 head, year ending September)

	1980	1981	1982
Cattle	3,174	3,240	2,900
Sheep	14,200	14,840	14,900
Goats	6,100	6,200	6,250
Camels	230	230	230
Horses	300	310	310
Mules	390	400	400
Asses	1,400	1,450	1,500
Chickens	24,000	23,000	24,000

LIVESTOCK PRODUCTS('000 metric tons)

	1980	1981	1982
Beef and veal	78	82	82
Mutton and lamb	43	55	56
Goats' meat	19	23	23
Poultry meat	100	75	97
Cows' milk	730	780	810
Sheep's milk	20	21	21
Goats' milk	26	28	29
Hen eggs	78.0	75.0	78.0
Wool (greasy)	12.7	13.1	13.1

MINING
('000 metric tons)

	1980	1981	1982
Coal	720	710	680
Crude Petroleum	24.3	18.6	13.8
Iron ore	62.9	61.7	78.0
Antimony ore	5.3	2.0	1.3
Cobalt ore	8.7	8.0	6.7
Copper concentrates	12.2	23.5	24.1
Lead concentrates	163.9	165.3	172.1
Manganese ore	126.2	135.7	132.1
Zinc concentrates	10.5	12.9	13.1
Phosphate rock	20,156.1	20,030.8	18,824.2
Fluorspar	59.2	63.2	64.4
Barytes	174.4	286.5	318.1
Pyrrhotite	190.4	197.1	136.1
Salt (unrefined)	17	18	67

318

PRINCIPAL TRADING PARTNERS (million dirhams)

Imports	1980	1981	1982
Belgium/Luxembourg	353.9	357.2	503.1
Canada	320.5	550.3	595.4
France	4,167.9	5,550.5	6,419.8
Germany, Fed. Republic	981.7	1,978.3	1,253.4
Iraq	1,986.2	362.6	1,047.9
Italy	957.9	973.3	1,069.0
Japan	220.7	411.2	617.4
Kuwait	0.6	657.8	865.4
Netherlands	402.0	551.7	610.0
Saudi Arabia	1,278.4	3,348.3	3,517.4
Spain	1,378.4	1,540.3	1,850.2
USSR	598.9	861.0	1,339.4
United Arab Emirates	275.5	549.4	n.a.
United Kingdom	496.6	516.4	911.6
USA	1,089.2	1,571.6	1,548.6
Total (incl. others)	16,792.6	22,455.1	25,990.3

Exports	1980	1981	1982
Belgium/Luxembourg	468.4	521.1	573.3
France	2,427.9	2,614.0	2,981.0
Germany, Fed. Republic	788.2	858.4	991.9
India	395.0	623.2	712.8
Indonesia	143.4	281.5	273.9
Italy	542.2	595.8	829.4
Japan	142.1	350.4	363.9
Netherlands	569.8	669.0	680.8
Poland	190.7	311.2	370.8
Spain	565.2	834.3	837.1
Turkey	65.3	212.8	280.4
USSR	485.8	684.4	253.7
United Kingdom	398.8	477.8	511.1
Total (incl. others)	9,645.0	12,002.6	12,439.7

319

Direct capital investment (net)	89	59	80
Other long-term capital (net)	1,270	1,233	1,228
Short-term capital (net)	-242	73	113
Net errors and omissions	16	63	40
Total (net monetary movements)	-286	-416	-418
Allocation of IMF special drawing rights	21	19	—
Valuation changes (net)	-62	-39	-13
IMF Trust Fund loans	37	1	—
Official financing (net)	13	132	—
Changes in reserves	-277	-303	-431

EXTERNAL TRADE

PRINCIPAL COMMODITIES (million dirhams)

Imports	1979	1980	1981
Food, drink and tobacco	2,143	2,833	4,613
Wheat	973	1,255	2,044
Sugar	269	627	1,054
Tea	190	153	278
Dairy products	200	252	349
Energy and lubricants	2,769	3,961	6,124
Crude petroleum	2,437	3,578	5,624
Animal and vegetable products	1,332	1,397	n.a.
Crude vegetable oils	531	481	538
Timber	307	434	470
Minerals	335	574	n.a.
Semi-finished products	3,287	3,542	3,890
Iron and steel goods	880	911	1,073
Chemicals and fertilizers	758	907	992
Plastics	265	316	281
Paper and carboard	191	228	232
Synthetic textile fibres	205	228	241
Agricultural equipment	161	119	134
Industrial equipment	3,130	3,052	3,726
Consumer goods			
Passenger cars and spares	261	308	309
Pharmaceuticals	131	153	151
Total	14,328	16,793	22,455

TOURISM

FOREIGN TOURIST ARRIVALS

Country of Origin	1979	1980	1981
Belgium	34,597	28,263	26,012
Canada	18,146	11,417	13,829
France	323,057	340,380	347,565
Germany, Federal Republic	100,393	118,359	129,491
Italy	32,018	34,155	35,956
Netherlands	28,114	29,046	27,688
Scandinavia	63,720	60,162	52,486
Spain	134,879	122,912	165,386
Switzerland	24,383	22,103	19,844
United Kingdom	108,316	131,937	150,421
USA	84,732	62,179	73,272
Moroccans living abroad	357,318	327,492	361,188
Cruise visitors (short-term)	113,458	92,495	79,536
Total (incl. others)	1,549,454	1,517,228	1,646,610

EDUCATION

	1980/'1	1981/82	1982/83
Primary school pupils	2,106,1\2	2,331,000	3,693,593
Secondary school pupils	754,542	826,500	968,150
University students	86,844	98,513	82,944
Student teachers	14,466	16,148	23,853

BALANCE OF PAYMENTS (US $ million)

	1980	1981	1982
Merchandise exports f.o.b.	2,414	2,283	2,043
Merchandise imports f.o.b.	-3,770	-3,840	-3,815
Trade balance	-1,355	-1,557	-1,772
Exports of services	856	801	902
Imports of services	-2,037	-2,174	-2,009
Balance of goods and services	-2,536	-2,930	-2,879
Private unrequited transfers (net)	1,004	988	840
Government unrequited transfers (net)	113	99	162
Current balance	-1,420	-1,844	-1,878

321

Exports	1979	1980	1981
Food, drink and tobacco	2,283	2,599	3,040
Citrus fruit	859	1,160	1,072
Fresh tomatoes			
Potatoes	384	392	334
Fresh vegetables			
Canned fruit and vegetables	270	263	284
Wine	36	40	79
Preserved fish	300	342	465
Energy and lubricants	276	467	543
Animal and vegetable raw			
materials	218	399	337
Olive oil	0.8	106	7.4
Cotton	1.6	34	57
Pulp for paper	90	122	125
Minerals	2,878	3,711	4,487
Phosphates	2,213	3,012	3,827
Lead ore	282.	281	208
Cobalt	119	138	92
Manganese ore	662	59	63
Semi-finished products	972	1,354	2,096
Phosphoric acid	504	793	1,342
Fertilizers	120	153	288
Refined lead	137	120	145
Agricultural and industrial			
equipment	27	28	n.a.
Consumer goods	997	1,115	1,499
Carpets	283	286	302
Clothing	261	296	420
Hosiery	101	113	156
Total	7,622	9,645	12,003

REFERENCES

[1] The Arab country that is located in the very western region of the Arab world.

[2] Mina'a el Hassan (Minda el Hassar)

[3] The International Monetary Fund

CHAPTER 13

SUMMARY

Mediterranean Africa is a huge region that extends
from the eastern shores of the Atlantic ocean to the
south eastern shores of the Mediterranean Sea. It is
considered as a transitional area between Africa south
of the Sahara and southern Europe. All of these
countries have been in direct contact with Europe;
nevertheless, they are still a part of the African
continent. The Islamic religion and the Arbic language
have made the region a part of the Islamic world, the
Arab nation and the Middle East.

The region in general and Egypt in particular,
played a great role in the ancient history of the then
known world. During the medieval ages, the capitals of
these countries were the bright lights in a dark era.
They carried their culture across the sea to Spain and
Italy and the rest of Europe. Due to political fueds
and unstability, as well as to economic decline, the
region fell into the hands of the Ottoman Empire, and
later, because of its strategic importance became a prey
for European domination. All the countries struggled
against the foreign control and were able to gain
independence after World War II.

Egypt regained its independence in three stages.
In 1921 it was declared an independent country by the
British and chose a king to head its government;
however, the independence was nominal because the
British were trying to stifle the strong nationalist
movement. In 1936, an Anglo Egyptian treaty was signed
to give Egypt more authority in its national affairs and
it also became a member of the League of Nations,
however, the British ambassador was the real governor of
the country. Egypt achieved complete independence in
1956 after the failure of the combined
Anglo-French-Israeli invasion.

Libya was the only country in the region that was
granted independence after World War II due to the
defeat of Italy. However, because of its strategic
importance and lack of any resources to support an
independent country, until 1970 it depended on financial
subsidies from the United States and the United Kingdom
in return for keeping two air bases there. The three
Maghreb countries gained their independence after
violent confrontations with the French authority in

324

which many people on both sides lost their lives especially in Algeria.

Both the U.S.A. and the U.S.S.R. recently have been trying to gain influence, or to get a foot hold in the countries of the area. Egypt was leaning toward the U.S.S.R. especially from 1967 to 1971, after the Arab-Israeli war of 1973, and since signing the Camp David treaty of 1978 the American influence in Egypt has been very tangeable. Libya is a problem area for the U.S.A.; however, the U.S.S.R. has no influence there. Libya considers the U.S.A. as the backer of Israel, supplying it with arms and money "to occupy the Arab land." President Qaddafi also accuses "American Imperialism" as being in the way of "Arab unity;" his sweet political dream. The U.S.A. accuses Qaddafi's government as being responsible for terrorism and financing and protecting terrorists. Certainly the American shooting of two Libyan fighter jets and bombing Tripoli and Benghazi in April 1986 will not improve the relation between the two countries in the near future. In the meantime, although the U.S.S.R. has been the main arms supplier for Libya, it has not been able to gain clear influence in Libya with the exception of allowing some Russian navy ships to call every now and then on Libyan ports. Lately there is talk that Libya may allow the Russian navy to have a base in Libya to encounter the American Sixth Fleet in the Mediterranean.

Both Tunisia and Morocco are keeping very good relations with the western countries in general and with the U.S.A. in particular since both of them are receiving considerable American economic aid and some military equipment. Algeria, until the beginning of the 1980's, was not friendly with the U.S.A. but did not act as a hostile country. Although the foreign policy of Algeria is leaning towards neutrality, it is trying to keep friendly relations with the U.S.A.

Physically, the region has two striking features: the Nile river and its valley in the east and the Atlas mountain in the west. The Sahara occupies most of the region. Hamatas, ergs, regs oasis and seas of sands are the main features of that extensive sparcely populated desert. Climatically the coastal plains of the Maghreb enjoy "Mediterranean climates" with hot dry summers and warm rainy winters. The Atlas peaks and high slopes are covered by snow and ice during the winter season. East of Tripoli, in Libya and south of the Atlas mountains desert conditions prevail.

Mineral resources are of considerable importance in Mediterranean Africa; especially oil, phosphates and iron ore. Libya is the major oil producer: its production in 1983 jumped to 1.105 million barrels per day. Egypt produced 0.726 million barrels per day and Tunisia 0.120 million barrels per day. Oil reserves in these countries are estimated, in 1984, to be (35.54 billion barrels) 21.27 in Libya, 9.00 in Algeria, 3.45 in Egypt and 1.82 in Tunisia. Morocco is the world's third largest producer of phosphate rock and the biggest exporter: the production in 1983 reached 19.8 million tons and the volume of exports in the same year was 14.7 tons. Algeria's production of phosphate in 1981 reached 916.00 million tons while Egypt produced 737,000 million tons. Iron ore is the third important mineral in the region. In 1982, Egypt produced 1.9 million tons, Algeria 1.8 million tons, Tunisia 211,000 and Morocco 29,000. Libya has extensive resources in Fezan that are not used on a large scale yet.

The economics of the countries of Mediterranean Africa are characterized by being dual: traditional and modern sectors exist, non-integrated, side-by-side. Modern agriculture exists on large estates owned by individuals or run by government cooperatives in Morocco, Algeria, Tunisia and Libya, while intensive agriculture in Egypt is on small plots not exceeding 50 acreas, but with very high yields. Traditional agriculture practiced by peasants, nomadic and semi-nomadic communities using primitive methods still exist in all the countries. The governments are investing heavily in the agricultural sector to expand acreage, increase productivity and building irrigation projects. However, due to the unbridled growth rates of population and more demand for food, all the countries are importing large quantities of grains and other food items. It should be noted that more than 60% of the population are rural, depending directly or indirectly on farming, and the agricultural products are constituting a large item of the exports.

In the industrial sector, modern and heavy industries have been established especially petro-chemical, fertilizers, steel, vehicle assembly and textiles. Most of this kind of industry is owned or run by governments or receive huge government subsidies, or were established in cooperation with foreign companies. In the mean time, traditional handicrafts such as leather products, wood work, silver and copper works, homemade rugs and homemade tapestry play a fairly important role in the economics of these countries.

The industrial development has had varying degrees of success in each country and in different industries. The main obstacle facing it is mainly the limited size of national markets and to some extent the relatively poor planning or management.

In spite of the financial problems facing each of these countries, their huge international debts and chronic budget and trade deficits, they are spending large sums of money on armament and arms industry. Each of them has its own reasons or excuses, but with the common result that the economy of the region is deprived because of these investments that are poured into armament.

The total population in the region is about 95.7 million and increases at an average rate of 3.1 percent, which is among the highest in the world. This high growth rate constitutes a severe socio-economic problem. The doubling of the population in less than 30 years is not matched with the economic growth, which prevents the development of the per capita income, and puts pressure on the national budgets to allocate the money needed for social services, especially education.

The overwhelming majority of the population are Moslems, with the exception of a relatively strong minority of Christians in Egypt. The Arabic language is the official language in all these countries; however, there are linguistic minority groups in the Maghrab countries: the Berbers and Tuareg.

The two major problems facing the countries are: modernizing their economies by both horizontal and vertical expansion, and crossing the religious and traditional barriers to control the high growth rate of population. Neither can be achieved without a large degree of political stability.

BIBLIOGRAPHY

Abdel-Malek, Anwar. Ideolgie et Renaissance Nationale/L'Egypte Moderne. Paris, 1969.

Abu-Lughod, Janet. Rebat: Urban Apartheid in Morocco. Princeton University Press, 1981.

Abu-Nasr, Jamil. A History of the Maghrib. Cambridge University Press, 1972.

Allan, J.A. Libya: The Experience of Oil. London, Croom Helm, 1981.

Amin, Samir. The Maghreb in the Modern World. Harmondsworth, Penguin, 1971.

Ansell, Meredith and Al-Arif, Ibrahim. The Libyan Revolution. London, The Oleander Press, 1972.

Baker, Raymond William. Egypt's Uncertain Revolution Under Nasser and Sadat. Harvard University Press, 1979.

Ball, John. Contributions to the Geography of Egypt. Cairo, Government Press, 1939.

Balta, Paul and Rulleau, Claudine. L'Algerie des Alge'riens. Paris, Editions Ouvriers, 1982.

Barbour, K.M. The Growth, Location and Structure of Industry in Egypt. New York, Preeger, 1972.

Bernard, Jean-Louis. Aux Originos de L'Egypte. Paris, Laffont, 1976.

Berque, Jacques. Egypt: Imperialism and Revolution. London, Faber, 1972.

Boateng, E.A. A Political Geography of Africa. Cambridge, Cambridge University Press, 1978.

Blunsum, T. Libya: The Country and Its People. London, Quee Anne Press, 1968.

Bovill, E.W. The Golden Trade of the Moors. Oxford University Press, 1958.

Briggs, Cabel L. Tribes of the Sahara. Cambridge, Harvard University Press, 1969.

Butzer, Karl and Hansen, Carl. Desert and River in
Nubia. Madison, The University of Wisconsin Press,
1968.

Chamberlain, M.E. The Scramble for Africa. London,
Longman, 1974.

Chi-Bennardel, Regine, Van. The Atlas of Africa. Jeune
Afrique, Paris, 1973.

Clarke, J.L. and Fisher, W.B. ed. Population of the
Middle East and North Africa. Cambridge,
Heffer, 1972.

Cooper, Mark N. The Transformation of Egypt. London,
Croom Helm, 1982.

Damis, John. Conflict in Northwest Africa. Stanford
University Press, California, 1983.

Dawisha, A.I. Egypt in the Arab World. London,
MacMillan, 1976.

Depois, Jean and Raynal, Rene'. Geographie de L'Afrique
du Nord-Quest. Paris, Payot, 1967.

Depois, Jean. L'Afrique du Nord. Paris, Universitaires
de France, 1964.

Esposito, John, ed. Voice of Resurgent Islam. New
York, Oxford University Press, 1983.

Fallot, Paul. Essai sur la geologie du Rif
septentrionel. Rabat, Imprimerie Officialle,
1937.

Fedden, R. Egypt, Land of the Valley. London, 1977.

Furon, Raymond. Geology of Africa. (translated)
Edinburgh, Oliver and Boyd, 1963.

Gabrieli, Francesco. Mohamed and the Conquests of
Islam. (translated) New York, McGraw-Hill,
1968.

Garas, Felix. Bourguiba et la naissance d'une Nation.
Paris, 1956.

Griffths, J.F., ed. Climates of Africa. New York,
Elsevier Publishing Company, 1972.

Halstead, John. Rebirth of a Nation: The Origins and Rise of Moroccan Nationalism. Harvard University Press, 1967.

Harmessi, Elboki. Leadership and Nationl Development in North Africa. University of California Press, 1973.

Harris, J.R. The Legacy of Egypt, 2nd Edition. Oxford University Press, 1972.

Hitti, Philip. Makers of Arab History. New York, St. Martin's Press, 1968.

_____. History of the Arabs. New York, St. Martin's Press, 1967.

Hoare, Ian and Tayar, Graham, ed. The Arabs. London, B.B.C. Publications, 1971.

Hodges, Tony. Western Sahara: The Roots of a Desert War. London, Croom Helm, 1983.

Hoffman, Michael. Egypt Before the Pharaohs. New York, Knopf, 1979.

Hopwood, Derek. Egypt: Politics and Society. Allens Unwin.

Hume, W.F. Geology of Egypt. Vol. I The Surface Features. Cairo, Government Press, 1926.

Ibrahimi, Taleb. De La Decolonisation a La Revolution Culturelle - (1962-1972). Algiers, SNED, 1973.

Julien, Ch. History of North Africa From Arab Conquest to 1830. London Routledge and Kegan Paul, 1970.

Kay, Shirley. Morocco. London, Namara Publications, 1980.

Kinross, Lord. Between Two Seas: The Creation of the Suez Canal. London, John Murray, 1968.

Knapp, Wilfrid. North/West Africa: A Political and Economic Survey. Oxford University Press, 1977.

_____. Tunisia. London, Thames and Hudson, 1972.

Lambotte, R. Algeria, naissance du'une socie'te', nouvelle. Paris, Editions Sociales, 1976.

Le Tourneau, Roger. Evolution Politique de l' Afrique
du nord musulmane. Paris, 1962.

Lebjaoui, Mohamed. Ve'rites sur la Revolution
    Algerienne. Paris, Gallimard, 1970.

Leca, Jean and Vatin, Jean-Claude. L'Algerie politique,
    Institutions et regime. Paris, Foundation
    Nationale des Sciences Politiques, 1974.

Lewis, Bernard. The Arabs in History. New York, 1950.

_____. Islam. New York, Harper and Row, 1976.

Mabro, Robert. The Egyptian Economy 1952-1972. London,
    Oxford University Press 1976.

Martens, Jean-Claude. Le modele Algerier de development
    (1962-1972). Algiars, SNED, 1976.

Moore, C.H. Politics In North Africa. Boston, Little,
    Brown, 1970.

Mountjoy, A.B. "Egypt Cultivates Her Deserts".
    Geographical Magazine, X:OV (1972), pp. 241-250.

Murdock, G.P. Africa, Its Peoples and Their Culture
    History. New York, McGraw Hill, 1959.

Murnane, William J. The Penguin Guide to Ancient Egypt.
    London, Penguin, 1984.

Owen, Roger. Libya, Royal Institute of International
    Affairs. Oxford University Press, 1961.

Quandt, William. Revolution and Political Leadership:
    Algeria 1964-1968. MIT Press, 1970.

Rabana, Abderrahama. The Prospects For an Economic
    Community in North Africa. London, Pall Mall,
    1973.

Raven, Susan. Rome in Africa. London, Evans Brothers,
    1970.

Richmond, J.C.B. Egypt, 1798-1952: Her Advance Towards
    a Modern Identity. London, Methuen, 1977.

Robson, P. and Lurry, D. The Economics of Africa.
    London, Allen & Unwin, 1969.

331

Ruf, W.K. Independence et Interindependence au Maghreb. Annuaire de l'Afrique du Nord. Paris, 1975.

Said, Rushdi. Geology of Egypt. New York, Elsevier, 1962.

Sylvester, Anthony. Tunisia. London, Bodley Head, 1969.

Talbott, John. France In Algeria, 1954-1962. New York, Knopf, 1980.

Thompson, B.W. The Climates of Africa. Nairobi, Oxford University Press, 1965.

Thompson, Virginia and Adloff, Richard. The Western Saharahs. London, Croom Helm, 1980.

Trimingham, J.S. The Influence of Islam Upon Africa. London, Longman, 1968.

Turnball, C.M. Man in Africa. London, Newton Abbot, 1976.

U.S. Naval Weather Service. Vol. IX, Part 1, Washington, D.C., December 1968.

Vutikotis, P.J. A Modern History of Egypt. London, Weidenfeldt, 1980.

Waddams, Frank. The Libyan Oil Industry. London, Croom Helm, 1972.

Waterbury, John. The Egypt of Nasser and Sadat: The Political Economy of Two Regimes. Princeton University Press, 1983.

_____ . "Land, Man, and Development in Algeria". American Universities Field Staff, Vol. 17, No. 1, 1973.

Wright, John. Libya: A Modern History. London, Croom Helm, 1982.

PERIODICALS

Africa Research Bulletins. Exter, England

L'Afrique et L'Asie modernes. Paris, France

American-Arab Affairs. Washington, D.C., U.S.A.

Jeune Afrique economie. Paris, France

Middle East Economic Digest. London, England

The Middle East Journal. Washington, D.C., U.S.A.

Mideast Report, Financial Times. New York, U.S.A.

Near East Report. Washington, D.C., U.S.A.

335

9918